IAL SCHOOL DISTR

A Pryor Commitment

"The true story of public service at its best, Pryor's memoir takes the reader through his career in an unusual and intimate way. A remarkable student of Southern politics, Pryor has been an outstanding leader for Arkansas and our nation as a member of the U.S. House, the U.S. Senate, and governor. David is a unique political leader who combines courage, intellect, and integrity with a rare ease of humility and humor."

—U.S. Senator Sam Nunn, Retired (D-Georgia)

"David Pryor's memoir could also be called, 'The Education of a Public Man.' It is a magnificent account of a life devoted to public service, with all of its problems, dilemmas, failures, and satisfying triumphs. Pryor's book is an inspiration to anyone who considers a life in government and politics. A *Pryor Commitment* should be taught in Political Science courses everywhere."

—Nick Kotz, Pulitzer Prize-winning author of
Judgment Days: Lyndon Baines Johnson, Martin Luther King and the Laws That Changed America

A Pryor Commitment

The autobiography of **David Pryor**

With **Don Harrell**

Butler Center Books is a division of
The Butler Center for Arkansas Studies
Central Arkansas Library System
100 Rock Street
Little Rock, Arkansas 72201

Cover photograph of David H. Pryor by Thomas Fitzsimmons. Used by
    permission.
Book and cover designs: H. K. Stewart
Project manager and photo editor: Ted Parkhurst
Acquired for Butler Center Books by Bobby Roberts, David Stricklin, and
    Ted Parkhurst
Project editor: Roger Armbrust
Project proofreader: Barbara Paddack

First Edition, 2008; ISBN 978-0-9800897-3-8
Library of Congress PCN: 2008927762

12 11 10 9 8 7 6 5 4 3 2 1

On the end-sheets: Pulaski County Special School District students show their enthusiasm for Governor Pryor (undated). Courtesy UA Special Collections.

Title page spread: Barbara and David Pryor visit as their sons Dee (David, Jr.), Mark, and Scott play in the yard of the Pryors' Arlington, Virginia, home during David Pryor's first congressional term. Photo by Bob McCord, courtesy UA Special Collections.

This book is printed on archival-quality paper that meets requirements of the American National Standard for Information Sciences, Permanence of Paper, Printed Library Materials, ANSI Z39.48-1984.

Printed in the United States of America.

For Barbara

Table of Contents

Acknowledgments

This book could never have been written without Don Harrell. We grew up in Camden only a few blocks apart, and our lives have been intertwined since childhood. In each Pryor campaign, for whatever office, Don would show up ready to work, and in time he served as press secretary, chief of staff, confidant, and overall adviser. With this book, he has been there once again, and I will always be grateful to him, and to his wife, Chris.

Much of this book was written in Fayetteville, and while Don spent his days in the Special Collections at the Mullins University Library, I tended to settle in at one of the small study rooms at the new Blair public library a few blocks away. I am grateful to the library staff for the help and assistance they gave me. And to Susie James, always an integral part of the Pryor extended family, who was more than generous with her time in pulling together various parts of our growing manuscript.

I also want to acknowledge the family and friends, campaign workers, and staff members who managed to keep me in office over so many years. In the chaos of major campaigns, they came to us as volunteers, many of them mothers who brought their children to the headquarters. I hope they know that without them I could never have been elected to public office, or stayed there.

Books on Arkansas history and politics have always helped to keep my thinking straight. The first edition of *Arkansas Politics and Government*, written by the late Diane Blair, went into a second edition in 2005, completed by her co-author, Jay Barth. I have read this book with unflagging interest and curiosity. It reminds me that our state enjoys a rich history of independent political thinking, always kept in action by a cast of unforgettable and public-spirited characters.

Ben F. Johnson's *History of Arkansas in Modern America 1930-1999* has repeatedly served as a valuable companion when I wanted to check specific dates or relevant facts of recent history. The case study on the Arkansas Plan, published in a UALR series in1979 by Cal Ledbetter, Beadle Moore, and Glen Sparrow, proved greatly helpful in recalling bittersweet memories of that project. And I was swept back in time by Rob Wiley's master's thesis dealing with the McClellan-Pryor debate in 1972. In a general sense and covering many years, I have continued to be enlightened by the quarterly publications of the Arkansas Historical Association, edited by Jeannie M. Whayne in the history department at the University of Arkansas.

My sisters, Cornelia Pryor Lindsey and Elinor Pryor, published a book of memories and family recipes in 1990, titled *Perfectly Delicious*, which was our Mother's way of describing particularly tasty food. The reminiscences they put together at the front of that book—from longstanding friends and family members—inspired me to write my own recollections of growing up in Camden, as well as the years beyond.

Several sections of this book appeared in altered form before finding their way to final passage, as we said in the Senate. A longer version of the first few pages describing my heart attack appeared in the August 1991 issue of the *Arkansas Times*, considerably modified here and included with the magazine's permission. My retellings of the Cherry race for governor in 1954 and of the short-lived Sovereignty Commission three years later were drawn from papers I gave before meetings of the Arkansas Historical Association. And the Kosovo experience comes in part from a speech to the Little Rock Rotary Club.

I'm especially indebted to the members of the press who have covered my years in politics. Two of them—Ernest Dumas, formerly the chief political writer at the *Arkansas Gazette*, and Roy Reed, first with the *Gazette* and later at the *New York Times*—have been friends for many years. Ernie, Roy, and I took part in a series of interviews telecast by the Arkansas Educational Television Network. These conversations helped to refresh my memory and gave me the idea of putting many of them in a book. I will always be indebted to Roy for his study of the career of Orval Faubus and the lasting effects his tenure had on our state.

Pulitzer Prize winning author Nick Kotz of Washington, D.C., has offered years of invaluable advice on history and politics. Especially during precarious times in my life and career, Nick always kept a steady hand on my shoulder. His wife, Mary Lynn, a distinguished author in her own right, has been a constant source of encouragement and counsel. Both have helped in shaping this book to its final form.

When it became clear that I had somehow collected a mountain of paper, I wondered who might go through it and put it in one place. I was fortunate to find that the Mullins Library at the University of Arkansas, and in particular its

Special Collections, would take on the task. This archive became known, somewhat grandly, as The Pryor Papers. I couldn't help thinking of it as "my stuff" and became grateful that it didn't wind up in our attic.

The decision to truck this collection to Fayetteville turned out to be one of the wisest moves I've ever made. Tom W. Dillard, the director of Special Collections at the Mullins Library, has been diligent in overseeing the organization and disposition of a wealth of paper. I'm indebted to him for his continuing articles on Arkansas history and in particular his concise account of Commonwealth College. I also appreciate his strong arguments for teaching the history of our state in the public schools.

I have also benefited from the counsel of Dr. Todd Lewis, a member of the Special Collections staff, who worked for five years organizing 821 linear feet of letters, memos, committee reports, speeches from the *Congressional Record*, newspaper clippings, photographs, ledgers, and hastily-scribbled notes.

A year before leaving the Senate, I was fortunate to acquire the professional services of Dana Lawrence, a former staff member in the office of Senator Fulbright. A native of Fayetteville, Dana knew Arkansas politics and had a strong kinship with the University campus. She prepared and cataloged hundreds of boxes before sending them to Arkansas.

My special thanks to the Richard C. Butler Center for Arkansas Studies, headed by David Stricklin, for the steady guidance it has given this book through its middle and final stages. Included in this number is Ted Parkhurst, a member of the Butler Center staff who is better informed about getting books to the public than anyone. I'm indebted to Roger Armbrust, whose sound judgment gave this sometimes rough manuscript meaningful form, and to H. K. Stewart, whose editorial skill contributed to the book's final design.

My particular thanks to Bobby Roberts, director of the Central Arkansas Library System, for his encouragement in moving this project along. The Library's *Encyclopedia of Arkansas History and Culture* has been a constant reference point for me. I appreciate the advice of Professor Willard Gatewood, who brings history to life at the University of Arkansas and who was willing to read this manuscript in its early form. Thanks to my niece, Katherine Ozment, for applying her editorial skills in the book's final stages, and to my friend, Sheila Anthony, and my daughter-in-law, Judith Pryor, for reading the book in its early form and offering their suggestions and advice.

Of course, the ultimate responsibility for errors and oversights, and for judgments and opinions, is entirely mine. I hope my recollection of names, places, and events has not been greatly diminished by the passing of years.

I wish to acknowledge my children and their families for their continuing love and support. David, Jr., his wife Judith, and their son Hampton, live in Washington, where David—or "Dee," as we have always called him—has been associated with FedEx for several years. Mark and Jill, and their son Adams and daughter Porter, are now residents of Little Rock, while Mark commutes to Washington as a U.S. Senator from Arkansas. And Scott and Diane, with their son Devin, live in New Jersey, near New York City, where Scott produces television commercials.

Whatever pleasure I take in my record as a public servant falls far short of the pride I feel when I look at the lives of these sons, their wives, and their children.

And finally, my lasting love and gratitude to Barbara, who has stood by me through victory and defeat and who never faltered, never failed to give encouragement and to prop me up when I needed a hand. Without her, this collection of memories could never have been written, and the life it describes could never have been lived. It is to her that I dedicate this book.

Barbara and David Pryor campaigning during the 1984 U.S. Senate run. Courtesy UA Special Collections.

Chapter 1
"The Fun's Done"

I'll never forget that Monday night, April 15, 1991. The Senate had not been in session that day, and none of my committees had met. It proved a good time to catch up, clean off my desk, and make sure everything was mailed to the IRS. That afternoon, I sat down with the staff and was briefed on the Tuesday schedule.

Here's what it looked like: The Arkansas Homebuilders Association would be in town for the day. I was scheduled to meet the Harrison ninth-grade class on the Capitol steps for a picture. Dr. George Haas from North Little Rock was coming in to discuss optometry issues.

In addition to joining these Arkansas visitors, I would attend the Senate Finance Committee meeting at 10:00 a.m., and the weekly luncheon with members of the Senate Democratic Conference, scheduled for noon. It promised to be a long and busy day, but not very different from most.

I was home by 7:00 p.m. and watched the news in shorts and a tee shirt. An hour later, I was walking up Connecticut Avenue, headed for a favorite eating place near our home on 19th Street. Over spaghetti and meatballs I scanned a folder on the Finance Committee hearings for the next day, read the current issue of *Golf Digest*, and was back home in bed by 10:30. Barbara was touring Thailand with a group of Senate wives, and with her out of town the house formed a tomb of silence. I downed my cherry-flavored Rolaids, turned off the TV, and fell asleep wondering how Dick Darman, the president's budget director, would answer my questions tomorrow about the exploding cost of prescription drugs.

Little did I know that within three hours my life would change forever.

I woke up at 1:45 in a pool of sweat. My chest felt not in sharp pain, but in something more like massive discomfort. I'd only eaten spaghetti and meatballs. Could it be indigestion? Had I actually eaten a live porcupine? Within minutes the pain's intensity increased. I thought to myself, I've got to get up. I'm getting light-headed. I grabbed a pair of warm-ups and a golf shirt and headed downstairs. I needed air.

As I reached the bottom step, I *knew* what it was. Rolaids and fresh air wouldn't help. It was a heart attack. Me, of all people. Heart attacks were for someone else. I didn't have time for a heart attack.

My health record was terrific. After every physical, I skipped out of the doctor's office as the man who defied his age and thumbed his nose at all the greasy cheeseburgers, French fries, and tons of salt. My heart rate belonged to a swimmer, my lungs were pure leather, and my blood pressure the envy of any athlete. I would sit in the Senate dining room in amused silence as my colleagues compared their cholesterol numbers. I didn't even know what mine were and, what's more, didn't care.

At the foot of the stairs, I reached for the phone and punched in 911. A recent horror story about poor ambulance service in Washington shot through my mind. The article pointed out that crews invariably arrived too late and even then didn't know what to do.

"My name is Senator David Pryor," I whispered into the phone. "I live at 1615 19th Street. I'm having a heart attack, and I need help. Please hurry."

I hung up the phone and walked out the front door to wait on the ambulance. I sat on the curb between two cars. What happens if the ambulance driver doesn't see me and drives right by? My chest tightened. My rib cage became a vise. I was losing consciousness. I stood up and spotted a white '73 Ford down the block—one of those vintage numbers with a long, wide hood. It looked like an aircraft carrier. I made my way to the car, climbed on the hood, and lay down on my stomach. It was wet with the April night's cool dew.

I don't know when the ambulance arrived, but I do remember being helped onto a stretcher. The light in my eyes was very bright, and the siren sounded as if it were far away. Someone covered my face with an oxygen mask. An attendant asked me, "From one to 10, how much pain are you in?" I held up 10 fingers.

A nurse got right in my face and chanted, "Breathe. Breathe. Breathe."

"Give him more oxygen," someone said.

"Do you smoke?" another person asked.

"No," I told him. "But I used to."

"When did you stop?" he asked.

"About 15 minutes ago," I said.

We careened from our row house at DuPont Circle down Connecticut Avenue and into the emergency dock at George Washington University Hospital. My only recollection of that room, apart from the freezing air and blinding light, was that all the unknown faces surrounding me seemed far too young.

"Are you allergic to any drugs? What about morphine?"

"Are you really a senator?"

"What state are you from?"

"How do we reach your wife?"

Someone in the room said, "We've got to find his next of kin." The voice could have come from *The Twilight Zone*.

My next of kin. Is this an obituary? In the movies, when they asked for "next of kin," that was it.

"You've had a heart attack, Senator. We're trying to get you stabilized."

Stabilized? I'm stable. I've always been stable.

Chaos. Shouting. People everywhere. For over two hours I fell in and out of a fog.

"Am I going to make it?" I asked someone hovering over me.

"You're okay," she said. "You're okay."

I didn't believe her.

"Senator, President Reagan was on this same bed 10 years ago. Mr. Brady was right next to him, beyond that curtain." The cheerful young doctor seemed to think this would pull me through. It occurred to me that he was probably in high school when President Reagan was shot.

I had the strange sensation that I was an inner tube being blown up to the point of exploding. Am I dying? Is this what it feels like to die? Don't I have some say in this? Things are moving too fast. I can't comprehend it.

The wall clock said 4:30 a.m. For nearly three hours I had been flat on my back—jabbed, hit, shocked, monitored, and gouged. I kept thinking of the phrase, "rode hard and put up wet."

One image repeated itself over and over: our family pew at the old Presbyterian Church in Camden. I was 14 years old, but I could have been 12. Or maybe nine. Nothing was clear. Nothing, anyway, except for the voice of Jac Ruffin, our minister in the 1950s. He had moved to Camden from Mississippi, and he spoke in deep Southern tones. I could hear him perfectly:

This is the age of the half-read page,
The mad dash, the quick hash,
The short hop and the brief stop
Until the spring snaps and the fun's done.

Until the spring snaps. That's me. The spring has snapped. And the fun's done.

Mr. Ruffin liked to quote this poem in his sermons on the hustle and bustle of everyday life. I had made a point to memorize it, even though I knew it didn't apply to me in any sense. I'm not in a rush or a dash. I've always taken time to read and sit down and contemplate. I couldn't imagine why that short poem rushed back at this time. But there it was. And along with it soared a host of other memories and recollections from my earliest years. For the first time, I understood how, in the final moments, your entire life passes before your very eyes.

I'm happy to say that, after all, these were not my final moments. I survived the scare and fright of that heart attack. It wasn't easy. They put me through angioplasty and a maddening series of tests and trials and examinations. My son David and his wife Judith appeared in the emergency room. Barbara rushed back from Thailand.

When they had moved me from intensive care, Jim Lehrer stood over my bed and said, "You're a lucky SOB. They don't like for senators to die in this hospital." Jack Valenti brought me a book, and Carl Levin brought an artist's paintbrush. He said, "You've got to use this." Max Baucus brought me a copy of John F. Kennedy's *Profiles in Courage*, and Dale Bumpers regaled me with Arkansas stories and news. He told me that he had introduced a sense of the Senate resolution expressing the hope that David Pryor would soon get well and return to the Senate floor. He was happy to report that it had passed 51-48.

On Friday of the following week, I was released from the hospital and allowed to go home. They warned me that nights would prove the hardest time, and they were right. I started to dread the dark. I also became more grateful every day for the doctors who attended me and gave me small daily assurances. And, of course, for the emergency team that saved my life. I invited the ambulance crew to lunch in the Senate dining room.

In a matter of days I was beginning to come back. Several weeks later, I experienced a minor crisis with chest pains and rushed back to the doctor's office, wondering if I'd spend the rest of my life suffering a series of medical emergencies. A year or so after that, I underwent successful bypass surgery, making it possible to live as a reasonably productive person. I've also become a proud member of an exclusive club: heart attack survivors anxious to share with each other the details of their narrow escapes. And mine had been narrow.

The lasting effect of that April night in 1991, apart from my profound gratitude, is a new grasp of my childhood experience growing up in Camden, Arkansas. It's as though a vivid light were cast on what had been a range of dim and uncertain shadows. They say an experience of this kind makes you stop and think, the current term being, I suppose, "a wake-up call." But I'm not sure it was a call, or a spiritual epiphany. I saw that I would have to change my way of life, including spending more time reading food labels in the grocery store. But most important of all, I'd been given a new appreciation for the considerable array of people who helped shape my life and guide me over the past 70 years.

Chapter 2
River City

All of us can point to a unique childhood that molds our adult lives. If we're lucky, we recall those early times as a string of happy days free from troubles and care. Looking back, I know my youthful experience couldn't have been as joyous and free as I remember it. A lot occurred that wasn't pretty. Southern towns in the 1930s and '40s endured firsthand the painful wrongs of racial and religious discrimination. Even more pervasive, the Depression hovered as a sinister presence in the daily lives of every family and community, black or white. The gap between rich and very poor created two disparate worlds within one small community. And while World War II eventually lifted the country back on its feet, it erupted in 1941 as a terrifying menace separating loved ones and threatening invasion of our shores.

As a child growing up in Camden, I was only vaguely aware of the troubles of our time. The third child of four, I followed behind Bill and Cornelia and before Elinor. Our parents did not overly protect their children, but they remained determined to shield us from troubles and provide what we needed. I'm grateful for my childhood—comfortable and secure by any standards—and for benefiting from a small-town upbringing. I'm also naïve enough to believe I experienced something unique.

History buffs relish our town's role in the Civil War. David O. Dodd, a 17-year-old from Camden, was arrested outside Little Rock with Union maps in his pouch, allegedly heading for Confederate lines. Union troops summarily hanged him as a spy—a story with fascinating details of local history and intrigue. It's still re-enacted from time to time on Confederate holidays. I could only imagine the mystery and desperation behind Dodd's capture and the swift trial that ended in his execution. His saga was the kind of tale that, in my view, should have been coming out of World War II, with its cloak-and-dagger stories of espionage behind enemy lines. And to think that it happened only a few miles away.

An even more stunning Civil War event took place on the outskirts of town. Major General Frederick Steele had commandeered the homes of both the Chidester and the Gaughan families on West Washington Street, setting up headquarters in their houses and on their spacious lawns. His goal was to supervise a substantial Union presence throughout the southern part of the state.

In April 1864, his command was running out of provisions. General Steele ordered his troops to move west of town and forage food supplies and staples wherever they could find them. He learned of a nearby supply of 5,000 bushels of corn and a livestock herd. But the Union's sizeable detail of 198 wagons quickly attracted the notice of Confederates camped in the hills nearby. The Grays ambushed the train. The conflict at Poison Springs resulted in a combined total of more than 400 men killed, but a decisive Confederate victory.

I could never find enough reading material about this conflict. I visited the site several times, trying to imagine the encounter that took place in the surrounding pinewoods. Too many war memorials seem to dwell on numbers and statistics, discounting the human element that makes up a battle's real story. Years later, as a freshman member of the Arkansas House, I introduced a bill to create Poison Springs State Park, and today a monument commemorates what Civil War buffs often describe as a "skirmish." I've always considered it much more.

History particularly came alive for me in Camden's old Ingham Library, a one-room frame house with a dilapidated porch and lattice railing. Propped up incongruously at the corner of Washington and Harrison Streets, the building was surrounded by appliance stores, gas stations, and bustling downtown traffic. For me, it embodied the spirit of history itself. With its white paint peeling and one side leaning out toward the street, this aged structure stood starkly out of place.

The library was also one of my favorite spots in town, my one guaranteed avenue of retreat. Miss Lalla Thornton presided over stacks of musty volumes and a card catalogue of seriously outdated books, but I had no concept of the collection's being obsolete or behind the times. My unflagging interest focused on clippings and pictures from Camden and Ouachita County going back a century or more, including detailed accounts of political races my grandfather, my father, and even my mother had run.

Some years after a new library rose a block away, Mother helped put together a group of local historians. Their efforts saw the old frame relic picked up and moved out on West Washington Street, to the side yard of the McCollum-Chidester home. It's there today, restored to a fine white polish as an adjunct to the historical museum. Coming full circle in a curious way, I was serving as governor when the library's move took place, and I dedicated its reopening as an archive of Camden history and tradition.

Like many young people of my vintage, I grew up assuming that life in my hometown pulsated with the stuff of high romance, along with only occasional touches of grit and hardscrabble labor. My youthful imagination never strayed far from the idyllic childhood of Tom Sawyer and Becky Thatcher. Like them, we thrilled at a river running through town, maybe not as wide as the Mississippi, but brown and swift enough to feed my boyhood dreams. It also seemed that in April or May of every year the river would flood beyond its banks, threatening the Camden Monument Works and the Maid-Rite Drive-In.

Unless the wide, flat fields remained under water, the Clyde Beatty Circus set up shop for a week every June at the river bottoms' lowest point. Three decrepit elephants announced the circus's arrival as they shuffled along in a morning parade down Washington Street. Any kid who didn't stick his toe in the piles of fresh dung left by the elephants was a sissy.

Not many years before my birth in 1934, the Chidester livery stable had finally gone out of business, selling its teams of horses and wagons for practically nothing. Driven into bankruptcy by the new-fangled automobiles, Mr. Frank Chidester, who lived well into his 90s, stubbornly refused to ever ride in a car. For years he took the bus to town—Camden even had a bus line in the early '50s—but most of the time he walked wherever he needed to go. His deliberate, defiant stride captured both his independent streak and utter refusal to accept change in any form.

A woman I met years later while serving in the Senate reminded me of Mr. Chidester. She lived in Hampton, next door in Calhoun County, and was celebrating her 100th birthday. "You must have seen a lot of changes during your time," I suggested to her. "Yes I have," she responded, "and I've been against every one of them."

The Chidester family had owned the stagecoach line connecting south Arkansas to points as far west as Fort Worth. When the railroad replaced overland coaches, the family transportation business downsized to a local taxi service that rented out horse-drawn wagons and buggies—a humbling substitute for a once-thriving enterprise. Pictures of the Chidester stable, located on Jefferson Street where the *Camden News* later opened its first offices, show evidence of their once-booming trade. One shot reveals throngs of merchants and travelers milling around the crowded, muddy street. Every day, teams of horses and wagons met each train that arrived at the Cotton Belt and Missouri Pacific railroad stations. Traveling salesmen, or "drummers," rented them for making commercial rounds throughout the county.

* * *

It's not that Camden was different from any other small town in Arkansas. If you study its layout from one of those Internet satellite maps, zeroing in from space and centering on the town's shape, it looks like Hope or Magnolia or Fordyce. Or even El Dorado (pronounced to rhyme with "see you latah") 30 miles south. El Dorado was a major city compared to Camden. We liked to consider the two towns rivals, especially on Thanksgiving Day when they usually beat us at football. But, in truth, Camden measured a good bit smaller, somewhat less affluent, and lacking the sheen and sophistication we attached to our neighbor named for that mythic city of fabulous riches.

An oil boom hit nearby Smackover in the early 1920s, when more than a thousand wells gushed into Standard Umsted. The surprise discovery spilled its riches directly into El Dorado's economy. This revenue infusion accounted for a sudden progressive rush unseen elsewhere in the state. By the time a second oil explosion hit in 1937, Union County was far outpacing any area around it. In this vicinity, H. L. Hunt first struck oil, after having worked as a night clerk some years earlier at the Orlando Hotel in Camden.

If Mother wanted the latest toys or fashions, she shopped at El Dorado's courthouse square. And if we needed a medical specialist, Mother and Dad carted us to one of the doctors at Warner Brown Hospital. The Rialto Theatre featured first-run picture shows, and the Dairy Queen premiered in 1950, a good two years before Willie Wilhite opened the one in Camden. When in El Dorado on Saturday afternoons, we always stopped at the DQ for ice cream after riding with Roy Rogers and Gabby Hayes at the Rialto.

If we moved at a slower pace than our Union County neighbors, we wrote it off simply as a difference in style and manner. They boasted their economic progress while we claimed a sense of history and tradition, pointing to our rich heritage and community pride. Although it remains open to question, local legend says that De Soto landed at our river bluff as he moved through the wilderness in 1541. It may be a fine point, but this slice of lore stretches beyond what any other southern Arkansas river town might claim. Most of his exploration followed the Mississippi, well east of us.

The French settled Camden as a trading post in the 1780s and originally named it Ecore Fabre for a Frenchman living near the river. Literally, it means "Fabre's bluff." The name changed when citizens incorporated the town in 1844, probably in honor of Camden, Alabama, the original home of General Thomas Woodward, whose family actually founded the settlement.

The county itself is named for the river—Ouachita—which some say comes from Choctaw for "clear sparkling water," but disagreement still exists on this point. Others say that in Choctaw the words "owa" and "chita" mean "big hunt." In any case, Camden is the county seat. Nobody outside Arkansas knows how to pronounce Ouachita. It's WASH-a-taw. It might be easier to pronounce if we had stuck to the Oklahoma spelling. Over there, it's Washita. I'm always amazed at how difficult we can make things, even the simple pronunciation of locations.

Its perch high up on the river—at a wide bend snaking through low-bottom hollows—accounted for Camden's early importance as a shipping port for cotton and other crops. The river's highest cliff, known as Fort Lookout, took its name during the Civil War when Confederate troops established a watch point. A fair amount of trade—including home goods, furniture, and finery—made its way up the river from New Orleans.

As in most small towns, commercial streets came to be named for national statesmen—Adams, Jefferson, and Washington—and residential streets for native trees—Maple, Chestnut, and Elm.

Antebellum homes sprung up along Washington Street as the wide avenue drew a straight line from the riverbank toward the hills west of town. This gracious stretch of homes makes a curious dogleg turn at the corner of the First Baptist Church, then straightens out and continues southwest toward Texarkana. The wide and welcoming front porches along Washington Street for years impressed me as evidence of the town's durability and cultural significance. I remember hearing tales of cotton farmers west of Camden bringing wagonloads of cotton along Washington Street and down to the river, headed for New Orleans.

Most of those great homes are gone now. And the downtown, like so many in the state, has undergone a series of radical changes since the 1940s. The local retailers that flourished after World War II—Watts and Lide's department stores, Copeland's, the Style Shop, and Morgan's and Snow Hardware—all shut down years ago. Naturally folks shop at WalMart now.

Chapter 3
Edgar and Susie

My father, Edgar Pryor, was born in 1900 in Holly Springs. A tiny hamlet bordering Ouachita and Dallas counties in southwest Arkansas, it runs straight up Highway 9, and lies about 20 miles from Camden, just past Eagle Mills. The village still cradles only two stores, a church, and a graveyard.

Dad knew what hardship meant. His father's early death, and later his mother's, had forced him to abandon school in the eighth grade. He worked in the family's general store, supporting his younger brother Judson and their sisters Annis and Grace. Sometime around 1920, he left Holly Springs and moved to Camden. His leaving proved difficult for everyone in the family, but financial hardship forced his choice.

Dad found a boardinghouse room, and took a job sweeping floors and working the grease rack at the N. S. Word & Co., a Ford dealership. Always gregarious and never one to shun a stranger, he soon made it his business to know just about everyone in Ouachita County. He found out the make of cars they drove, and the likelihood of anyone who might buy a new one. From the country school of trade—horses, cows, chickens, or hay—he understood the basics of barter and demonstrated uncanny skill in buying, selling, and swapping. He was a master of human nature.

As Dr. Word became older and more infirm, he asked Dad to make an offer for the auto agency. While Dad had done well by the day's standards, he didn't possess the assets or the bank credit to buy the dealership on his own. But he knew an opportunity when he saw one. The developing Smackover oil field promised major growth throughout southern Arkansas, especially around El Dorado and Camden. Determined to grab this rare chance to build a business, Dad went to his brother-in-law, Fred Laney, who had married my Aunt Annis. With his brother Ben—who would become governor of Arkansas in 1944— Fred had struck a financial geyser through oil leases in the Smackover field. Dad offered Fred a partnership in the Ford firm. Fred agreed.

Despite the early Depression's withering years, the business ultimately flourished. Dad didn't read much, but early in his career he discovered *Fifty*

Years with the Golden Rule, an inspiring book by department-store wizard J.C. Penney. Dad became so enamored with Penney's message, he bought dozens of copies and gave them to friends. He also often quoted, unknowingly, Tammany Hall's George Washington Plunkitt: "I seen my opportunities and I took 'em."

Meanwhile, Dad also set his sights on the local Chevrolet franchise. But Ford's corporate heads in Detroit refused to allow this maverick dealer in a small south Arkansas town to own two competing franchises. They forced him to make a choice. He picked Chevrolet. Almost immediately, Chevy challenged him: the company would ship him 40 new automobiles—all of them white. They would arrive by train within the next three days. He had a month to sell them or he would lose his franchise.

This surely would prove impossible for any small-town dealer. The nation, state, and town lay stuck in the Depression. Practically in tears, Dad crossed the street to the Citizens National Bank, his prime lender, and threw the dealership's keys on bank president Garland Hurt's desk.

"I'm finished, Garland," Dad muttered. "You can take my business now. I just can't make it."

Mr. Hurt, also experienced in dealing with human nature, dropped the keys in a drawer and said, "O.K., Edgar. But I didn't know you were a quitter."

Dad lunged over the desk, grabbed the keys, and marched back across the street to his shop. He went on to build Pryor Chevrolet into an institution, a gathering spot for business, local politics, and friendly commerce that lasted another 25 years.

Mother's father had served as a sheriff, and my father also decided he wanted to assist the public in that position. In Dad's first race for Ouachita County sheriff, he ran against Arthur Ellis, the incumbent and actually a family friend. At that point in Ellis's career, he and his comrades pretty much ran the courthouse. But even his old friends now agreed—he had held court too long.

It was 1938, and Dad helped lead a reform movement to take on the whole courthouse crowd. "Sweep the courthouse clean" became the battle cry, and each reform candidate announced his mission with a coat-lapel symbol: a two-inch broom.

Actually, Dad hadn't planned on running for sheriff at all; his friends pressed him into service. One afternoon while reading the paper, he discovered he had become a candidate. "How did this happen?" he asked a regular seated in the Chevy dealership office. "Well, we paid your filing fee because we thought you should be in that race," the man responded matter-of-factly. "So there you are. Good luck."

Dad approached a campaign so informally folks today wouldn't recognize it as political strategy. He wanted to neutralize the opposition upfront. (As it turned out, I adopted this method in many of my campaigns.) He went to all of Arthur Ellis's friends around the county and said, "You have to vote for Arthur, and I understand that. I won't hold anything against you. I just want you to support me whenever you find you can't go with Arthur." As a result, Arthur Ellis's friends—although casting votes for him—clearly didn't expend their energies in his re-election.

Dad served four years as sheriff. As his popularity peaked, he retired from elective office to become a full-time Chevrolet dealer again. He called it the wisest professional move he ever made. His neighbors knew him as a genial, fair, but shrewd and competitive dealer. With a cigar and a keen eye, he could look through his office window and see nearly every corner of the place. Possessing a prodigious memory, he called all his customers by name, and always knew the current state of their credit.

Dad's trading ability grew legendary in the county. Negotiations with Edgar Pryor might include a mule, a horse, a new saddle, or even cows and hogs. His gentle reach especially affected those he fondly referred to as the country folks he knew best. He was one of them. In many cases, he sealed a deal with nothing more than a county resident's handshake and a promise to pay as soon as possible.

Dad was most proud of the loyal team that ran the place. Calvin Tuberville and Theo Money worked the two Texaco gas pumps in the filling station fronting Pryor Chevrolet. Many nights, Theo, a large black man with a native understanding of nature's work, would guide me in hunting rabbit at the river bottoms. He showed me how to attach a charcoal lantern to my hat's front bill. In the dark night along the river's edge, a rabbit's red eyes appeared almost incandescent. For me, this exhilarating thrill matched any adventure Alan Ladd might experience; for Theo, it meant rabbit stew.

Martin Gaston managed Pryor Chevrolet's parts department, and his brother Zann shared bookkeeping and accountant chores with Ray Joiner. Zann, a chain smoker, incessantly whittled away on cedar sticks, leaving a shavings trail in his wake. After World War II, Harry McGuire filled the place with legendary stories about the Pacific. According to town lore, after one disputed track meet between Camden and El Dorado, Harry's brother Pat, who worked at the paper mill, fought an El Dorado fan down by the railroad tracks. The El Dorado man bit off the bottom part of Pat's ear.

Owen Fincher returned from the Pacific to sell Chevy parts for older cars and trucks. People drove for miles to buy a new tire or even a used carburetor. Dad's goal was to interest them in a shiny, new BelAir Chevy displayed in the garage or on the lot. He once told me that I might live long enough to see Chevrolets sell for as much as $2,000!

Robert E. Lee, known as "Bookie," was in charge of the wrecker. Frequently called upon to tow cars in distress, he knew more about the town's nightlife and culture than anyone around. But Bookie stayed stubbornly close-mouthed, never giving the lowdown on Camden's elite.

Odie Vaughan ran the used car lot. He constantly cleared his throat with such ferocity that Dad once offered him a $50-a-month raise to quell his disgusting habit. It worked. Somehow Odie controlled his urge and got the pay boost. He flaunted a unique angle for selling used cars. Parking at downtown Camden's main intersection, he'd sit on his front fender, enticing customers with a sign boasting his nickname: "Po-Boy Vaughan."

Before automobile air-conditioning became common, Pryor Chevrolet sold a makeshift contraption for cooling: a narrow metal cylinder shaped like a torpedo and fixed atop the passenger window. Each morning, you could fill the cylinder with chipped chunks from one of Camden's two icehouses. Then, if you drove fast enough, wind flowing over the ice and into the car guaranteed a cool ride. The problem was that an Arkansas summer could melt ice quickly. Still, on many an August afternoon, Po-Boy Vaughan showily drove around Camden wearing a hat and an overcoat, enjoying the luxury of an air-conditioned car. Sam Walton was clearly not the first Arkansan born with marketing genius.

Miss Mollye Anderson answered the phone at the Chevrolet place. The phone number 628 eventually became so popular, Dad had to install a switchboard. With that improvement, Miss Mollye could plug in the parts room, the back shop, or the used car lot. The first switchboard in Camden, it drew people from around the county, especially on Saturdays, to watch Miss Mollye juggle the switchboard wires.

Bell Telephone in Camden operated from Morgan Hardware's second floor. All local calls went through an operator. You'd simply pick up the receiver and tell her the number you were calling. In every small town like ours, callers referred to her as "Central."

Camden's Central was Lucy Mae Phillips, seemingly on the job every hour of the day and night. "Lucy Mae never sleeps," Mother often quipped. Of course, Lucy Mae knew all. Many days after school, I would get home, pick up the receiver, and listen as Lucy Mae informed me where Mother was spending the afternoon. Usually she visited the church circle, played bridge with her friends, or worked at the Community House. Three days after having my tonsils removed, and dressed up in a white satin suit, I served as ring-bearer in Lucy Mae Phillips's wedding. Mother fretted I'd keel over during the ceremony. My body may have swayed a bit, but my legs remained sturdy!

* * *

My mother, Susan (Susie) Newton, married Edgar Pryor on April 6, 1927. She came from a Camden family of long-time public servants, pillars in the Presbyterian Church. Like many families at the time, the Newtons marched in strict adherence to bluestocking Protestantism. On Sundays, her mother allowed no music except for hymns, no sewing, and no kitchen-stove fire; food had to be prepared on Saturday. Children couldn't attend the circus because female performers wore tights.

Despite her narrow views of good and evil, my grandmother had a softer side. She once persuaded the churchwomen to admit a woman from Camden's red-light district, a convert who had married a young man from the congregation. My grandfather was Ouachita County sheriff at the time. He later said he never grew accustomed to coming home and finding "that woman" in his living room, visiting with his wife—the same woman whose past business he had raided many times. He suggested that she stop coming to the house. But the woman remained a frequent and welcome visitor.

Mother's younger brother, Robert Newton, stood out as all the Pryor children's favorite uncle. Known by everyone as "Bud," he excelled in athletics both in Camden and later at Hendrix and the University of Florida. For many years, he held Hendrix's broad jump record. In his two years at Florida, he lettered in four sports each year. He was named to the *New York Sun*'s all-

America football team. When he was growing up, he used to ask my grandmother to fry him a dozen eggs for breakfast every morning, but she never cooked more than nine.

As a young woman of 20, Mother served as deputy circuit clerk of Ouachita County. When the circuit clerk retired in 1926, she ran for the position—the first Arkansas female to seek public office after women earned the vote. England Plunkett, a veteran who had lost a leg in World War I, defeated her. She returned to politics in 1947 as an elected member of the Camden School Board.

Mother was always an organizer. Her concept of good consisted in loving God and doing the job at hand. She put together a women's Bible class, and spoke at any political rally that needed a Pryor voice. Whatever the activity, she added a major force.

In the midst of the Depression, Mother led a group of Camden women in founding the Community House, a children's activity center for families unable to afford suitable housing. In many cases, they had to share homes with other families. For most of World War II, the Community House became a refuge for many children whose parents either served in the armed forces or worked at distant defense plants. Many mornings, Mother drove from one town to another across the county, soliciting money and pledges for the project. I still recall her standing on the Rialto Theatre stage between features, making impassioned calls for Community House volunteers.

Mother was a cook, a seamstress, a landscape painter, an amateur photographer, a graduate of the Famous Writers' School, an accomplished musician with a gorgeous alto voice, and a local historian. Five years after Dad's death, when she was 57 years old, she spent several months as a British-Guinea missionary, tutoring children in English and helping construct new family quarters in the jungle. She lived in a thatched hut; her legs carried deep scars from insect bites from that time until she died at age 84. She bathed in a nearby river as village tribesmen protected her from crocodiles. As a parting tribute, the tribe gave her a seven-foot python, which, on returning to the States, she promptly presented to the Miami zoo.

In her Christmas letter of 1950, addressed to friends and relatives around the country, she described me this way:

(David) still hasn't decided what he wants to make of himself. I don't think he could be hard-boiled enough to be a good business man as he would probably write off too many accounts and give away all the cash on hand ....
He declares he is considering politics as his vocation but he can't be serious. I think it would be too disillusioning.

She was right about my lacking a head for business, but I have to confess that, disillusioned or not, politics has always fulfilled my life. When people ask me, "How did you get into politics?" I have to answer that I was born with that instinct—an irresistible pull. It's all I know. Dr. J. B. Jameson, who delivered me at the old Camden Hospital, once joked that I came from the womb asking the nurse for her vote.

Our house at 307 West Washington was uprooted and moved away years ago, over to Locust Bayou in Calhoun County. Mother sold it to a man for $300. I have never driven over there to see it, fearing it won't rise as large and imposing and as filled with life as I remember it. Every room remains vivid to me. Of course, we lived without television or air-conditioning. A large, screened sleeping porch stretched across the house's back. In the summer, our whole family slept out there, listening to crickets share the stage with Dad's constant snoring. A huge fig tree spread high and far, just a few feet from the sleeping porch. We claimed it to be the biggest in Ouachita County.

Miss Annie Newton lived in the large house next door. She took in boarders who often sat on her massive front and side porches; we could hear them talking into the night. In the summer, with rocking chairs scattered about, the male boarders would sit in the front yard under one of the enormous magnolia trees, smoke, and tell stories. Choirs of sparrows added to the chorus. In the house's front, lightning bugs and an old street lamp helped illuminate Washington Street. Behind her house, Miss Annie kept a chicken yard.

Our backyard bordered on the Presbyterian Church's grounds. An English-style chapel, it was torn down years ago to make way for a new sanctuary and education building. For years our minister was Horace Villee, who preached in a morning coat and striped trousers. Dad served as a church elder, and mother a Sunday school teacher and an alto in the choir. In my memory, it seems we went to church every time the doors opened. Once a year, Mother promised Dad that—when she turned 50—she'd leave the choir and sit with us in the family pew. But that never happened.

A major part of our religious exercise consisted in observing the Sabbath, which meant refraining from any work or frivolity. Most of the time, we remained faithful to this obligation. But one Sunday afternoon, Dad and I slipped away to a baseball game at Kraftsman's Park out by the paper mill. As we entered the ballpark, a foul ball hit Dad on the head, crushing his new straw hat and knocking him temporarily unconscious. Dr. Jameson, who brought him around, teased that Dad had paid for his sin.

Religion in those days never confined itself exclusively to Sunday mornings and church buildings. Out-of-town evangelists routinely made yearly visits to the high school, appearing on Friday mornings at an all-school assembly. They'd preach the gospel and invite students to come down front and repent their wayward lives. No one questioned separating religion from public education. Since the high school principal also acted as a deacon in the Baptist church, he gladly scheduled the visiting preacher for a revival meeting on campus. Students had to attend, and, if we didn't get worked up, the visiting preacher sure did.

Toward each meeting's end, the choir sang, "Just as I am/Without one plea," and one by one, students seeking redemption joined a long line of fellow pilgrims marching to the stage. Those who stayed in their seats were supposed to close their eyes and bow their heads, but most of them—most of us—stole a glimpse to see who had joined the host. We regarded the "saved" students as warriors who had narrowly escaped the devil's temptations. We gave them a hero's welcome.

Chapter 4
Jessie and The Glass Hat

The Lides' and Usreys' large homes lined the next block from ours, on the way to town. Rumor held that, when Mr. Usrey died, his widow ordered embalming with a special fluid from their family drug store, for years storing his body in the upstairs bedroom closet. True or not, the story took on its own life, becoming established fact for neighborhood children.

Along with the Merchant and Planters Bank, three drugstores cornered downtown's main intersection. At Patrick's, an "old fashioned"—made with milk, chocolate syrup, and ice—cost 15 cents. I ran up my first charge account at Patrick's, buying my friends and classmates rounds of that tasty beverage for several days after school. Dr. Patrick kept a charge tablet, every month or so sending a statement to Dad. I reveled in my first experience of announcing, "Charge it!" No credit cards, no signatures, no problem. But Dad paid with a frown.

From our breakfast-room window, I could sight Charles England Plunkett every morning, walking through a vacant lot from Jackson Street, across Washington, heading toward our house. I would grab my book satchel and join him for the five-block amble to Cleveland Avenue Elementary School.

I realized my earliest political ambitions at that school, hoping to get elected president of Mary Bragg Wheeler's third grade. Three of us received nominations, and Miss Wheeler asked us to wait in the hall while the class voted. Sweating under the tension, I promised God that if He would let me win this election, I would never again run for political office. Our teacher called us back into the room. I had won! Before I sat down, I was already planning my race for fourth-grade president.

As things turned out, Charles Plunkett and I remained friendly rivals for years. In 1951 we became co-captains of the Camden Panthers, our high-school football team. Eleven years later, he unsuccessfully opposed me when I sought a second term in the Arkansas legislature. Ironically, Charles's father had defeated Mother for Ouachita County circuit clerk. Charles would move on to a distinguished law practice and chancery judgeship in south Arkansas.

After our district championship season in 1951, Charles won a coveted berth on the high school all-American team, and that's where our friendly competition stopped—in sports, anyway. I couldn't compete. Maybe some inherent value in becoming a football standout escaped me. That didn't mean I wasn't aware of football stars or failed to follow their flashy careers. Every Saturday afternoon in the mid-'40s, I sat by the radio, listening to Army take on foe after foe. Everyone I knew hovered near their Philcos or Zeniths, experiencing the latest gridiron exploits of the Touchdown Twins—Doc Blanchard and Glenn Davis—also known as Mr. Inside and Mr. Outside.

I still recall seeing them on *Life* magazine's cover, realizing for the first time what they actually looked like. They matched pretty closely the image shining in my mind—No. 35 Blanchard, a powerhouse well over six feet tall, and No. 41 Davis, small and swift, able to dash 100 yards in 10 seconds. I was thrilled in 1946 when the Associated Press named Glenn Davis athlete of the year, beating out even Ben Hogan and Joe Louis.

Closer to home, my boyhood hero was Clyde Scott from Smackover, outstanding as No.12 on the University of Arkansas Razorback football team, and a track star. He later received a Naval Academy appointment, where he also excelled on the field and cinders. He became an Olympic medalist, and later an NFL player. I admired him as much as anyone in the world, our connection melded by the significant omen that our birthdays both fell on August 29. Even today when I see this 80-year-old icon, I start to stutter as I try to make conversation.

It was one thing to idolize a football hero, quite another to become one. I did the best job I could for someone whose heart wasn't in the game. To be honest, I never enjoyed playing football, dreaded the practices, and would cheerfully have left the team, but social pressure forced me to stick with it. Any Camden boy in the 1950s who entertained the slightest interest in peer acceptance—and who could circle the practice field in a heavy uniform without crumpling to earth— went out for football. Even now, I still cringe if someone mentions August 20, the day football practice began every year. Memories linger of blistering heat, gritty shoulder pads, and 200-pound linemen smearing me in the dust.

I preferred the Saturday morning scrimmages with friends at Coleman Stadium. We refused to play any sissy touch games. Our sport was brutal and often resulted in sprained limbs and bloody noses. Somehow, recreational collision and pain seemed worthwhile when with buddies, as an individual choice, not sanctioned by any official. Also, these games stood as rare experiences when white and black players came together, amiably and equally. That felt right to me. It also made me wonder why we weren't meeting in other places like school, movies, Teentown, the country club, and even more puzzling, Sunday school and church.

For all its placid calm, our neighborhood offered a well-scrubbed collection of families involved in fair amounts of real undercurrent. The Rineharts lived across the street from us. By the time I came along, the parents had turned feeble, but Dr. Rinehart showed considerable energy, continuing a limited medical practice well into his 80s. Their large home flexed with masculine granite fronted by a wide porch across the house's length.

We often longed to glimpse their only child, Jessie, a town curiosity and easily our street's most intriguing person. Only once in a while did we catch even a glance. By the early 1940s, Jessie was probably 30 years old. Whisperings insisted his mind had been damaged in Camden's 1936 tornado. How that injury came about, we were never sure. Rumor also married Jessie to a rich and beautiful movie star in California—we pictured Linda Darnell—but she left him, and he went insane. According to this fantasy tale, the Rineharts had rushed to Los Angeles and fetched him back to Camden to straighten him out.

Miss Annie Newton swore that Jessie was a chicken thief. She alleged that once, in the dark of night, he had stolen two hens from her back yard. She claimed, furthermore, he buried them alive behind his house.

Jesse stories abounded. His hair hung to his shoulders. A yarn goes that once some neighbors walking to town spotted him on the front sidewalk, draped in a white sheet. Terrified, they shrieked, "Jesus has come! Jesus has come!" We were never lucky enough to witness such a second coming.

But one night when I was 11 years old, I sat alone in our front porch swing. I saw Jessie suddenly fly out his front door and jump into the bushes. He began firing a pistol in the air. I dashed into our living room, bolted the door, and peered out from the window. Soon a police car arrived, and I could see them putting Jessie in the back seat. I never learned the reason for this incident, or how it concluded. As a child, you didn't question such things.

Jessie was only one of several fantasy sources in those early years. I used to imagine mobster figures slipping into Camden via Chicago or Miami. Most of these whimsies rose from Warner Bros.'s black-and-white crime movies playing at the Rialto every Wednesday and Thursday—those tough-guy adventures with Richard Widmark and Robert Mitchum. Once the images of sinister double-crossers and con men ingrained in my mind, they suddenly appeared everywhere. In fact, I was puzzled when Dad, the county sheriff, refused to wear his .357 magnum on his belt at all times to protect us.

For a short period in the late 1940s, a private bar and nightclub—an "establishment," as such places were known—flourished in downtown Camden. Located just off the corner of Washington and Adams, and next door to the Merchant and Planters Bank, it operated as The Glass Hat. A parrot's image colored the front door, next to a peephole for checking out potential patrons.

The place somehow came into being without protest from the local ministerial alliance. Its shrouded origins remain a mystery. A set of rather flashy brothers, Bill and A. B."Buckaroo" Turner, seem to have founded the Hat. They originally came to town from around Stephens, some 20 miles south of Camden, after winning considerable oil holdings in a crap game. Buck Turner drove a yellow Cadillac convertible with leopard-skin upholstery.

The brothers hired a club host, actually a bouncer, named Nubbin Smith. Nubbin hailed from Chicago, sported a thin moustache, alligator shoes, and a "zoot suit." He spoke hardly a word to any Camden resident. In no time, Nubbin became the object of conjecture—a sure fugitive from justice. Buzz offered he had worked for Al Capone, been "sent out of town" until things "cooled off." In other words, the perfect anti-hero.

When I was about 17, B. T. Fooks, a prominent businessman who years earlier had invented Grapette soda, traded in his seven-passenger limousine for two pickup trucks at Pryor Chevrolet. Dad parked the limo on the used car lot. One afternoon, along with a couple of friends, in particular James "Bum" Atkins, we drove the fancy blue auto off the lot and parked in front of The Glass Hat. Bum, who years later founded one of Arkansas's most successful insurance companies, had fixed on Nubbin as a model of high crime and intrigue. He assured me that the limo—with its glass screen separating driver and passengers—would lure Nubbin into taking a ride.

Bum said we should get to know Nubbin. We suspected he'd be somewhere around the club, getting ready for the night's business, and soon he walked out the front door. Bum approached him gingerly, introduced himself, and asked if he would like to take a ride in this impressive, dark blue limo. Nubbin said that he wouldn't mind, and flopped in the passenger seat.

We drove out across the river, then circled back to town. Nubbin stayed silent. No one else dared say a word. We pulled back up to The Glass Hat. All got out of the car, and stood on the sidewalk, still mute. Finally, Bum asked Nubbin how he liked the limo. We all held our breath.

Nubbin looked down, kicked a tire, took a long drag on his cigarette in an exquisite onyx holder, then breathed out a long hiss: "*It's a water moccasin.*"

That was all. He turned and walked into the club, leaving us again speechless. I thought Bum would faint on the spot. Even today, we're not sure what Nubbin meant. Still, Bum and I use *water moccasin* to describe anything truly impressive and worth remembering.

Chapter 5
Mary Elizabeth McFadden
Cooper Heard Wilburn and Biggie

E ven The Glass Hat's raucous image couldn't incite my imagination like the vibrant tales that flowed from our long-time maid, cook, and surrogate parent, Mary Elizabeth McFadden Cooper Heard Wilburn. My parents doubted her story, but Mary claimed to have been married four times.

In every way, we considered Mary a family member, though she lived at 501 Short Street, the "other part of town." I still recall being captivated by her elderly mother's image whenever we dropped Mary off. A former slave— striking with her inky, black skin and snow-white hair—the old woman always sat quietly in her front-porch rocker. I never heard Mary's mother speak a word.

Like Miss Annie, Mary raised chickens in her backyard, and she warned us never to eat a chicken born in May. It could sicken or kill us. She would point to her huge palms' light skin, gravely revealing that, as a little girl, she had told a lie and her flesh had turned black—all but the inside of her hands. She also swore that, one winter during the Depression, her family lived only on black walnuts; their nutritious value kept all of her 11 brothers and sisters from taking sick.

We spent most summers at Mustin Lake, actually a large backwater pond formed by the Ouachita River nine miles east of Camden. Here Mary taught me how to fish. In her starched white dress, she'd share a communion with fish unlike any person I've ever known. She caught bream, perch, and bass that today would win national awards. She would stand regally erect, her scepter a cane pole, its line offering a worm or balled-up bread. After chewing the bread, she'd slip it from her mouth, molding it around the hook. Then she'd toss the line in the water. She kept a clump of Garrett's snuff in her mouth, claiming it attracted fish. Sometimes she only caught a turtle. A turtle that bites you, she warned, won't let go until it thunders.

On special days, Mary took us to one of Camden's three movie theatres— the Rialto, the Strand, and the Ritz. They're all torn down now. Children's admission was 10 cents.

The Rialto remained our favorite. It featured Tex Ritter and Gene Autry on Saturday afternoons. Going with Mary could have created an awkward problem, since the "colored" had to sit in the balcony. We solved this by joining her upstairs with her family and friends. Even though we loved going to the show, especially with Mary, I knew at the time (I was 10) this segregated arrangement made no sense at all; it would have to change. I hoped I would be there when it did. I would take Mary to the show with me. She could sit with my family and friends downstairs.

Despite our love for Mary, social separations insuring a segregated world stood firmly in place, going more or less unquestioned. This system also guaranteed that white and black students would attend separate schools in distinctly different parts of town, just as "they" had separate water fountains, churches, and even undertakers.

In Camden, Ben Williams—a devoutly religious man—served most black-community families from his North Adams Street mortuary. Respecting his leadership in a small Presbyterian church, Mother crossed all racial barriers, teaching an adult Bible class there every Sunday morning.

Some people used to say Ben Williams kept more cash on hand than most white folks. I considered that an effort at salving guilty consciences by the very whites responsible for racial wrongs. As long as he was rich in cash, what's the problem? Of course, nobody criticized this attitude. In fact, many things went unsaid. Propriety required looking the other way, or else being regarded as impertinent.

References to Ben Williams's alleged mounds of money meant he might have as much as Mike Berg, a Jew and the richest man in town. At the age of 10, I never quite knew who or what Jews were. I knew the Bergs had money, a houseboat and a swimming pool, and they drove Cadillacs. The Bergs were among the few Jewish families in town, along with the Newmans, the Zavelos, and Judge Stern in municipal court. Judge Stern was in something of a vanguard, when Jews were beginning to take part in Camden's civic affairs.

The Felsenthals were another Jewish family in Camden. They had moved from St. Louis and, along with the Rosenbaums, owned vast south Arkansas timber acreage. The Felsenthal land eventually became an enormous wildlife refuge, and Lake Felsenthal was regarded as one of the state's premier fishing and camping areas.

But it was Mike Berg who garnered our youthful attention, almost as much as Nubbin Smith. We thrilled to see him glide Camden's streets in his new Cadillac convertible. "There goes Mike in his Caddy," we'd say. The mystery of being Jewish intensified with his phobia against germs. He always wore gloves in public, and never shook hands with anyone. Rumor allowed how he required boiling a can's contents before he'd eat it, of course with his gloves on. Never, ever, did he dine in a café or restaurant. Since Mike was Camden's wealthiest person, I simply assumed that all Jews were rich.

We often ate at Newman's Café on Washington Street across from the post office. But the Newmans never mingled with us, there or anywhere else. Their children went to their own church, something called a synagogue, over near Helen Street Grocery. I always wanted to sneak in and see what a synagogue looked like, but I strongly sensed it remained off limits to Presbyterians.

I had other questions.

Why didn't Jewish families belong to the country club? In accordance with the time's custom, we swam at the club's carefully restricted pool, and safely played our nine holes on a closed golf course with sand greens—a club of white people, Christians all, who could afford to pay the dues.

Weren't all Jews rich? Did they all own a houseboat on the Ouachita? Were they all afraid of germs? Wasn't Jesus a Jew?

My questions matched those on many young Southerners' minds. No answers came forth, resulting in confusion on all sides. One day, during a pickup basketball game, I said something unkind about Jews. I don't recall what, or where it came from. I suppose childish ignorance lay behind it. I hope it was nothing more than that. But I still remember how my friend Burton Zavelo shook his head, painfully gazing at me. Then he turned and walked off the court.

We were in the fifth grade. I've never fully forgiven myself for that hazy but cruel remark. Every time I saw Burton until his death a few years ago, I had the urge to tell him I was sorry.

In our house at Mustin Lake, we built a special screened-in porch for Mary Elizabeth McFadden Cooper Heard Wilburn. She traveled with us to Hot Springs and Myrtle Beach, and to Santa Fe to visit Mother's cousin. But in those places, we knew that, according to long tradition, she would quietly keep her distance and spend her nights away from the family.

Still, I probably spent as much time with her as with my own mother. Her influence on my thinking—on my *life*—has remained profound and real. She lived with our family almost every day for 30 years. After losing a leg to diabetes, she spent her last years alone in a Camden nursing home.

Mary knew Mother better than anyone else did. Between them glistened a code of respect, friendship, admiration, and love—a solid bond never openly discussed, but obvious to any family observer. The warm relationship's silence assured its acceptance. A hug between them would have been unthinkable.

Their attachment existed very much like other close domestic unions in many Southern white homes. The pattern defined the lady of the house and her trusted black maid. This delicate balance goes back more than a century. It continues today, in spite of integration and the progress in civil rights.

Actually, it carries little connection with civil rights. The custom survives more like an ancient dance with clearly defined roles. And while it may be misunderstood or condemned outside the region, this odd twinship accounts for much of the civility among southern families. With only a change in gender, the play and movie "Driving Miss Daisy" describes clearly the unique relationship between many whites and blacks in yesterday's South. And some in today's as well.

During Dad's tenure as Ouachita County sheriff, Mary cooked breakfast in our kitchen for the county jail's inmates. She'd arrive at the kitchen before 6:00 every morning, brewing an enormous pot of coffee, and preparing eggs and buttered toast for "the folks downtown."

At 7:00, Biggie Young, a jail trusty, would knock on the kitchen door, place the tin plates of Mary's fixings in a big wicker basket, hang it on his arm, and head downtown to the jail.

Biggie seemed straight out of a Rialto movie. A large black man with a gold-crowned front tooth, he bore a huge forearm scar, the result, we were told, of a knife fight years earlier. I'd never seen muscles bulge like his. He could hold an arm parallel to the ground and let me swing from it. Yet, though he always arrived in crisp khaki shirt and pants and seemed outwardly jovial, I'd see a constant sadness in his eyes.

Biggie took the path from our kitchen in back of the house to Washington Street. Then he turned left, walking three blocks to the county jail, separated from the courthouse by an alley. Sometimes Biggie let me walk with him so that

I could watch him feed the prisoners. The jail, dark and dank, swelled with an awful stink. Biggie's belt held a ring with enormous iron keys—the only way to open the huge steel doors.

Though Biggie was a gentle and good-natured man, Mother always seemed nervous when he threw me high in the air, or when I walked with him to the jail. Any jail paraphernalia I came across fascinated me. One afternoon, I found a pair of handcuffs and stuck them in my pocket. Back home, I handcuffed my sister Elinor to a bedpost, where she remained a prisoner until Dad returned from Little Rock late that night to release her.

Biggie provided a special treat when he'd open the safe, showing me the wooden box of knives confiscated from jail inmates. He would tell a story about each knife, elaborate tales with characters and plot. I imagined hoards of people killed or robbed from their horses and wagons and stagecoaches.

Brass spittoons squatted in two corners of the sheriff's office, usually filled with stale cigars floating in creepy black liquid. One wall displayed a stand of rifles and shotguns, off limits to me, which only made them more compelling. A deer head hung on the wall, along with pictures of past sheriffs. These included two bearded grandfathers from my mother's side. As Newton family members and pioneers in settling Ouachita County, they filled me with a sense of history and the possibility of my following them. Even as governor and later as senator, I often met people who suggested I return to Ouachita County and run for sheriff. They meant I should get a job that really mattered.

Chapter 6
War, Mustin Lake, and Dixiecrats

In all America's communities, December 7, 1941, changed our lives in a single stroke. I was seven years old, and remember sitting in the living room, hearing the radio announcement: the Japanese had bombed Pearl Harbor.

That December day in Camden shone clear and balmy, almost like spring. One by one, bewildered families began gathering downtown, their car radios blaring the news.

We didn't know it then, but every Camden family would in time feel the direct pain of that far-off tragic event. I didn't understand when my parents said we soon would be at war. I asked why. Dad reasoned that people fought most wars because they want more land. The two main questions I wanted answered: Where was Pearl Harbor? And who were these Japanese?

Young men began to leave for Camp Joseph T. Robinson outside North Little Rock, and distant training grounds in California and Texas. Overnight, the city started gas rations and paper drives. At school, we conducted air-raid drills every week, ending each orderly march at safe zones, feigning collective calm.

On Fridays we pooled our money, buying war bonds and defense stamps for a dime each, the proceeds going to manufacture tanks and guns. President Roosevelt filled our living rooms on Sunday evenings with a magical, paternal voice that inspired and assured us. The radio fueled our imaginations, but the Rialto's newsreels offered our only means of actually witnessing the war front. Maps of Europe and the Pacific—at Miss Lalla's library down the street—became a buzzing gathering place.

The war came directly to Camden when the Navy began building a rocket manufacturing plant in Ouachita County. Soon after the war began, the government bought the old Berry Murphy farm. Overnight Camden became a boomtown. In my young aroused imagination, it represented a return to the old Wild West.

Plant workers' housing disappeared as people set up pup tents and lived in residents' side yards until finding more permanent places. Schools became overburdened, inadequate in numbers of faculty and classrooms. Cafes and dives rose haphazardly to accommodate the flood of service people and construction workers.

The Naval Ammunition Depot—commonly called N.A.D.—changed Camden's face for years to come. Traffic jams actually became regular occurrences on our downtown streets. At the Sanitary Café on East Washington Street, hoards of famished customers nearly grabbed burgers off the grill. Children packed into schoolrooms. Kids dug backyard trenches, playing G.I. and Nazi, of course with the good guys winning. Herschel McAnulty, the Maid-Rite Drive In's owner, when leaving for the Army posted a door sign: "Will Reopen After Hitler's Funeral."

During the war years, our family spent two weeks every summer in Hot Springs at Grasby's Cottages on Lake Hamilton. One August afternoon in 1945, we gathered around the radio on our cottage's screened-in porch, listening with intensity. The announcer told us we had just dropped an atomic bomb on Hiroshima; the war would soon be over. I was 11 years old.

During those war years, our trips to Hot Springs were with the Harrells. Our mothers would sit on our bungalow porch drinking Grapettes and would watch the children—the three Pryors and two Harrells—fire steel-tipped arrows at each other. B. T. Fooks had invented Grapette in Camden, first selling it in 1940. We always knew if people worked in the Grapette plant. They all smelled like grapes.

Because of severe rationing, our Chevy's gas tank would barely allow our making it back from Hot Springs to Camden. We also planned on at least one flat tire when hurdling the gravel road between Gurdon and Bluff City. Sometimes Mother kept the speed down, letting us ride the running board.

For shorter and more economical summer trips, we took off to spend several days at our Mustin Lake house. As soon as school let out in June, Mother would load the station wagon with children, neighbors, dogs, fishing poles, bedding, and groceries. We also packed slingshots, Daisy Red Ryder rifles, and bows and arrows. George Benson, older and bigger than the rest of us, always beat us to the car, hollering, "Dibs on the window!" While he sat on the front, breezy passenger's side, we had to endure the torrid back seat, like worms stuffed in Mary's bait bag.

The lake road's final leg exploded with dust and sand as we drove. One year some driver had hit and killed a horse, leaving the carcass in a ditch. Each time we traveled the nine miles to the lake, we stopped first at Woolworth's, buying a bottle of cheap perfume. We'd douse our towels and handkerchiefs, holding them to our noses, the only way to bear the stench. Mother would gun the station wagon past the horse's carcass while buzzards flew off in all directions, their feast interrupted.

In 1938, Mother had drawn up the Mustin Lake house's plans on a paper napkin and handed it to a local carpenter. She explained that she was leaving town for a month. Could he have it finished by the time she returned? He guessed he could. Built to accommodate the masses, the house possessed nothing intimate or classical in its design. Screened-in porches surrounded a kitchen and three large bedrooms. Dad used to say there was enough screen to wrap around Texas. Somebody called our place a barn on stilts, but the high supports protected the house from the Ouachita River's spring flooding. A corrugated tin roof played thunderous music when it rained.

Six double beds filled the main room; wooden rockers and Army cots with hard, musty mattresses crammed onto the various porches. The kitchen offered near-pioneering essentials: a large sink, a linoleum-topped table, and an iron wood-burning stove.

The nights were best of all. Every Friday evening at dark, the radio sparked with the Gillette Cavalcade of Sports, easily my favorite program. As the cypress trees' long shadows faded, a hush came over the lake. Stars appeared over the tops of trees, and bullfrogs bellowed and croaked against the night sky. From our front porch, you could hear a bass attack a minnow in the lily pads. A turtle would slide off a log into the water. Thad McDonald and Colin Threadgill fished the lake at night, and we could hear a whoop whenever their Lucky 13 or green jitterbug raised a big one.

At Mustin over many years, Hezekiah King cooked for our family. On special nights, he'd barbecue for the 20 or more folks who might gather. All afternoon, he stood at the backyard pit, nearly hidden in a huge hickory-smoke cloud, practicing his art. After supper, he and his guitar transformed the big screen porch into grand theater. Mother gathered the children in an intimate circle, weaving her tales of Ol' Weary Willie. Mother's best friend, Annie Lea Harrell, performed her Mrs. Gotnuthin' routine. Others revealed favorite heroes they had read about, ranging from Joe Louis to Doc Blanchard and Glenn Davis, Fibber McGee and Molly, and Johnny Mack Brown.

Then came time for bed and the mad dash to grab a cot nearest the fan. We put Unguentine on sunburns, and Mother pulled splinters from our feet.

We'd lie quietly and eavesdrop. The adults would mingle on the porch, discussing the local sheriff's race, President Roosevelt's health, the war, and whose boy wouldn't be coming home from the fighting.

We also listened fearfully as they named kids our age coming down with polio. How many had gone to the hospital in Little Rock last week? Were some of them simply checked and examined, then sent back home? Only one evil scared us more than polio and being trapped in an iron lung: a Nazi invasion, and fear we would all end up in a concentration camp.

One of Mother's most impressive talents was floating on the lake's surface. In the early mornings, we raced down to the dock. We'd find her in her scratchy, black-wool bathing suit, stretched out on her back, floating calmly on the still water—reading a book. We knew nothing of plastic rafts or high-tech flotation.

Summer every other year brought the state's political primaries. Dad's car business, often called "the Chevrolet place," could just have easily been dubbed "the political huddle." Politics always held forth as a main discussion topic. Spirited debate fired from stools and cane-bottom chairs remained a showroom staple, particularly during the summer primaries of my youth.

On election nights, the political establishment moved a half block from the Chevrolet place to a public viewing stand at the *Camden News* building. Returns poured in by phone from 33 Ouachita County boxes and from the state's other 74 counties. Tally keepers posted the returns on the newspaper's marquee, which had transformed into a giant scoreboard.

Chidester. Louann. Elliott. Stephens. Harmony Grove. Red Hill. Each box glowed with its own history and voting culture. The crowd waited intensely for each count. Political elections always promised a long and raucous night, particularly spirited contests for county judge or sheriff. W. R. "Chicken" Holleman would man the loudspeaker and announce the results.

My clearest memory of those rallies spotlights a hot summer night in 1948, when Sid McMath won the Democratic primary for governor. I didn't know much about him then, and even less about the issues, but I felt a kinship with the young Hot Springs prosecuting attorney. I had heard Dad talk about McMath's determination to keep Arkansas in the national Democratic Party, opposing the Dixiecrats' revolt. That was enough to get my full, 13-year-old attention.

Toward the end of that July, Mother and Annie Lea Harrell gathered their five children in a red Chevrolet station wagon. We headed out for two weeks in Myrtle Beach, South Carolina, to romp in the Atlantic Ocean.

Throughout the trip, I kept thinking about the coming Democratic National Convention, and the party's struggles with the splintered Dixiecrats. Strom Thurmond, the Dixiecrat presidential candidate, had campaigned in Camden earlier in the summer. He had also made known his number one choice for a running mate: our next-door neighbor, Governor Ben Laney.

Now we were spending two weeks in Thurmond's home state. I looked for him everywhere we went. I had made up my mind to set him straight: he should have stayed within the Democratic fold. I didn't track him down until exactly 30 years later. We became Senate colleagues, although on opposite sides of the aisle—and just about every issue.

Chapter 7
Leaving Home

Early in 1951, I plopped down my 25 cents at the Strand and saw "Born Yesterday," a romantic comedy about Washington politics starring Judy Holliday, William Holden, and Paul Douglas. It captured a world I had only dreamed about. Caught up by the magical film story, I immediately ran home and wrote our Congressman, Oren Harris. I asked if he would consider assigning me as a page that summer. He did. I spent three months in Washington, my first exposure to politics's real world.

On my first day, I followed instructions and reported to the House of Representatives doorkeeper's office, where I found William "Fishbait" Miller pacing the floor.

"I'm David Pryor from Arkansas," I told the venerable doorkeeper, who came from Pascagoula, Mississippi. "I'm here to be a page for Congressman Oren Harris."

"We've been looking everywhere for you," he blurted. "There's an emergency situation over in the Senate, and we want you to go over there. They've had an all-night filibuster, and their pages have all gone off to rest. They need help. Quick. Get yourself over to the Senate floor."

I didn't know where the Senate floor was. I figured it was at the Capitol's opposite end, so I headed there. As I entered the Senate Chamber, I saw Senator Joseph R. McCarthy of Wisconsin standing in the well, that area directly in front of the desk. He snapped his fingers, motioning for me.

As I came closer, he reached in his pocket, took out a $10 bill and a set of keys, scribbled an address on a piece of paper, and handed it to me.

"Here, son," he said. "Get a taxi and go to this address, and on the floor of the closet in the bedroom you'll find my bedroom slippers. Bring them to me."

I was experiencing my first day in the Capitol, my first Senate Chamber moment, my first meeting with a U.S. senator, and my first taxi ride. What a memory for a teenage boy. But, as I learned more about our government, I came to see McCarthy as a stain on the democratic system.

The next year, I graduated from high school. In early June, Mother and my sister Elinor and I joined a group of 11 Arkansans for a European trip. We sailed from New York on the *Britannic*. Over the next several weeks, we visited seven countries. For some reason, I kept my watch on Camden time during the entire trip. Maybe I suffered lingering homesickness, but I suspect I was keeping mental tabs on a hot race for governor back home. Judge Francis Cherry of Jonesboro had won the Democratic primary, pulling a major upset over several better-known political figures. I didn't want to lose touch with that unfolding drama. Somehow, by leaving my watch on Central time, I felt connected.

I was set to enter my freshman year at Baylor University. But one night in Geneva, Switzerland, I suddenly awakened, as if by a loud clap of thunder. No, I shouldn't go to Baylor. What was behind this sudden epiphany, I have no idea. In any event, I called my Camden cousin, Gordon Newton, who had just finished his freshman year at Henderson State College in Arkadelphia. I asked if he could use his influence to help get me admitted for the fall. It worked. By airmail—problematic at that time—I paid tuition, scheduled my classes, secured a room in Womack Hall, and withdrew from Baylor.

That summer was tough for Dad. He stayed alone in our house on Graham Street, only dabbling in the governor's race, and not showing much interest in the car business. Only a year before, he had moved the Chevrolet place from its traditional location on Jefferson Street down to Van Buren, to a new art-deco building near the river. The facility featured separate hydraulic lifts for each mechanic. A wide new showroom spread across the building's entire front. Opening the new dealership became a major social event in town, but Dad quickly seemed to lose interest in its shiny newness. The spiffy surroundings simply didn't have the old shop's comfort and culture. Or its openness. In the old shop, he loved to hang out his office window and see everything that went on. But in his new sheltered office, that old love escaped him.

When we came home in late August, Dad's appearance concerned us. He was listless and tired much of the time, with his normally healthy complexion given way to jaundice. Just before Labor Day, news came that General Eisenhower would speak in Little Rock at MacArthur Park's bandstand. A Republican, he was running a close race for president against Democratic candidate Adlai Stevenson. I knew if Ike came to Arkansas, I had to be there to hear him, even though I wasn't old enough to vote, or claim staunch Democratic credentials.

I left Camden early the morning of the rally, driving the hundred miles to Little Rock. As I approached the center of Bearden, Bradley Gilbert, a friend of

Dad's, jumped in front of me at the red light, waving his arms and yelling for me to stop. He hurried to the window, asked, "Are you Edgar's boy?" I told him I was. Dad had called ahead and asked him to flag me down. He had decided to hear Ike as well, and was headed up the road to catch me.

The crowd was enormous and wildly enthusiastic. At that time, Eisenhower was probably the world's most recognized figure. Only seven years earlier, he had commanded the European forces who fought and defeated Hitler. Americans saw him as a hero who had freed the world. Even though Arkansas stood solidly in the Democratic fold, everyone wanted to see and hear him. His speech was short. That scorching afternoon, among the summer's hottest, demanded too much attention.

After an hour in the park, we headed back to Camden. Dad napped most of the way to Bearden, where we picked up his car, and he talked very little. This wasn't like him at all. I asked if he wanted one of his trademark Roi Tans. He said that he didn't want to taste a cigar today.

A week later, while shaving, Dad cut himself on his right cheek. It seemed nothing more than a nick, but he couldn't stop the bleeding. He checked with the doctor that morning, who referred him to specialists, but no one could tell what was wrong. Within a week, he was facing a diagnosis of acute leukemia at the Scott-White Clinic in Temple, Texas. He died less than a week later at the age of 52.

My brother Bill was holding down the fort at the Chevrolet place while Mother and Dad stayed in Texas. For some reason, he woke up the morning of September 15 and decided he should join them at the clinic. They had spoken with Bill every day by phone, insisting the prognosis would be good, surely bringing them home before the week's end. But Bill's instincts told a different story. He arrived in Temple only hours before Dad slipped into a coma.

Late that night, Bill drove Mother back to Camden, both still in shock at Dad's sudden death. She later described how she dreaded returning home. The house would hover empty and dark, unfriendly, far from the open and gracious home Dad had always prized. As she and Bill drove down Graham Street, nearing the house, they saw people clustered on the lawn and in the street. She wondered who they could be. Soon she recognized our neighbors, friends, and family. Every light in the house was burning. She said, for the first time in her life, she understood the meaning of being a survivor.

On the day of Dad's funeral, even Camden's ever-churning paper mill closed for an hour. The Presbyterian Church was packed with neighbors, friends, judges, and sheriffs from all over the state. Most of the town made the short trip to Greenwood Cemetery. Later, in Dad's wallet, we found bits of paper—notes from people promising to pay for loans and car parts as soon as they had money. Most of these accounts receivable were scribbled in margins of torn envelopes and blank checks.

Dad's good heart and his willingness to extend credit without questions formed the fabric of conducting local business. One freezing January Saturday afternoon, he was scheduled to deliver seven log trucks to Anthony Lumber Company in Bearden. He gathered several men from the Chevrolet place to drive the trucks 20 miles north of town. I rode with Dad.

When we reached Bearden, we learned that the mill owner, Garland Anthony, was back in his office, sick with the flu. His office was actually an old temporary outbuilding at one corner of the mill property. When we walked into the overheated room, we found Mr. Anthony lying on a cot.

Dad said, "Garland, we brought you those trucks you've been wanting." Mr. Anthony fixed us with an uncertain gaze and whispered, "Edgar, look under the cot and get what I owe you out of the coffee can." Dad reached down and counted out the several thousand dollars Mr. Anthony owed him. Then we went on our way—never a discussion of contracts, prices, or sale terms.

Open trust of this kind sometimes yielded mixed results. At war's end, and after the enormous production of armor, a serious lack of resources hampered production of cars, stoves, refrigerators, and other heavy household items. The demand for automobiles easily topped every list, even old and rusty used cars barely able to roll off the lot. A new car or truck represented a dream most people waited years to realize.

Dad posted a price list on a roll of white butcher paper, hanging it in his showroom window. He made it plain that anyone buying from him would pay the same amount. Then he went a step further. He included names of people who had requested a new car or truck, and the order in which they had applied. Everyone knew what each person was paying, and when the delivery might take place—usually within a three-to-six-month period.

A Pacific-theatre veteran had lost an eye. He was returning to Camden, desperately needing a Chevy pickup truck to help his aging parents bring in their crop. The man's parents came to Dad, pleading their case: Please move their son to the head of the list. Dad's sympathy prevailed, and he agreed to assist them. But he insisted on one condition: contacting each person on the list, who must consent to the move up. That would postpone for weeks or months each person's delivery date. But Dad required 100% agreement, or the deal was off.

Dad, Miss Mollye, and Zann Gaston, plus others at the Chevrolet place, made nearly a hundred calls. They explained the situation, stressing requirement for unanimous approval. Without even a moment of hesitation, all those on the list agreed. Of course many were disappointed, but patriotism and a sense of community prevailed.

The following week, the veteran with bandaged eye received the keys to a fully gassed, blue 1946 Chevrolet half-ton pickup. The full Pryor Chevrolet contingent, plus many in town who had followed the story, witnessed the occasion. The *Camden News* sent a reporter and photographer. Everyone waved proudly as the young man drove away. He turned right at the Jefferson Street traffic light and drove straight into a used car lot. There, someone handed him a check for the pickup, plus a $300 profit. It was the one time I saw Dad break down and cry.

At the time of Dad's death, I had spent only a few days on the Henderson campus. Like every family member, I was stunned by the swift turn of events. It's never easy to accept a parent's death, or the loss of any close family member. At age 18, it's doubly hard for a young man to come to grips with his father's passing.

Bill was 22 at the time, and everyone expected he would own and manage Pryor Chevrolet. My older sister Cornelia had married, and her husband, Lloyd Lindsey, was establishing a CPA practice. Elinor was a sophomore in high school.

I spent several days in Camden after the funeral. The Sunday night I drove back to Arkadelphia, I turned into the campus and saw a large banner across the drive: "DAVID PRYOR FOR FRESHMAN CLASS PRESIDENT." Without my knowledge, a group of fellow freshmen, most of them I hardly knew, had started to run my campaign. And thanks entirely to those friends and their efforts, I won.

Dr. Dean David McBride was president of Henderson. I thought "Dean" was a title, not actually his given name. For several weeks, when I saw him on campus, I would respectfully call out, "Good morning, Dean!" I thought I was really making some points. Then one day, the president's office phoned, asking me to come by during the noon hour. It turned out that Dr. McBride's secretary wanted a few words with me:

"Did you know that as a freshman here it is improper, even impertinent, to call Dr. McBride by his first name?" she asked. "Even full-time faculty don't refer to him in that familiar manner."

I wrote him a long letter of apology. In time we became close friends, a warm relationship lasting until his death many years later.

After my freshman year at Henderson, I worked that summer on the Chevrolet place's used car lot. And without much success. I sold only one car the whole summer, a 1950 Plymouth coupe. In my spare time, I baled hay at the Holly Springs farm; at nights I made house calls selling Electrolux vacuum cleaners. Wilbur Redwine, Electrolux's district representative, encouraged this venture, telling me I had a knack for sales.

This talent evaluation turned out to be wrong. I drove fruitlessly around the county in a new Chevrolet convertible, top down, back seat and trunk packed with vacuum cleaners, hoses, bags, and sacks of special dirt to sprinkle on potential customers' floors. Actually, I did manage to sell two cleaners—one to Mother and one to Bill and his wife Mary Lou. I just knew I'd sell the third one to a woman on Old Smackover Road. I sprinkled a generous amount of designer dirt on her shag carpet, then she let me know they didn't have electricity.

I roomed at Henderson with Ben Hale from Altheimer. One late Saturday night, with nearly everyone in the dorm gone for the weekend, we suddenly woke up, startled by screams from down the hall. Ben and I raced to the room. Eldon Wallace of Carthage was doubled up on the floor, writhing in pain. We picked him up, carried him down two flights of stairs, and laid him on my car's back seat. Doctors at Clark County Hospital quickly discovered that Eldon's appendix had ruptured. They performed emergency surgery, saving his life.

To make ends meet, Eldon had taken a night job downtown at the Royal Theatre. I took over for him during his two-month recuperation. Taking tickets and boxing popcorn, I met nearly every person in Arkadelphia. Without knowing it, I had formed a support base throughout Clark County. Nearly two decades later, as I campaigned for Congress throughout Clark County, people would ask, "Didn't you used to work at the Royal Theatre?"

That fall I transferred to the University of Arkansas in Fayetteville. I wanted to take advantage of a wider course range, and meet more people from all parts of the state. Already I was thinking of some kind of political future.

I entered rush week, pledged Sigma Alpha Epsilon, and moved into the old fraternity house overlooking Razorback Stadium. We rotated rooms every three weeks, so in one year, you lived with literally dozens of roommates. It presented a sure way of becoming acquainted with the maximum number of pledges and members. That helps explain the legions of University alumni who, over the years, showed up in the governor's office, and in Washington, saying they had been David Pryor's roommate. All of them were correct.

I took a horse to Fayetteville that fall, boarding him at the old Gene Goff farm south of town. Not a good decision. I didn't have the time, or the expertise, to pay proper attention to the colt. At Christmas that year, I brought him back to Holly Springs, where Dad had held onto a farm long after he moved to Camden. He had raised whiteface cattle on its wide expanse of fields and meadows. Driving there in a pickup truck became an exciting family adventure, something like exploring primal wilderness. The reality (it was 10 minutes off Highway 9) didn't diminish the romance. Riding horses represented a major part of the fun.

Looking back after 50 years, I wonder why it seemed appropriate to bring a horse to college. Maybe I was holding on to home: earlier times when my life felt safely bound to simple assurances of parents, family, and a shelter with a wide sleeping porch. It also had something to do with my favorite picture of Dad, taken at his career's pinnacle—sheriff, businessman, farmer, politician, father: he sits, with a wide grin, astride his horse in the 1952 Ouachita County Fair parade—it was the last time I saw my father alive.

Chapter 8
Cherry Pickers

The May 1954 balmy afternoon was inviting serenity into the U of A's old SAE house. Then suddenly someone downstairs yelled up to my third floor room, "Pryor, you've got a phone call from some guy who claims he's Governor Cherry."

I couldn't believe it. Was this a joke?

The voice on the line began with no introduction or fanfare, "Would you be interested in driving me during the campaign this summer?"

Sure enough, it *was* Governor Cherry. Anyone who had heard him on those 1952 radio marathon broadcasts would know that voice in a second. He had started that campaign with less than 1% name recognition, but hit on a new way to carry his message: the "talkathon." He would ride into town, sign on at the local radio station, and stay for as long as anyone paid for airtime. Some days, as calls poured in, he'd sit and respond for 10 or 15 hours.

Now he was running for re-election. And that famous voice was calling me.

"I don't think there'll be much of a race," he said. "Looks like we'll be facing Mutt Jones and Gus McMillan. Oh, and there's a fellow named Faubus who's the postmaster up in Huntsville. He's making noises about running, but he'll probably drop by the wayside before much longer."

My heart could have challenged Bill Haley's drummer. "Governor, right now I have to finish this semester. But if it's O.K., I'll be in your office on June 1."

That was two weeks away, and it felt like forever. Driving a governor during a re-election campaign, for this 19-year-old political animal, seemed a dream come true. And especially this governor. I had watched Francis Cherry from a distance in 1952, and greatly admired his first-term record.

I wondered how he got my name. Perhaps through the Presbyterian Church. I had met people from Jonesboro—his hometown—at Ferndale's Presbyterian summer camp. But I had lost touch with most of them. When a freshman at Henderson, I sat in Gable's Café with friends one night when Cherry, returning to Little Rock with staff members, stopped to have supper. I introduced myself as Bill's younger brother; the governor responded that he had known Bill for many years. Maybe he somehow filed this brief visit in his memory.

Now my head raced. I had to take final exams, move out of the SAE house, and find a place in Little Rock. But, first things first: I hurried down to the Fayetteville square and bought a blue seersucker suit and some white shirts—the right style for a hot campaign. Then I called Watts Department Store in Camden and asked Tommy Watts to order a pair of black and white wingtip shoes. He said he'd mail them to me.

In a few days, I had finished classes, passed my exams, packed the car, and set out for Little Rock. That five-hour drive in 1954 seemed like two weeks. I found a room at 2021 Arch Street, near the governor's mansion, for $13 a week. The bathroom was down the hall.

A few minutes before 8:00 a.m. on June 1, I parked near the capitol, walked up the steps to the governor's office, and found the front door locked. I sat on the marble steps outside. Finally someone opened the door. I stuck out my hand and announced to a startled Jean MacGregor, "Hello. I'm David Pryor."

She shook my hand and gave me a puzzled look. "Okay," she said. "Let's see now. What is it you're doing here?"

"Governor Cherry has asked me to drive him this summer," I said.

"You must have misunderstood," she said. "A state policeman drives the governor."

I was stunned. Surely there was some mistake. "Well, could I see the governor?" I asked.

"He's gone to the governors' conference in South Carolina. Won't be back for a week."

About that time, Ken Francis, the governor's executive assistant, came through the door. I gave him my name and my mission. He and Jean huddled near the water cooler and in a few minutes he came back and said, "Son, we don't know anything about this. But you can do some stuff around the office until Governor Cherry gets back. Then we'll talk."

Just being inside the governor's office seemed a great start to me: the paneling, the aroma of granite and cigars, the plush carpet, and the soft-toned conversations. The space projected an unreal sense of importance and security, as though crucial decisions and actions swirled all around me. I felt like *somebody.* When the phone rang, you knew someone important waited on the other end. I had become a part of something big.

On my first day, I stamped justice-of-the-peace credentials and framed Arkansas Traveler certificates. The JP applications flowed in from the state's every region. I tried to learn the names of every town and county, and memorize details of Arkansas geography.

During that week, I made sure I met each member of the governor's staff, running errands for anyone who asked. Still, the nagging thought stayed with me: had my phone call two weeks earlier been a hallucination? Was the caller an imposter, some cruel practical joker?

Late that first afternoon, when no one was looking, I ventured back to the governor's private office. I literally caressed the leather chairs, studied the pictures and plaques lining the beautiful oak-paneled walls. The room commanded respect. Tall windows gazed out on the capitol's front lawn. Above all, the room's warm comfort held me. I silently stood at the governor's desk. I couldn't bring myself to sit in his chair. It belonged to him and nobody else.

Even to this day, I still respect the privacy of someone else's chair, careful never to invade the space of a person I deeply respect. Years later, as a freshman state legislator, I joined a House-Senate delegation to meet with Governor Faubus. While waiting for the governor to arrive, I saw a veteran and powerful state senator from southeast Arkansas step behind the governor's desk, taking a seat in the executive chair. From that day on, that senator remained suspect in my mind.

Governor Cherry returned to Little Rock, the confusion cleared, and my concern vanished. Yes, in fact, he did want me to drive him. I was to report immediately to the Spring Street campaign headquarters.

The Cherry campaign headquarters's small assortment of people seemed confident and unconcerned. The barny open space, set up in an old auto-repair garage, smelled of oil and tires. Memories quickly came back of our old Chevy place in Camden.

Two small glassed-in offices, both with a view of the main room, flanked a desk near the front door. One office housed a tough little 60-something man, red hair slicked down with an ample Vitalis coating. I didn't know it then, but J. C. "Steve" Stevens would become a friend and protector.

"Just call me Steve, son," he rasped. A three-packs-a-day smoker of unfiltered Camels, Steve was a seasoned pol. He had worked in Cherry's first campaign only two years earlier. After that, he had taken a job as a part-time revenue agent. Whatever that was.

"Come here, I want to show you something," he said. We walked to the building's rear. With a sweeping gesture he drawled, "See them seven cars? They're what we call 'loaners' from car dealers around the state. Friends of the governor's. Me and you, we're in charge of them. Somebody'll come and take 'em back after the election. Our job for now is to check 'em in and out, and keep 'em gassed up and ready to go. We keep track of 'em. You never know what's gonna happen in a campaign, you know."

But Steve Stevens *knew*. Among the cars, our favorite was a green and white BelAir Chevrolet. It sat like a prince at one end of the shop, its white sidewall tires gleaming.

Three days later, I got *the call*. The governor wanted me to drive him to south Arkansas the following day. The next morning, I steered through the governor's mansion's grounds for the first time—a fully alive 19 year old, charged up with the realization of holding a gubernatorial campaign's front-row seat.

I parked my car in back, and a state trooper escorted me through the kitchen and into the breakfast room. Suddenly, I stood 10 feet away from Governor Francis Cherry himself. He was talking on the phone—shirtsleeves rolled up, smoking a Pall Mall and sipping coffee—reviewing the day's schedule with Ken Francis or Jean MacGregor. Suddenly, I felt terrified, and my heart pounded.

"C'mon, we're late," he said, jumping up from his chair.

We took off in the governor's car, a blue and white 1953 Oldsmobile. The people of Jonesboro had presented it as an inauguration gift. It stood in a rare class: one in a handful of the state's air-conditioned cars. Winthrop Rockefeller and B. T. Fooks, Grapette's founder in Camden, owned the other two. We hoped no one would notice that the governor's car was air conditioned.

We drove to Fordyce, my part of Arkansas. On the way down, I wanted to point out favorite sites, like the mansion halfway to Sheridan. It sat on a lake off the road and looked like a castle. My peers and I had always heard the mansion housed a monastery, with monks appearing now and then on the front lawn. But none of us had actually seen a monk.

Silence reigned all the way down. The governor read the *Gazette*, always the sports page first. If the Cardinals were streaking, he was happy. I kept my mouth shut, but I was a nervous wreck all of a sudden, driving the governor of Arkansas.

Heavy road construction suddenly leaped at us just south of Sheridan, and I accidentally swerved the car off the road onto a gravel siding. "Good Lord!" the governor exclaimed. "Don't get me killed. Remember that if something happens to me, Mutt Jones could be governor of Arkansas!" The governor's attention remained focused on Senator Jones. He seemed, at that time, the only real challenger.

In Fordyce, we arrived at the Redbug Café for the noon Rotary Club luncheon. Somebody told the governor he was wasting his time coming to Dallas County. He could expect to get 95% of the vote. Almost everywhere, he heard this message: don't worry.

He told the Rotary Club of his accomplishments and repeated his campaign's constant theme: "Don't turn this state back to the professional politicians!"

Of course, we ate cherry pie. Throughout that summer, we faced mountains of cherry pie, cherry tarts, cherry cokes, cherry cake, cherry ice cream. Naturally we'd pretend each cherry offering surprised and pleased us.

I felt privileged to work closely with Governor Cherry. Here he was, the distinguished judge and white-haired Presbyterian elder from Jonesboro, elected by an overwhelming majority two years earlier. He had broken what many considered a political machine, and with the Highway Audit Commission in place, politics would vanish from road construction. With an incumbent's public support, Governor Cherry seemed assured of winning a second two-year term. Only the unpopular Tom Terral had lost a second-term race in 1926, the result of a major life insurance scandal.

So most Arkansans that summer focused on "the real race": former Governor Sid McMath challenging U.S. Senator John L. McClellan. A white-hot fight from the opening bell, it ranked as a match of true heavyweights. McClellan was emerging from Washington's celebrated "Army-McCarthy" hearings. McMath, the aggressive and dynamic former governor on the comeback scent, hounded the veteran McClellan. McMath's support included the labor unions, black organizations, and the political spectrum's progressive elements. McClellan's solid backing rose from the business community, including construction, insurance, and banking interests. The early political money flowed into both channels of the Senate campaign. The public, press, and Cherry's staff felt history would mark the governor's race with a mere asterisk. Cherry had ruffled feathers in his first term, to be sure. But no force could counter his record and support, or so it seemed.

Meanwhile, malcontent special-interest forces had multiplied. Poultry farmers thought he supported a feed and fertilizer tax exemption; the legislature approved it, but Cherry vetoed it. His constitutional amendment on property taxes angered many. Major printing companies bucked at his desire to reform government methods of purchasing stationery and printing supplies.

What hurt him most: his 1954 infamous line "we're going to get the old deadheads off the welfare rolls." Little noticed at first, the general statement usually struck people as a pretty good idea. Who wants deadheads on the welfare rolls?

Then the crafty hill politician, Orval Faubus, couched the governor's quote in language slapping people's faces. Faubus indicated that Cherry was condemning white-haired grandparents and lovable next-door neighbors who struggled through years of hardship. The challenger pointed to one old woman who government had threatened: she'd lose her benefits if she didn't spend the $200 in her bank account. She was saving that money to have a decent burial, Faubus stressed. He knew how to make a point hit the heart.

Cherry preached taking politics out of road and highway construction—an idealistic stand hard to oppose, except close to home. He soon found that people wanted nonpolitical highway decisions for *other* parts of the state. In their own towns and counties, the old system worked just fine, thank you.

The uproar caused by the U.S. Supreme Court in *Brown vs. Board of Education* also affected the gubernatorial race. We didn't know at the time how the court decision—handed down in May, and at first an early summer storm—would soon become a high-intensity hurricane.

Cherry issued a "support the court" statement soon after the decision came down, but when powerful opposition crystallized, he altered his moderate stance, trying to cool the boiling issue.

The Fayetteville, Charleston, and Sheridan school boards had announced they would implement full compliance with the court ruling, but Sheridan recanted when its school board received threats of a recall election. Fayetteville stuck by its word. But a majority of the state's districts remained tentative and wary, hoping other districts would move first and show the way.

Cherry also lacked a warm relationship with many legislators and local politicians. He shunned county leaders who he thought tried to take advantage of him. A man of little patience, sometimes his short temper would snap. Give and take in Arkansas politics could become noticeably foreign and distasteful to him. One *Arkansas Gazette* editorial noted, "He needles easily, is blunt to the point of harshness at times."

I recall a trip to Bradley County for a fish fry at a Saline River overnight camp. House Speaker Carroll Hollingsworth, a political icon in the General Assembly and a major power broker in south Arkansas, introduced Governor Cherry to some hundred invited guests. We spent the night on the rustic camp's cots, and I vividly remember sitting up late, listening to the card players murmur their discontent with Cherry and his administration. I knew then that something was wrong, but I couldn't put my young finger on it. Even with contacts in every Arkansas county, the governor and his administration had found it difficult to connect. And in politics, connecting is the key to survival.

Chapter 9
The Man from the Hills

The Cherry campaign's entire tempo changed in late June, not long before the sultry July primaries. If a close vote required a runoff, it would come in August, the summer's most torrid month.

It seemed clear that State Senator Gus McMillan's campaign had stalled. But Senator Guy "Mutt" Jones was suddenly whipping up crowds, ranting how Cherry couldn't be trusted. All of 5'2" and with fiery tongue, the Conway legislator had been dubbed by the press as the "Bantam Rooster." And the little-known postmaster Orval Faubus, low-key at the race's beginning, was now developing a magnetic rhythm with his stump speeches and mountain manners.

The son of Sam Faubus, an avowed socialist and prolific letters-to-the-editor writer, Orval had received little formal education; his first job, as a teacher, brought in only $100 a month. After he received the rural-postmaster appointment, Sid McMath plucked him out of the Ozark hills, planting him on the powerful state Highway Commission. From there, he leapt into Governor McMath's office as an administrative assistant, craftily forming contacts for future political use. Later in his life, McMath admitted his "terrible mistake" was paving Arkansas Highway 23 out of Huntsville, giving Faubus an "escape route" from the hills to the state capitol.

Faubus's candidacy carried a stain: the highway scandals that damaged McMath's second term, leading to Cherry's defeating the governor in 1952. Fully aware of this black mark, Faubus publicly swore he would not run for governor; in fact, he would not seek any office in 1954. Witt Stephens, ArkLa Gas Company's president and the state's premier kingmaker, had told him earlier in the year, "If you run against Francis Cherry, we'll whip your ass."

But Faubus surprised the political mavens, ducking into the Marion Hotel just minutes before the ticket closed, paying his filing fee. He put down cash, fearing officials wouldn't accept his personal check. A complete unknown in those early days, he saw many newspapers misspell his name "Orville."

Faubus could masterly blame an unpopular action squarely on his opponent. When Arkansas Power & Light announced a rate increase in July, Faubus charged Cherry with "raising the costs of your light bills."

Soon after that, I drove Cherry to Brinkley for a campaign appearance. When he rose to speak in front of the courthouse, more than a hundred women also stood up. As one, they silently pinned their current utility bills to their blouses. They continued to stand, not saying a word. This sea of faces once had strongly supported the governor.

When Cherry fought against the feed-and-fertilizer exemption, Faubus cleverly engineered the poultry and livestock interests into a statewide juggernaut. Cherry's one move cemented northwest Arkansas and the fledgling poultry interests behind Faubus; as a highway commissioner, Faubus earlier had gained support there by replacing gravel roads with paved highways.

The two candidates' vocabulary also benefited Faubus in the Ozarks. Cherry talked about "a highway system throughout the rural sections of Arkansas" or "non-urban roadways." Faubus spoke simply of "country roads."

Perryville, Perry County's seat, had scheduled a major July evening rally on the courthouse lawn. Arkansas's smallest county, it's located only 45 miles from Little Rock. Candidates for every office arrived, ranging from locals to the state's top foes. Over 3,000 people showed up in the sweltering July heat wave.

McClellan and McMath represented the bill's major draw. Gubernatorial candidate Gus McMillan led off by inciting a boisterous response with a new fox horn. As an impertinent youth, I went up to McMillan, introduced myself, and asked him to define his platform. He reached in his pocket with a deft gesture and pulled out a worn Gideon New Testament. "It's all right here, son. It's all right here." Then he moved off into the crowd.

The governor ordered me to park down a shadowy street two blocks from the rally. He sent me ahead to scout the territory while he sat alone in the darkened Oldsmobile, listening to a Cardinals baseball game. Just before they introduced him, he shuffled the two blocks to the podium. The heat had sapped his energy, or maybe the Cardinals trailed in the eighth, or both.

Standing before the crowd, he asked them if they really meant business two years ago, sending him to Little Rock as a reformer determined to clean up corruption. He actually seemed to want a response. But his audience consisted of hard-working people wearing overalls and brogans, hands rough from fieldwork and patching tractor parts, trying to make ends meet. They had no idea how to respond.

Of course, Faubus spoke that night. A newsman later complained he was too shrill, telling him to present a calmer demeanor. But I had watched the crowd closely, how they responded to this man's mountain smarts and down-home talk. Anyone really watching and listening could feel the crowd stirring, see they identified.

Representative Paul VanDalsem, Perry County's long-time political boss, had invited the governor to his home after the rally. VanDalsem possessed incredible political power. Only a few years later, he would establish a lasting reputation, proclaiming how in Arkansas men keep their women "barefoot and pregnant."

Because of VanDalsem's influence—the unbridled and belligerent control he wielded in the state House of Representatives—Cherry felt obligated to accept his invitation. When we arrived, VanDalsem and County Judge Carl Adams greeted us in the living room.

"Governor," VanDalsem said, "Judge Adams here wants to be state director of welfare. What I want to know is, will you appoint him?" He made it clear he would accept no hemming or hawing.

Cherry, ever guarded and suspicious, especially of Paul VanDalsem, demurred. The conversation went on. I walked to the kitchen at the back of the house. From the hallway, I noticed someone through a bedroom's cracked door. There on the bedside sat Orval Faubus. At the house's opposite side, Mutt Jones perched in a breakfast nook. His two nervous hands stroked a 10-gallon hat, his trademark. None of the three candidates knew of the others' presence. All had received the Carl Adams ultimatum. Judging from Perry County's election results some weeks later, Faubus had offered the winning answer.

As the July 27 primary neared, Faubus continued to hammer away at Cherry. Gradually, more talk arose about a runoff, something never discussed before. Cherry made minor gains by linking Faubus and the past highway scandals. Faubus countered that if your grandmother was on welfare, Cherry considered her "a dead head," and he would force a state lien on all her real property.

Election night brought a seemingly impossible result: Cherry, 154,000; Faubus, 109,000; Jones, 41,000; McMillan, 19,000. Faubus had forced Cherry into a runoff. Arkansas election history showed an incumbent could not survive a runoff.

During the two-week runoff's first three days, the Faubus and Cherry camps fought for Mutt Jones's and Gus McMillan's support. Together, their combined vote totaled some 60,000. Jones played coy for only a few hours, then wilted under his former supporters' pressure; they sensed momentum moving toward Faubus. McMillan endorsed Faubus as well, but later switched to Cherry. He cited "recent, unexpected developments."

On Friday, July 30, the race took a surprise turn: the *Arkansas Recorder* asked Faubus if he had ever attended Commonwealth College in Mena, a town in southwest Arkansas. At first, the question seemed innocent enough, simply a small inquiry into Faubus's education. The following day Faubus spoke in Tuckerman and then in Newport. He seized the question, accusing the opposition of igniting a "whispering campaign of smears," trying to label him a subversive.

"I am as free of subversion as the spring that flows from the mountain to form the White River," proclaimed the incensed Faubus. He seemed to make much out of very little.

Later he told newsmen he had never attended Commonwealth College, not a class, not as a student or a faculty member. For the next 10 days and until the election, Commonwealth College and its surrounding mysteries would dominate the governor's race. When a reporter asked Cherry if he was accusing Orval Faubus of being subversive, the governor denied raising the issue, but vowed to "look into the matter."

Faubus knew Cherry had purchased live television and radio time for August 2. So, on August 1, the challenger declared to the press he had, in fact, spent a few days on the college's campus, but never enrolled as a student.

Late on a Saturday night, when Governor Cherry and I returned to the mansion from several campaign stops, a trooper informed him of a visitor. In the living room sat a Mr. St. John, the *Mena Star*'s publisher. I walked inside with the governor, and Mr. St. John presented him with a bound copy of *The Commonwealth Fortnightly*, Commonwealth College's campus newspaper. I sat on the piano bench as Mr. St. John unfolded to Governor Cherry the school's details. The *Fortnightly*'s aged, yellowed pages peeled back Faubus's fascinating relationship with the college.

Situated near Mena in Polk County, Commonwealth based its founding and teachings on socialism. Its original founders, Frank and Kate Richards O'Hare—along with their associate William Zeuch—wanted to train leaders for the country's industrial workers. Originally intending to form a colony in Louisiana, the founders searched for inexpensive rural land, enabling the commune to grow its own crops and become essentially self-sufficient. With support from the American Fund for Public Service, a philanthropic organization with radical ties, Commonwealth moved to Mill Creek Valley, some 13 miles west of Mena, opening its doors in 1925.

By 1932, the campus had grown to 22 buildings, all erected by student labor. Even at its highest, enrollment never reached more than 55 students, most of them from Arkansas and surrounding states.

The Mena publisher told Cherry that a later investigation found Commonwealth's administration advocated forceful overthrow of the federal and state governments. On a more symbolic level, the school had refused to display the American flag, raising instead the unlawful communist symbol of the hammer and sickle. The school was forcibly closed in 1940. In 1944, the House Committee on Un-American Activities declared the school to have been "a Communist enterprise," and in 1949 the United States Attorney General cited it as "a Communist organization."

On the Sunday and Monday following Cherry's meeting with St. John, pandemonium reigned at the governor's mansion. Then finally, consensus: on Monday night, eight days before the election, Governor Cherry would deliver the speech of his political life. He would show Orval Faubus as, while not necessarily subversive, blatantly untruthful with the public about his involvement in Commonwealth College. The governor would hold up photographs as proof: Orval Faubus in the school newspaper, being *elected* student body president, and receiving other school honors.

The governor's frenzied staff brought 10 typewriters into the mansion's living room and east conference room. They banged out drafts and redrafts, argued over words and expressions, rehearsed and reacted to each suggested change. The pressure swelled as Governor Cherry grew closer and closer to addressing the state on live television.

That Monday evening, I prepared to drive the governor the short distance to the KARK television studio at 10th and Spring streets. As reporters gathered at the mansion's back gate, I brought the Oldsmobile around front and waited for him to come out. Finally, he walked through the front door. Before he reached the car, he turned and vomited in the shrubbery.

He said nothing on the drive downtown, or in the reception room at Channel Four. He went before the camera, and the red light went on. He began a halting address, his voice weak, with little inflection or energy. It was a statewide hookup. He read from Faubus's claims of never being a student at Commonwealth, then he showed the photograph of Faubus as student body president. For 45 minutes, he wove an elaborate quilt of fabrication and deception around Faubus and his stories. Finally, he concluded, "The truth in the record of Orval Faubus has risen up to shame him for his deception."

After the speech, Cherry came out the studio's side door, finding a crowd gathered in the parking lot. Many wanted to cheer him on, but most were simply curious about the whole election that was ending in a few days. But we clearly saw that even his supporters questioned his decision to make the speech.

"How'd I do, kid?" he asked me in the car.

"Pretty good, Governor," I said.

The mansion looked like a huge haunted house. I recalled the night, nearly two years earlier, after Dad had died, when Mother had driven in from Temple, Texas, expecting darkness but finding people and lights instead. Now a ghostly darkness prevailed.

But the governor quickly ordered all the lights turned on, inside and outside the house. The atmosphere instantly changed. A host of people flowed in and out of the mansion. Telephones never stopped ringing. Radio stations wanted transcripts for replay. Even late-night radio editorials were calling on Faubus to withdraw.

We thought the crafty mountain fox had finally been cornered. Then the counter-attack began. Mutt Jones called a press conference, cited Faubus's military record, and stressed his unwavering patriotism. Faubus charged at a Heber Springs rally that Cherry had cast a cloud on his good name and the peace of his family. He claimed his rights as an American citizen had been jeopardized, and anyone listening at that moment could also be in peril. He challenged Cherry and John F. Wells of the *Arkansas Recorder*, who had editorialized against him, to call him a subversive. Then he threatened a libel suit against anyone who would do so.

Cherry continued to paint Faubus as lying to the public, but the message was backlashing. In the voter's mind, Cherry was labeling Faubus a subversive. In a way, Cherry wanted to have it both ways: he accused Faubus of having ties to the Communist party while, at the same time, only calling him a liar and not a Communist. Even the *Arkansas Gazette*, furious at Cherry's tactic, endorsed Faubus in an editorial.

But Cherry never relented in his attacks. He blanketed the state with television speeches using photographs and props. On August 6, he spoke to 5,000 in Paragould and 1,000 in Jonesboro. On the same day, Faubus had a crowd of 3,000 in Batesville and 2,500 in Blytheville, ending his campaign before 6,000 in Jonesboro, Governor Cherry's hometown. Anyone following the campaign saw that Faubus's counterattack was moving voters into his camp.

On election day, August 10, the Cherrys voted in Jonesboro. In mid-afternoon, I drove Mrs. Cherry back to Little Rock while the governor flew to other election-day stops. A huge crowd gathered at the Cherry headquarters after the polls closed. For the first hour, Cherry led Faubus in most of the boxes reporting. But as the rural vote began coming in, the governor lost his lead and never regained it.

Faubus won Madison County, his home turf, by 103%. He explained the questionable percentage resulted from military personnel serving overseas; that vote had skewed the returns, and nothing about the counting was amiss.

At midnight, Cherry had fallen 6,000 votes behind. The headquarters emptied, and television and radio stations signed off. Mrs. Cherry and the children left for the mansion. The governor and his staff went through the motions of working the phones one last time. At about 3:00 a.m., Governor Cherry climbed in the Oldsmobile's backseat, and I drove him back to the mansion. He was a sobbing and broken man, and kept muttering that only he and Tom Terral had lost a second term. I felt crushed as well. My political hero, the man who would clean up the state, now slouched in humiliation.

Trying to help him somehow, I blurted out that if the opportunity ever presented itself, I would settle the score for him. Ah, the impertinent promises of youth. What could I conceivably have had in mind? How could I even imagine settling a score of this magnitude? Among my Presbyterian mother's teachings, what were the strict lessons concerning revenge? Stop even thinking about it.

For years to come, I would replay that election, trying to understand what went wrong with Cherry's campaign, and how he might have set it right. He had stayed aloof, turning away potential supporters, reacting coldly to their offers of help. His idealistic proposals—to reform the state's taxation and assessment policies—reflected a naïve lack of political experience. He had supported a constitutional amendment to equalize property tax assessments, then later changed his mind; that couldn't have helped him. The Supreme Court's *Brown vs. Board of Education* decision, coming down in May, had further unsettled a wary voting public. Maybe he should have acted tougher in the face of an aggressive and crafty opponent.

But, more than anything, the Commonwealth speech's manner and timing proved tragically misplaced. After considerable debate within his camp, Cherry decided to deliver his address on a Monday night—to a live audience on Channel Four—eight days before the election. This seemed ample time to let the facts soak into the public consciousness, then bolster the initial charge with follow-up arguments, hammering home the issue's full meaning.

It was a disastrous decision. Far from giving Cherry the advantage of elaborating his accusations, those eight days handed Faubus time to counterattack each point in detail. To the shrewd mountain sage, the opportunity came as an unexpected luxury, almost too good to be true. Delivered several days later, or over the final weekend, Cherry's speech might have devastated Faubus, leaving no time to reply. But the carefully planned address boomeranged, dealing the sender a fatal blow.

I doubt that Cherry's defeat surprised people. Faubus had dramatically entered the political stage, gaining attention from all sides. It resulted in a classic contest between two starkly different figures. In the minds of many Arkansans, the McClellan-McMath clash overshadowed the governor's race. Their battle for the Senate took on national proportions. McClellan called for personal appearances from Senate colleagues Lyndon Johnson and Hubert Humphrey. McMath, battle-tested through two statewide races for governor, came close to defeating McClellan. But their contest turned into an old blood feud that inevitably ended as the established order's victory.

Cherry didn't concede defeat for nine days, hoping some miracle might take place. Somebody figured that a change of three votes in every box could have turned it in his favor.

The day following the election, I went in the late morning to the mansion, wanting to say goodbye to the governor and his family. He and a few friends sat in the east conference room. The cartoon in that day's *Arkansas Democrat* showed Cherry reading a granite slate with the inscription: "The first duty of a politician is to be re-elected .... The rule he failed to follow." The governor tore the cartoon from the paper and wrote across the bottom: "Dave, don't ever forget this lesson. F. Cherry." He handed it to me.

I left the mansion and drove to the Spring Street headquarters. The front door stood wide open, and I walked in. An AP&L crew was turning off the electricity. Scattered everywhere lay wreckage from the previous night—old posters, half-empty Coke bottles, stale sandwiches, cigarette butts ground into the green linoleum floor.

I heard someone call from the back. It was Steve Stevens.

"Hey, kid, guess what happened?" he said.

"What?"

"Remember the green BelAir?"

"Sure," I said.

"Well, it's gone. I've called the police, but they didn't know anything about it. They say it could be in St. Louis by now. Damn'dest thing. I told you, you never know what's going to happen in a political campaign."

Steve died within the year. In our last conversation, we still wondered what could have happened to our favorite, the green BelAir. Even today I still speculate about it. Like most things political, and most politicians, no doubt it was traded in years later for a new and sleeker model.

That Christmas, I received a card from Governor and Mrs. Cherry postmarked Jonesboro. Inside it, I found a $100 gift certificate for a new suit from Bauman's Men's Store—my pay for the summer campaign of 1954. I made it a matter of principle not to buy another blue seersucker.

The following year, President Eisenhower named Francis Cherry to the Subversive Activities Control Board, and he moved his family to Washington. The board, set up in 1950, was the federal government's response to the postwar Red scare. In line with the House Un-American Activities Committee and the early McCarthy hearings, the board was charged with tracking Communist influence throughout the United States. Several years later, Governor Cherry became chairman. He held that position until his death in 1965. The board disbanded in 1972.

Cherry's board service presented an appropriate historical irony. Many Arkansas voters looked at his Commonwealth attacks on Faubus as an unwarranted witch hunt against a valiant World War II veteran. Whether accurately or not, the public had come to see Faubus as a war hero. By 1954, even with the Cold War very much alive, few Arkansans welcomed any citizen being viciously accused as a Communist, and certainly not a fellow Arkansan who, as a G. I., fought in the Battle of the Bulge.

The ultimate sign of this mood came when the feisty Senator Joseph McCarthy rapidly fell into national disfavor. On June 9 of that summer, Joseph Welch had openly confronted McCarthy in the Army hearings, asking, "Have you no decency, sir, at long last?" Senator McClellan's loyal Arkansas constituency—seeing him turned against McCarthy some months earlier—considered it a gesture of patriotism. Cherry's attempt to link Faubus to Commonwealth College, thereby questioning his loyalty, led Senator Mutt Jones to publicly refer to the governor as "Joe McCarthy Cherry."

Chapter 10
Moving On

That fall, I returned to the U of A campus disillusioned with politics and determined to give up the campaign life. The bitter taste of Governor Cherry's defeat wouldn't leave me. From here on, I resolved, I'm majoring in business administration. No more of this dirty politics. It leaves deep wounds—too emotional and upsetting.

Cherry's loss marked my first major disappointment in elective politics. Eisenhower had defeated Adlai Stevenson two years earlier. But the general had gained widespread popularity, coupled with the lingering boost of our war success. So his outpacing the more intellectual, somewhat brainy Stevenson came as no surprise. Also, that letdown occurred much farther from home. We always regard presidential elections from a certain distance that rarely holds true to our own statewide campaigns. This difference proves especially true in Arkansas, where politics is unquestionably local. To see a hero, a mentor, rejected by our state's voters devastated me. Even worse, Cherry's own people abandoned him near the end. His own insurance commissioner went over to the Faubus side before election day.

With the political game firmly behind me, I enrolled in business school, signing up for courses in accounting, money and banking, and statistics. I even became editor of the *Guild Ticker*, the campus magazine for business majors. My friend Randy Tardy served as assistant editor, his primer for a later business-reporting career with the *Arkansas Democrat*. As my editorial ally at the *Ticker*, he promised to introduce me to profit-and-loss statements and actuarial tables.

Continuing my grudge against the Cherry deserters, I even invited Pratt Remmel, a Republican, to the SAE house for a speech. That's how far my resentment was taking me. He was running against Faubus in the general election. An astute politician and Little Rock's seated mayor, Remmel hoped to gain a number of disaffected Democrats—those wary of Faubus who might cross over to vote Republican. These "Cherry pickers," as they were called, made up a healthy voting block. A U of A alum, Remmel found a cordial reception on campus and, for that matter, throughout the state, especially in the larger towns. Although an appealing candidate, and articulate on Arkansas issues, Remmel fell in November. Faubus easily beat him two to one. The man from the hills's deep imprint had just begun.

I found that fall semester tough going. About Thanksgiving week, I realized I had made a mistake, thinking I could become an accountant or a banker. Frankly, I was bored stiff. Debentures and balance sheets clearly didn't rev my engine.

I longed to dive back into American government and Arkansas political history. I remained obsessed with Faubus's sudden, surprising rise to the governor's office—beating Cherry on August 10 and then sweeping past Remmel on November 2. Those two dates haunted my memory.

The stressful political year and my inner struggle for academic direction struck me like an unexpected knockout punch. Something close to a mental and physical collapse hammered me three weeks after the general election.

On Thanksgiving Day, I drove with friends to El Dorado for the annual football game between the Wildcats and the Camden Panthers. As I looked out across the field, vision in my left eye became blurred. Driving back to Camden, it became significantly worse. Our family optometrist sent me to a noted ophthalmologist. He discovered scar tissue on my eye, and recommended a Dr. Jack Guiton, an eye-disease specialist, at the Henry Ford Hospital in Detroit. To give this eye problem proper attention, I had to drop out of the University.

Mother and I took the train from Camden to Detroit. At the hospital, they assigned me to a ward with five other patients. For the next four weeks I went through a series of tests and procedures. My parathyroid glands were removed for tests. The diagnosis: some infection had invaded my body, but its nature and extent remained unknown. The doctor advised me to go home.

Folks in Camden tried to mask their expressions, but their faces showed genuine horror at seeing my jaundiced skin and bony frame, down to 130 pounds. Friends would go to Mother and ask if I could possibly be as sick as I looked. One day I grew restless at home. I dropped in on Camden's municipal court, checking out the town's political scene. Suddenly I doubled over in pain, unable to stand up. A policeman drove me to Mother's Graham Street home and helped carry me upstairs to my bedroom.

Mother summoned Dr. Sam Jameson in El Dorado, and that night he drove the 30 miles to Camden for an emergency consultation. He decided I had a damaged ureter, insisting he operate early the next morning at the Camden Hospital. He brought in a team of doctors and nurses. Due to the surgery's unusual nature, Dr. Jameson had the entire procedure filmed for later showings at medical schools. For the unprecedented surgery performed in a small-town hospital, Dr. Jameson was recognized the next year at a national medical convention in San Antonio.

I stayed in the hospital for two weeks, nearly blind in my left eye and barely able to walk. Full-time private nurses cared for me. One night, someone knocked on my door. As the nurse leaped up to answer the door, I jumped with her, pitching out of bed and onto the floor. They rushed me back into surgery, repairing a ruptured incision encircling half my left side.

So we started the healing process all over again. Physicians told me time was my friend, but I have seldom been so irritated or anxious to get on with my life. After another two weeks, the doctors declared the surgery a success and predicted full recovery.

That was the good news. The bad news was that I had lost an entire year out of school. When I got back to the university campus in the fall of 1955, I was determined to settle into political science as a major. Upcoming political events had grabbed my attention, and I could feel the old tug.

The Democratic Party was making plans for its national convention in Chicago, scheduled for August 1956. During the school year, I read every day about candidates wanting to unseat Adlai Stevenson as the party nominee and take on President Eisenhower. Even from Fayetteville, I could smell the sweet aroma of politics wafting from Chicago's south side.

My prospects of getting to the national convention and playing some small part came roughly to zero. I was involved in campus activities, running for this or that, but these clubs and councils didn't do the trick. While my appetite for politics grew insatiable, my contacts remained non-existent. I decided to aim at Washington for the summer, and brush up against a real politician or two.

Congressman Harris had brought me to Washington as a page back in 1951, and I had stayed out of trouble during my service. Also, he was a long-time family friend. I hoped he might help me land a job in the summer of '56. I fired off an air mail letter asking for whatever help he could extend.

Luckily for me, he came through. Patronage jobs existed on the Capitol police force, on the Hill buildings' elevators, and in the House and Senate post offices. Almost all these workers were enrolled at one of Washington's many universities. The trick was getting a senator or congressman to sponsor you, extending the patronage to a constituent. The salary would barely pay for rent and gas, but the experience would be invaluable for this wide-eyed political enthusiast, eager to soak it all in.

Congressman Harris found me a job delivering mail in the House office buildings. In no time, I had rented a room on Capitol Hill and joined the post office's 3:00 a.m. shift, one I wanted to work because I'd get off at 10:00 a.m. It would free me to attend committee hearings and watch the House or Senate from the gallery. These legislative sessions carried me a long way from Camden's municipal court proceedings.

Congress was buzzing that summer. Both parties were gearing up for their national conventions. I eagerly attended Congressional committee hearings on both sides of the Capitol. It soon became clear the real work took place here. Over two days in July, I watched the House Un-American Activities Committee try to get the best of playwright Arthur Miller, but he skillfully resisted their taunts and jabs. I still recall his eloquent use of language. His play *The Crucible* had told the story of 17th century witch hunts in New England, pictured as a close analogy to the House's anti-Communist hearings. Committee members regarded Miller as a hostile witness. Most would have preferred him in leg irons.

The committee subpoenaed Miller ostensibly because he wouldn't name writers who had attended scriptwriting sessions during his early years in Hollywood. But everyone knew the real reason: Miller was about to marry the actress Marilyn Monroe. Forcing Miller to testify would also draw the press, and the committee needed to gain as much attention as possible. As Miller said, the HUAC's tide was ebbing.

Later news accounts revealed what Chairman Francis Walter of Pennsylvania had told Miller's lawyer—he would cancel the hearing if Marilyn Monroe would consent to be photographed with him. As the story went, she turned him down, so the hearing took place. Did Arthur Miller have Communist leanings? Probably not. But predictable politics in 1956 required asking the question.

One day I sat in the Capitol rotunda next to one of the statues, eating a sandwich and reading *Profiles in Courage* by John F. Kennedy, the young senator from Massachusetts. Published earlier in the year, the book sat high on reading lists of everyone I knew.

Somebody came up to me and tapped me on the leg. "Son, how do you like that book?" I looked up and saw John F. Kennedy. I told him I liked it just fine. I didn't have the good sense, or the presence of mind, to ask him to autograph the book, and I have long regretted how I stumbled through that brief, friendly encounter.

Chapter 11
Conventional Wisdom

When my mail-delivery job ran out at summer's end, I took off to spend a few days in Virginia Beach, not far from Washington. I then planned to head back to Arkansas and my senior year at the university.

Getting to the Chicago convention looked more and more impossible, but at least I had enjoyed a stimulating summer in the halls of Congress. Or in the House post office, to be exact.

Then, out of the blue, I received a call from Paul Chambers, one of south Arkansas's young and rising businessmen. He had obtained my number in Virginia by calling Mother in Camden.

Paul had unsuccessfully campaigned two years earlier for Arkansas's U.S. Senate seat. A relative unknown who dived into the major clash between McClellan and McMath, Paul Chambers wasn't expected to make a strong run against those Arkansas political titans. Still, he had mounted a respectable campaign, which gained him a position within the state party.

"Listen," he told me on the phone, "I'm the Democratic national committeeman from Arkansas. I have great tickets to the convention. I have a suite reserved at the Palmer House, and I want you to come along and act as sergeant-at-arms to the Arkansas delegation. We leave on August 11."

I said, "You bet," without giving it a second thought, even though I hardly knew Paul Chambers. Acting as sergeant-at-arms seemed even more unlikely than being chosen to join the delegation, but if it got me in the convention, I was ready to go.

A special late night train from Little Rock pulled into Chicago in the early morning. It had proved a riotous trip. Only party delegates and their families traveled on this "midnight special," and they were calling the Hogs as though we were headed for the Cotton Bowl. This unique cheer, with its swooping start and its loud crescendo, always swells the hearts of Arkansans, but to people in Chicago it came as a major shock.

A band met us at the station, along with Gressie Carnes, Arkansas's Democratic national committeewoman. She was also a native of Camden and a long-time friend of my parents. Her father, Sidney Umsted, originally farmed vegetables, but then struck oil in the Smackover fields back in the '20s. Since then the family had taken a prominent role both in Camden's social life and state politics. Gressie's husband, Jack Carnes, an enterprising inventor, founded Camark Pottery; he sold thousands of ceramic cats and swans to streams of tourists visiting the Camden plant. For eons it seemed, Gressie had attended national conventions, acting as the grand dame at numerous breakfasts and official dinners. We thought of her as the Perle Mesta of Arkansas, but in truth, Perle Mesta took Gressie as a model for her own efforts at playing political hostess.

The Arkansas delegation proceeded in a caravan from the train station to the Palmer House. There Gressie threw open the doors to her elaborate suite, welcoming just about every distinguished party bigwig from Adlai Stevenson to New York's Governor Averill Harriman and Tennessee's U.S. Senator Estes Kefauver. Crowds of excited delegates filled the hotel lobby, with tensions unusually high.

Stevenson and Kefauver had become the leading candidates for the presidential nomination following their televised debate on civil rights and school integration—the first debate of its kind on nationwide television. It set a pattern of political confrontation for years to come. Harriman had recently thrown his name into the hat, upsetting the two-way race. Even with that complication, the abiding question remained whether the convention would give Stevenson yet another round against the popular Eisenhower.

As delegates swept into Gressie's suite, Chambers and I were working our way through the hotel lobby and up to the front desk. We suddenly found a stone wall. The desk clerk told us we didn't have a room. We stood there baffled. Paul suggested they'd made a mistake; he not only held suite reservations but had received confirmation some days earlier. "I am the Democratic national committee chair from Arkansas," he explained with some stiffness to the woman, "and this young man is the sergeant-at-arms."

The woman excused herself. In a few minutes she returned with the hotel manager, an elegant man in white tie and tails. He checked the register, made a call from the house phone, and came back to the front.

"I'm sorry, Mr. Chambers, but you don't have a room at the Palmer House."

"But I made a reservation. Here's the confirmation." Paul brought out a piece of paper, which the manager brushed aside.

"Yes, of course," he said, "but your suite was cancelled last week by—let me see—Senator McClellan and Governor Faubus. And your credentials were cancelled as well."

Paul was infuriated. His mouth fell open. "Two years after a Senate campaign, and I'm still paying the price," he said. "And on top of that, I came in third!" His embarrassment was painful to see.

Considerable turmoil arose at that point, including outrage and confusion. As a result of Paul's refusal to leave, they reluctantly assigned us a salesman's sample room at one end of a long dark hall. Hotel workmen removed the stands and racks of suits and dresses, leaving just enough space for twin beds. From these reduced circumstances, we handed out floor passes and credentials to the Arkansas delegation.

Without a pass, Paul couldn't get onto the convention floor or attend any official functions. As for the sergeant-at-arms, I had full access to activities from speeches to luncheons to caucuses and everything in between. I took advantage of every opportunity.

Bill Bowen—originally from Altheimer and years later a major player in Arkansas politics, legal circles, and banking—was serving on active-duty reserve training in the Chicago area. We gave him a floor pass, and he and I sat together that first night, hearing Governor Frank Clement of Tennessee deliver the keynote address.

Clement attacked the Republicans as the "party of privilege and pillage." He swore the GOP would eventually cross the Potomac River, sweeping into the "Solid South" in the greatest water crossing since the children of Israel took on the Red Sea. His voice rang out across the amphitheatre's wide expanse. "How long, O America, how long?" he cried. He hoped the convention might draft him as a compromise nominee, but his expectations would crumble. In fact his passionate address, for all its drama, received a poor response. Later, Kentucky Governor Happy Chandler's speech met a similar fate.

As things played out, the real jockeying took place between Stevenson, Kefauver, and Harriman. Only two days before the vote, President Harry Truman shook things up by endorsing Harriman, and then Eleanor Roosevelt made a passionate speech favoring Stevenson. The stem-winder of all, however, came with Stevenson's nomination by the young Massachusetts Senator John F. Kennedy. His address grabbed everyone's attention. The one we all remember, it pretty much cinched Stevenson's selection. He easily won on the first ballot with more than 900 of just over 1,100 votes.

Then a funny thing happened. Stevenson surprised everyone by throwing open the vice-presidential nomination and sending it to the floor. Wildly inspired by the youthful Kennedy's speech, people naturally expected him to get the nod. It seemed Kennedy's for the taking, and in the beginning he put up a fierce fight for it. But many people considered him too smart to want it, knowing that Stevenson would likely lose to Eisenhower. They figured the Massachusetts senator would wisely look ahead to 1960.

In the end, most speculated that he quietly turned it down. I learned later that, in the midst of these negotiations, Joseph P. Kennedy, patriarch of JFK's family, sent a telegram to Senator McClellan. The two men had a connection, since McClellan had hired Robert F. Kennedy as chief counsel in his committee investigations, giving national prominence to the younger, more aggressive Kennedy brother. I've never known whether this story is political truth or fiction. Supposedly, the brief message read, "Senator McClellan, Jack is not ready. Joseph P. Kennedy."

The convention broiled, rambunctious and divided, in Democratic tradition. It went to an unprecedented three separate ballots, finally choosing Kefauver over Hubert Humphrey as Stevenson's running mate. Meanwhile, the Kennedy organization, far from lamenting the outcome, began to gather mailing lists and names of important contributors. Looking toward 1960 and the possibility that JFK might capture the grand prize, they began a tradition of sending personal Christmas cards to every convention delegate, political novice, and hanger-on.

The 1956 convention has gone down as one of the unexpected highlights in U.S. political history. Everyone anticipated a cakewalk, but it turned out more like a fraternity food fight. Here's a lasting measure of the convention's mesmerizing effect: young NBC reporters Chet Huntley and David Brinkley's coverage proved so popular that in late October they received their own nightly news broadcast. *The Huntley-Brinkley Report* started a long tradition of popular newscasters.

For me, the convention opened wonderful doors.

First, it provided me an opportunity to witness firsthand a major political party at its most absorbing and compelling level.

Second, and more important, it introduced me to a gallery of Arkansas politicians, officials, party operatives, heroes, rascals, and characters that in time would play a part in my own political career.

Third, that week I established an enduring friendship with Ray Thornton, then in law school at the University. He escorted his grandfather, A. J. Stephens, who was attending his first Democratic convention. Mr. Stephens, a distinguished and successful businessman, legislator, and farmer from Prattsville, was the father of Witt and Jack Stephens, then establishing their wide-ranging Stephens investment firm in Little Rock. In spite of his considerable background, age, and experience, Mr. Stephens seemed as awe-struck by the proceedings as I did.

Ray invited me to join them in the Palmer House ballroom to hear the singer Harry Belafonte, and I jumped at the chance. The room was already packed when we arrived. The doorman said no space would become available for the rest of the night. I was ready to turn around and find some less crowded and imposing spot for a hamburger. Then I saw a smooth maneuver by my friend Ray Thornton—a subtle and elegant move I have never forgotten. He slipped a $50 bill to the *maitre d'*. In a flash we had the best seats in the house—Ray Thornton, his grandfather, and me. We could reach out and touch Harry Belafonte.

The convention ended on August 17. The night before we were set to leave, I came back to our tiny room to pack and prepare for the trip home. A note lay pinned to my bed. "Dear David," it said, "I'm sorry, but business has called me back to Little Rock, and I'm leaving tonight. I'll see you back home. All the best, Paul."

When business calls, you have to answer. I understood that. Except, in this case, the Arkansas delegation's sergeant-at-arms stood holding the hotel bill. I called Mother in Camden, and she wired enough money to get me out of the Palmer House the next morning. So I didn't have to work off the bill in the hotel's mailroom. But I could have if they had one!

After the convention excitement, my return to campus and classes struck me as a crushing letdown. I tried to follow the political maneuverings in Little Rock now that Faubus had completed more than a year in office. But the main attraction unquestionably remained the Eisenhower-Stevenson rematch. Through the newspapers, I followed Stevenson's every move as he traveled

50,000 miles, delivering over 300 speeches on his vision of "A New America." His ability to define and discuss important issues inspired me to make plans for the years ahead.

Chapter 12
A "Sovereign" Commission

Early in 1957, soon after Ike's second inauguration, an unsettling dark cloud of racial tension spread over the South, and Arkansas in particular. Before the year would end, a storm would descend on our state's people and our educational system. Anger and resentment would seethe even among neighbors who for years had trusted each other and valued their close associations.

The U.S. Supreme Court's decision in *Brown vs. Board of Education* was three years old. Arkansas schools had responded with very little compliance to the court's mandate to desegregate public schools "with all deliberate speed." Faubus had begun a second two-year term in January. The previous summer, he had faced down a challenge for re-election from Jim Johnson, Crossett's former state senator and an ardent segregationist. Johnson had built his campaign around charging Faubus with being "weak on segregation."

The following year, voters would elect Johnson to the state Supreme Court, his surprising victory a major upset over the court's highly respected Justice Minor Millwee. By then, "Justice Jim" had become a household name in Arkansas politics. And the ugly emotions of white resistance to school integration were igniting throughout the state.

As the state legislative session reached its mid-point, two Crittenden County legislators, Senator Charles "Rip" Smith and Representative Lucian Rogers, filed duplicate sets of bills to protect "the sovereignty of Arkansas."

Each package contained four measures.

The first would create a 12-member body known as the State Sovereignty Commission, patterned almost identically after one Mississippi had recently established. A second proposal would make attendance non-compulsory at integrated public schools. The third bill required people and organizations engaged in "certain kinds of activity" to register with the state and make regular income and expenditure reports. The fourth would allow local school boards to spend public money for hiring lawyers in integration lawsuits.

This proposed commission provided, in fact, the ideal fuel for stimulating fires of hatred and fear. Using Mississippi as a model, the bill's writers empowered the Commission to defend the state's sovereign independence from national or federal attempts at control. The legislation clearly aimed to ward off forced integration in public schools and elsewhere.

The Mississippi Sovereignty Commission was already paying $100 to $150 to any person providing information on civil-rights workers' activities. The panel further provided additional awards for license numbers of cars parked at any interracial gatherings. In other words, an underground spy operation had received the legislature's and governor's full statutory support. A legalized, state-sanctioned bounty hunt, the Commission used fear, hatred, and citizen intimidation to thwart the law of the land.

The Arkansas House received the proposed legislation with enthusiasm, suspending the rules to automatically place it on the calendar. Within 48 hours, Representative Rogers rose to speak for the bills, only to be shouted down with demands to "call the roll." The almost unanimous vote saw only one member dissenting, Ray Smith of Garland County—truly a profile in courage. Most observers concluded that voters would never again elect Ray Smith to public office. As things turned out, he ran unopposed in the following election, and continued to serve until 1990.

The Senate attempted an identical parliamentary ploy, but two members began questioning the legislation's purpose. One bill sponsor moved to suspend the rules and place the package on the calendar for an immediate vote. By a one-vote margin, however, the Senate refused to suspend the rules, and several members called for a public hearing.

Earlier on the same day, Governor Faubus had designated the package as administrative bills, thus giving them preferred standing. But when he saw the Senate's reluctance, he sided with those supporting a public hearing. Senator "Rip" Smith, the chief sponsor, angrily denounced the governor, saying, "We don't like our allies deserting us!" He threatened to withdraw the package.

After visiting with legislators over the next several days, Faubus called a press conference. He announced that the legislation had sufficient safeguards to prevent harassment of the public. He said, further, that he saw no harm in passing the legislation, but admitted not knowing if the package was constitutional. Only months before, the voters had approved an "interposition" act holding that a state could intervene between the U.S. Supreme Court and individual school districts.

In a politically savvy move, Faubus supported Winthrop Rockefeller's move in opposition to the Sovereignty Commission. Faubus had earlier appointed the respected and popular Rockefeller to head the Arkansas Industrial Development Commission, because the high-profile New Yorker had wanted to play a role in public service but was not yet ready to run for office. He had fallen in love with Arkansas, establishing a cattle ranch on Petit Jean Mountain near Morrilton. When he learned of the Sovereignty Commission legislation, Rockefeller went to Faubus and threatened to resign his post if the bills became law. He claimed that such a commission would establish a political gestapo, setting Arkansas back into the Dark Ages.

The most far-reaching of the four bills would create the Commission itself. The legislature would grant the new body huge and unchecked powers, leaving it accountable to no one. The panel alone would determine what constitutes an "encroachment" upon the state's sovereign powers, then it could subpoena any person, group, corporation, or firm accused of advocating encroachment. It could further subpoena private records of any person or group accused of such advocacy, and conduct its investigation either in public or behind closed doors.

In a front page editorial, the *Gazette* said, "The real issue posed by the creation of the Sovereignty Commission bill is whether the people of Arkansas are willing to undertake the unprecedented step of granting to a state commission unlimited powers to suspend traditional guarantees of the individual rights of our citizens." Many small and courageous independent newspapers opposed the package, among them the *Pine Bluff Commercial*, the *Crossett News Observer*, and the *Baxter Bulletin*. Several church groups and ministerial alliances also voiced concern and opposition.

Rev. W. O. Vaught of Little Rock's Immanuel Baptist Church devoted an entire Sunday sermon to "this oppressive legislation." He was joined by Rabbi Ira Sanders, Msgr. James O'Connell, and Rev. Charles A. Higgins in encouraging their congregations to attend the hearing on Monday night, February 18, in the House chamber.

But legislative voices of reason remained in short supply. That Monday morning, Representative Rogers noted that the morning newspaper editorials should be printed on pink paper, and concluded that Harry Ashmore, the *Gazette*'s editor, was trying to "brainwash" the state of Arkansas. Senator C. E. Yingling of Searcy responded by defending Ashmore and reading into the record several of his editorials. He referred to the legislative package as "these damnable bills."

Citizens jammed the House gallery that Monday night. My roommate, Ken Danforth, and I had driven from Fayetteville for the hearing. A native of El Dorado and editor of the *Arkansas Traveler* (the U of A's student newspaper), Ken possessed a passionate social conscience. Totally without portfolio, I came along simply as a committed opponent of the legislation. We hoped they would let us speak on the opposition's side. Ken and I represented a sizeable bloc of the University's students who opposed the Commission; they had assured their support if we could only receive a chance to voice our views.

The public could take whatever empty seats remained available on the House floor. Many legislators boycotted the hearing, claiming they had already voted on the package and nothing would change their minds. Each side received an hour to make its case.

Dr. Hoyt Chastain, pastor of the Second Baptist Church in Malvern, received thunderous applause when he rose and said, "One of the principal reasons I'm for segregation is that the Communists are against it." R. B. McCullogh of Forrest City, later hired as the new Commission's lawyer, said that if someone comes here to stir up trouble, we have a right to know the person's identity. And former Governor Ben Laney pleaded for the package's quick passage, asking, "Will the people stand for integration?"

Laney, whose brother Fred had married Dad's sister Annis, came from Camden and was a long-time friend of my family. But politically we seldom saw eye-to-eye. Nine years earlier, he had teamed up with Governor Strom Thurmond of South Carolina to form the Dixiecrat Party—renegade Southern Democrats opposed to racial integration. Laney had become bitter with the national Democratic Party, and spent considerable time traveling the South, demonizing the Democrats. Though Thurmond, the Dixiecrats' presidential candidate, wanted him as a running mate, Laney hesitated to take on a major campaign, however agreeable he found the cause. He turned Thurmond down.

Daisy Bates, head of the Arkansas NAACP, along with other civil rights leaders, spoke against the package. Her allies included Odell Smith, leader of the state Teamsters Union, who declared, "It's un-American. In fact, it's communistic!" Rev. W. L. Miller, Jr., of Rogers claimed that the bills would set up a secret police.

Justice Jim did not speak, but he was roundly applauded as he strode through the crowded House chamber. Since his run against Faubus the summer before, outdoing Faubus on the segregation issue, he had become the titular leader of anti-integration forces. Many believed that Johnson, with close ties to segregationists such as U.S. Senator James O. Eastland of Mississippi, was instrumental in drafting the Arkansas package.

After some wrangling over procedure, the lawmakers refused to let Ken and me speak. They said that too many speakers had shown up on both sides. We learned later that the University administration had quietly squelched our testimony, fearing slashes in the school's appropriations. Dejected, we attended the emotion-packed hearing anyway, then spent the night at the Marion Hotel, returning to Fayetteville the next morning.

That night at the Marion, however, we heard the major participants continue their arguments through the wee hours in the hotel coffee shop. We received an eye-opening and inspired education in practical politics. For generations of Arkansas history, the Marion stood as the state's unofficial center of political and social activity. Its wide front porch and grand white columns offered the solid appearance of Southern manners and respectability. Even the old State House, a classic structure enfolded next door in a thick tangle of magnolia trees and verbena, seemed less authoritative and historic than the Marion Hotel. Someone said that more negotiations and deal-making went on in the Garhole, the hotel basement's bar, and in the spacious dining room upstairs, than in all of Arkansas's restaurants, dives, auction houses, racetracks, and churches put together.

Of that night-long wealth of spirited opinions, Ernie Deane, the *Gazette*'s political writer, wrote in his Sunday column, "What a beating logic takes at an event like this, what a terrible beating."

Before the Senate voted the next day, Senator Robert Hays Williams of Russellville rose to the floor and asked, "If we can go after the NAACP today, then what about the Rotary Club tomorrow?" Even the feisty Mutt Jones from Conway, a Faubus supporter, declared, "This is the most vicious legislation a democratic body ever enacted upon its people."

Only 12 of the 35 senators voted against the package, and it went to the governor for his signature. In less than two weeks, the legislation setting up the Sovereignty Commission included an array of segregation bills. They passed with almost no debate, were signed into law, and the panel received $50,000 to begin operations. Commission members would include the governor, attorney general, lieutenant governor, speaker of the house, two senators, and three House members. The bill required the governor to complete the Commission's membership by appointing three public citizens.

Faubus appeared hesitant to cast his entire lot with the most rabid segregationists. In any case, he failed to designate his choices, and the commission couldn't become active until he did. Johnson, ever the segregationist and antagonist, needled the governor for timidly dragging his feet. Legislative leaders also grew perplexed at his hands-off attitude. On July 2, five months after the Commission's birth, a lawsuit was filed mandating that Faubus name his appointees. He responded, "This appears to be Jim Johnson's strategy and might have a political tinge."

On August 1, the governor appointed Dr. Joe Rushton of Magnolia, J. C. "Bex" Shaver of Wynne, and Connie Shields of Shirley as the Commission's public members. Days later, the group's brief first meeting took place in the governor's office.

On August 19, ten black ministers filed suit in federal court challenging the constitutionality of both the Commission and the anti-integration laws passed by the legislature. Bruce Bennett, Arkansas's attorney general and an avowed segregationist, fired back by filing suits against the NAACP Legal Defense Fund for failing to register with the secretary of state's office and not paying $350 in franchise taxes.

After two years and a flurry of litigation, the state Supreme Court ruled the Commission unconstitutional on the grounds that sitting legislators could not be appointed to any commission. It also ruled unconstitutional the panel's investigative powers to examine the books of any person without notice, search warrant, or judicial process. The Commission had met only once.

My memory occasionally returns to that Monday night, two years earlier, when crowds packed into the House chamber. I sensed a historic moment then, and my insight to its importance has grown through the years. I had witnessed the subtle art of social and political manipulation with a dangerous meanness that squelched the voice of reason. I saw the sinister ease with which headstrong leaders sow seeds of suspicion and hatred among an unsuspecting public. I also observed men and women of courage openly lay their reputations on the line, standing tall against bullies and racists. And I learned that at the bully's core lies a coward.

The fear and hatred didn't end that night in February. Seven months later, many of the same participants would gather as agitators at Little Rock Central High School. Justice Jim Johnson, Rev. Wes Pruden, and Amos Guthridge would play leading roles in both public spectacles. Many of us found it astonishing that these men would publicly identify themselves as the reactionaries they really were.

Despite his segregationist actions at Central High in '57, for some reason Faubus remained lukewarm to creating the Sovereignty Commission. He seemed suspicious of both Jim Johnson and Bruce Bennett, considering neither of them a friend or ally. Johnson had called Faubus "a race mixer" a year earlier, and Bennett had recently won the attorney general's post on a states' rights platform. Faubus surely saw him as a future political adversary. The governor's friends said he was always "keeping a keen eye on ol' Bruce." He was right to feel concerned. Bennett ran against him in 1960, mailing thousands of photos showing Faubus shaking hands with Daisy Bates, the civil rights leader. Faubus beat him anyway.

That spring of '57, I finished my degree at the University. I was ready to face the world. But not a single person in Arkansas or anywhere else offered me a job. This came as a genuine surprise. I had fully expected someone from International Paper or General Motors to meet me at the far end of the ceremonial platform, inviting me to join them in their executive offices.

That didn't happen. With no prospects on the horizon, I decided to go home. I didn't know why I was going or what I would do when I got there. It would be a long drive back to Camden.

Chapter 13
A Whole New Life

So I packed my car and struck out for home, a 300-mile trip south through the heart of Arkansas. I had made the journey many times before along those pre-interstate roads, crooked and narrow, filled with variety and character. Highway 64 takes you over the hills and right through the heart of towns—Clarksville, Russellville, Morrilton, Conway. Then you're crossing the bridge at North Little Rock, where Broadway Avenue leads you out past the stone quarries to the winding road toward Sheridan. You pass that mysterious monastery on the right, fronted by a tranquil lake and barefoot monks walking the grounds. Then the road suddenly stretches out straight through the Saline River bottoms, beelining all the way to Fordyce, where it starts a new small tangle through Bearden, and then Camden. It's not like that now. The new cutoffs make driving easier, but the fun is more or less gone.

This drive to and from Fayetteville always stimulated me. The contrast between the southern flatlands and the northern mountains promised something different and unexpected through to the end of the line. This distinction held true in either direction, whether I was headed to Camden or Fayetteville. But on *this* trip home, I had no exciting expectations, no future plan, no grand life design. Not even for the summer. I wasn't even sure what I would do that night when I pulled into our Graham Street driveway.

The one bright spot in my life was Barbara Lunsford, a beautiful freshman from Fayetteville. I had met her the previous fall, a total but welcome surprise. I knew I wanted to marry her, to have her with me on whatever trip or adventure lay ahead.

The only daughter among four sons, three of them younger, she stood heavily outnumbered and surrounded by males in the Lunsford household. She shared in raising those brothers, keeping them decently fed and dressed, helping address and correct their childhood misbehaviors, or keeping those misdeeds hidden from view. Always a serious reader, she matched excellent school grades with her efficiency in keeping a neat house and the welcome mat highly visible on the front porch.

Thanks to her houseful of brothers, she learned early to form opinions, and to defend her position if someone tried to tell her what to think or how to act. This refreshing determination counted as a rare trait among young women in the mid-50s, and increased my attraction to her. I knew this self-reliance would come in handy later on, if and when she became a politician's wife. I knew I wanted her at my side.

Barbara also benefited from her bigger-than-life father's sense of humor. Bruce, or "Poppa Bear," passed this endearing quality on to all his children. Given his size and demeanor, the "bear" description fit him exactly. Bruce and Barbara spoke the same hill language and laughed at the same jokes.

A close-knit family, the Lunsfords looked out for each other, but also willingly shared their home and warmth with any strangers who showed up at their doorstep—including me, and a lot of other people. A crowd always seemed to gather at the Lunsfords' place. They lived in a rambling house on the sheer edge of Mt. Sequoia, looking down on Fayetteville's rooftops and the University's Old Main tower. The house overflowed with antiques collected by Rosalie, Barbara's tireless mother better known as "Momma Bear." A pot of coffee constantly sat brewing on the kitchen stove.

Barbara's mother grew up in the Boston Mountains near Fayetteville. When Rosalie was two, her mother died, and her grandmother raised her. She met Bruce when he was working in a Civilian Conservation Corps camp outside Cass, in Franklin County. Born and raised in DesArc, Bruce had joined the old CCC during the Depression, when jobs were almost impossible to find. A master carpenter and builder, his entire life he took special pride in the public trails and stone picnic tables he constructed throughout the Boston Mountains' many parks.

For years, the Lunsfords operated one of those wildly stocked antique shops, forever in disarray, that still dot the Ozark hills's back roads. Poppa Bear always answered the phone with "The check's in the mail!" much to Rosalie's chagrin. I can still see her racing to beat him to that ringing phone.

Barbara and I were formally introduced at the SAE house. She and a friend came for a visit, and, near the front door, she greeted me with a dazzling smile. I had spotted her much earlier. One day at fall semester's beginning, I sat with friends on the student union's porch. I saw this superb freshman coed walking down Maple Street with a group of her friends. Her bright smile and way of moving seemed a perfect combination: grand style blended with simple undergraduate modesty. As I watched her, I certainly didn't have these terms right on the tip of my tongue. But, as I look back with a 50-year perspective, I can see my instant evaluation landed right on target.

Our first dates followed the usual courtship patterns seen on '50s university campuses. I invited her to a Blue Key honorary fraternity dinner. We had supper at Heinie's Steak House and took in a movie. We studied together. But unlike many couples then, we ventured into the small Ozark towns outside Fayetteville, dropping in when sale barns held auctions. Several times we drove to War Eagle River, some 25 miles from the University, and to the comfortable family farm owned by Blanche Elliott. There's now an Ozark crafts show every fall at War Eagle, where the surroundings' perennial appeal attracts visitors from all over the South. But for us, it provided a quiet place to get away from campus, and to learn more about each other in the midst of great mountainous beauty.

We planned a wedding for that Thanksgiving weekend in Fayetteville. It was the fall of 1957. With no prospects, no job, no place to live apart from one of Mother's upstairs bedrooms, I longed to get married and take on new responsibilities. So much for college-educated reasoning.

Once back in Camden, I thought I might teach political science in high school, even though no high-school curriculum included anything like political science. On top of that, I wasn't qualified to teach political science or anything else. But acting out of impressive self-assurance, I drove 15 miles from Camden to Stephens, where I asked to teach in their school system. Of course, I was turned down there, as well as in Fordyce and Camden. Education and teacher training: that's another subject I hadn't bothered to investigate as a student. You can't go far in the teaching profession unless you've earned at least a teacher's license.

For a couple of years at the University, I had written an occasional column for Ken Danforth at the student newspaper. Expressing opinions in print, seeing my name in a byline, getting feedback from friends—all this provided a rush, and convinced me I might have a future in journalism. I had not taken a single journalism course, and knew nothing about the newspaper business. But that in no way slowed me down. Even though I had no money, apart from a small nest egg Dad had left me, I thought I might finance and support a weekly paper in Camden.

My inspiration for this venture came from one of my heroes, Hodding Carter, Sr., editor and publisher of the *Delta Democrat-Times* in Greenville, Mississippi. His memoir, *Where Main Street Meets the River*, had come out in 1953, the year after I graduated from high school. It had lingered in the back of my mind, and became more vivid as I started thinking about editing a small-town newspaper.

Hodding Carter brandished the reputation of a vigorous and independent thinker with great skill and courage. As editor of a paper in Bastrop, Louisiana, in the 1930s, he had taken on Huey Long and his political machine. But his real fame rested in Mississippi, where his series of fierce editorials defended minorities' civil rights and, more than that, the essential dignity of all people. Nothing intimidated or stopped him from writing the truth about the unfairness and cruelty he saw in Southern society. I was young and idealistic enough to think I could set my sights on Hodding Carter as a model, and become that kind of editor and publisher.

But first, I needed to approach Barbara with the idea of starting a newspaper, since whatever route I took would necessarily become hers. She confessed that she knew no more about the newspaper business than I, but she found the prospects interesting and the idea exciting—if I was sure that's what I wanted. Of course, I wasn't sure at all, but I told her that I was. With that open commitment, I was on the hook to find out something about publishing.

As my first foray into gaining newspaper experience, I visited the *Pine Bluff Commercial*. Hire me for the summer, I asked, and give me a chance to learn the business firsthand. No way, they told me. They weren't doing public or private charity. I received a similar reaction in Fordyce at the *News Advocate*. And at the *Arkansas Gazette*. To add insult to injury—when I went back to the same editors and offered to work three months *for free*—they shook their heads and narrowed their eyes as if I was mentally unbalanced. Maybe I was.

Meanwhile, somebody told me about a Camden printing plant on East Washington Street down near the river, an area fallen into serious neglect. The Cotton Belt railroad station was long shut down, as well as the nearby hotel, once a gathering spot for socials and weddings. An icehouse across the tracks had folded some years after the hotel closed.

The printing operation worked out of a storefront shop around the corner from the *Camden News*'s new location. Dr. Lawrence E. Drewry financed the shop. He had bought an old press from some place in Iowa and moved it to town, hoping to attract local businesses' printing accounts. Dr. Drewry reportedly might be willing to expand the printing business into a local newspaper. He was a distant family friend, but I had never known him myself, and had no idea whether a newspaper would interest him. But I hoped the family connection might help me get my foot in the door.

Entering the back shop, I first spied an enormous man sitting at a huge linotype. The size of man and machine matched each other. He introduced himself as Preacher Rhodes, explaining that he served as an itinerant Baptist minister, preaching Sunday and Wednesday nights around south Arkansas, and working in the print shop during the week.

We hit it off right away. He told me to pull up a chair, then plunged into stories about his experience in the newspaper business. I didn't need to encourage him, either, as he spun tales about putting out the paper in El Dorado and surrounding towns. These were exactly the firsthand experiences I wanted to hear. I touched on the idea of starting an alternate paper in Camden, maybe covering the town's colorful characters and goings-on, and expressing opinions on the editorial page. He encouraged me to approach Dr. Drewry with the plan. I told him I didn't exactly have a plan. Preacher said, that's all right, just give the doctor a point or two. He promised I would get a sympathetic hearing.

He was right. Dr. Drewry could not have been more receptive. Most of my projections sprang right off the top of my head, and I think he knew that. But I guess something about the raw excitement, even the inexperience, grabbed his attention. He possessed a far more adventurous spirit than I had expected.

We prepared to introduce a weekly newspaper called *The Ouachita Citizen*. It would cover the county, and take progressive positions on state and local issues. Exactly what those issues were we didn't know, but we felt sure we either would track them down, or they would find us. We set a target date for late fall, probably around Halloween. With that in mind, we invested in a typesetting machine and another press that, when fired up, roared like six locomotives.

Suddenly my plate had become full. What started as a season of dark uncertainty had now rocketed with prospects of a new business and, even more sobering, a Thanksgiving wedding. Barbara had remained in Fayetteville making plans, and we spoke on the phone twice a day, discussing the wedding and the newspaper. We weren't sure which one loomed larger in our minds.

At our Thanksgiving Day wedding, family members formed our main backup. We married at 10:00 in the morning in the First Methodist Church on Fayetteville's Dickson Street, only a few blocks from the campus. Nearly a hundred of our friends came.

We took part in one of those traditional services where everyone divides up between Friends of the Bride and Friends of the Groom. After the ceremony, we all came together at the Lunsfords' house on Assembly Drive for punch and cake. Barbara's younger brothers turned on the black-and-white television set as loud as it would go. Since it was Thanksgiving morning, everyone was anxious to watch football games or hit the road and get back home. Following the reception, our collected families took over the old Mountain Inn Hotel for two or three days.

We enjoyed a quick honeymoon trip to New Orleans, stylishly driven in a black 1957 BelAir Chevrolet with a bright red interior. Then we landed back in Camden, trying to meet a payroll, and hoping to get some version of the *Citizen* in the mail on time.

We moved into an apartment at the back of Miss Sat Smith's house on Agee Street, at the corner of Maple. Wisteria covered the front porch. By funny coincidence, our apartment sat directly across the street from the first house my parents moved to when they married. Our rent was $35 a month.

It still seemed smart to seek advice on putting out a paper, and a little on marriage as well. I found those points of view, sometimes conflicting, more help than I had imagined. Bob Newton at the *Warren Eagle Democrat*, Bob McCord at the *North Little Rock Times*, and Bill Whitehead at the *Fordyce News Advocate* all came to my aid when I showed up at their doorsteps. So did Cone and Betty Magee in Cabot, and Frances Bestershea in Malvern. A closely-knit community of the state's newspaper people proved more than willing to assist a new editor filled with questions and uncertainties. It was also remarkably easier seeking advice than it had been asking for a job.

I hired Robert Maxwell from Smackover to operate the new linotype. The only one in the shop who actually knew how it worked—he could even change the ink—he had to always show up on time and stay longer than anyone. We kept a cardboard box in the back where Robert could nap. With Thursday as our publication day, we would put the paper to bed on Wednesday night, dumping the heavy bundles on the Camden post office's mailing dock sometime after midnight. Often our delivery came closer to 4:00 in the morning.

We took notes on Big Chief tablets, recording who had gone to the hospital, whose horse became sick, where people were visiting relatives, the week's activities in Red Hill, Chidester, Reader, and Harmony Grove. In time, we were receiving articles from 20 reporters around the county who became known as our "country correspondents."

Barbara carried a camera with her everywhere. I sold and laid out advertising in every issue, and she wrote a weekly column describing "good news" about a person in town. She also operated the stamping machine, a device run by a foot pedal that addressed each paper separately before folding it for delivery. Stamping meant hard physical work, especially trudging through the early Thursday morning hours before sunrise, as we prepared to deliver papers to the post office.

Mother compiled society news, obituaries, and cooking items in what we called the Food Fair. I edited copy and wrote editorials based on what seemed hot issues for Ouachita County or Little Rock. These ranged from sewer stoppages and trash pickups to potholes and animal rescue efforts. Now and then a tax measure in city court might require our taking a stand. Before long, I was beginning to take on the Ouachita County courthouse organization, as well as Governor Orval Faubus and Attorney General Bruce Bennett.

Sometimes our former college friends would drop by during vacation and write a story or two. We took anything they turned in. Hoping to gain public notice and increase circulation, we hired a writer with experience in society news. She had promised to put us on the map. On her first day at work, she looked at me and said, "Are there a bathroom in this building?" I could hear the map falling in the trash can. So much for public relations.

Chapter 14
A Public and Private Citizen

W alter Hussman and the Palmer media empire owned and operated our chief
rival, the *Camden News*. Palmer stood as the forerunner of today's WEH
Corporation, run by Walter Hussman, Jr. in Little Rock. His father, Walter, Sr.,
had married Betty Palmer of Texarkana, the daughter of Clyde Palmer, the media
magnate with a string of local newspapers in Hot Springs, Texarkana, Hope,
Camden, El Dorado, Magnolia, and other south Arkansas towns.

The elder Palmer had started his business in 1909. By the time he died on
July 4, 1957, the company had added a healthy round of radio stations including
KAMD in Camden. His son-in-law remained a major political force in south
Arkansas for 50 years, until his death in 1988.

Friends of my parents, thinking that "Edgar's boy" had lost his mind,
warned me against going up against the Hussman organization. It could only
result in despair and bankruptcy. But the challenge attracted me, so I went
ahead anyway, blithely unaware of the financial stakes and potential threats. I
suffered from either foolish rationalization or youthful brashness, but I felt
Camden needed a new voice, and that healthy competition represented "the
American way." While the older sages warned, my close friends encouraged:
"Sure, we need another voice in this town," they told me. "We should have a
paper that takes positions and concentrates on local issues."

The Hussmans weren't so sure. I had nothing against their family and, for
that matter, they seemed to have nothing against me. In fact, young Walter
attended a Sunday school class that Barbara and I started teaching at the
Presbyterian Church, and I had known their elder daughter Gale through
high school and at the University. We had always been on good terms. But
soon the Hussman-Palmer gargantua set its sights on the *Ouachita Citizen*—
and specifically on me.

Advertising sales depended on local business, since Camden store managers
at Safeway, Western Auto, or Chevrolet could spend only what their national
budgets allowed. If we couldn't sell a placement to the local representative, then
we went without. I took advertising from any source I could find. Once I

accepted an ad from Zales Jewelers in Magnolia. When the ad appeared, John Stinson, a major local jeweler who descended from generations of Camden business people, became so infuriated he pulled his account. He refused to speak to us for several months over what he took as a betrayal.

We operated in the black only around Christmas and Easter holidays. The Hussman team of ad salespeople pressed countywide merchants to remain loyal customers. Our ad sales team—me—saw every day how the Camden News elephant regarded a challenge from a mouse.

The competitive issue never exploded into open warfare. After all, this was a family competition, and Camden families and businesses remained too civilized to engage in outright conflict. What's more, Betty Palmer Hussman attended a women's Bible class in Mother's living room every week, and the indelicate business-rivalry issue never arose. Every Sunday at church, we sat in a pew next to the Hussman family, both sides demonstrating the strength of a weekly detente.

But as our struggle continued, I could hear echoes of family friends' warnings. I began to see my paper sinking deeper into a financial hole. Each issue usually came to eight pages, and I strived for a minimum of 65% advertising space. Making that goal proved tough. With increasing frequency, I'd hear Mr. Garland Hurt's voice on the phone, asking me to come in to Citizens Bank and cover the overdraft. This personal humiliation ran deep. Mr. Hurt was our next-door neighbor on Graham Street and a long-time friend of my parents. And here I was, digging into the Pryor-estate share Dad had left me, then walking into the bank every other week with hat in hand. The estate, not large by any standards, was comfortable. And it, including some insurance policies, was all I had to my name.

In late 1958, the Citizen had been operating just over a year. I cashed in my insurance policies to keep the paper afloat. This cash infusion of about $15,000 represented my heaviest personal investment in my brief business career. It covered only a few existing debts, enough to satisfy our paper contractors and the linotype company.

My self-confidence was dwindling even more rapidly. Barely scraping by, I was surrounded daily by my Camden heritage's tattered gentility, constantly reminding me of my family's high hopes for me. I was disappointing those expectations on every level.

Over and over, the critic inside me warned of life's greatest burden: an impressive potential. The Presbyterian Church had tapped me to become a deacon, and the Rotary Club had extended membership, as well as the Jaycees and the Chamber of Commerce. I joined up, but my heart never did. I tried to become a community participant, but nothing seemed to work. I felt like a failure—and worse—a hypocrite. One day at the Rotary Club, C. M. Sizeland, who owned the Ford dealership, asked why I had stopped shaving. It hadn't fully dawned on me until then, but when I looked in the mirror, I was ashamed of what I saw.

Barbara and I took off nearly every weekend, traveling somewhere in the state. We wanted to visit places we had never seen, but chiefly our journey distracted us from the fear that our dreams were rapidly evaporating.

We would struggle to publish the week's edition, dropping the final at the post office very early Thursday morning, then strike out for Hot Springs or Little Rock or, even better, the peace of War Eagle and north Arkansas's mountains. We financed our weekend stays in local hotels through a kind of barter system, known then as a "due bill," between our paper and the hotel. I would run an ad for the hotel, and instead of being paid, Barbara and I would get a night or two on the house.

At one point, we considered moving to Rogers in Benton County. The local paper was about to go up for sale. An owner of a successful Rogers baking company called, promising to back me in buying and running the paper. Even after visiting Rogers twice, and seriously considering the deal, I still couldn't make up my mind. In the meantime, Don Reynolds of Fort Smith heard about the sale prospects, swept in, and added the paper to his growing communications empire. I took this as a sign that, for the time being, I should stay put.

Meanwhile, emerging political issues loomed far more threatening than any media rivalry. Orval Faubus had reached his heyday, and I was staking out strong positions against nearly every move his administration took. He had defeated Cherry only three years before, and that painful memory remained with me. On top of that, I felt he was wreaking havoc on Arkansas and its future. I came to believe that—while our state's national reputation remained in tatters from the '57 integration crisis—our own sense of self-esteem had fallen even lower due to Faubus's despotic ways. Always verging on demagoguery, he surrounded himself with political cronies, cozied up to the utility giants, and packed state commissions with campaign loyalists.

It's difficult now to recall the kind of raw power Faubus had come to wield. Every board was a Faubus front; he expected non-loyalist members to resign before their terms ended. Cherry had appointed my brother Bill to the State Police Commission when Bill was still running the Chevrolet business in Camden. Two years remained before Bill's Commission tenure expired. Nevertheless, Faubus pressured Bill to resign at once. My brother initially refused, but resignations were flowing throughout state government, many at the governor's insistence. Bill soon left the Commission, and Faubus replaced him with Camden's Mike Berg.

Like most local papers, the *Camden News* and, in fact, the entire Hussman chain supported the Faubus administration. When Faubus took what I regarded as an objectionable stand, I would step into the breach, perhaps foolishly, writing a fist-swinging editorial. But the Hussman papers usually stayed discreetly quiet. Meanwhile, my reputation was growing as, not only a brash upstart, but a potential threat to the old order. On top of that, I was going broke. It was only a matter of time.

But I couldn't ignore Faubus's ominous presence in Camden and Ouachita County. In addition to putting Mike Berg on the State Police Commission, he named Mose Zavelo, an early Faubus ally, to the Alcohol Beverage Control Board. This meant anyone wanting a new liquor or beer license, or even to stay in business, had to go through Mr. Zavelo. It always impressed me that, while he owned the Style Shop, Camden's closest thing to high fashion, Mose Zavelo also exercised raw power over people's licenses and livelihoods.

As a member of the State Police Commission, Mike Berg stayed involved in all aspects of southern Arkansas law enforcement, especially hiring and firing state troopers and other police personnel. Mike's Cadillac convertible, front grill brandishing a gold star, cut a wide swath gliding through Camden's downtown streets. Reportedly, his office desk would instantly plunge to the basement if he sensed a bomb threat or a political enemy's or intruder's attack. Mike continued to be obsessed with germs, wearing his slick and expensive leather gloves everywhere he went. In his new power position, his long-time personal habits only added to the political mystique.

Everywhere I traveled in Arkansas—around town, county, or state—it seemed Orval Faubus resided there. His tentacles wrapped tightly around the fabric of our lives, and that influence and power seemed to go unchallenged.

Chapter 15
Hitting the Trail: The First Campaign

The Faubus machine reached a trial by fire on September 2, 1957, when the governor called out the National Guard to prevent integration of Little Rock Central High School. This precipitous action—its drama magnified by its unexpectedness—would precede an eruption of political warfare unfamiliar to anyone in Arkansas.

Small towns in Oklahoma and Kentucky had ended segregation with little trouble. In midsummer, North Little Rock, Ozark, and Fort Smith schools had announced plans to integrate in September. While not all Arkansans were happy about it, these efforts at integration stood as clear signs of progress, and a public preparing to initiate equal education for all the state's young people.

Many believed that Little Rock citizens would passively open their major high school to a handful of minority students. But Southern towns' acquiescent actions had only inflamed Arkansas's vocal segregationists, and a bitter resentment began to swell in our small towns and rural communities.

Toward August's end, rumblings grew, sometimes loud and threatening. If the Little Rock school board had its way and integrated Central High, then whole armies of protesters might descend on the city. Goaded by an unrelenting segregationist trio—Amis Guthridge, the Reverend Wesley Pruden, and Jim Johnson—Faubus decided to prevent nine students from entering the school. That action, which many found unnecessary and unwise, inflamed the most serious federal-state confrontation of its kind since the Civil War.

Throughout September and into the fall, Little Rock flared into a political battleground uniting true believers from all sides of the issue: teachers and students, parents, political officials at every level, national and international writers and press, education experts, and impassioned hangers-on. The world's eyes focused on Little Rock.

Faubus and President Eisenhower met in Newport, Rhode Island, on September 14. There the governor asked the president to give the state a little more time. Eisenhower thought the governor had agreed to admit the students at least on a temporary basis, but Faubus later maintained he had never given any such indication. This two-way misunderstanding resulted in a stalemate. On September 23, the nine students entered Central High amid a violent crowd's jeers and threats. Television and newspaper images of Central High School became familiar throughout the world.

The next day, Eisenhower—claiming Faubus had betrayed him—took federal command of the state National Guard. He also ordered a thousand troops from the U.S. Army's 101st Airborne in Kentucky to Little Rock. Ironically, as things turned out, Frank White, who served as Arkansas governor for one term from 1981 to 1983, piloted one of the C-130 transport planes that brought in federal troops.

Eisenhower's decision, and the army's ominous presence in the city, set off Arkansans' emotions ranging from sadness to fury, from elation to relief. These varied reactions aimed in many directions: at Faubus or Eisenhower, the *Arkansas Gazette*, the Little Rock school board, or lesser local figures. Most folks I knew believed Faubus had fueled the rabid segregationists' fire, and his public fearful warnings of violence were only a hoax. Many suspected he had quietly orchestrated the entire spectacle to guarantee a third term as governor. This opinion grew as fall gave way to winter.

I never doubted that—if Faubus had not staged the events—he certainly seized the moment and made them work in his behalf. His character manifested in entering with a grand gesture to protect the "public welfare," even if that meant totally disregarding nine students' rights and igniting a states' rights war with the federal government. This is what I could not forgive: he had implanted in the nation's mind a vicious image of all Arkansans fired with racial prejudice. And I knew that image was false, despite photographs of angry whites venomously protesting at Central High.

Frightening pressures spread throughout the state as well. High-school and college teachers grew cautious about their own free speech in the classroom, particularly in government and history classes. Instructors who became objects of suspicion feared for their jobs. The next legislative session approved Act 10, a bill requiring teachers to list their organizations, an effort to weed out members of the National Association for the Advancement of Colored People. This new law amounted to requiring an oath of allegiance, since the legislature had earlier passed a law forbidding any state employee from belonging to the NAACP.

Within two months of the Little Rock crisis, I became identified as an unwavering anti-Faubus editor and publisher. Every Sunday, the *Gazette* reprinted selected editorials published that week in the state's local papers. Pryor vs. the Faubus administration became a regular feature in this column, as many of my editorials began to appear.

My anti-establishment reputation expanded the following year when I joined with Camden friends openly supporting Chris Finkbeiner's gubernatorial campaign. At that time, Jeff Davis stood as Arkansas's only three-term governor (1901-07), and we did not want the two-term Faubus to follow in his footsteps.

The general unrest among most Arkansas people seemed palpable. Other candidates were trying to unseat Faubus—Joe Hardin of Grady and Lee Ward from Paragould—but we picked Finkbeiner as the most likely to win. He had become a household figure in Arkansas through his TV ads for the local family meatpacking company. His familiar image—calling "Ship Ahoy!" as he hawked wieners before the camera—had proven him a compelling if somewhat goofy public spokesman.

One night we put together a TV watch party at Mother's house when our candidate was scheduled to speak in Pine Bluff. His performance was a crushing disappointment. By the primary, we could see Faubus had bagged the election.

The governor came to Camden toward the campaign's end, speaking at the rodeo grounds before nearly 5,000 people. Barbara and I covered it for the paper, and stood at the front of the crowd. Faubus held up copies of *Life* and *Time* magazines, declaring, "*Life* is a magazine for people who can't read. *Time* is for people who can't see. And the *Ouachita Citizen* is a paper for people who can't think." With a flourish he held up a recent copy of our paper. The crowd roared its approval.

I knew nearly all the people in that crowd by their first names, many of them well. But something in that moment's tension made me sense a threat. People gazed at Barbara and me with a cross between a frown and a scowl. Actually, they glared. I said, "Okay, it's time to leave." And we got in the car and went home.

Perhaps my imagination got the better of me. But I felt a lot of those people were choosing Faubus's inflamed rhetoric over long-held friendships. I had never witnessed this type of crowd mentality before. Fear, I found, is an easy sell. Originating in the previous year's school crisis, a narrow vision of suspicion and hatred was spreading into the summer's Democratic primary. Faubus was emerging as one of the most effective communicators in the state's history. With a mixture of homegrown cynicism, humor, and fear, he could mold a crowd's emotion and turn it into a mob.

He won the 1958 election in a walk, with 69% of the vote. The arch-segregationists seemed to be having their way. Justice Jim won his race for the state Supreme Court, defeating the progressive and wise Judge Minor Milwee. Even a large percentage of the black vote had surprisingly gone to Faubus. We couldn't imagine why. Manipulating black voters—a result of the poll tax—even should not have accounted for nearly 70% of the state's votes. And no one was taking on the governor's unbridled power seizure. It seemed reformers had nowhere to turn.

Totally frustrated, I became determined to initiate some kind of change. I went to our Ouachita County representative, William S. Andrews, a friend and a good and decent person. It was late in the year. I asked if, in the coming legislative session, he intended to continue his unqualified support of Governor Faubus. Yes, admittedly a leading question.

He looked surprised, responding more than likely he would. "I have to work with the governor," he said, "if I'm going to get anything done for Ouachita County."

I told him that, if he continued to move in that direction, I would oppose him in his next re-election effort.

Throwing my hat in the ring seemed to make sense, even though the race would prove a hard, uphill battle. We were looking toward 1960's election cycle, and Senator John F. Kennedy was gearing up for what promised to be a thrilling presidential race. I was 26 years old. As small and infinitesimal as my arena might be, I was inspired by Kennedy's example to play a cameo role in whatever political drama I could find.

Before announcing for the legislature, however, I had to sell the *Citizen*—or rather get out from under it. So I went to Ernest and Charles Looney, investors in Progress Printing, the business side of the paper. I asked if they might want to buy the *Citizen*.

The brothers had become close colleagues over the past three years, and they supported my editorial efforts as well as the paper's general aims. Between them, they figured it a good idea to take over the paper. With one brother from

Magnolia, the other from Texarkana, they had grown familiar with south Arkansas politics and business. They believed it would work. We struck a deal, and I agreed to run the newspaper until after the election. Barbara had been at my side in the newspaper and never questioned my decision to seek a seat in the Arkansas legislature.

Barbara gave birth to our son David, Jr., or "Dee," in March. The new addition inevitably changed the family's entire chemistry. We were excited about the arrival of this big, healthy baby who, from the beginning, behaved like the perfect child.

But we hardly had time to enjoy him. Within a week or 10 days after his birth, I announced for the legislative seat Bill Andrews had held for the past 10 years. Then Barbara and I set out on our first campaign. We carried Dee in a large wicker basket with us to fish fries, picnics, birthdays and anniversaries, school programs, ice cream socials, and church singings. Anywhere we could find a crowd, we three arrived early and met as many people as possible. We became a blizzard of activity, and her political acumen quickly became legendary.

Our initial challenge involved neutralizing a strong pro-Andrews labor vote. By that time, his voting record almost entirely favored labor, a mighty force in Ouachita County. International Paper Company employed some 2,500 workers, most of them union members. Their leaders had endorsed Andrews before I announced. I paid a visit to several of them, hoping to sway their support, but to no avail. In 10 years as a legislator, Andrews had cultivated firm relationships with union figures throughout the county.

As the campaign moved into full swing, I felt the strong rush between politician and voter that one never forgets. I loved it. It became my energy and strength, coupled with a new realization of this remarkable young Fayetteville woman who had become wife, mother, and now full partner. She possessed stamina and intellect, as well as an uncompromising sense of justice.

Still determined to attract the labor vote, Barbara and I drew a grid of Fairview and Cullendale, both large south-Camden sections with homes of paper-mill workers. We planned to focus on the millworkers' families—the wives, aunts, and relatives who were not themselves union members. We decided to campaign hardest in their neighborhoods, systematically visiting every block and every house on every street. Almost every afternoon at sunset, Barbara and I walked the streets, knocked on doors, and asked people for their vote. She soon grew into the best campaigner I ever saw. One of our neighbors commented that, when Barbara met the voters, she "melted 'em."

We also targeted the African-American voter bloc, representing a quarter of the county's total population. These minority citizens were emerging from a long, intimidating period that had kept them from voting. The U.S. Supreme Court remained still four years away from declaring the poll tax unconstitutional. Meanwhile, we continued to witness the fear pattern that had defined the black community for more than a century.

Here's how it worked. Local political bosses and plantation owners would pay black voters' poll taxes, then cast those ballots in any way they saw fit. Without the tax, those minority voters would eventually stand up and cast ballots of their own, not fearing for their jobs or homes. We hoped that time would come soon. But for now, we had to begin encouraging them to open their minds and vote independently. We also knew we would need them as active participants in our campaign.

Wanting to split the black vote, the Faubus organization convinced R. A. Sharpe, band director at Camden's segregated Lincoln High School, to announce against me. Sharpe had performed commendably at the all-black school in south Camden. A well-intentioned man and a friend, he knew exactly why he was in the race. But the people pressuring him operated with such strong authority that he found it impossible to resist. His campaign presence brought home the obvious truth that I was running against R. A. Sharpe, William S. Andrews, and, to a greater extent, Orval E. Faubus. Add to that mix the county judge, the sheriff, the *Camden News*, and other courthouse officials.

As the campaign progressed, public rallies drew crowds nearly every night of the week. Promoted widely on radio and in local papers, the action began at 6:00 p.m. and went on past 10:00 or later. Food and local entertainment could always attract a crowd, but well-known candidates with any flair could pack a schoolyard or church parking lot on their own.

We drew straws for program positions, and all hoped to land a slot around 7:00 or 7:15. Earlier than that, people were still munching catfish and hush puppies, deaf to the bands, the speakers, or even their own children. Many busily bid on pies and cakes. By 9:00 or 9:30, heat and mosquitoes had driven off most of the crowd.

Faubus and I both appeared one sultry Saturday night at the Bearden bandstand. The state police swarmed thick as fleas. This proved the only time we both shared a public platform, and it felt like the hottest night of the summer.

Faubus had carried the deeply conservative town handily in 1958, slicing his way through segregation's fleshy meat with a surgeon's precision. Everyone expected him to carry it again. The people of Bearden were turning out to hear the old warhorse talk about "protecting the sovereignty of our state" and "securing the public good."

Everyone knew these phrases as code words for segregation, and only three years had passed since the Central High crisis. Were a vote taken of that huge and frenzied crowd, Faubus would have won a lifetime term as Governor of the Universe.

Two items formed my agenda.

One, address Andrews's puppet status. I lit into him directly for being an administration stooge. I asked the audience if, in fact, they really wanted a legislator who's nothing more than a rubber stamp. "Is it right to give up your independence to an administration that's out only for itself? Stand up and be strong!" A surefire theme at any political level, it went over rather well. At least I wasn't run off the platform.

Two, I wanted to undermine the credibility of the Faubus candidate for Ouachita County judge. Once a friend of Dad's, Judge Milas Reynolds had held a reputable office. But by 1960 he ran the county for himself and his list of friends. Orval Faubus sat at the top of that list.

My clan of Camden-area co-conspirators was backing J. B. Cross to defeat Reynolds, and we knew the chances were slim. Cross, a concrete-block manufacturer, made an uncertain and painfully awkward candidate. Especially on the stump, where he recited in perfect rote exactly the speech text we had prepared for him. Dooley Womack, my friend and future legislative colleague, and I started coaching J. B. Cross in every gesture and voice inflection.

His Bearden appearance that night offered a classic attack on Reynolds and, therefore, on the governor. I can see J.B. still, taking out a worn piece of paper, starting his stock speech: "I ... am ... a ... Methodist .... And ... I ... am ... a ... Mason .... Cross ... your ... ballot ... for ... Cross!"

Chapter 16
A Fresh Young Turk

J. B. Cross won his election. And so did I. In fact, I carried every box in Ouachita County. My victory directly testified to how a candidate can succeed with a door-to-door, hand-to-hand campaign—particularly when he's joined by a tireless, politically talented young wife carting a beautiful baby in a basket.

I have never forgotten that invaluable 1960 lesson in what consultants today call "face time." Then, we knew it as "pressing the flesh." Many modern professionals dismiss this one-on-one approach, but I not only believed in it, I loved doing it. When political historians write the definitive story of Arkansas politics, they are bound to agree that Clinton, Bumpers, and Pryor all had one thing in common—the belief that politics is more than local; it's exceedingly personal.

I learned other lessons as well. After all, in this first-time effort, despite my passion for anything political, I knew very little about personal campaigning. As a novice, while I knew I loved direct contact with people, I was also learning one of politics's most important lessons: ask people for their vote. This simple request, often forgotten or overlooked, can actually cement the personal political relationship, the importance of both the voter and the *vote*. The bond formed in that brief instant between politician and voter sometimes lasts a lifetime. It's one of the great mysteries of self-government.

One day I drove the 15 miles to Chidester, a small sawmill town west of Camden, introducing myself to a handful of old-timers sitting in front of the town's main-street filling station. I was proudly driving a new Opel, just purchased at Doyne Hunnicut Motors, a trade-in for my old Chevy.

Exiting the car, I handed a Pryor thimble to each man sitting near the station's door. Thimbles had become my campaign's familiar symbol, a holdover from my Dad's and my grandfather's earlier county-sheriff campaigns.

We greeted each other with a handshake and a nod. This brief, friendly visit would prove the close tie between personal and political. I sat down on a bench by the screen door and opened a cold Grapette.

We discussed the heat, the lack of rain. Finally, one old-timer stopped whittling for a minute and asked, "What kind of car is that?" The others didn't even turn their heads to view the auto. One just kept whittling.

"It's an Opel," I said. "Pretty good car, too. Gets good mileage. It's made in Germany."

"They killed my boy," the man said. He never looked up.

I got in the car and drove back to Doyne Hunnicut. I told him I wanted my old Chevy back.

That campaign also connected me to national and world politics. In the early fall, Dr. Shade Rushing, a distinguished dentist and civic leader in El Dorado, invited me to a fish fry at a camp on the Ouachita River's lower reaches. I had just won my Democratic primary battle, with no Republican opponent in November, assuring my January swearing in as Ouachita County's newly-elected state representative.

Hundreds of people rode barges and walked along the river banks while a band played under several oak trees' protective shade. The afternoon broiled us, one of those steamy, sun-drenched days when you feel humidity creep clear to your bones.

On one barge, Senator J. William Fulbright—then one of the U.S. Senate's most powerful members—shook hands and visited with the crowd. I sidled right up to him and sat down. It was thrilling to hear him comment on the presidential race between John Kennedy and Richard Nixon.

After catfish, hush puppies, and barbeque, someone hooked up a small TV set, placing it on the picnic table so most folks could see it, and adjusting the rabbit ears. We viewed the first Kennedy-Nixon debate, a crucial event in American political history. Everyone watching shared in the excitement. It created a dramatic turning point in that election, when the savvy, young Kennedy coolly pummeled the shady-faced, hesitant Nixon. And it set the stage for all presidential debates to come.

I sat next to Senator Fulbright, and noticed through his body language and occasional low grunts that he took the candidates' sparring very seriously. "Not a bad argument, Jack," he would say at one point, and "Oh, no, that's not right" at another. I asked him how he thought the debate was going. He said he was proud of Senator Kennedy. In fact, he had briefed him on foreign policy issues only that morning in Washington before flying to Arkansas.

This casual piece of information made a stunning impression on me. Here I was—sitting on the Ouachita River banks deep in south Arkansas—next to a U.S. senator who only that morning had advised a colleague and presidential candidate on such crucial issues as Quemoy and Matsu, the Cold War, and nuclear disarmament. And I had just been elected to the state legislature. My political passions were beginning to blaze.

That December, a month following the general elections, the Camden Chamber of Commerce invited Senator Fulbright to address its annual banquet. I met his plane at the local airstrip. As we drove up to the Camden Hotel, a policeman stopped us, notifying the Senator of an urgent phone call. Hotel management had set a private spot off the lobby for him to take the call.

It was John Kennedy, just elected president. He informed Senator Fulbright that he would *not* become Secretary of State. The position would go to Dean Rusk.

I have often wondered how history might have unfolded if Senator Fulbright had received that appointment. How America would have dealt with the Vietnam conflict if he had advised Kennedy, and later Lyndon Johnson. Surely, he would have insisted on ending the war before our mistakes and pride cost us those unbelievably high death tolls and America's confidence in its leadership.

In 1961's first week, Barbara, Dee, and I moved into an $85-a-month old house in Little Rock, not far from the governor's mansion. We had won our first election, sold the *Ouachita Citizen*, and I was ready to begin the legislature's 60-day session. I felt I had gone to heaven.

The state capitol's Old Guard considered me something of a curiosity. I had survived the Faubus organization's attempts to defeat me, and, in fact, I had licked one of their own lieutenants. The administration had counted on Bill Andrews as a prime mover, and a fair amount of press centered on how I would fare as his replacement.

Reporters and editorial writers speculated on whether Paul VanDalsem, the veteran legislator and Faubus friend, would take to this whippersnapper, and how the whippersnapper would take to VanDalsem. They wondered about my relationship with J. H. Cottrell, a Faubus loyalist who loved to start fights, then stand back and watch them play out. Other key legislators also had taken an interest in seeing me lose. Now their chance had arrived to exact a pound of flesh.

The session saw the legislative battles between Old Guard and New grow to fever pitch. As a result, the Arkansas Education Association bowed to public pressure, sponsoring an open debate on where the two sides stood. The AEA chose me to represent the New's view; who else but Paul VanDalsem would carry the status quo's torch. People packed the AEA auditorium, with standing room around the walls. The statewide press covered the event, as well as a live radio hookup which carried the debate to Arkansas's four corners. We sparred over everything from teachers' salaries to school curriculum to the months, days, and hours required for student attendance. We spread everything on the table, and agreed on nothing.

W. R. "Witt" Stephens had just been elected to the House, a freshman power broker holding forth at his desk, chomping a cigar and dispensing favors. His legislative tenure was short, but dramatic. At one point, Mr. Witt suggested, with a dose of sly humor, a bill should be passed naming him Speaker of the House. He had helped several members succeed in both politics and business. So we often speculated on which legislators he would admit to his inner circle or relegate to the back row. From the beginning, he was always friendly to me, even though he and Faubus united on just about every issue.

Before long, I had aligned with other young, progressive members such as Jim Brandon, Ray Smith, Hayes McClerkin, and Hardy Croxton—all of them willing to take on the Faubus administration. I found a comfort level with these Young Turks, as we were called, that seldom held true with other groups. Our primary goal involved change, in almost any form.

One *Gazette* editorial named me a "wandering evangelist with a passion for reform." It declared I was pushing change of any kind, achieved through whatever means necessary. While flattered by this description, I still wondered if I was tilting at windmills. Did the editorial paint a true picture, or simply toss out a catch phrase describing a new and unsophisticated novice?

Almost at once, my leading issue became constitutional reform. The 1874 constitution had grown outdated with antique phrasing and anachronisms. One provision even disallowed dueling in the legislative halls. But, more important, this ancient relic of old-fashioned, even obscure prose permitted the continuing abuse of local power. County judges, for instance, still acted as fiefdom lords, ruling without legal authority, directing unilateral equipment purchases, and building roads at whim. No control existed over their power, resulting in no competitive bidding, and no means of recall except at biennial elections. These rituals had basically become formal rites for further entrenching the despots in office.

Unwilling to wait for a new constitution, which could take years, I sponsored a bill to place more accountability in county purchasing. I considered that a good first step. By any standards, my bill offered a modest reform, requiring competitive bids for any purchase over $300. But when the vote came up, the state's county judges descended on Little Rock, filled the Marion Hotel, and packed the House galleries. The first round, the bill received 10 votes, then 20, then 36.

Faubus had told me confidentially that the bill would not pass, but that if it should, he would sign it. He assured me privately that it was the right thing to do.

Our progressive flock increased. Virgil Butler of Batesville, well into his 70s, became our "senior" Young Turk. He was fearless, taking great glee in needling Faubus's allies. He soon became a favorite with the capitol press. They loved nothing better than a good fight, and they could always depend on him to start one.

Through serving on the Ouachita County grand jury, I had learned about county government's inner workings. A year before I went to the legislature, we had indicted the county clerk for misuse of his office. We had to rely on scant information mustered from disorganized files and county employees willing to testify. Understanding a county government's business practices would have required a double master's degree in political science and journalism.

In a speech to the statewide Jaycee convention, I angered county judges by accusing prosecutors of neglecting to charge county executives with malfeasance. The same with state investigators. These political relationships had become far too cozy. We desperately needed, I argued, a law requiring "an investigation of the investigators and the prosecution of the prosecutors." I liked the sound of that phrase, but the idea naturally built a wall between me and county officials that remained for some time. The idea went nowhere. One prosecuting attorney wrote me a letter with a distinctly nasty tone, implying I had slandered him and his colleagues.

I also fell short in rewriting county purchasing procedures. In fact, that much-needed reform didn't become law until 1965. When it finally passed, the required minimum purchasing figure had risen from $300 to $500. What's more, the Faubus administration stripped my name from the bill. They refused to allow the Pryor name any connection with legislation that, by then, enjoyed vast statewide support and editorial endorsements.

As another signature cause, I took up poll-tax repeal. At that time, Arkansas remained one of only five states with the repressive tax. Repeal efforts in the 1930s and '40s always met defeat. Sid McMath was the only governor to give it any serious attention. My cohorts and I took up the fight. While repeal had surfaced in nearly every legislative session, it continued to receive strong opposition. Final repeal didn't come until 1964, and on the national level, when the country ratified the U.S. Constitution's 24th Amendment.

We grew similarly frustrated in our efforts to clean up election procedures. Faubus had received 103% of the Madison County vote in 1954, and when this glaring discrepancy came to light, the administration only shrugged its shoulders.

Our continuing reform efforts grew into larger and more pointed civil rights struggles. As we studied the state's delta and southern counties with large black populations, we discovered how seemingly separate activities actually formed elaborate patterns of repeated abuse.

In 1962, Barbara and I wanted to assure fair elections in Ouachita County, but we weren't entirely sure how to go about it. We personally paid for 35 portable voting booths, with one to be installed at each county precinct. They were nothing more than tall, slender cardboard boxes resembling outhouses. But we hoped they'd protect people's privacy. That would represent a major change from marking ballots on a fire-truck fender or open table, where election officials could often intimidate with constant stares.

The night before the primary, we borrowed a pickup truck and delivered the voting booths to the county's precincts. We never learned if voters used them. I have always wondered if any good came from our efforts.

Almost since settlers first came to the state, decent roads and highways have remained a major political issue. The Mack Blackwell Amendment, passed in 1955, had supposedly taken politics out of highway construction. A popular measure backed by the Cherry administration, it set up a five-member highway commission, each representing a section of the state. Landmark legislation, voters placed it squarely in the Arkansas state constitution.

Nothing in Mack Blackwell defined qualifications for the commission's executive director, a crucial post requiring both professional knowledge and sound judgment. When the commission director died, Faubus appointed his friend and ally Mack Sturgis. Many people in state government were aghast. Sturgis possessed no qualifications for the job, being neither an engineer nor an administrator with state-agency experience. He had served several years as a highway-department purchasing agent, but held little if any responsibility. No one could testify to his character or judgment.

Faubus's power play prompted our Young Turk coalition to introduce a bill requiring a professional engineer in the post. Of course, it met an overwhelming defeat. But we made the point that professionalism had taken a back seat to politics. In retrospect, Mack Sturgis did a commendable job, and in time became a friend and supporter in my statewide elections.

When I served in the legislature, committees functioned only on paper; any rare meeting remained customarily informal and brief. Lawmakers commonly discovered their committees had met the previous afternoon "at Mr. VanDalsem's desk" or in some spot off the capitol grounds, like the Marion Hotel dining room. No one took minutes or kept records.

This haphazard business often led to two or more bills covering the same issue. For instance, the public school teachers' retirement system was woefully inadequate, but a lack of coordination led Faubus to write one bill and the state education department to prepare another. Faubus's staff informed us what the governor's proposal included, then the education director offered an entirely different approach. Faubus even asked a General Assembly joint session to pass both bills, then let him decide which one to sign.

The governor's appeal brought on my first floor speech to a legislative body. I advocated better teacher retirement benefits, plus fair and equitable treatment in whatever legislation the education committee drew up.

A young civics teacher from Pine Bluff was sitting in the House gallery that afternoon. After my speech, she sent a note down to the floor: "Thank you for your speech," it said. "I'm going to help you in future races." She signed it, "Anne McClaran." Anne ultimately became the bellwether of my 1966 Congressional campaign.

Chapter 17
A Good Life

The legislative session ended in April. I clocked out on my $100-a-month lawmaker's salary. We left Little Rock for Camden with no means of support and, once again, no future plans. Fortunately, we could live with Mother in her Graham Street home.

While there, one night I lay in bed with a cold and high fever. My condition somehow led to a white-light epiphany—a valuable way to *use* my recent legislative experience and the blood-rush of its political battleground: I should go to law school. I was almost 28 years old.

Still, Barbara agreed. Far from suggesting we were bouncing around the state, she began plans to move. I passed the U of A's law school entrance exams, and was admitted for that fall semester. So I would work both as legislator and law student, a rugged dual obligation I'd hardly recommend to anyone.

We moved into a small Fayetteville house that belonged to Barbara's aunt, turning its old garage into a study. I attended day classes, while on weekends making speeches calling for constitutional reform. I also strove to keep my fences mended in Ouachita County.

Through it all, I still felt I was playing catch-up while my old college friends stayed ahead of the game, progressing in their professional lives. To complicate matters further, Faubus called a special session during my first two weeks of class. I spent most of that time phoning classmates back in Fayetteville, reviewing missed lectures and briefing cases, trying to stay afloat.

Money remained a problem. Barbara worked at the Palace Drug Store, bringing home just enough to pay the babysitter and buy food. I grabbed a part-time job with a company installing restaurant equipment on campus, but it ended in three weeks.

How do young people get by in such situations? Family. Barbara's parents invited us to supper several nights a week. Her brothers gave Dee hand-me-down clothes, and Mother kept us in baby shoes. An accomplished seamstress, she made clothes for Barbara. She also sent us $100 a month, which went a long way in the '60s.

Then I answered an ad for a dispatcher at a Springdale trucking company. At the interview, the plant manager said they didn't ordinarily hire students. If anything should become available, he'd let me know.

Six months later, the legislature was considering the truck-weight bill—controversial legislation allowing heavier trucks on Arkansas highways. The Springdale trucking company sent an emissary to lobby me: the same manager from my job interview. He explained his company's position favoring heavier vehicles, asked for my support, then added, "Oh, by the way, that job you wanted has just become available." I went back to the floor and voted against the truck-weight increase.

In 1962's early summer, a *Camden News* story revealed that Charles Plunkett, my childhood friend and fellow co-captain on the Camden Panthers, was running against me. We had grown up in the same neighborhood, daily walked together to Cleveland Avenue Elementary, even stayed in touch through our college years. Still, Plunkett had no reason not to run, except friendship. I knew that seat didn't belong to me. In fact, I had occupied it for only one term. I fully expected that, given my trouble-maker reputation, someone would certainly announce against me.

But not Charles Plunkett. That came as a shock. Within a week, he began newspaper ads picturing a Fayetteville telephone-directory page highlighting my address and phone number. "Fayetteville is 300 miles from Camden," the copy read. And it went on: "Here's an absentee representative who lives in Fayetteville and pretends to represent Camden and Ouachita County."

I saw no way of defending myself successfully against the absentee-legislator charge, and I quickly saw his argument having an effect. I could sense people looking at me as a con artist trying to save my hide. And the Faubus machine seemed to lurk in the race's back stretches. I've never believed the governor's people convinced Plunkett to oppose me, but they relished the chance of replacing me with someone they thought would be easier to influence.

A tough summer awaited the Pryor family. Barbara and Dee joined me again in visiting the district's every town and neighborhood. By then, Dee had become a rambunctious two-year-old who had outgrown his basket. But he had also become our chief campaigner as we repeated our route from two years earlier, attending every church or school supper. I defended my staying in the legislature while also trying to better myself through law school—a tough sell, but my only credible defense. In the end, I won by a comfortable margin. I even kept my friendship with Charles Plunkett.

One of my bitterest state legislative struggles involved Faubus's attempt to remove Winthrop Rockefeller as chairman of the Arkansas Industrial Development Commission. In 1953, Rockefeller temporarily moved to the state, hoping to secure a quick divorce. Much to his surprise, he fell in love with Arkansas. He set up Winrock Farms on Petit Jean Mountain near Morrilton, a truly scenic spot, and successfully began raising Santa Gertrudis cattle. Rockefeller quickly became a highly effective salesman for his new home state, and in 1955 Faubus appointed him AIDC's chairman.

But in 1957, Rockefeller warned Faubus that his defying the Supreme Court's school desegregation case was damaging the state's reputation. Unless the governor changed direction, Rockefeller would leave the commission. Faubus resented Rockefeller's threat. He brushed it aside, continued defying the federal government, and never regained his confidence in the rich heir to an oil fortune.

By 1963, Faubus's resentment had festered long enough. Most of all, the governor feared this high-profile Republican might oppose him in his coming re-election bid. With the backing of Paul VanDalsem and other legislative members, he decided to remove Rockefeller as chairman.

Faubus wanted to keep the dismissal quiet, but it was impossible to silence VanDalsem. He told everyone he knew, and reaction came swift and heated. Along with several others, I wrote the governor, opposing his move. I joined in House chamber speeches defending Rockefeller, emphasizing how removing him would reverse progress in bringing the state business and industry.

Opposition from legislators, press, and public forced Faubus to change his mind. Rockefeller stayed on and, sure enough, did run against Faubus in 1964. A bitter race, it was easily Faubus's toughest to that point. Still, he won it by carrying 65 of the state's 75 counties.

Our son Mark was born in Fayetteville on January 10, 1963. Barbara and I began my second legislative term by moving with our two boys to the Grady Manning Hotel at Markham and Main streets in Little Rock. The entire hotel staff helped Barbara feed, care for, and babysit Dee and Mark. They even issued us a key to the main kitchen downstairs.

That summer, I took the Arkansas bar exam in the LaFayette Hotel basement, fortunately passing it the first time. Juggling classes with representing

Ouachita County in legislative sessions and speeches around the state had me expecting a second try at the exam. When that intense period ended, I was ready to return to Camden and set up a law practice.

But politics remained my first interest. This was early 1964, the year of LBJ, Goldwater, and the Goldwater book, *The Conscience of a Conservative*. Wherever I went around south Arkansas, billboards demanded we get out of the U.N., and reaffirmed our right to bear arms. People voiced resentment over the Civil Rights Act that Congress would soon pass.

As the Democratic Party seemed to move toward the left, old diehards were leaving the Democrats and joining the Republicans. By moving away from Strom Thurmond and the Dixiecrats in 1948, Sid McMath had reaffirmed the state's Democratic ties. But 15 years later, the surge of party strength had spent itself.

I was discouraged to see hardcore racism resurge along with quarrels over states' rights. Lyndon Johnson carried Arkansas against Goldwater with the same percentage as Faubus's win over Rockefeller. But 1964 proved the last election when a Democratic Arkansas would be a sure thing. Only four years later, the majority of Arkansas voters endorsed independent candidate George Wallace for president.

Running for a third state legislative term, I watched daily for someone to announce against me. On the final morning for filing, I circled the Camden courthouse, fully expecting an opponent to show up, but nobody did. I felt fortunate. A wave of hardcore conservative thinking—if one were actually forming out there—would have become my major opponent.

The time had come for me to return to Camden and start my new law career. Harry Barnes, a former Marine and among our class's brightest students, had been one of my good friends in law school. I asked him to consider joining me in a Camden law practice. I could not have chosen a better partner to move there with his young family, but I doubted he would accept my offer. Why should he? He could follow any number of our colleagues to a major law firm in Little Rock. But he did accept. When the law school's dean heard we planned to open a practice in Camden, he predicted we would starve to death.

In our first notable case, a local man hired us to sue his neighbor for stealing a prize coon dog from his pickup truck—a hard charge to prove due to an absence of dog tags or markers. We also knew the case could become notorious, because coon-hunting ranked almost as a religion in south Arkansas.

Far from simply a financial investment, a hunter's coon dog invariably attached itself to its owner and became a subject for backwoods myth.

Word got around about the trial, and folks packed the courtroom the morning Judge R. W. Mason called us to order. Every coon hunter in south Arkansas seemed to have traveled to Camden to witness the drama to come. Judge Mason cast himself as a rare figure from another world. He dressed in tails and a high starched collar, conducting his proceedings in the British Inns-of-Court's stilted tradition. Stern, somber, and eccentric, he still had become known throughout south Arkansas as a fair and evenhanded judge.

After hearing formal arguments from Harry and me, and from the opposing side, Judge Mason confessed he could not make up his mind as to the animal's ownership. So he ordered the dog brought to the courtroom, to let the animal seek out the rightful party on his own.

An oversized, mangy hound, it smelled of the wild, with straw and dried grass covering his paws. His head hung down almost to the floor. As he sniffed around the room, slowly making his way toward the front, everyone silently watched in rapt attention. You could have heard a hiding coon breathe. Finally, the hound swayed over to our client, slowly raising his paw to the man's knee. Half the room broke into cheers, the other half in jeers and boos. Judge Mason declared the case closed.

Not long after that, Judge Harry Crumpler, our district's circuit judge, appointed Harry and me to represent a man from Hampton, some 25 miles from Camden. It looked like a tough case from any angle. Claiming the victim was having an affair with his wife, our client had shot the fellow six times, then he had reloaded his gun and shot him again. Several witnesses had stood by in disbelief, watching the spectacle. The simple truth was that he had no defense, and neither did we.

Our first visit with him came on a cold January morning at Hampton's county jail. When we introduced ourselves to Sheriff Doyle Duncan, he said, "I know who you are and why you're here. The killer is across the street, top floor of the jail. Here's the key."

We found the defendant in his cell, hovering over a bucket of burning charcoal and wrapped in an Army blanket. Harry explained every aspect of the law applying to his case, starting with the Magna Carta and moving through the Constitution, the Bill of Rights, and the full history of Arkansas case law. This took some time, and Harry's grasp of legal history greatly impressed me, and also the alleged perpetrator, who listened intently.

When Harry finished, he asked the man if he had any questions or comments. "Yeah," he said. "I think I can get up $500 to bribe the judge."

We allowed that wasn't an option.

Our practice found good things came our way when we least expected them. One day, Mr. Emmett Gaughan, member of a pioneering Camden family, walked into our office, handed over some 30 files, and said he didn't need or want them any longer. The Gaughan firm ranked high among the state's distinguished law partnerships; John L. McClellan practiced law there in the 1930s. Inheriting a partial list of their clients represented a welcome meal ticket for two young lawyers starving to death.

We worked through the mountain of material. In one folder, I discovered a long overdue debt of $15,000 an oil-field supply company owed our new client. Calling his office, I explained that, with his permission, Harry and I would try to collect the debt. He said okay, but doubted we would have any luck.

On a late summer afternoon, Harry and I drove to Stephens, halfway to Magnolia, approaching the house address listed in the file. A man sat on the front porch, eating watermelon. He looked out, squinting at us, and called, "Is that you, David Pryor?"

I said it sure was, and I had my law partner with me. We had been in practice all of a month, but I left that part out. I explained how we were following up a debt he seemed to owe from some time back, and wondered if he would like to discuss it.

We were prepared for an argument, even a big one, including being thrown off his property. After all, $15,000 was no small sum, and here we were, showing up on his porch out of the blue.

He got up from his chair, saying in a friendly voice, "Here, let me get you boys some watermelon. Then I'm going inside and write you a check. I know I've owed that money for some time, but I just didn't like the way that company treated me." Harry and I ate a piece of watermelon, then drove home with more money than our small partnership had ever seen.

Circuit Judge Harry Crumpler, a Magnolia native, belonged to an old guard that boasted some stout Faubus backers. I assumed from the beginning that Judge Crumpler and I would not get along, and would likely work at opposite ends of the district's legal system. But he soon became one of my closest friends and mentors. In fact, he had as much influence on my professional thinking and conduct as anyone I know.

At one point, I was representing a Bearden man who was suing the city jail's night marshal for the false arrest of his son. I was gearing up to make a long and impressive closing argument when Judge Crumpler called me to the bench, along with the opposing attorney. He said the jury was clearly leaning toward my client; if I wanted to win this case, I would wisely keep my argument brief. "If they see you getting cocky, you're going to lose it," he said. So I went back and made a two-minute closing argument. Sure enough, the jury ruled in our favor.

Judge Crumpler taught me a lesson I've always valued: you don't always have to say everything you want to say. Sometimes it's better to keep your mouth shut. I can't count the number of times I drove the 35 miles to Magnolia to seek Judge Harry Crumpler's advice. His answers to my questions often proved oblique and indirect; many times he would respond by simply telling a story. But whatever form they took, his comments helped me, and were exactly what I needed to hear.

By the beginning of 1966, Harry and I actually represented paying clients. We were also making a place for ourselves in Camden. For the first time, I felt secure about myself and what I was doing. I came to believe that nothing could upset the balance between work and family, or set our direction off course. Even if some higher political office should open up and tempt me to go for it, I would have to say I wasn't interested. I might consider it at some time in the far-off future, but not right now. My life as a father of two healthy young sons, and husband of a splendid wife and partner, was literally all I cared about in those early '60s. It was a good life.

Photo Section I

"I'm a Pryor" fan made for David Pryor's 70th birthday party, August 28, 2004. Courtesy UA Special Collections.

Pryor's father, Edgar Pryor, Chevrolet dealer and Ouachita County Sheriff. Photo courtesy Pryor family.

David Pryor, age 14, beside Pryor family Chevrolet. Note the rabbit's foot hanging from his right pocket. Photo courtesy Pryor family.

From left: David Pryor, age eight, Don Harrell, Gordon Newton, Cornelia Pryor (later Lindsey), Dottie Harrell, and Elinor Pryor. Photo courtesy Pryor family.

The Panther's Echo

VOLUME XXXXI   CAMDEN, ARKANSAS, OCTOBER 27, 1950   NUMBER

SCHOLARSHIPS EXPLAINED

On October 3, Miss Rema Hutchinson, vocational guidance counselor, spoke to all seniors concerning scholarships for college educations. Miss Hutchinson stated: Scholarships are offered by colleges, foundations, societies, fraternal groups, churches, business organizations and individuals. Requirements for these scholarships vary greatly, many stress high scholastic achievement; others emphasize need. Some must be used in specified colleges, others may be used anywhere in the United States.

The assurance that the applicant will succeed in the training he undertakes is one common requirement. For high school seniors, success in the Scholastic Aptitude Test and the achievement tests of the college board together with high marks in high school are accepted as proof of this ability.

Applications for scholarships and enrollment in colleges should be applied for as early as possible in the senior year. As each month passes, the number of opportunities is reduced. Some colleges have full enrollments in advance of the freshman year; therefore

Pictured above on the school steps are the class presidents and sponsors for the three senior high classes. They are (left to right, first row): Harold Campbell, sophomore president; David Pryor, junior president; Gordon Newton, senior president; (second row) Mrs. Diamond Sewell, sophomore sponsor; Ben Hines, junior sponsor; Wyley Elliott, senior sponsor — (Photo by Ernest Nipper.)

High School Classs Officers Elected

Gordon Newton, David Pryor and Harold Campbell have been elected to head the senior, junior and sophomore classes respectively.

This is Newton's second time as president of his class. He's vice-president of the Student Council, one of the Co-Captains of the football team, a member of the track team and basketball team and a Thespian.

Pryor has been president of his class since the first grade. He is vice-president of the F.T.A., a member of the Student Council and on the football and basketball squads.

At all of the football games you will see a blond-burr headed boy helping to lead the yells. This is Harold Campbell, president of the sophomore class. He is a member of the "B" team.

Other officers of the senior class are: Richard Rushing, vice-president; Jane Skinner, treasurer; Kay McCord, secretary; and Evelyn Gillespie, reporter. The senior class sponsor is Wiley Elliott. Tinker Urrey, vice president; Sara Redding, secretary; Barbara Biggers, treasurer; and Jimmy Westbrook, reporter are the other junior officers. The junior class

Camden High School Panther's Echo, October 27, 1950, in which David Pryor is pictured among class presidents and sponsors. Photo courtesy University of Arkansas Special Collections.

David Pryor astride his horse "Bill" at Circle C Riding Club, Camden, AR, age 21. Photo courtesy UA Special Collections.

David Pryor as a sophomore quarterback at Camden High School. Photo courtesy UA Special Collections.

David Pryor and Barbara Lunsford prior to their marriage. Photo courtesy Pryor family.

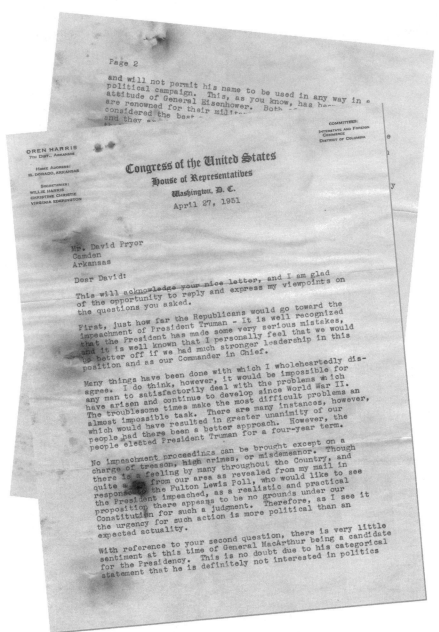

Page 2

and will not permit his name to be used in any way in a political campaign. This, as you know, has been attitude of General Eisenhower. Both -- are renowned for their milit-- considered the best -- and they a--

COMMITTEES:
INTERSTATE AND FOREIGN COMMERCE
DISTRICT OF COLUMBIA

OREN HARRIS
7TH DIST., ARKANSAS

HOME ADDRESS:
EL DORADO, ARKANSAS

SECRETARIES:
WILLIE HARRIS
CHRISTINE CHRISTIE
VIRGINIA EDERINGTON

Congress of the United States
House of Representatives
Washington, D. C.
April 27, 1951

Mr. David Pryor
Camden
Arkansas

Dear David:

This will acknowledge your nice letter, and I am glad of the opportunity to reply and express my viewpoints on the questions you asked.

First, just how far the Republicans would go toward the impeachment of President Truman - It is well recognized that the President has made some very serious mistakes, and it is well known that I personally feel that we would be better off if we had much stronger leadership in this position and as our Commander in Chief.

Many things have been done with which I wholeheartedly disagree. I do think, however, it would be impossible for any man to satisfactorily deal with the problems which have arisen and continue to develop since World War II. The troublesome times make the most difficult problems an almost impossible task. There are many instances, however, which would have resulted in greater unanimity of our people had there been a better approach. However, the people elected President Truman for a four-year term.

No impeachment proceedings can be brought except on a charge of treason, high crimes, or misdemeanor. Though there is a feeling by many throughout the Country, and quite a bit from our area as revealed from my mail in response to the Fulton Lewis Poll, who would like to see the President impeached, as a realistic and practical proposition there appears to be no grounds under our Constitution for such a judgment. Therefore, as I see it the urgency for such action is more political than an expected actuality.

With reference to your second question, there is very little sentiment at this time of General MacArthur being a candidate for the Presidency. This is no doubt due to his categorical statement that he is definitely not interested in politics

A letter from Congressman Oren Harris to David Pryor, then age 16, acknowledging the young Pryor's interest in serving as a Congressional page. Document courtesy UA Special Collections.

Newspaper ad after successful campaign for State House of Representatives. Barbara is pregnant with Mark, and son Dee (David, Jr.) is age two. Photo courtesy of UA Special Collections.

David and Barbara Pryor campaigning in Harrison, Arkansas, 1974. Photo courtesy UA Special Collections.

David Pryor with bucket of thimbles at Pink Tomato Fest in Warren, 1966 (with Mrs. Walter Tate in background). Photo courtesy of UA Special Collections.

Pryor (standing in auto driven by Matthew Rothert) tossing thimbles to crowd at Warren Pink Tomato Festival during a congressional campaign, 1966.

David helping Barbara aboard Walt Thrasher's plane during Pryor's unsuccessful bid to unseat John L. McClellan, 1972. Photo courtesy of UA Special Collections.

Following second State-of-the-State speech in the Arkansas House of Representatives chamber: Pryor family left-to-right: Mark, David, Jr., Scott, Barbara, and David. Also pictured: Senator Stanley Russ, John Paul Capps, Bud Canada, and Bill Moore, 1977. Photo courtesy of UA Special Collections.

Governor Pryor greeting Mr. Issac Sanders of Mississippi County, Arkansas, a 108-year-old participant at the 1975 Governor's Conference on Aging. Photo courtesy of UA Special Collections.

At a London, England, press conference, (l. to r.) Ambassador Elliott Richardson, then-director of state industrial development Frank White, Governor Pryor, state senator Robert Harvey, and state representative Cecil Alexander. Photo courtesy of UA Special Collections.

David Pryor (standing) and Barbara (not shown) initiated a new tradition, a barbecue for all state police troopers, in 1975. Photo courtesy of UA Special Collections.

Pryor speaking at Fayetteville fairground rally during 1972 U.S. Senate race. Photo courtesy of UA Special Collections.

Barbara Pryor taking a break from campaigning, c. 1972. Photo courtesy of UA Special Collections.

Governor Pryor speaking at dedication ceremony of Ouachita Technical School in Malvern, c. 1975. Photo courtesy of UA Special Collections.

Pryor sons (l. to r.) David, Jr., known as "Dee," Scott, and Mark, at Pine Bluff Fish Fry, 1971. Photo courtesy of UA Special Collections.

David Pryor with President Lyndon Johnson. Photo courtesy of UA Special Collections.

David Pryor holding son Dee at campaign rally in Camden, 1972. Photo courtesy of UA
Special Collections.

Pryor campaigning for governor, 1974. Photo courtesy of UA Special Collections.

Governor Pryor (second from right) visits with Ann Bartley (l.), and Jeanette Rockefeller (r.), c. 1976. Photo courtesy of UA Special Collections.

Barbara and her father at a campaign event. Photo courtesy of UA Special Collections.

Governor Pryor, discovering that long-time governor's mansion cook, Eliza Jane Ashley, was unfairly underpaid, promoted her to the newly-created position of Food Production Manager, thereby eliminating a longtime inequity. Photo courtesy of UA Special Collections.

After unsuccessful 1972 U.S. Senate campaign, Pryor thanked many for "reaching into cookie jars to help me with my campaign," an image George Fisher could not resist.

The Pryor family on the backyard steps of the Arkansas Governor's Mansion, c. 1977.
Standing (l. to r.) Governor Pryor, Barbara Pryor, son Scott; sitting (l. to r.) sons Mark and
Dee Pryor. Photo courtesy of UA Special Collections.

Chapter 18
A Sudden, Surprising Opening

On a Monday evening in April 1965, Fred Coleman called. A Washington railroad lobbyist originally from Lewisville, Fred had become a friend the summer I delivered the House of Representatives' mail. We had stayed in touch because of mutual interests in Democratic politics and the workings of Capitol Hill.

Fred's inside track on Arkansas politics came from closely associating with both Senator McClellan and Congressman Harris. Both wielded considerable weight in Washington, McClellan as the Government Operations Committee chairman and a senior member of Appropriations, and Harris the chairman of the House Commerce panel. Fred's American Railroad Association bosses paid him to provide McClellan and Harris whatever they needed in transportation and incidental comforts—all above board. In fact, in those days, a commonly accepted practice involved lobbyists being "assigned" full time to powerful Congressional members.

"This is a heads up," Fred quickly whispered. "Congressman Harris is about to resign his seat in the House, and President Johnson is appointing him to the federal bench. Nobody knows about this. If you're ever going to run for his House seat, now's the time. But you better move quick because it's happening fast." He hung up before I could say a word.

Suddenly everything had changed. Barbara and I agonized that night and into early morning. Dee was five and Mark had just turned two. She stressed it was my decision. She would go along with my choice. I had always assumed that Oren Harris would serve in Congress for life. It seemed impossible that the Fourth District seat would actually open up.

Early the next morning, I called Harry and asked him to meet me for coffee at Horne's drugstore's back booth. I didn't mention Fred's news because it was still top secret.

An hour later, as Harry sat down, he said, "Guess what. I just heard on the radio that Oren Harris is resigning to become a federal judge." Then he added, "You gotta run. Let's saddle up. I'll feed your family while you make the race."

Harry's encouragement pushed me over the line I had felt wary to cross. We went to the office. I sat down and started making lists of people, county seats, possible contributors. We didn't know whether a special election would occur or, if so, when. My stomach was tied in knots.

I knew I'd better hit the phone. My first list contained names I needed to reach right away. Line up key supporters before anyone else reached them. Then I thought, "Who would 'anyone else' mean?" There could be a crowd of people in this race. A coveted House seat opening up surprised us all; for our generation, it was almost unheard of.

My first call was to Richard Arnold in Texarkana. A lawyer in private practice, he was married to Gale Hussman, whose father ran the Palmer chain of newspapers and radio stations. Richard had set scholastic records as an undergraduate at Yale and later at Harvard law school. He had clerked at the U.S. Supreme Court. His father and grandfather were both distinguished attorneys. Richard Arnold's wide connections throughout the district could prove invaluable, and I wanted him on my side before anyone else got to him.

"Richard," I said when he came to the phone, "Oren Harris is resigning his seat, and I plan to announce today. I'm calling to ask if you'll manage my campaign in Miller County."

Long pause.

Then he said, "I've just heard that myself, David, and I was about to call and ask if you would head *my* campaign in Ouachita County. I'm also announcing today."

Another long pause.

The fat was in the fire.

Chapter 19
A Grueling Race Begins

When Congressman Harris resigned to accept the federal judgeship, everyone questioned whether Governor Faubus would call a special election, or let voters pick a new congressional representative in the general election 18 months away. A costly special election would disrupt the state's familiar voting pattern, but it would quickly fill the vacancy.

On the other hand, if the governor let the process work its normal cycle, those 18 months would allow unknown candidates to organize campaigns and meet the voters. But a delayed election would create a lengthy vacancy, leaving the district's citizens with no representative.

Naturally, as one of those new and unknown candidates, I was pinning my hopes on November, a year and a half in the future.

A special election would almost guarantee a victory for Jimmie "Red" Jones, the state auditor and a close Faubus friend. Originally from Magnolia, in the Fourth District, Jimmie "Red" held credentials: a decorated war veteran, popular leader in the state's Young Democrats and Jaycees, and effective public speaker. As a constitutional officer and auditor, his name appeared both on state letterhead and every poll-tax receipt.

Soon after Congressman Harris's announcement, word got out that Jimmie "Red" had rented an apartment in Pine Bluff, the district's largest town, and had transferred his official residency from Little Rock to the new address. Accepted wisdom held, given a special election, Jimmie "Red" Jones would probably win in a walk.

Hearing rumors of Jones preparing to announce, Farrell Faubus, the governor's son, went to his father and asked him *not* to call a special election. Or rather he pleaded with him. He argued that a special election would assure Jones the office and—here's the startling part—David Pryor would not receive a fair chance. He added, David Pryor is my friend.

Despite our years of disagreement and contention, the governor listened to Farrell. Risking his friendship with Jones and a host of loyal backers, he decided not to call a special election. His move seemed even more remarkable since his relationship with Farrell was strained at best, and why the governor would assist David Pryor in any way rocketed beyond anyone's imagination.

Having made his commitment, Faubus announced that a special election's expense would cast too heavy a financial burden on the counties; voters would fill the vacancy in the November 1966 general election. In fact, two elections would occur at the same time: one to complete Congressman Harris's unexpired term, another to elect a full-time successor. Several weeks later, Jimmie "Red" Jones announced he would seek another term as state auditor. That opened the field.

The governor's decision at once altered the campaign's complexion and momentum, and the force behind it was Farrell Faubus. Even though Farrell well understood how I opposed his father and the entire Faubus program, he and I had become friends as fellow University law students. As the governor's son and only child, he naturally stood out as a curiosity at law school. He possessed an awkward shyness and hesitancy, isolating him from classmates. Maybe it came from being the son of a world-famous, controversial governor.

Farrell impressed me as being painfully uncertain of himself, wanting to please others but never quite certain what anyone wanted from him. People in Huntsville, the governor's hometown, considered him a turncoat who had picked up Little Rock's city ways. Little Rock acquaintances seemed to see him as a country bumpkin from the hills. In any case, I had become his friend. In law school, we played a few rounds of golf, and shared notes when our study group prepared for exams. I liked Farrell and valued his friendship.

Early one morning before class, he led me to a back office, pulling out blueprints for his father's planned house in Huntsville: an enormous mansion designed by noted architect Fay Jones—a structure figured to cost perhaps two or three million dollars.

I never really knew why Farrell wanted to show me the plans. He swore me to secrecy, which of course I honored, but the promise was unnecessary. Before long, the public learned about the project and started asking questions. In no time, this palatial home—built by a governor drawing a $10,000-a-year salary—became a major issue, and a milestone in Faubus's legacy of mistakes and embarrassment.

My political credentials in 1965 did not appear significant, and in no way predicted victory. In fact, the race for Fourth District Congressman was shaping up as a major contest of will, stamina, background, and money. What's more, the heavy 18-month battle would seem interminable.

My campaign began with a group of supporters asking me to act as master of ceremonies, crowning Miss Dallas County at the annual fair in Fordyce. This was always the summer's big event. Friends assured me that a couple thousand people would show up.

Revelers packed the rodeo arena that Saturday night. Probably 20 or more local contestants performed in talent and swimsuit competitions.

At the evening's climax, the judges sent their selections to the stage so I could announce the winner. At the microphone, I received the paper slip with the top three contestants' names. No one told me the list proceeded in reverse order. With full confidence, I announced the third place winner as Miss Dallas County of 1965. In horror, the judges rushed to the stage. What could I do? I apologized and begged forgiveness. But the worst was yet to come: they told me I had to ask the young girl to return the crown. When the dust had more or less settled, the sheriff provided a police escort, assuring I made a safe exit from town.

We planned a Pine Bluff rally for the following weekend, and hired two organizers who, we were told, were Jefferson County's best. We depended on them to draw a crowd, set up the Holiday Inn ballroom, and recruit volunteers to help with the overflow of Pryor supporters cramming the place. Barbara and I arrived an hour early, expecting a rush of campaign supporters and excited potential voters. No one came. Not a soul. The cavernous ballroom featured only a long table holding a pitcher of ice water with two lonesome drinking glasses. We learned a painful lesson: take nothing for granted, least of all a crowded turnout.

* * *

A few days later, a man showed up in my office with a delivery from his boss, Mr. Napoleon Bonaparte Murphy, the Ford dealer over in Hamburg. He handed me the keys to a new Ford, along with a Gulf credit card. Mr. Murphy, a fellow member of the Arkansas legislature, wanted to wish me well, the messenger said, in my race for Congress. "Nap" Murphy, from that moment, became not only a lifelong supporter but a lasting friend.

During the campaign's early weeks, I was spending an afternoon in Sparkman, working the lumber mill, shaking hands with anyone willing to talk with me. At the top of a 100-foot fire tower, a workman yelled at me, "Hey, David Pryor, if you'll climb up here and ask for my vote, you can have it!"

I climbed the tower ladder's full length while everyone in the lumberyard watched and applauded. They thought I was crazy. I thought the challenge made perfect sense, and felt certain that I would gain the man's vote. I also felt his cohorts would side with me just because I had accepted the challenge.

From the start, I kept very close watch on Richard Arnold. His formidable family connections, with the Palmer chain of newspapers, radio, and television stations, threatened any opposing campaign. Even though Texarkana's location, in the state's very corner, isolated it from the Congressional district's 20 counties, the city had always played decisive roles in Arkansas politics. The legal and social status of Richard's distinguished family guaranteed him a blue-blood stamp no other candidate could claim. His father and grandfather were established lawyers in Miller County. His maternal grandfather was Morris Shepherd, a former U.S. senator from Texas. Richard would surely set a high tone to any confrontation. From the beginning, he ran a brisk and well-financed campaign.

In addition to Richard Arnold, the slate included three other candidates. Dean Murphy of Hope, shrewd owner of a large and successful truck stop, was making a second run for the seat. Two years earlier, challenging Congressman Harris's bid for an 11th term, he had surprised everyone by receiving 44% of the primary vote. At the time, Oren Harris was chairman of the House Committee on Interstate and Foreign Commerce, and a formidable congressional member. Yet Murphy's campaign showed that Harris was vulnerable; some opined that the congressman took the judgeship because he didn't have the heart or stomach for another tough race. Murphy promised serious opposition; he was street-smart, boasted a wide circle of support, and already had a campaign operation in place.

A surprise candidate also entered: John Harris Jones, a quiet and introspective Pine Bluff lawyer and banker. A relative unknown, he still had developed a highly-respected law practice. And, with Pine Bluff as the district's largest city, he commanded a wide range of contacts and supporters in a crucial area. At any other time, I would have wanted John Harris Jones in my camp, even as a Jefferson County coordinator. But as an opponent, I was betting his temperament and intelligence—so close to Richard Arnold's—could well be cancelled out by Arnold's more aggressive and expensive campaign coming out of Texarkana.

Chuck Honey, a Prescott lawyer and former staff assistant to Congressman Harris, announced last, but he proved first to step out with mailings and ads. Having assisted in obtaining grants and projects as a Washington aide, Honey had forged alliances with every county courthouse in the district. Local officials for years had known, if they wanted something out of Congressman Harris's office, they could call on Chuck.

But through his early campaign charge, Honey overdid the back-slapping, good-old-boy swagger, and he overstated claims of favors to mayors and county judges. While many of them remembered David Pryor as a nuisance to their free-wheeling spending styles, they still refused to join Honey's hoedown. His musical jingle appeared to deluge all south Arkansas radio stations at once. Even our children knew the words by heart:

> Honey in the morning
> Honey in the evening
> Honey at suppertime
> ... And your best bet is Chuck Honey for Congress!

Far from winning supporters, this refrain, though catchy, grew tiresome and overblown.

At last, old power politics was beginning to fade as voters became aware of civil rights and needed election reform. Not to say 1966 brought a whole new day, or past political alliances' demise, especially in south Arkansas. But power bases that had ruled state politics since the 1930s were showing cracks. We could sense change in the air.

This distinctly new atmosphere rang particularly true with the race question. Both sides, black and white, still had to travel a long road toward trust and cooperation. But the journey had begun. Anyone viewing the political horizon could see light beginning to appear.

Meanwhile, in the governor's race, Justice Jim Johnson was doing nothing to encourage a new age in Arkansas politics. He continued to preach just the opposite. A native of Crossett who had served one term in the state senate, he had risen as a major force in persuading Faubus to close the Little Rock schools in 1957. He had played a role in establishing the now-abolished Sovereignty Commission, and his narrowly defeating Justice Minor Milwee in 1958 had encouraged him to seek higher political office.

Johnson played a waiting game until the right moment. History turned when Faubus announced he would not run in 1966. Winthrop Rockefeller decided to seek the Republican nomination for governor, which led several Democrats to consider the race. Justice Jim quickly dropped his name in the hat for the Democratic primary. Surprising everyone, he ultimately defeated moderate Frank Holt, a thoughtful and progressive Democratic Party voice.

During that campaign, I met young Bill Clinton, then 19 years old and working to elect Holt. We introduced ourselves in front of the Arkadelphia fire station, and fell into conversation about the summer's major races. He had a surprising grasp of my campaign, as well as every other political rivalry. As Barbara and I got in the car, she asked the name of the young man I had just spoken with. I said his name was Bill Clinton. "And we're going to be hearing more about him in the future."

Justice Jim publicly relished his general-election race against Winthrop Rockefeller, whom he described as "this multi-millionaire carpetbagger from New York." Fresh out of the gate, Justice Jim's campaign bellowed of a shrill racist crusade. In frequent television appearances, he drew in viewers with calls to "friend" and "brother." He attacked Lyndon Johnson, the ACLU, and the *Arkansas Gazette*, ending with a fixed stare at the camera and, with outstretched arms, pleading, "Precious Savior, lead me on!" In November, he lost to Winthrop Rockefeller, who became Arkansas's first Republican governor since 1874. Many lifetime Democrats understandably defected to Rockefeller and his moderate positions.

During the congressional campaign, anyone who mentioned race did it primarily with subtle winks and in whispered conversation. One night in a Malvern truck stop, a man came up to me at the cash register and handed me a card. With a knowing look on his face he said, "If you ever need me, give me a call." When I got home I pulled out his card. He was a member of the Ku Klux Klan. Later in the campaign, I chose the issue of "hate" in a speech before a local civic club in El Dorado. I denounced the cowardly activities of the Klan. At that point, three club members got up and stormed out of the room.

That September, just minutes before the annual Miller County fair's parade in Texarkana, Barbara and I were sitting on the back of a convertible, waiting to ride through town and join the festive crowd. Virginia Johnson—Justice Jim's wife—her eyes and mouth narrowed in a tight frown, stepped up to the car and handed us two Johnson for Governor buttons. "Shame on you for not supporting our party's candidate," she snapped, and stalked off.

Chapter 20
Answering a Letter

R ace became a campaign issue only once: in the Democratic primary runoff
between Richard Arnold and me.

Here's how the election unfolded. Murphy, Harris, and Honey fell short in
the first vote on July 26. Murphy had endorsed me, even joining my runoff
campaign on an almost daily basis. Polls showed I held a modest-to-healthy lead
over Arnold. My tactic to maintain that lead was to avoid rocking the boat. We
concentrated heavily on Pine Bluff and Jefferson County, which housed a fifth
of the district's population. I felt holding our own there could win the runoff.
Poll results in every county encouraged us.

Then a devious and unexpected move wrenched open the race issue. Early
Friday morning, August 5, only four days before the runoff vote, anonymous
drivers stuffed the district's rural mailboxes with circulars from some mysterious
group called Arkansas Committee of Concern. The circular headline read, "Black
Power Supports David Pryor." It followed with two paragraphs about the Student
Non-Violent Coordinating Committee (SNCC), and Stokely Carmichael's
fabricated endorsement of me. It described SNCC as an organization advocating
violence in the streets and at courthouses, quoting Carmichael as saying, "We will
bring whites to their knees every time they mess with us."

In an ironic twist, the circular listed positions I had taken defending
minority rights. It also expressed more favorable opinions of my civil-rights
efforts than I had received from any newspaper editorials. I knew the flyer
couldn't go uncontested.

That afternoon, I announced with radio and newspaper ads that I would
formally "answer a letter" the following night on El Dorado's Channel 10.
Arnold and his campaign had reserved airtime following my five minutes (all
the broadcast time I could afford). They were loading to fire a reaction at what
I would say. Naturally they assumed I would come out swinging, responding to
the SNCC circular and Carmichael's so-called endorsement.

I came on the air at 10:20 p.m. I didn't mention SNCC in any way. Instead,
I "answered a letter" from a 13-year-old Arkadelphia boy who had saved change

in a fruit jar and sent it to me, wishing me luck in my campaign. I encouraged him, and anyone else who might be watching, to tell the truth in politics, to fight clean campaigns, and to wage only honest battles. A little corny, perhaps. But my brief broadcast earned a couple of favorable editorials the next day. The young boy from Arkadelphia was Phil Herrington, who later established a successful investment business in Little Rock and brought my Camden friend Bum Atkins and me into the firm.

The bogus circular represented a deceitful attempt to bring fear into the campaign. Stokely Carmichael had not endorsed me—I had never met or talked to him—and I knew about SNCC only through news stories. The ploy created a firestorm throughout the district, but its effects lasted only a day or so.

We never determined whether the Arnold campaign instigated the circular. Knowing Richard Arnold as I did, I felt certain that, if he had learned of the plan, he would have stopped it. In the long run, it probably helped more than hurt me. The lack of effect on voters indicated that racial tensions, and their attendant fears and suspicions, were starting to wane. The general reaction to that blatant racial hoax confirmed my positive belief in Arkansas voters' awareness and intelligence.

I faced the far more pressing campaign charge that I was under Chicago and northeast labor bosses' thumbs. These accusations typically involved my three-term record as a state representative. The only candidate in the race with a legislative voting record, I had strongly supported issues the AFL-CIO had endorsed. These included a minimum-wage increase and expanding the food-stamp program. I had also voted for a shorter workweek and additional firemen benefits.

Labor unions also strongly opposed the poll tax, another major cause I had supported. The AFL-CIO had endorsed almost every reform effort in the early 1960s, and with few exceptions, I had taken the same side. Ouachita County, and Camden in particular, stood as a labor stronghold. Unions were prominent in other district cities from El Dorado and Texarkana to Benton and Pine Bluff. These areas burgeoned with heavy concentrations of oil and gas interests, paper mills, and manufacturing plants. Aluminum production had become a major economic underpinning in Saline County. So with my progressive record, I was depending on a strong labor vote, but I didn't expect my union associations to become a negative campaign issue.

Chuck Honey had questioned my labor ties before the runoff. Then Arnold brought the first formal charge in a television speech on August 1, the runoff period's sixth day. The speech would last a full half-hour—a lengthy period for any talk uninterrupted by an interviewer or reporters panel. When I heard of the airtime, I knew something serious was in the works.

Holding up a thick sheaf of papers, Arnold said that in 1961, and again in '65, I had voted "100% in favor of labor's positions." He accused me of lacking the courage to accept labor's endorsement and admit publicly who my friends were. Finally, he said I had received money directly from my pals Jimmy Hoffa and Walter Reuther; if I went to Congress, I would become nothing but union bosses' rubber stamp.

In a televised speech the following night, I addressed Arnold as an old friend who should know better than to distort my legislative record. I shamed him for suggesting I was Jimmy Hoffa's tool, or anyone else's. I declared that people throughout the district knew me and my record, and would respond to his negativism by making up their own minds. Then I outlined programs in education and jobs, highway construction, and ways of attracting industry. I suggested that these valid goals mattered to voters, not his negative charges.

The next day, the *Pine Bluff Commercial* wrote that Arnold should not attack my legislative record, since it stood out as one of my strongest points as a candidate. The editorial brushed aside Arnold's calling me a labor-boss tool. I hoped that would settle the matter, and felt particularly good about the Pine Bluff support.

Then on Thursday night, five days before the runoff election, Arnold fired again on the labor issue. It was an odd appearance. Halfway through the speech, he suddenly halted discussion of my legislative record, and dropped the gentle hand-waving gestures that usually punctuated his speeches. The camera dollied in close.

"David Pryor has charged me with *insinuating* the Hoffa affiliation," he said. "But, ladies and gentlemen, this was no mere insinuation. This was a statement of fact." His eyes narrowed. "Two union officials told me this about two weeks before the primary, and the other time on July 27, the day after the voting. David Pryor, in other words, is controlled by labor union bosses, and he has received money from them."

Arnold's initial "labor bosses" charge had met with public disbelief and some outrage. From what we could tell, most people dismissed his suggestions that anyone controlled me, least of all union officials in Chicago and New York.

His new charge—given with an intense, confidential air—brought different results. When I met people, I saw traces of doubt in their faces, sidelong glances as though Arnold's charges might have substance. Dooley Womack, my long-time friend and political colleague, encouraged me to take a strong offensive stand, stressing his point by complaining that every night parents were scaring their children to sleep with stories about me and labor unions.

Pressure rose for me to return to television and denounce Arnold's tactics, and then repeat it the following night. Memory took me back to 1954 and Francis Cherry's dilemma of whether to charge Orval Faubus with hiding his communist background. This labor issue was different, but its intensity and pressing demand for action, for a *decision*, was painfully similar.

I clearly had to answer Arnold's charges. But a problem persisted. My campaign was out of money. I couldn't afford to pay airtime on El Dorado's Channel 10 or Pine Bluff's Channel Seven. Or anywhere else, for that matter.

Then, the late afternoon before the runoff, Barbara and I stood in the El Dorado TV station's parking lot, wondering how to raise $1,069 needed for my speech. A large black, chauffeur-driven limousine pulled up beside us. Out stepped Miss Bertie Murphy—the mother of Charles Murphy, Murphy Oil's chairman and a major backer of Richard Arnold. In open but friendly disagreement with her son, Miss Bertie had long supported me, even publicly endorsing me at the campaign's beginning. And Theodosia Murphy Nolan, Charles Murphy's sister, also stood firmly in the Pryor camp, along with the entire side of her family. Her son Bill was one of our mainstays in Union County.

"David," Miss Bertie said, "of course you have to answer Richard Arnold's charges."

I told her that I agreed, but didn't have the money for airtime.

"You have it now," she said. She took out her checkbook and began writing. "I have no idea what this will cost, but you go in there and buy the time you need and say what you need to say." She got back in her car and the chauffeur drove her away.

I chose a course different from Cherry's, and different from any I had seen before. My short speech—we had only 15 minutes—was a personal address to Richard Arnold.

"Richard," I said, "you have attacked me in a personal way that you know is wrong and without any basis in fact. You know that I have no association with labor bosses, that I never have, and that I have not taken money from them." I then went on to deflect his charges by saying that I would not fight personally with him and would not dignify his outlandish charges with a reply. Finally, I chided my friend Richard Arnold for his tactics and his willingness to circulate hatred in what should have been a clean campaign.

My "Shame on you, Richard" approach was a calculated risk. I also took a chance by refraining from a detailed defense of myself and my record. But it proved the right choice. It left Arnold with no retort but to repeat his attack on my legislative record. He could not make the Hoffa accusations again, since I had not taken the bait.

His next half-hour TV speech covered a lengthy discussion of legislative bills I should have supported and did not, along with others I favored but should have opposed. Then he brought out what he hoped to accomplish in Congress. As always in Richard Arnold's manner, he intelligently discussed the issues, but without the political passion required in a closing campaign speech. Much to my relief, his appearance lacked the strength I had feared. In his unfailingly magnanimous way, Richard told me years later that—during the runoff's heated two weeks—he had received, and followed, a lot of poor advice.

Chapter 21
Turning on a Dime

I won the Democratic primary's special election on August 9, 1966, which designated me to fill Congressman Harris's unexpired term in the 89th Congress. This also nominated me for the 90th Congress's full term. Still remaining was November's general election. But contesting with a Republican opponent would seem like a pillow fight compared to the Democratic primary's contentious rivalry.

I could never have won that race without a strong showing in Pine Bluff, Jefferson County's seat and major town, where nearly 20% of the voters lived. Without the help of Anne McClaran, Stanley McNulty, and their tireless team, I doubt we could have made it. Through them all, I discovered another timeless lesson in state politics: you must have the volunteers to succeed in a campaign. And volunteers had arrived in force, vital in identifying potential voters, getting them to register, and making sure they went to the polls and voted.

My general-election opponent was Lynn Lowe from Texarkana. I had known Lynn for a number of years and respected his family and their district leadership. His brother Bob, also a friend, had served on Senator Fulbright's staff in Washington. Arkansans interested in federal policy knew him well. Bob was as much a Democrat as Lynn was a Republican.

Lynn's campaign repeated many issues Arnold had raised. But by the time November's chill winds and winter promise rolled around, politics's searing heat had cooled. What's more, the primary battle had dissected my record so thoroughly, voters had grown weary of Pryor and Lowe. They just wanted the campaign to end.

Following the November 7 election, we threw a victory gathering at the Camden Hotel. But it lacked the luster and excitement of our Democratic primary win in August, when we had celebrated in the same ballroom.

Early the following morning, I stepped on to our front porch at 929 Banner Street to grab the paper. The *Arkansas Gazette* headline read, "Winthrop Rockefeller Elected Governor over Jim Johnson." Below that, "Congressman Jim Trimble, after 20 Years in the House, is Defeated in the Third District by

John Paul Hammerschmidt." And finally, below the fold, "State Representative David Pryor of Camden wins the Fourth District Congressional Seat."

The bold print of the *Gazette* headline, right there in black and white, shook me with a stunning moment of recognition. I truly realized voters had elected me to Congress. Inevitably, I wondered what the future held for Barbara and me, and for our growing family.

Scott had been born on April 2 after serious complications and a difficult pregnancy. He arrived right when the campaign was reaching fever pitch, and despite our concerns, Barbara brought us this big, beautiful blond boy— a family victory, indeed.

Still, through his first six months, Scott had hardly felt our presence on Banner Street for even two straight days. What kind of life could he expect, growing up in a politically-obsessed family like ours? Or, for that matter, what could Dee and Mark hope for? I wondered if it was fair to pass my political obsessions on to my family's innocent and unsuspecting members.

Despite a full schedule of rallies, speeches, and courthouse visits, I always managed to spend time with Dee, Mark, and Scott. I found it essential to take a few minutes—and often no more than that—pitching a football in the backyard, or reading a Dr. Seuss book, or picnicking with the family whenever time allowed. Barbara, of course, constantly encouraged all these efforts. She never lost sight of the family's needs and demands.

When the long campaign had finally concluded, I came to realize how Barbara had developed into the best campaigner I had ever seen. From our first legislative run only five years earlier, she had hit the road with a truly impressive gusto. Friend and foe alike had come to respect and admire her political perception and her response to a campaign's everyday challenges. She had become not only wife, mother, and friend, but also my compass and rock.

Because I was filling an unexpired Congressional term, the rules gave me seniority over other new House members. They had been elected to full terms, but wouldn't be sworn in until the following January. Texas would send a new House member, a moderate Houston Republican named George H. W. Bush. He would be selected to head the House's freshman Republican class, and I would garner the same spot for the Democrats. That leadership post would bring little responsibility, but still would serve as a nice vote of confidence from our peers.

Just after dawn on that post-election-day morning, I had finished reading the paper when Texas Congressman Wright Patman called to congratulate me, welcoming me as a colleague. A grizzled, 40-year Congressional veteran, Patman served a district including Texarkana. As a politician familiar with Texarkana hierarchy, he had known generations of Richard Arnold's family. He possessed firsthand knowledge of our hard-fought race, as well as my recent and less prickly run against Lynn Lowe. Both of my opponents were long-standing Miller County residents, and Congressman Patman knew his political landscape better than any ward boss or county sheriff in the country.

When the caller identified himself, I was curious what tack he would take, half-expecting him to reprimand me for some political gaffe during one or both campaigns. But he couldn't have been more gracious, or more politically savvy. After extending the warm welcome from the Democratic House caucus, he reminded his new neighbor that Texarkana's federal post office building sat half in Arkansas and half in Texas.

"But don't you worry about that, son," he cautioned me, "or the rural mail carriers either. I'll take care of those postal jobs. You have enough to worry about as a fresh young member of that fine Arkansas delegation." He hung up with a friendly laugh. I had just received my first dose of power politics from a Texas charmer who had played the game since 1927.

So the morning had already turned busy. A man I had never seen before arrived to discuss that job I'd give him—the one promised by my friend, Dooley Womack. Johnny Harrell at Station KJWH called to line up an interview.

Ralph Scott, the local FBI agent, dropped in, wanting to chat. A friend and fellow Presbyterian Church member, he had taken an active interest in the campaign. His manner was unusual, asking if we could sit alone on the back porch. Sipping a glass of lemonade, he seemed to avoid getting to the point. Finally, he reached over, patted my arm, and held my attention: "Mr. J. Edgar Hoover just wanted me to extend his personal congratulations."

Early the next morning, with grandparents moved in as babysitters, Barbara and I headed for Washington and my swearing in to finish Oren Harris's unexpired term. On the way to the Little Rock airport, we stopped by the Marion Hotel for a necessary and somewhat formal interview with Congressman Wilbur Mills. He was practically holding court, and as a recently-elected freshman House member, I was high on his list of expected supplicants.

His powerful standing as the Ways and Means Committee's chairman included an unwritten rule: no one ever called him anything but "Mr. Chairman." Not "Congressman Mills" and certainly not "Wilbur." For as long as I knew him, even after he had left the House, he was simply "Mr. Chairman."

More important for me, Wilbur Mills also chaired the Committee on Committees. He would ultimately decide, more or less on his own, committee assignments for all newly-elected Democratic representatives. Even Speaker of the House John McCormack didn't wield that degree of raw control.

Our visit proved cordial but somewhat stuffy. Senator Fulbright, whose status permitted him to call Mr. Mills by his first name, had once commented, "Wilbur is not too cozy." Over the years, my relationship with him was always pleasant, but also a bit stiff and reserved.

The formality of our Marion talk had to do with the new look of Congress. The November elections had seen the Democrats take a beating, with only 14 newly-elected Democrats. Republicans had gained 44 House seats, mainly because President Johnson and his party bore the blame for escalating the Vietnam conflict. On top of that, Johnson and the Democrats had advocated civil rights legislation, leading many Southerners to leave the Democratic Party and turn Republican.

We didn't fully comprehend how the 1966 election signaled this major American political change. The once solid Democratic South had begun to crumble. I had survived the first giant wave, but would need to contend throughout my still-young political career with this reality: Democrats—especially liberal and progressive ones like me—were becoming an endangered species in the former Solid South. Voters were already sweeping Democrats from office in Alabama and Mississippi.

The country's few winning Democrats were making their pilgrimages to the Chairman, either in person or by phone, plugging for specific committee assignments. Even today, new members observe these rituals every two years, the political dance's manner and timing familiar to those few who hold power and the many who seek favors.

Of course, everyone wanted the Appropriations Committee. That's the power of the purse, where public-works action always centers. But the Chairman was clear and emphatic. "No, David, there are no vacancies on Appropriations," he explained with an impatient frown. "All our committee members survived their elections. What about Agriculture?"

Silence.

"Well, let's think about this for the next few weeks." And that was that.

Except for one thing. He almost offhandedly had mentioned the Agriculture Committee. I took his cue as a default assignment, until something better came along. Instinctively, I wanted a high-level panel that determined policy, an inner group with star appeal and political intrigue. Foreign Affairs or Ways and Means—in my dreams—would be the ticket. But it was not in the cards.

Barbara and I left Little Rock late that afternoon. The next day in Washington, I signed the necessary legal documents and was sworn in. We rented a small house in Alexandria that featured an all-pink kitchen. That night, my law school friend George Jernigan took us to dinner at a small and popular Italian pizza place on M Street. We celebrated the beginning of our new life in the nation's capitol.

We would make it a swift trip, anxious to get home, pack up the children, and move back to Washington.

Still, one chore remained before we could return to Arkansas. Actually, I was keeping a promise I had made 15 years before, when I worked as a teenage House page the summer of '51.

Late one afternoon, I had indulged my superstitious juvenile nature, making my way to the U.S. Capitol building's deepest bowels. Climbing among the pipes and rafters above a basement hallway, I placed a dime—far back as I could reach—in a crevice between two giant granite columns. I was extending my romantic political fantasies, fed by having grown up breathing the air of campaigns, elections, and political parties.

"O.K., dime," I said, "stay there until I come back for you—someday when I'm a Congressman."

So before Barbara and I left for Arkansas, I stole down that afternoon to my secret hiding place. Making sure no one had seen me, I reached behind the columns and into the crevice. Sure enough, there sat my good luck dime—portraying the head of Franklin D. Roosevelt—waiting for my return. I picked it up and turned it in my hand. Then I put it back. Despite the Capitol basement's recent construction projects, so far as I know, it's still there today.

Chapter 22
The New Kid on the Block

Entering the House in late 1966, I became junior member of a truly distinguished Congressional delegation. Its strength rested in longevity leading to seniority. Like so many southern states, Arkansas kept re-electing legislators once they assumed office and kept delivering for constituents.

But this veteran Arkansas delegation also possessed an impressive collection of political intelligence and power. In Washington, anyone wanting to pass meaningful legislation knew, at some point, they would have to deal with McClellan, Fulbright, Mills, Harris, Trimble, or Gathings—sometimes with all six.

The subtle power shift in 1966 promised to change all that. Political certainties were breaking up throughout the South. It looked more and more like a new day, particularly for Arkansas. I was taking the seat of Oren Harris, who had distinguished himself over many years as chairman of the House Commerce Committee. John Paul Hammerschmidt had defeated Congressman Jim Trimble, known to everyone as "the Judge," who had represented the state's third district for 20 years. Hammerschmidt, a young and upcoming politician, was a Republican. Someone jokingly told me that when I got to Washington, I'd see a real Republican for the first time in my life. That's how solidly Democratic our state had always been. But times were changing.

From the beginning, John Paul knew he was an Arkansas political anomaly, and he played his new role with impressive understatement. In time, he found a ready niche for himself, especially in air safety, highway funding, conservation, and veterans' affairs. His constituency services provided a model for every office on the Hill. People realized he could secure a wayward passport or Social Security check quicker than anyone in Congress. He was also known as the man who gave Bill Clinton his first defeat, when the future president ran against him in 1974.

The twin losses of Harris and Trimble presented a major and perhaps unsettling change for many Arkansans. But an incredibly stable foundation remained: Wilbur Mills, as chairman of House Ways and Means, carried in his head the entire U.S. tax code. He had written most of it himself. His committee members felt so confident of his knowledge and leadership that—in many cases, knowing his position—they didn't bother to vote.

J. William Fulbright, known worldwide for the international exchange program that provided thousands of Fulbright scholarships, chaired the Senate Foreign Relations Committee. He had taken that role in 1958, during the Eisenhower administration's waning years. Gaining respect as the University of Arkansas's president while still a young man, he served for a short time in the House, coming to the Senate in 1945. Far ahead of his time, he stood as the lone Senate member to vote against funding Senator Joseph McCarthy's investigation committee.

Senator Fulbright combined intelligence and country manners like no one I had ever seen. Friends would tease him for piling up a supply of gingham sport shirts every six years, leaving his ancient Mercedes in Washington, and driving a rented Pontiac through Arkansas for another campaign. He took the joke with a laugh. Arkansans knew he rose intellectually above the crowd, loved him for it, and kept returning him to Washington.

The delegation's senior member, Senator John L. McClellan, originally hailed from Sheridan. He ran for the Senate as a resident of Camden, where he practiced law. My father was a friend of Senator McClellan's. At one point in his initial Senate run, with the candidate out of money and ready to abandon his campaign, Dad rounded up a group of businessmen. Entering McClellan's office on a Saturday afternoon, they found him at his typewriter, pecking out a concession letter. But they raised the necessary funds to keep him running. Dad, W. A. "Red" Daniel, Don Harrell, and B. T. Fooks each signed a note for $2,500. They asked Garland Hurt, president of Citizens Bank, to come downtown, open the doors, and make good on the loan.

McClellan had previously served a short House tenure, and in 1938 had challenged Senator Hattie Caraway in the Democratic primary. His campaign slogan claimed Arkansas "needs another man in the Senate." While that effort failed, he finally gained election in 1943. He built his reputation during Government Operations hearings, then went on to become chairman of Appropriations, a highly powerful position. He made possible numerous public works projects around Arkansas. As chairman of the Senate Permanent Committee on Investigations, he became a revered symbol of right moral conduct in both the Army-McCarthy hearings and while investigating Teamster union activities under Jimmy Hoffa.

A natural chasm spans the House and Senate, its size at times seeming to rival the Grand Canyon. This split involves aim and purpose, and even how each body communicates with constituents. Frequently, relationships within a state delegation become strained due to competition, jealousy, and suspicion. I've seen this frosty give-and-take occur in many instances.

As our House session's opening day approached, Congressman E. C. "Took" Gathings of West Memphis introduced me to House procedure's methodology. He became an informal preceptor to several young Democrats. As vice-chairman of the House Agriculture Committee, he prided himself on becoming "the farmer's voice," and on his impeccable dress and courtly manner. I never became comfortable with his social and political conservatism, and I think he knew it. But we willingly overlooked our basic differences and got along.

Congress convened on Monday, January 10, 1967. I walked onto the House floor well before the first gavel came down, my eyes wide and pulse racing. Awake most of the night before, I kept imagining who I'd see, and what our first call to action might be. Something to do with Vietnam probably, or an appropriations measure funding the brand-new Medicare program. As it turned out, my maiden voyage had little to do with national policy.

When I first reached the floor, I saw Representative Adam Clayton Powell, Jr., Harlem's high-profile and notorious African-American congressman. He was moving around, greeting colleagues, making a point to shake hands with everyone. The next thing I knew, he spied me and came striding across the room with his hand out. My heart pounded. What could he want from me?

"You're Pryor from Arkansas," he said, almost like a declaration of fact. Without giving me a chance to answer, he said, "Oren Harris is a gentleman and a good friend of mine. We got along just fine." He pulled me over to the chamber's side. I half expected to hear him come out with his signature greeting: "Keep the faith, baby!" But his concerns were far more serious.

He wore a silver suit with red tie and matching pocket handkerchief. Along with his brilliant white shirt, his character seemed almost surreal. I was frankly dazzled by this bigger-than-life figure seeming to spring directly from a cover of *Time*. Or the *National Enquirer*. I was thoroughly familiar with his flamboyant reputation as a playboy and flouter of Congressional rules and customs.

As chairman of the House Labor and Education Committee, Powell had written key legislation covering every issue from desegregation to anti-lynching bills, the poll tax, minimum-wage increases, and education of the deaf. He had laid crucial foundations for President Johnson's war on poverty. I think his committee still holds the record for initiating Congress's largest number of bills.

But on January 10, 1967, his star hung distinctly tarnished—and for good reason. The House that morning would consider whether to seat him, or delay until a special House committee could investigate his recent activities.

Powell had been accused of mismanaging committee budgets, and questions abounded regarding his expensive global junkets. The press had flashed numerous pictures of him, shirtless, perched on his Bimini house's deck. Most recently, he had refused to pay a slander judgment, making him subject to arrest. Yet in spite of all this, a huge majority in his Harlem district had re-elected him. His constituents revered him, despite his exploits remaining embarrassing page-one items.

The day before the opening session, the Democratic caucus had stripped Powell of his committee chairmanship, and a strong movement rose for immediate expulsion. But Congressman Morris K. "Mo" Udall of Arizona had offered a compromise resolution delaying any action until the special committee could gather evidence and make a recommendation.

"Let me tell you something," Powell said to me in a low voice. I felt like every House member, plus a packed spectator gallery, was watching us. "I know your district," he went on, "and when your name is called, I don't think you should vote to seat me. Maybe in another couple of years, if this thing drags on, but not today. Don't do it."

I followed his advice, and sure enough, the House voted to withhold judgment pending a committee report. Then in March, the House voted to exclude him, and I favored the provision. Two years later, after he and the leadership had reached a restitution agreement, I joined a sizeable majority of Democrats and Republicans that voted to reseat him. This was the right thing to do. But by then, Powell had decided not to retake his seat. Charlie Rangel won election in 1970, and has represented that district ever since.

Powell clearly was guilty of power abuses that merited censure. But on reflection, a number of white members of Congress, guilty of the same kind of abuses, went unscathed and unpunished.

That January 10, for all the Powell suspense, involved even more drama. That afternoon, Congressman John E. Fogarty, a Rhode Island Democrat and senior member of the Appropriations Committee, fell dead of a heart attack. A much respected member, he had come up through a bricklayers union. His name, attached to two decades of significant health legislation passed in the House, remains on a major Providence hospital.

I learned later that Chairman Mills, standing at his office window, happened to see Fogarty cross Independence Avenue, then crumple to the sidewalk. As the Chairman watched the emergency team put him in the ambulance, he picked up the phone and called Speaker John McCormack. "Looks like John Fogarty just died," he said, "so there's a vacancy on Appropriations. I think you should see David Pryor this afternoon."

A day after the Fogarty funeral, I was named to the Appropriations Committee, leap-frogging colleagues who had worked and waited patiently, expecting this reward for loyal service. One of those, Congressman Freddie St. Germain, also of Rhode Island, had served many years on the Banking Committee. He felt he deserved the move up to Appropriations. He also thought Fogarty's seat more or less belonged to Rhode Island. I'm sorry to say he never quite forgave me for securing that coveted spot.

Still, St. Germain knew I was from Arkansas and enjoyed the patronage of the powerful chairman of Ways and Means—and the Committee on Committees. Because we both understood that, we were able to remain friends for many years thereafter.

Mo Udall of Arizona became a good friend. On a number of spring evenings, we slipped out for a quick nine holes of golf, although neither of us scored very well.

I admired him as a model of right conduct during my House years. His sense of justice had made possible the fair and decent treatment of Adam Clayton Powell. A committed defender of the environment, Mo also came out early for campaign reform and Congressional standards of ethics, long before these became rallying cries for both Democrats and Republicans. He was the first Democrat to oppose President Johnson on Vietnam.

More than anything else, Mo's sense of humor attracted people to him. When the Hill buzzed that Mo Udall might run for the oval office, David Broder, the *Washington Post* columnist, wrote that he was too funny to be president. Mo picked this up as the title for his autobiography. It somehow struck an accurate note in defining his character. I still wish we would have given Morris Udall a serious chance to lead this country. He continued to be a friend long after we left the House.

Congressman Tom Gettys, an old-style Democrat from South Carolina, became an early mentor and advisor. A former high-school principal and football coach, Tom knew all the Capitol policemen, the elevator operators, and the cafeteria workers. An accomplished public speaker, he could woo audiences with a great story.

Our friendship started on a surprising note, typical of Tom Gettys. One afternoon soon after the session opened, he summoned me to meet him in the Speaker's Lobby off the House floor. The message contained a fairly urgent tone. As I hurried to the Capitol, I couldn't imagine what a senior House member wanted with me. I found him waiting near the Democratic cloakroom door. He ushered me to two leather chairs near the back. When we sat down, he leaned toward me.

"Dave, you're new here," he whispered, "and you're finding your way around the Hill and learning a lot. You're also hearing things from many people." He leaned in a little closer. "I need this to be very confidential. Just between us, have you heard any rumors about me and Congresswoman Charlotte Reid?"

My eyes widened. Charlotte Reid was a greatly admired Republican from Illinois. She had come to the House in 1963 to fill the term of her late husband. She was then elected twice on her own. A beautiful woman, at one time a professional entertainer, she had appeared in the 1940s as Annette King on the Don McNeal Breakfast Club out of Chicago. I regarded her as a true celebrity.

Gettys could see the shock in my face. "No, Congressman," I assured him. "I haven't heard anything of the sort."

"If you do hear anything about us, promise you'll let me know," he said. "And if you *don't* hear any rumors, I want to know that, too. Because I'm getting ready to start some." Tom Gettys loved telling everyone about his "initiation" of young David Pryor.

During my first year as a House member, Camden's post office employees requested four rubber mats—foot cushions to ease their long days standing on concrete floors, sorting and routing mail. Ritchie Morgan, our local postmaster, was known as a stern and somewhat humorless little man. He could quote at length the post office's intricate and arcane rules and regulations. His answer to the employees took five seconds: "No. If your feet hurt, wear rubber-soled shoes." The employees appealed that negative decision to higher authorities in St. Louis.

They also came to me. I was both their congressman and also a Camden native who knew most of them by name. As Wright Patman had reminded me the morning after my election, postal jobs were choice patronage, and Congressional representatives dispersed them among constituents. The local post office occupies a vital place in many Arkansas towns, affecting social, political, and business life. The local postmaster, as well as postal clerks and rural mail carriers, were highly coveted positions. I took seriously these employees and their need for rubber floor mats.

Complicating the request, Ritchie Morgan was a cousin of mine, on my mother's side. Not a close cousin, but close enough to be considered extended family. Congressman Oren Harris had appointed Ritchie our Camden postmaster back in the '40s. And my cousin had a long history of infuriating his fellow workers. Truth was, Ritchie actually appeared more interested in Civil War history than in the U.S. Postal Service. His grandfather was Colonel Asa Morgan of the Confederate Army, a distinction Ritchie proudly acknowledged by wearing a wide, gray and red necktie featuring a graphic image of the Confederate flag.

In short order, the St. Louis officials mandated Ritchie to purchase four 4' x 6' black rubber mats for the Camden, Arkansas, post office employees. Whereupon Ritchie, almost blinded with outrage, appealed the decision to the U.S. Postmaster General.

Some months later, I was having lunch in the House dining room with constituents. Ernie Petrand, the maitre d', rushed excitedly to the table and whispered, "Congressman, the Postmaster General is on the line for you."

Sure enough, Larry O'Brien was calling about the Camden employees. O'Brien had been confidant to both John F. Kennedy and Lyndon Johnson. A no-nonsense administrator, he got right to the point.

"Congressman, do you want the employees in the Camden, Arkansas, post office to have rubber mats to stand on?" he asked.

"Yes," I said. "Absolutely."

My cousin Ritchie became livid when he learned his kin had humiliated him in this way. He drove to Mother's house and protested at length, letting her know that he would never forget this insult. We could count his side of the Morgan family o.u.t.

Two years later, with construction of a new Camden post office, the employees went to Ritchie and asked for a wall clock in the new mail room. They knew from government catalogues that the General Services Administration stored thousands of them.

"No," Ritchie told them. "If you want to know what time it is, you can wear a watch."

Once again, the employees appealed his decision to the St. Louis authorities. In short order, the higher-ups again ruled in the employees' favor. Ritchie again appealed to the Postmaster General in Washington, and—again—Larry O'Brien called me.

"Do you want the employees in Camden to have a clock in the mailroom?" he asked.

"Yes, of course," I told him.

Upon order by the Postmaster General of the United States, Ritchie requisitioned the clock. When it arrived, he hung it in a closet, locking the door. And only Ritchie Morgan had the key.

Chapter 23
Vietnam

Certainly my first year in the House overflowed with learning experiences, opportunities to meet new friends and colleagues, and humorous encounters. Every day broadened my cultural awareness of this world I had always wanted to join.

But we also had to address serious, often grave, questions. It impressed me that members from all backgrounds and regions approached these vital matters in a spirit of good will and cooperation. I can't comment on the current U.S. House and Senate's collegiality, but in the 1960s and '70s, both bodies' members shared a mutual trust and understanding that still seems unique.

The principle of Crossing Party Lines, which now draws attention as a remarkable feat, we considered a given fact—an accepted protocol needing no amplification or underlining comment. You'd often see two House or Senate members rip each other over a disputed bill or personal opinion, then walk off the floor, arms around each other. In my early Congressional years, such acceptance and cordiality were simple facts of life. Without them, the country would never have seen the G.I. Bill, civil rights laws, Medicare, and many other social and educational programs.

For me, 1967's early days moved very fast. The seemingly-endless Vietnam War loomed like a dark cloud over every issue, committee action, and the entire country. The Southeast Asia quagmire moved from every newspaper's back pages to page one. It dominated the 6:00 news every night. Conflicts of war intruded upon American living rooms as part of our daily routine.

Almost overnight, I found myself thrust into decision-making circles that included not only President Johnson, but Secretary of State Dean Rusk and Secretary of Defense Robert McNamara. Far from my normal life as a spectator of world events, I now served on the Appropriations Committee, finding our country's leaders asking *me* to grant money for national security.

At one breakfast briefing, I sat next to Richard Helms, the CIA director. I asked him where, exactly, his jurisdiction began and ended. And in particular, what about the FBI? He didn't hesitate. "We begin at the water's edge," he replied. "The FBI has everything else." It was an enigmatic answer to what I considered a simple question, but it seemed an accurate description of these two classically secretive agencies' rivalry.

One night early in 1967, LBJ invited all 14 of the newly-elected House Democrats to the White House—an informal gathering in the cabinet room. Finding a scheduled event cancelled, he suddenly summoned us to one of the world's most awe-inspiring rooms. He wanted to convince us that escalating the Vietnam War was necessary and deserved our support.

We sat there for three hours while the president sipped Frescas and munched potato chips, but never offered us so much as a cracker. "One thing you have to remember," he said, "is that Republicans exist for two reasons: to investigate the Democrats, and to take care of the rich people."

Every day during my first months, we followed bitter struggles of U.S. forces literally driving Viet Cong out of the Iron Triangle. But whenever a military operation appeared successful, the Viet Cong would re-enter the zone for another bloody confrontation. Americans wondered why we couldn't enter that small country and simply bring off a victory. We had done as much at Guadalcanal and Iwo Jima. What had happened to our country's military spirit?

By 1967, this back-and-forth struggle had become a familiar story. The U.S. forces wanted open warfare, but somehow this never happened. We possessed superior firepower and more effective weapons, but the Viet Cong forced us to respond to primitive sniper attacks and booby traps. From 1965 to 1968, Americans bombed the Ho Chi Minh Trail almost every day, but to no avail. By early 1967, some 20,000 North Viet troops were using the Trail each month.

Then escalation gripped our attention: growth of combat encounters and troop numbers. The two increased simultaneously, each beginning as a trickle and quickly becoming a flood. General William Westmoreland repeatedly requested more men and arms, and almost without notice LBJ—ever the commander-in-chief—would grant his wish.

At the beginning of 1966, American troops numbered roughly 250,000. During the early months of 1967, when I first began keeping track, this number had reached 485,000. And by April of 1969 the figure had risen to 543,000. At the end of 1967, the death rate among U.S. forces had doubled, to more than 800 per month.

We know from subsequent histories and memoirs that even Secretary McNamara had begun to see no way to "win" in Vietnam. He came back from Saigon in October 1966, declaring we had exceeded all expectations, but in private he knew better. By the summer of 1967, he had abandoned hope. In Senate hearings held that fall, he admitted that the Rolling Thunder campaign, touted as our best and strongest effort, had failed.

One of the war era's truly mystifying and tragic figures, McNamara held his post until February 1968, when President Johnson replaced him with Clark Clifford. McNamara moved on to head the World Bank. Johnson announced in March he would not seek re-election as president.

Early in my term, anti-war demonstrations erupted in our country's state capitols and on college and university campuses—the culmination of young people's long pent-up frustrations over the war and the draft.

These public expressions of outrage were not confined to young men bent on avoiding military service. Older people, parents and relatives, grandparents, public officials, writers, teachers, and union members all took to the streets, repeatedly demanding an end to the conflict. The twin peaks of antiwar sentiment crested in October 1967 and August 1968. The first was the march on the Pentagon that drew an estimated 100,000. The second was the demonstrators' nightly riots at Chicago's National Democratic Convention.

Even now from my 40-year perspective, it's impossible to definitely say when President Johnson first realized our Vietnam efforts were failing. My son Scott asked me in the 1980s to "explain" the Vietnam War to him; I was hard pressed to find an answer that made sense. I wrote him a long letter, attempting to describe our country's frustration, our bewilderment at seeing our president entirely unable to find a solution. Johnson's secretly-recorded phone conversations indicate he felt early on we could not win, but he believed our fire power could force Ho Chi Minh to beg for peace. I concluded my letter by confessing that we'll never know exactly what went through Johnson's mind.

Early in 1967, I was invited to travel with President Johnson and his staff on Air Force One—a quick trip to Austin to bolster his sagging Texas support. He included me hoping I might become the administration's future ally.

When the huge convention-center rally had ended, the president's entourage sped out of Austin—at least 20 cars in the pack. Johnson radioed back to the procession's last car. "Stop this parade at the next street," he ordered. "Send somebody into that Dairy Queen and get me a triple dipper." No sooner said than done. The president's entire entourage—Secret Service and all—came to a halt … before a Queen.

On the return trip to Washington, LBJ disappeared into the presidential quarters. Soon he emerged in pajamas and bathrobe, mingling with the rest of us back in the cabin. I sat across from Congressman George Mahon of Texas, and the president joined us. It was a treat to hear the two of them, long-time Texas natives and prominent political figures, recount some of their early adventures in state and national politics.

Mahon had entered the House in 1934, the year I was born, and had only recently become chairman of Appropriations. The phrase "power of the purse" is most often associated with George Mahon, due to his long chairman's tenure. He was known for strict discipline and rigorously organized style. His wife drove him to the Capitol every morning from their Arlington home. Mahon would sit in their old station wagon's back seat, working on correspondence and committee reports.

He received other members' close attention as they exercised in the House gym. After his workout, he always dressed from the top down, a rigorous and precise series of disciplined moves. First the 10-gallon cowboy hat, then the undershirt, the dress shirt and tie, and finally the briefs, the trousers, and the socks and shoes.

When I attended my first House Appropriations Committee meeting, the full room included no table seat for me. So I pulled up a chair at the table's end, opposite Chairman Mahon. When the session adjourned, I told the chairman I felt awkward sitting at the head of the table. He put his hand on my shoulder and said, "No, son, you were at the *foot*—and don't forget it."

Returning from Austin that night, we flew over south Arkansas. I leaned toward the window, pointing to the swiftly streaming earth 35,000 feet below.

"Mr. President," I said, "it looks like we might be flying directly over Camden, Arkansas. That's my home town. If you look straight down at the ground, you might see Jim's Café on Washington Street."

For a moment, he was no longer leader of the free world, just a big Texan with a hefty Southern way of talking. I could see him simply as LBJ. He looked pained and troubled, the wrinkles lined on that famous thick brow. The world literally weighed heavy on his shoulders.

He leaned over and looked out the window. Then he shook his head. "God a'mighty," he sighed, "I wish I was at Jim's Café right now."

When we arrived at Andrews Air Force Base in Washington, a military driver returned Congressman Mahon and me to the Capitol. As we entered the District along South Capitol Avenue, Mahon told the driver to circle the Capitol building. "I love to ride around the Capitol at night," he said. "It's such a sight to see; I never get my fill."

Sometimes I suspect that LBJ already saw, by the summer of 1966, our Vietnam involvement's inevitable and tragic end. Not to say that he changed course then. Clearly, he kept up his determined efforts until deciding to withdraw from the presidential race in March 1968. But I do know that, at one point early in 1966's summer, Senator Fulbright went to the White House, telling Johnson in a private face-to-face meeting that he could no longer support the war effort.

Fulbright had begun public hearings that January. In the succeeding months, he had grown increasingly skeptical of the Johnson administration's war escalation. In particular, he had publicly questioned the "domino theory" that predicted our Far East allies' systematic collapse if we pulled out of Vietnam. The Fulbright hearings had a major impact, raising public interest and doubt about our continued participation in the conflict.

Johnson had to see this breach coming long before it happened. He couldn't speak a foreign language, but he could read body language better than anyone. He and Senator Fulbright had been close colleagues as Senate members. They shared similar minds on a range of issues and, with their two states as neighbors, they had worked together to benefit both Arkansas and Texas.

Their connection in many ways exemplified how the U.S. Senate cemented friendships and associations that otherwise might never have come about. For all their similarities, the two were very different. Johnson was an openly confrontational, spirited hand shaker who welcomed public exposure, while Fulbright was scholarly and sometimes withdrawn. Johnson got his information from conversations with colleagues, Fulbright from long hours with a briefing book or history text. Regardless of their differences and likenesses, after that summer the two long-time colleagues would never be personally or professionally close again.

The war played out long after LBJ left the White House. Nixon came in with the November 1968 elections. The secret bombing of Cambodia followed in February, and we invaded that country in April 1970. Kent State's brutal shootings came the next month.

The last U.S. combat troops didn't leave Vietnam until August 1972, and we co-signed the Paris Peace Accords in January 1973. Our embassy was evacuated in April 1975.

By that time, I was serving as Arkansas's governor, preparing for a rainy-morning helicopter trip from Little Rock to Fort Chaffee, to welcome the first wave of Vietnamese immigrants.

Chapter 24
Turning Point

One night on *The Dick Cavett Show*, writer Mary McCarthy called 1968 the year everything changed. When I think back on the swift and colossal movements taking place then—almost every week—I'm surprised we didn't realize fundamental revolutions were occurring. The ground beneath our feet was shifting.

Not only the war, but racial and political divides were taking their toll. When Martin Luther King, Jr., was assassinated in Memphis on April 4, instant riots caught fire in Boston, Baltimore, Chicago, Detroit, Kansas City, Washington, D. C., and other cities. Fourteenth Street and the H Street corridor behind Washington's Union Station became flaming centers of violence. City police declared curfews and martial law.

From our house in Arlington, we could see fires glowing across the Potomac. Some friends who lived in the District came to spend several nights, afraid for themselves and their homes. Mayor Harold Washington ordered that looters would not be shot, angering FBI Director J. Edgar Hoover, who argued for extreme measures to quell the violence. Their public disagreement underscored much of the racial tensions that embroiled the whole country. Once the smoke cleared in Washington, 11 people had died, some 1,000 had been injured, and more than 8,000 had been arrested. Property damage totaled nearly $100 million.

On top of social unrest and fierce war opposition, Robert F. Kennedy's assassination in June added to the general population's anger, whether they supported his candidacy or not. Earlier in the spring, before Johnson withdrew from the presidential race, Kennedy had gone to the White House to tell the president he would challenge his nomination. Word spread that the conversation moved quickly from cordial to icy, Johnson sitting behind his enormous desk, forcing Kennedy to stay walled on the other side.

Robert Kennedy carried not only his late brother's legacy, but the promise of peace. With his death, the presidential race took on a special urgency. Opposing administration policy, Eugene McCarthy's followers pushed for settlement of the war.

The 1968 Democratic National Convention met in Chicago during the last week of August. History has stamped it with images of riots in the streets and violent confrontations between anti-war activists and Mayor Daley's police forces.

Several close friends advised me not to attend the convention. Two issues will rule the day, they warned me, and if you're a delegate you'll have to take a stand on both. First, Mississippi's Freedom Democratic Party will try to be seated, and second, the party surely will include a platform plank on the Vietnam War. Ignoring their advice, I went anyway, as a credentials-committee member and Arkansas delegate.

Credentials-committee meetings started a week before the convention's August 26 opening. The committee decides which state groups should be formally seated with full convention voting rights. Normally, only one group seeks credentials, so the panel usually functions as a routine approval stamp.

But in 1968, two distinct bodies of Mississippi delegates applied as the state's official representatives. Right off, we knew trouble was brewing. The so-called "regular" delegation was entirely white, the "loyalist" delegation racially balanced. The national Democratic Party had decided to no longer tolerate state delegations that excluded blacks. But Mississippi chose to thumb its nose at both the rule and the reality. The nation had changed with passage of the 1964 Civil Rights and 1965 Voting Rights acts.

Along with the committee majority, I voted to seat the loyalist group. In no time, I began to receive angry letters and phone calls from constituents. My Congressional District's eastern border lay just across the river from Mississippi.

One Star City woman reminded me, "Politicians, like band wagons, rise, engender rot, and then fade away." A Camden friend sent me a one-line note defining me as a traitor and a Red. While casting my vote was difficult, I felt unquestionably right in doing so. Later, when I mentioned to House Speaker Carl Albert of Oklahoma that I had received over 100 critical letters, he told me to drop by his office; he would show me 15,000.

For the next two or three years, Mississippi's House members gave me a distinctly cold shoulder. This included William Colmer, Jamie Whitten, and, for a time, Sonny Montgomery. Colmer's administrative assistant, a young lawyer named Trent Lott, put on a friendly face, trying to offset his boss's chilly disregard. Lott eventually would become a Republican U.S. senator and Senate majority leader.

Another of my convention positions has haunted me to this day. Senator Edmund Muskie of Maine asked me to make a short speech supporting the majority plank on Vietnam policy. My first reaction was negative; I suspected this might side me with the war's defenders. I was becoming increasingly worried about the Vietnam quagmire, yet also felt we could not enter the Paris Peace Talks in a weakened position.

Eugene McCarthy and his supporters were forcing Humphrey and the so-called majority plank into a hawk's position. Fully aware of Senator Fulbright's well-known opposition to our war involvement, I tried to reach him on the phone. Before I would agree to speak, I wanted to make certain I wouldn't embarrass or compromise him. Unable to connect with him, I spoke with Lee Williams, his administrative assistant, who assured me that Senator Fulbright would not object. I have often wondered if Lee were not simply being polite to me. I felt the Democrats needed to emerge from the convention unified to defeat Richard Nixon. Many of those convention wounds remained open at election day, and that lack of unity may in fact have cost us the election.

Convention leaders assured me that my speech would state the moderate position. Then Vice President Humphrey made his personal plea to me. So I accepted the invitation, giving a two-minute endorsement of the majority plank. Little did I realize then how closely our position would be identified with LBJ and the war's continuation.

In my speech, I asked for an end to war, but also made an appeal for unity, strength, and wisdom, and for putting aside emotional slogans and empty phrases. I said we should not give the world the impression that America seeks an escape from the hard realities of surviving in today's international community.

Recently I came across a copy of this speech. It's now yellow with age. It's also tortured beyond anything else I've ever written, with whole sentences and paragraphs re-phrased, added, or crossed out altogether—a clear sign of my discomfort with the speech's position. Across the bottom of the first page, clearly written at some later time, I had spelled out in big red letters, "This speech was a *horrible* mistake. DP."

Senator Eugene McCarthy claimed firm support from many Arkansas people, but our delegation went for Humphrey 30-2. Sadly, in my view, the state was slipping away from its ties to the Democratic Party, and from all logical predictions and prognostications. In 1968, Arkansas supported George Wallace for president on the American Independent ticket, Senator J. W. Fulbright for the Senate as a Democrat, and Winthrop Rockefeller for governor as a Republican. Maybe I had won my re-election campaign, but fellow Southern Democrats continued to lose their Congressional elections.

Not long after the convention, I called for withdrawal from Vietnam. There had been rays of hope, but they had all been false, face-saving, and merely convenient. I also endorsed an end to funding and an immediate return of our troops. "Vietnam," I wrote in a newsletter to constituents, "is not worth one more American life." I regretted everything associated with the war, and my deepest regret was that I had not opposed it earlier. This sense of remorse lies at the heart of that letter I wrote to my son Scott 20 years after the fact. Making it more poignant today, I realize this sad chapter in our country's past mirrors the quagmire of our long war in Iraq.

One day, on a plane trip from Little Rock to Washington, I fell into conversation with a young serviceman, a constituent from south Arkansas. He was going to Vietnam. A few months later, I was flying from Washington to Little Rock and recognized the same young soldier. He sat with a blanket spread over his lap. We exchanged greetings, and I asked him about his tour of duty. He pulled back the blanket, showing me he had lost a leg in combat.

"Congressman Pryor," he said, "I would not have minded losing my leg, if only someone had told me why we were there in the first place."

Chapter 25
Senior Citizens

With the distant war commanding our attention, I was tempted to ignore problems at home. But my sudden awareness of nursing-home abuses wouldn't wait for more convenient times. I found myself thrust into the elderly-care issue almost without warning.

In 1969, Mother sent me a letter about her great aunt confined in a nursing home. Doctors, nurses, and administrative staff all were providing her unbelievably poor attention. A few days later, Mother called me about the untenable situation. She detailed how all the patients were receiving squalid treatment; she also had discovered similar situations in the area's other nursing homes.

"You're in a position to do something," she said, her voice tinged with impatience. "What are *you* going to do about it?"

Mother's impressions struck a familiar chord. As a state legislator, I had remained frustrated by our constantly approving welfare payments to support the nursing-home industry. Its members consistently assured us they would spend the additional money *only* for elderly patients' better care and attention. Yet we never saw those services provided or patient care improved. Maybe Mother was alerting me to a much greater problem than abuses just in Arkansas. When I asked federal authorities about my aunt, I began to uncover a hidden national scandal.

Over the next few weeks, I tracked down the addresses of Washington-area nursing homes. I then spent several weekends volunteering at various facilities in Maryland, Virginia, and the District. No one asked for identification or suspected I served in Congress. The teams I joined in some 11 nearby homes seemed relieved to have an extra hand. They knew only my name, that I lived somewhere nearby, and that I willingly pitched in to help with any chores. One night, I took along Dennis Brack, a *Time* photographer, who passed himself off as my brother. In fact, he looked enough like me so that no one questioned us.

Every night, I'd arrive home and fill a notebook with my findings. Even now, I recall clearly the loneliness, neglect, despair, anxiety, and boredom—in particular, the *boredom*—of those cold and sterile homes—essentially human warehouses for old people. A resident's only relief came when an attendant brought a meal, or simply peeked in to poke and prod, seeing if the patient was awake—or *alive*.

We commonly found up to 15 beds in one room. One nurse told me an elderly woman might have suffered a slight heart attack, but no one called a doctor, afraid to disturb him on a Sunday. As I clipped one 80-year-old man's toenails, he warned me not to let the attendant see, because he charged $7 for the same service. A home with 80 patients depended on only one attendant. At one facility, of four men lined up in wheelchairs, three sat in their own excrement.

A nursing-home owner in suburban Maryland explained his patients' common situation. "Look," he said, "let's say your father is getting old and he's hard to handle. So you bring him here for a few weeks and maybe one day you get him home. But the first thing you've got to show these old people is who's boss." The brochure he handed me boasted of a "pleasant home atmosphere."

One Baltimore facility adjoined a funeral home, so patients received commanding, front-window views of handsome granite tombstones the mortuary marketed.

I discovered several popular misconceptions about the nursing home industry.

- All homes for the aged are strictly licensed, regularly inspected, and staffed by a health team present at all times. Pointedly untrue. Frequently, health inspectors gave advance warnings of visits, so staff could prepare residences well ahead of time.
- If an institution claimed approval by Medicare and Medicaid, then it at least would provide acceptable service. Also untrue. I found no governmental control over the industry, no consistent guidance from federal or state agencies, and general indifference among administrators and nursing personnel.

At the same time, the nursing home industry showed no indifference to Congress. Lobbyists' political contributions resulted in relaxed safeguards and the poorest care for millions of seniors.

Such abuses form unfortunately familiar landmarks in the current health-care landscape. Many people have become calloused to the sad consequences of elderly mistreatment. But the fraud and abuse we see today was just beginning to gain public attention in 1969. Even though nursing homes had existed since the 1930s, Medicare and Medicaid's establishment in the 1960s accounted for their startling growth, and the resulting criminal abuse of patients and elderly clients.

Shocked by what I found, I spoke on the House floor in late February 1970, describing my series of *in cognito* nursing-home weekends. My report made clear I did not oppose profit-making, but I condemned those exploiting elderly, defenseless citizens who lived in deplorable conditions. Bringing it to a personal level, I pointed out only two homes I had visited where I would willingly place my own mother. But I didn't think I could afford either one on my $42,500 Congressional salary.

Admittedly, I was getting wound up at the end of my speech. I concluded with a jab at many nursing-home inspectors' relationships with owners of the profiteering firms.

A fiery reaction resulted. Dr. Matthew Tayback, head of the Maryland Department of Mental Health and Hygiene, called my speech "reckless and lacking humanity." He added that "hundreds of people reading the report will be upset for months …. People are being treated well in nursing homes, and there is no segment of business or industry which is 100% pure." One nursing home director called Speaker Carl Albert, requesting a conference with Congressman Pryor of Arkansas, who had caused his company stock to plummet.

The Associated Press published a timely series on the nursing-home industry, revealing a national scandal. The articles exposed negligent physician care for elderly patients, many wrongly-administered drug prescriptions, most meals valued at less than $1 per day, and fire prevention figures listing nursing homes at the top of unsafe living places.

A *New York Daily News* reporter, also undercover, found filthy rooms, abominable food in several area homes, roaches in glasses, and often indescribable bathroom conditions. Outlining growth in nursing-home profits, *Business Week* headlined one article "Nursing Homes Offer an Investment Lure."

Other news reports uncovered startling facts: a nursing home administrator listing only one qualification—junk dealer; 87 nursing homes failing to meet federal standards, yet the government paying them $380,000 in a six-month period; and one 317-bed home operating three years without regular inspections.

With the press's encouragement, I hoped to receive the House leadership's approval as well. Confident the issue needed national attention,

I called for creating a Select Committee on Nursing Homes and Homes for the Aged. The House resolution received 235 votes, a clear majority, and in private, members assured me overwhelming support. Unfortunately, the resolution was non-binding.

Representative William Colmer of Mississippi, the 80-year-old chairman of the House Rules Committee, then surprised me by blocking the move, preventing further discussion. He said he had conferred with Speaker Carl Albert; they determined no space was available for a new committee. Therefore, he saw no reason to plan hearings. Besides, 16 resolutions were already introduced to establish a myriad of new House committees. The Committee on Government Operations could gather all needed information.

The *Pine Bluff Commercial* predicted that, given the Rules Committee's history, my resolution "seems doomed to languish there indefinitely." In truth, any change or reform effort sent to the Rules Committee entered the proverbial black hole.

My argument also received opposition from committee chairmen who feared a Special Committee on Aging would steal their authority and weaken their own, well-established political fiefdoms. They were partially right. Tax measures, a great number of health and welfare issues, and some regulatory areas would all come under any new committee charged with writing elderly-care legislation. Old-timers, with their built-in suspicions, also resented any young whippersnapper like me who threatened the power balance between legislators and lobbyists.

With firm determination and a strong dose of youthful optimism, I set out to hold hearings of my own. Down the street from the Longworth House Office Building, our staff found a vacant lot attached to the Capitol View Gulf station, near a railroad viaduct. The station and lot's owner, Joe Jarpoe, was eager to help, and later received a citation for his cooperation. He assisted us in setting two house trailers on the lot. The mobile-home industry came through with the double-wides.

We dubbed these improvised rigs the House Trailer Committee on Aging. We also referred to the project as our "Government in Exile" location. We wanted to probe for ourselves what the House leadership did not want investigated. Many dedicated people from Washington-area schools, Arkansas, and surrounding states came to work as volunteers.

Operating on a shoestring of $1,300, we held a fish fry on July 13, 1971, to help pay for rent and expenses. Tiny Meeker and his Dixieland Band provided the entertainment, which began immediately after the Southern Railways passenger train had chugged through the neighborhood. Congressman Jim Symington of Missouri sang folk songs. Several thousand people showed up for catfish and hush puppies, and Senator Hubert Humphrey delivered the blazing, featured speech.

The *Washington Post* and other national media gave us extensive coverage. Ken Schanzer, now head of NBC Sports, showed up one day out of nowhere, announcing he would take charge of our press operation. Then things took off in a big way. During his year on the job, our profile doubled.

Over those months, I traveled to conferences in Dallas and other parts of the country, trying to drum up national support for legislation. Ralph Nader's Raiders, a band of fired-up young activists, conducted nursing home inspections that showed clear collusion between inspectors and owners. Nick Kotz, an investigative reporter at the *Washington Post*, wrote a front-page story, strongly impacting the city and surrounding counties.

The House leadership, both Democratic and Republican, continued to cast a skeptical eye, even with 235 members' signatures on the resolution to create a House Committee on Aging.

At one function, several of our young volunteers heard Speaker Albert comment it was high time somebody got "those wagons" moved out of Washington.

One day Congressman Tip O'Neill of Massachusetts called me aside. He asked in confidence if he should divest his holdings in a nursing-home chain located in his district. Reluctant to offer any direct advice, I suggested the industry would undergo considerable scrutiny in the near future. Two days later, I learned he had sold his stock.

Months of improvised hearings resulted in a wealth of data. I widened my target, calling for a House Committee on Aging as a counterpart to the Senate Special Committee. But again this effort failed. I filed a discharge petition in the House, calling for immediate action; the leadership buried it.

Senator Tom Eagleton of Missouri hoped to bring provisions including our research before the Senate Special Committee. He soon became a friend and mentor through some rather dark days. By underscoring our work's importance, he helped provide a degree of credibility.

Reacting to years of pressure, the House finally voted in 1974—some two years after I had left—to establish a Select Committee on Aging. The venerable Claude Pepper of Florida, a stalwart friend, became the committee's chairman, and rose as the undisputed voice for America's elderly people. He told me many times that serving as the Aging Committee's inaugural chairman was the best job he ever had.

* * *

One night in October 1967, the people of Camden held a testimonial dinner honoring Senator McClellan. Those were the days of appreciation rallies built around Chamber of Commerce dinners. Local citizens routinely turned out, celebrating a popular elected official's career or an esteemed local citizen's contributions.

At that point, I had served in Congress less than a year. Before the dinner's proceedings began, Senator McClellan and I met at the community center, located at the old Naval Ammunition Depot north of town. We had both experienced a long and grueling day of speeches, presentations, and press conferences through south Arkansas.

As we changed into fresh shirts and ties, Senator McClellan suddenly admitted he was tired. He wondered how much longer he could keep up a senator's hectic pace. He appeared worn down by the day's schedule, but so was I. In fact, at 71 he showed more raw energy than I could muster at 33.

His tone of voice and confidential manner held me. He seldom spoke in confidence and, like Chairman Mills, was almost never "cozy." I felt he was referring to more than his health, that he might be thinking of retirement, and how I might consider moving to the Senate in another five years. Was he saying, "Get ready," and giving me the nod, or at least a head's up?

He stated nothing specific, and of course, I didn't pursue the point. I had been happy and challenged by my work in the House, and had seen no reason for grander plans. But his brief comments immediately entranced me. I literally felt my eyes light up and my heart pound. I jumped to a conclusion that night, and this totally unwarranted leap turned out to be the major political miscalculation of my life.

Chapter 26
Aiming at Goliath

In 1980, CBS News's Roger Mudd asked Ted Kennedy why he wanted to be president. Kennedy stumbled with an unclear answer to that simple question, and it may have cost him the election.

It may be simple to ask why a politician wants to serve. But the answer can often appear too simplistic or too complex. Complex if you begin to discuss issues. Simplistic if you attempt to explain your own nature. Voters expect politicians and seekers of public office to reveal themselves. In reality, politicians love both the thrill of the race and winning, and the tough challenges of governing.

That night in Camden, when Senator McClellan dropped what I took as a hint to replace him, my mind rushed to a future campaign and then serving in the Senate. And exactly in that order: the campaign, then the service.

This process unfolds as the natural order of things. It doesn't rank the importance of either campaigning or serving as a Senate member. It just reminds you that, before you can enter that hallowed chamber, you first have to put in the hard work. And you have to hope you'll be lucky, that your timing is just right, and that the moon and the stars perfectly align.

I love a campaign, whether it's one-on-one with a constituent, speaking in front of a small group, or—probably my least favorite—a formal address at a sit-down dinner. Arkansas has always offered these various private and public platforms. A politician would never miss certain events—like the Gillette Coon Supper, Toadsuck Ferry Day in Conway, the Mt. Nebo Chicken Fry, and Ding Dong Daddy Days in Dumas. I've always said that if you don't like catfish, don't run for office. Following the Warren Pink Tomato Festival parade, the mayor whispered to me that a certain regional candidate hadn't shown up since his first election; because of that, he wouldn't get 30% of the Bradley County vote. The mayor was right. These are command performances.

A campaign's best moments come when you least expect them. Maybe you're driving into a small town on a hot afternoon, and find a parking spot near the courthouse. You get out of the car in full sweat, open the trunk and pull out yard signs and maybe some printed material with your picture that's still not quite right. Barbara and I always carried straw buckets of thimbles with "Pryor" printed in small letters. These became our familiar campaign brand in my first state legislative race, and I never saw a need to change.

So you gather up your goods. If it's a major stop, maybe you have a second car alongside with a loud speaker announcing your arrival at the courthouse steps, or outside the bank or drug store. Anyone wanting to visit is welcome. You never know who's likely to drop by. Campaigns by nature attract plenty of characters who should probably be finding something more important to do than listening to a candidate speak.

Barbara and I especially valued the women volunteers who expended great time and energy running the office, answering phones, and getting out mail. Many were supporters' wives with children in school. They got involved in our campaign because they felt strongly about the issues we were defining— education, better pay, health care, and opportunities for women. Our initial races came just as the full-fledged women's movement got under way in the '60s. Even in those early days, we recognized the strength of the mothers and single females who joined with us, wanting to make a political difference.

One hot afternoon in my first Congressional campaign, Barbara and I drove to Sparkman in Dallas County to see how many people we could stir up on the main street. Nearly everybody in town sat at home running their electric fans, trying to stay cool. But one old man, scrawny in his overalls and shirtless, saw us get out of the car, and followed us through town.

It turned out that he lived off in the woods, four miles down a dirt road. He had written me in the legislature, asking me to help him get a telephone installed. I made contact with everyone I knew at Southwestern Bell, but the utility turned us down; his house was so far from the main line, the installment expense proved far too high. Sorry, but case closed.

Every time we exited a store or bank, heading for our next stop, this old man would hunker down on the sidewalk. He'd cup his hands around his mouth and chant, almost in a whisper, "Didn't get me no phone .... Didn't get me no phone .... Didn't get me no phone."

Luckily for us, the crowd that day remained thin. In fact, not a dozen people had ventured out onto the street. As I started my speech, our friend hunkered down again in front of the few straggling spectators, still chanting, but this time with a new mantra: "Had a big crowd .... Yessir! Had a big crowd .... Didn't get me no phone .... Had a big crowd."

I was drawn to that man, tough and resilient and stubborn. And angry at me. Where else could you gather such experiences except in the streets of Arkansas? I didn't get him a phone—no one could have brought off that demand for a miracle—but I've always recalled his forthright determination to remind me of my all-too-human limitations.

You soon learn that the best in a campaign occurs when somebody talks straight about his or her life, or what's going on in the family. That "least expect it" part shines here. Maybe they need help getting a long-overdue Social Security check, or clarification on one of those Medicaid regulations nobody understands. Maybe the old woman who puts down her grocery bag just wants someone to talk to. Nothing more than that. But that connection matters—the brief minute or two of honest exchange, when there's nothing for you to do but listen.

I'd never want to give up a campaign's physical and mental rush. But then, giving it up was not the question at the end of 1971. The question persisted of whether to stay in the House—probably a safe choice—or risk reaching for something higher. Like the U.S. Senate. Here I was, serving my third House term, with no opposition since that first race in 1966. I had put together a fair amount of political accomplishments I could point to with pride. I was the father of three sons and married to an extraordinary woman.

On Thanksgiving Day 1971—in fact, on our 14th wedding anniversary— Barbara had undergone surgery at Sibley Hospital in Washington. Without warning, she developed a massive blood clot that stopped her heartbeat. Code Blue all around. Teams of doctors and experts pulled her through, but that narrow escape made both of us seriously question the future: which road fork should we take in this defining moment of our lives? She was 33, and I was 37.

During her convalescence from Thanksgiving until New Year's, we had time to sort things through. We asked ourselves, Is this what we want for the rest of our lives? Should we continue the frenzy of traveling nearly every weekend to and from Arkansas?

The long absences, the mad dash and quick hash—as Rev. Jac Ruffin had described it—was this any way to live? As long as I served in the House, we would face an election campaign every two years. In other words, we'd never really stop campaigning. We had to make a major decision, and knew it would take both of us to resolve it.

Chances were good I could escape opposition for one more term. But I was getting restless. I asked the House Appropriations Committee's chief counsel to run a computer study determining when I might become a committee chairman. He reported it would probably occur sometime after the year 2000. At least a 30-year wait. In other words, an eternity.

I had been looking at past Arkansas election results, peering back to 1948 and 1954, and up through 1966, trying to ascertain Senator John McClellan's strengths and weaknesses. I studied just about every precinct and county. I felt reluctant to confide in anyone about possibly challenging the Senator, knowing news would instantly travel to his third-floor suite at the Dirksen Senate Office Building. Word of that kind, however scant, always spreads in an eye blink.

If Senator McClellan heard I was even considering such a race, he could make my life miserable. Even worse, if I publicly considered making the run, then backed off and sought re-election to the House, he would revel in my loss of nerve. That alone forced me to withhold my private ruminations.

McClellan was no stranger to political ambition's sting. He had felt defeat's lash in 1938 as a young Congressman who gambled and lost a tight race against Senator Hattie Caraway. She had taken her husband's seat after his death in 1931. The next year, when she decided to run on her own, legendary Huey P. Long of Louisiana barnstormed with her across Arkansas, helping secure her win.

When Mrs. Caraway defeated McClellan, he moved to Camden to practice law with the Gaughan-Sifford law firm. McClellan was a smart lawyer. He had begun studying with his father at home and passed the state bar exam at 17.

Once in Camden, he swore off elected politics, but that resolution didn't hold up. In 1942, he ran for the Senate after President Roosevelt appointed then-Senator John E. Miller as U.S. attorney for the Western District of Arkansas. McClellan won that election in a runoff, and remained virtually unchallenged until the 1954 race against Sid McMath.

I steeped myself in the senior senator's career details, especially his record at the polls. I was intrigued by returns from 1966, the year I first won election to the House. McClellan had faced a minor challenge from Foster Johnson, a perennial office-seeker from Little Rock who spent less than $10,000 on his campaign. Johnson received 33% of the vote. That impressed me as a healthy number, especially since two years later, in his race against Fulbright, Johnson barely mustered 10,000 votes.

Most people would assume that trouncing an opponent by 67% showed supernatural strength and, granted, McClellan's victory was impressive. But, given McClellan's powerful reputation, plus Johnson's weak financial efforts, the Senator should have won by an even higher percentage. His soft spots showed me where a respectable challenger might weigh in.

I felt that in the state's southern counties, those I crisscrossed constantly, I could get at least two votes for every one Foster Johnson had received. What's more, Little Rock and Pulaski County, as well as the band of counties north of Interstate 40, had loosened their consistently tight McClellan support. The returns showed that.

I projected how, later in 1972, McClellan would turn 76; many of his kingpins had died out or grown too old to deliver support. With his record of strenuously opposing civil rights legislation, a sizeable black vote should oppose him. On top of that, 18-year-olds were able to vote for the first time. Surely a younger candidate would draw them.

I wasn't alone in considering a possible Pryor-McClellan race. As early as May, 1971, Washington columnist Marianne Means had suggested it as a hot contest, and the *Arkansas Democrat* had reprinted her article.

I figured the field might also become crowded. Everyone knew that Senator McClellan was heading toward his career's end. A group of young politicians like me would inevitably be looking at the race. This included Jim Guy Tucker and Bill Alexander, both seated Congressmen, and Attorney General Ray Thornton.

Frequent speculation ran through the Arkansas press about McClellan's vulnerability, most of it supporting what I had found. Editorial writers are always anxious to see a heated race, and hope to light a fire under one or more candidates. "Let's you and him fight," in other words. They were predicting that, in any re-election campaign, McClellan would find little support among organized labor, minorities, or young people. All three groups had come to see him as too conservative, too "old guard," and not responding to demands for minority voting rights and opposing the war in Vietnam.

I found myself agreeing with the editorials. What this state needs, I came to believe, is a good, old-fashioned shootout. Not entirely to my surprise, Barbara said, "Okay, let's give it all we've got."

By mid-January, I had talked to so many friends that the word had leaked out. Of course, Senator McClellan was the first to hear it, and his stiff body language indicated that he was mounting protective defenses. He hit the phone every day, lining up commitments and raising money. I could feel his strong and deft hand everywhere I went.

Meanwhile, editorial writers continued to speculate about "that young Congressman from Camden" who just might have the audacity to challenge John L. McClellan, hoping all the time that I would. Incredulous state leaders were calling my staff and expressing disbelief. The more discouragement I heard, the more determined I became to make the race. If you want to climb a mountain, why not pick the highest one?

Chapter 27
Caught in Firestorms

Senator McClellan announced for re-election on February 11, 1972. Ted Boswell, a 39-year-old Bryant attorney, announced the next day. He had run an impressive race for governor in 1968, receiving strong backing from labor and young people for his stances on education, civil rights, and health care. Last to announce was Foster Johnson, the constant candidate who had opposed McClellan in 1966 and Fulbright in 1968.

On February 18, Barbara and our three sons and I drove to Camden, spending the night at Mother's house. The next morning, we walked into the Whiteside Junior High School cafeteria to announce my candidacy. Over a thousand hometown friends and supporters turned out, waving posters, cheering, and whistling.

We brought in Razorback football heroes Bill McClard and Joe Ferguson. After the high school cheerleaders delivered a rousing, "Go, David, Go," the Presbyterian Church youth choir sang "The Battle Hymn of the Republic" and "America."

I stressed that voters should never consider a political office one person's property. I quoted FDR. "This election is not about power and influence," I reminded the crowd. "It's not about what one man can do, but what we can all do together." It turned out to be a pretty good day. I thought we might make it happen. After all, I had never lost an election.

On March 1, ten days after announcing, I appeared on KARK-TV, Channel Four—the local NBC affiliate—as a guest on *Challenge '72*, the Jaycees' public-affairs interview show. At that point, the two-week-old campaign was moving at a glacial pace. One *Gazette* columnist said it languished because Arkansas voters refused to respond to campaigning during February's freezing days. Dooley Womack, my long-time family friend and Camden state senator, told me I'd better find something to jazz things up. We needed an issue.

A handful of Jaycees conducted the Channel Four interview, a routine question-and-answer session dealing with the Senate race. Why was I running— that old question again—and what did I hope to accomplish if elected? We talked a little about education, affordable housing, and elderly health care.

Then, almost out of the blue, somebody asked, "What do you think of these draft dodgers?"

I said that after wars, we've always forgiven our enemies, and I think we should also forgive our sons. Even before the rest of the country, many young people had realized our tragic mistake of Vietnam military involvement. Because of their perception and foresight, the nation should readily forgive those who chose not to fight. I added that they should go through an individual screening process, then be assigned some term of public service. The word "amnesty" never came up.

Taped on Wednesday, the interview would be shown the following Sunday. But reporters were present for the taping, and that Wednesday night the Channel Four news opened with this announcement: "Congressman Pryor favors amnesty for draft dodgers." The *Gazette* and the *Democrat* followed up with almost identical stories the next morning. I still recall the *Gazette* headline—"Pryor: 'Forgive' Draft Evaders."

That spark quickly became a firestorm. Editorials and radio talk shows roundly condemned me. Senator McClellan didn't mention the amnesty question for a couple of weeks. In fact, at one point he said he would review the issue from all sides. But in the long run, when he realized its explosiveness, he grabbed it as manna from heaven.

Our campaign literally came to a halt. One *Democrat* columnist said I had nearly knocked myself out of the race. And Dooley came back with, "Good God, Dave, when I asked for some action, I didn't mean *this*."

Two days later, I held a press conference, trying to explain my position. In the first place, I said, amnesty shouldn't be discussed until the war ends and American prisoners of war return. What's more, I was not talking about deserters. Draft dodgers and deserters were different breeds, and deserters should never receive special treatment. I emphasized that an independent review board should examine all draft evaders—I studiously avoided saying "dodgers"—and evaders should fulfill an alternative service obligation. I even brought in the Prodigal Son parable and Truman's amnesty program after World War II.

Nothing seemed to help. The amnesty issue dogged my entire campaign, from early March through the June 13 primary. We never successfully put it to rest.

Gun control proved equally persistent, and almost as emotional. My first involvement in that thorny issue had come in 1961, when I served in the state legislature. A Camden boy accidentally killed himself with a shotgun. His mother had left him in a Safeway parking lot while she briefly went inside. He spied the weapon in a nearby truck's gun rack. Filled with curiosity, he climbed in the truck's cab, took the gun, and accidentally shot and killed himself.

The following Monday, I introduced a bill preventing drivers from transporting a loaded shotgun or a rifle in a moving vehicle within city limits. Fellow House members and the Arkansas Game and Fish Commission endorsed it without qualification. It seemed a way to curb future deaths or injuries. The House passed the bill with only two negative votes. But by the time it reached the Senate, the National Rifle Association had issued a nationwide alert. It warned members of the "Pryor bill" down in Arkansas—the first step, the NRA said, to taking away your guns.

Senators scurried to the House chamber, asking what the hell was going on. A former University roommate wrote me, saying he had always liked me all right, but back then he didn't know I was a communist. I held an open town meeting at the Camden courthouse. Angry voters packed the room, their fists waving and voices shouting. It seemed like every south Arkansas hunter had turned out. Not one person there supported the bill. Finally, the next week I pulled the legislation down. It was going nowhere, and I was forcing good legislative friends into a no-win situation of having to vote Yes or No.

Yet even in 1966, five years later, the issue remained alive. In my campaign for Congress, my Republican opponent Lynn Lowe ran a TV spot showing him with his son, walking through the woods on a beautiful misty morning, rifles on their shoulders. The message said, "David Pryor wants to take this privilege away from you."

I learned from that 1961 experience the power of fear, suspicion, and half-truths. I particularly came to understand the NRA's tactics, and how the organization plays political hardball. The NRA endorsed Senator McClellan, put out numerous mailings, and sent people to work in his headquarters.

By 1972, you'd think the rage from a decade earlier would have died away, but it had not. Wherever I went—campaigning at a paper mill's midnight shift or speaking at an industrial park or church fish fry—some fellow would come up, give me a narrow look, and ask why I wanted to take away his guns.

The controversy of mandatory prayer in public schools came up only once. I was speaking in Jonesboro the day the House of Representatives voted on school prayer. A local reporter asked me how I would have voted, had I been in Washington. I said I would have voted against the proposal as written. Any mandate by a school board, or by any school system, would force students to pray as they were told, and I was against that.

Another firestorm. The next day, the newspaper reported that David Pryor opposed school prayer. McClellan used it against me, mailing postcards across the state. One postcard signer was Justice Jim Johnson. Somehow, despite initial furor, the issue soon simmered down. But it still smoldered.

Amnesty, guns, and school prayer became the warm-up acts in 1972. Labor rose as the main attraction, particularly big union bosses' alleged influence on my campaign. Senator McClellan's opposition to labor hailed back to his 1950s hearings, when he investigated corruption in the International Brotherhood of Teamsters run by Jimmy Hoffa and Dave Beck.

The story went around that Senator McClellan had seriously considered not running at all, until he saw how forcefully labor courted David Pryor. He couldn't abide that, so he had to run again as the state's protector from union bosses. Whether true or not, it made a good campaign story.

The rhetoric used against me echoed the 1966 campaign and Richard Arnold's charges that labor unions controlled me. But McClellan introduced new dimensions. In his campaign's early phase, he almost never used the terms "labor" or "unions." He spoke of "outside influences" the public had to watch. McClellan used these as code words for "labor bosses," hoping that, by avoiding a direct attack on the unions, he might gain some of their support. By 76 years of age, he had practiced his craft long and well.

To counter this, we changed the issue's image, lowering the focus from labor leaders to the individual worker. In a Hot Springs talk, I declared I'd rather receive contributions from carpenters and retail clerks than from high-powered heads of corporations and conglomerates. I also used that idea a time or two in later speeches.

Justice Jim Johnson sent a feverish letter to 50,000 voters praising Senator McClellan for "taking off the gloves and letting those sniveling liberals have it with both hands." He charged that anyone opposing the Senator was nothing more than "a mess of trash." This term, along with "labor goons," who were reportedly tearing down McClellan yard signs, gave the campaign two of its long remembered catch phrases.

One afternoon before I had even announced my plans to run, I stopped outside a Conway barber shop and was shaking hands. The barber stepped out and said someone inside wanted to see me. I followed him back in. There sat, of all people, Justice Jim Johnson.

"You're running against John McClellan?" he asked.

I told him I wasn't definitely sure, but it looked like I would probably enter the race.

"Are you going to ask him about those shares of AP&L stock they gave him for free?" Johnson asked. "And about all that property they've given him on those Corps of Engineers lakes and dams? And what about all that bank stock in First National of Little Rock?" He kept naming charges I should bring up in a campaign.

"But I didn't know any of this was true," I said.

"Wait a minute," he came back. "I didn't say any of it's true. I just wondered if you were going to *ask* him about it."

At a fish fry in Okolona, the mayor asked me if I knew about a rash of McClellan signs showing up in some local front yards. I told him that's the first I had heard of it. He shook his head, frowned and said, "Well, we've had a bad run of termites this spring, and I suspect they'll probably eat up those signs later tonight or tomorrow."

Early in the campaign, I didn't fully appreciate the deep split between many union leaders and their rank-and-file members. This division came home one night when Barbara and I were working a Fort Smith plant's late shift. We stood at the gate with the local union president. Wearing a new suit, he stood by a slick convertible with his girlfriend, speaking to his members with a better-than-thou tone.

Barbara immediately noticed the look on members' faces. When we returned to the Holiday Inn that night, she predicted we would lose that plant's labor vote. Later, I checked the returns; sure enough, we did. The vote count made clear how union members disapproved of their own local officers leading the high life. It also reminded me once again of Barbara's sharp perception.

Chapter 28
A New Pair of U.S. Keds

The campaign seemed to turn around on April 27 at a Jonesboro rally. In fact, things went so well I rather grandly referred later to "the Jonesboro miracle." The *Democrat* declared, "Pryor's campaign is finally in full swing."

McClellan had predicted a Pryor rally in Craighead County could never draw more than 100 people, but we estimated 3,000. The free catfish and hush puppies may have drawn them.

For the first time, I went after McClellan's record. My camp had questioned whether I should go on the offensive or leave the dirty work to Ted Boswell. Finally, we decided I couldn't simply discuss the need for change and what we could accomplish together. I had to level direct and aggressive charges.

That night in Jonesboro, I complained that McClellan represented only the upper 5% of America's money earners, and was plagued with conflicts of interest. What about the bank stocks he holds in First National of Little Rock? And his cozy relationship with corporate heads at ITT? I also listed his negative votes, especially on education and benefits to veterans and the elderly. I pointed out that, while he boasted of supporting Social Security, he had actually voted against it 26 times.

The momentum we felt from that night carried the campaign through most of May. I carefully avoided any reference to age. Nobody wants to hear a younger candidate attack his opponent for being 40 years older. Much of my House record involved fair treatment to the elderly, and pushing for a full-time aging committee.

Given that recent background, I could hardly come out with a direct statement that Senator McClellan had grown too old for the job. So I indirectly suggested his longevity was impressive, but not necessarily helping the state. Arkansas remained near the bottom in education, health care, and per capita income.

By late May, the race had grown unquestionably tighter and, I thought, encouraging. I aimed for voters to associate me with Arkansas progressives like Dale Bumpers, and going back to McMath and Fulbright. Only two years before, Bumpers had started his gubernatorial campaign with 1% of the vote, and yet he overturned a long-established status quo, defeating both Orval Faubus and Winthrop Rockefeller.

Bumpers's success against formidable odds demonstrated a weak spot in the state establishment's armor. New public support had risen for prison reform, legislative reorganization, and racial acceptance. New industry and television's growth had transformed the state's political life. Old-fashioned populists railing against big business were disappearing. Even my old push for constitutional revision had seen new life.

I wanted to latch onto Bumpers's progressive appeal to the young, reform-minded, and moderate voters, without alienating the traditional old-line Democratic stalwarts. Successfully balancing these various camps called for delicate maneuvers. The *Northwest Arkansas Times* alluded to this high-wire act when it said, "Pryor counts on a coalition of the very young and the very old."

In my February Camden announcement, I predicted no one would personally attack Senator McClellan; the state's mood opposed that kind of race. While I carefully stood by that in my campaign, Ted Boswell came out swinging.

In a stunning May 4 speech at Bryant, Boswell hit McClellan harder than anyone could have expected. He called seniority the only reason the Senator's supporters had kept him in Washington. Without that, he charged, McClellan stands helpless and ineffective. No one praises the Senator's talents, Boswell said, or his vision, his foresight, or soundness of his representation.

McClellan lives in a world of the status quo, Boswell complained, following the premises of a half-century ago. And, while he labels himself a law-and-order candidate, he does nothing about crime's causes.

I've always thought Boswell's harsh and direct attacks hurt *him* more than they did Senator McClellan. No one knows for sure how such a barrage affects a campaign. I've often considered that question over the years, because the dilemma of whether to "get tough" comes up in every race. Many in my campaign loved Boswell's full-bodied charges, believing I benefited without delivering the blows myself. But any advantage I might have gained gave me very little comfort.

McClellan scored a narrow lead in the May 30 primary. He came in with 220,000, to my 204,000 and Boswell's 62,000. Foster Johnson got just over 6,000. McClellan carried 51 counties, and I carried 24. Neither Boswell nor Johnson carried any. Especially encouraging were the results in Ouachita

County, where I got 72% of the vote. In the runoff, I would remind people that both McClellan and I came from Camden.

More than 35 years later, I can still respond to the great excitement I felt—the excitement the *entire* Pryor camp felt—in the runoff's first few days. My initial impulse was to saddle up and ride off in all directions. But I concentrated on nailing down my organization, working out a feasible schedule, and pushing hard to raise money. Most of all, I warned my team not to gloat. To win that runoff, we would need every one of Boswell's votes, and any appearance of smugness or over-confidence would jeopardize our chances.

Arkansas's whole political chemistry was in flux. This campaign shattered families and kinships—sons and fathers, brothers and brothers, long-time partners in established businesses. I didn't want to tip the fragile scales toward Senator McClellan. I knew the initial turnout disappointed McClellan's people. They believed his supporters, too complacent to vote, had assumed he would win without a runoff. I didn't want to energize those voters and bring them back to the polls by saying something foolish. Barring some major catastrophe, any challenger traditionally defeats the incumbent in a runoff. That had always rung true in Arkansas, and I certainly didn't want to break tradition.

Two minor, almost fleeting incidents warned me of the difficulty we'd face in winning the runoff. One came at Searcy's outdoor rally before a very large crowd, with both Senator McClellan and me on the program. He spoke first, then we passed each other as I stepped up to speak. "Pour it on me, David," he said, his face forcing a grin that seemed more like a grimace. He reached out and patted my shoulder. Warmed up and ready for battle, he had regained his footing.

Several McClellan campaign members had started calling me "Little David." That diminutive term had never bothered me, or anything else they had said, for that matter. But McClellan's greeting that day in Searcy, along with the light pat, flashed "Little David" directly to my mind. It caused me to stiffen defensively and wonder: could he, in fact, bring off a victory that none of us expected?

The second incident occurred one afternoon when Tucker Steinmetz, our campaign press person, bounded into our headquarters. He had just seen Senator McClellan in a brand new pair of U.S. Keds. McClellan's staff had scheduled him for a visit to Blanchard Caverns in Stone County. They had stopped on the way, buying him that pair of tennis shoes. We saw the clear message: he might be 76 years old, but brandished enough energy for a fight with young David Pryor. He wasn't about to roll over for any 37-year-old upstart Congressman.

People began to see Senator McClellan in a new light. One newspaper photo featured him folk-dancing at a picnic. Ted Boswell commented to one reporter that his vigor was exceeded only by his arrogance, and the *Gazette*'s George Fisher even drew a cartoon of Senator John L. McClellan in his new pair of Keds.

Everyone got a kick out of the story and drawing. I reacted differently. The Senator could not be counted out. Not by me, not by anyone. This election was going down to the wire, and in most counties, we were the only race on the June 13 ballot.

On May 26, the Associated Press reported that a cache of letters indicated national labor leaders had promised me help twice in recent months. This led Senator McClellan to step up the old charge that out-of-state bosses controlled me.

In fact, I had met with union representatives and asked for their support, but the meetings were not secret, as the AP story and McClellan suggested. My sessions involved political action committees, attended by aides on both sides, no cloak-and-dagger, clandestine back-alley gatherings. The Senator's angry attack revealed the labor-control issue would likely dominate the race to the finish. Sure enough, it did.

Chapter 29
The Old Warrior

The runoff climaxed on Sunday, June 11, two days before the final vote. A *Gazette* editorial later dubbed it "the much-debated debate." Gallons of ink have spilled, analyzing that one crucial primetime-television hour—the first of its kind in Arkansas history. It still reverberates in the minds of many who saw it.

I first challenged McClellan to debate early in the race, well before the May 30 vote. He responded that he wouldn't consider it until he received a formal invitation, not just a challenge he'd read in a newspaper article.

Two days after the primary, Shirley McFarlin from my campaign delivered my personal letter to McClellan at his Little Rock headquarters. That afternoon from Fort Smith, the Senator said we must work out the debate's details, but he thought we could arrange it. "I'm not afraid to debate David Pryor at any time, under any circumstances," he added.

McClellan's accepting my second challenge shocked and dismayed my supporters. They even questioned the wisdom of confronting him in the first place. Why didn't I drop the subject when I had the chance? With my clear edge going into the runoff, I should have left well enough alone. Several advisers reminded me that McClellan had honed his own confrontational style against some of the very labor bosses who were now supposedly Pryor supporters. Just think what he would do to me.

Later I learned similar questions ran deep within McClellan's camp. As a powerful incumbent, he owed me nothing. His older and established backers advised against the debate, claiming he had nothing to gain and a lot to lose. But the younger faithful argued that a debate would lift the McClellan campaign from its doldrums and send inspired supporters to the polls.

The debate took place at 9:00 p.m. I had gone to Warren and ridden in the Pink Tomato Festival parade a day earlier. The crowd had been friendly but strangely cautious. This was home territory for me. Everyone along the parade route seemed to feel the gravity of the moment.

Senator McClellan arrived at KATV Channel Seven, the local ABC affiliate, an hour before the scheduled time. He was ushered into an office upstairs; a monitor there showed the studio where the debate would take place. I reached the station soon after him, stopping to check out the studio's seating arrangements.

Much later, I learned that McClellan had intently watched me on the monitor as I made adjustments, and reviewed the text of my opening remarks. I felt nervous and uncertain. Apparently, from all subsequent reports, my fidgeting heartened him.

McClellan came downstairs, and we greeted each other with a handshake. When he entered the room, my mind flashed with quick, instant images: Camden in the 1940s, and our house on Graham Street, only a block from the McClellans' home, and next to them, my grade school on Cleveland Avenue. I was surprised to see Senator McClellan in full make-up. He wore a snow-white suit and white patent leather ankle boots—consummate picture of a Southern gentleman on an Arkansas summer night. As the studio's clock moved toward nine, my heart raced. I felt my entire life depended on the next 60 minutes.

The hour debate allowed both sides equal time, as agreed. I started out determined not to show sympathy for Senator McClellan because of his age. I opened from an essentially defensive position, answering charges on amnesty, labor, gun control, even prayer in the schools and busing.

McClellan, on the other hand, came out swinging. He jumped on me for down-playing labor's support. I said my campaign money came from Arkansas workers' cookie jars. He came back citing $79,000 I received from out of state. He ridiculed my innocent workers' image. "Cookie jars!" he said in a loud voice, almost a shout, "Ha!"

I called him "Senator McClellan," and he called me "David." I appeared naïve and inexperienced, he appeared the seasoned veteran. Despite long hours preparing, I seemed disorganized and rushed, while he poured out facts and statistics, holding up documents for the huge television audience to see. The old lion had cornered his prey.

We entirely left out key issues any substantive debate would include: Vietnam, tax reform, health insurance, inflation, agriculture. Looking back, I regret the lack of a genuine debate, exchanging views on issues vital to Arkansas and the country. We owed as much to our statewide audience, 89% of that night's television viewers. But it was his night, not mine. Most voters tuned in for a verbal prize fight, and they had wanted blood.

Senator McClellan won the runoff by 18,000 votes: 242,000 to 224,000. Our crowd gathered election night at the Sheraton Hotel, in a banquet room filled with hundreds of friends, family, and supporters from around the state. Everyone entered in high excitement. But soon the returns began pouring in, and by 9:30 it was over.

Never before had I felt the deep ache that stabbed the pit of my stomach. I was a loser. How could I face my family, especially my three sons; their faith in me must be shattered. I had snatched defeat from the jaws of victory. Election Day had literally turned to a night in hell.

I hadn't even prepared a concession speech. Now I knew I had to come up with one. And it would have to be positive. The hotel was packed with campaigners who had worked their hearts out, and I needed to show my appreciation. I tried to put up a good front and encourage young people not to give up. Barbara, of course, stood with me, self-composed and trying to hold back the tears. If anyone knew what it meant to stay positive and encourage others not to give up it was Barbara, especially on this night of all nights.

But I really wanted to crawl under the sofa, or just lie alone in a dark room. At the same time, Senator McClellan was my senator. I had to show my respect for him and his people. I've always known that Arkansas voters judge you, not by how you win, but by how you lose. I remembered Dale Bumpers telling me years earlier: "You never make a mistake by being magnanimous."

I don't know how magnanimous I sounded that night, but I gave it every effort. Most of what happened in that ballroom, and in the hours after, still hovers as a blur in my mind. Despite the deep pain I was experiencing, I also felt genuine respect for Senator McClellan.

The next morning you could have mistaken our Quapaw Towers apartment for a morgue. No phones ringing. A battlefield stillness, where everyone either had died or moved on.

As the sun came up, I heard a knock at the door. A delivery man handed me a pair of white shoes, like those McClellan had worn in the debate. "Good luck in your next life," the note said. It was signed by Channel Four. What was this all about? Did it come from newscasters? Or station managers? Was it a sarcastic message aimed to make me feel even more like a loser? I've never found out.

Soon Bill Overton, my friend from law school, showed up with a box of doughnuts. He had the final tabulations from around the state. We made coffee and sat in the living room, looking out over the city, not saying a word or even glancing at the returns. He appeared ashen and bleary-eyed. Barbara walked into the room and said, "Well, we gave it our best."

The truth is, she did give it her best. So did our workers and friends, the idealistic young people who moved mountains in my behalf. I felt I had let them down, and regrets began rushing through me. Why did I make that stupid remark about amnesty? Why didn't we debate earlier in the campaign? Why did I miscalculate, feeling I shouldn't go for the jugular? Had I been too cocky, too tentative? Maybe I should have avoided those last-minute call-in shows, giving people a chance to voice complaints. Maybe I counted too much on Ted Boswell's voters turning out for me, when they preferred to stay at home and sit on their hands. Maybe I was hoping for greater support from 18-year-olds, who had just received the right to vote. And maybe I should have avoided that runoff debate at all costs. Immediately after the primary, Ted Boswell had told me, "Whatever you do, don't debate him." I should have listened.

Maybe I should have gone to Senator McClellan in 1971, explained in person how I was ready to leave the House, and how I hoped, after 30 years of serving Arkansas, he might consent to retire, and give me his blessing. He might very well have thrown this suggestion back in my face, but at least I could have given him that option. To tell the truth, I had been unable to summon the sheer nerve to make such an offer to Senator McClellan. You simply didn't take that approach with a man of his stature and demeanor.

One night during the runoff, I spotted Bruce Bennett at the Leather Bottle, a steakhouse on Cantrell Road, and a campaign hangout. Bennett, remembered chiefly for his openly racist record as state attorney general, sat on a bar stool. As I walked in with Barbara and several campaign workers, he signaled me to come over.

Dropping his voice to a whisper, he told me that, if I called up Senator McClellan and "said the right things," he would back out of the race. He said the Senator was depressed, thought the race a sure loss, and was prepared to throw in the towel. He's tired, Bennett told me, and he thinks he's beaten. His people were the only thing keeping him from pulling out.

Bennett didn't tell me what "the right things" would be, and I didn't ask. I've wondered since then if he knew what he was talking about. Even though Bruce Bennett didn't rank as a close member in any McClellan circle that I knew of, his conservative credentials were first rate, and he knew all the anti-Pryor people.

Bennett may have been sharing confidential advice based on good authority. But I was too self-confident, too assured of my prospects, to place that call. Would it have made any difference? I'll never know.

At least, I had sense enough in the Sheraton Hotel ballroom to get up and personally thank those who had worked so long and hard. And we had to get back to Washington and hug our sons. We still had six months left in the Congressional session, and personal decisions awaited. Should we stay in Washington or move to Little Rock? What about returning to Camden and starting all over again?

Truth comes in many shapes and sizes, always tempered by time. I see now the blind self-confidence I possessed throughout that campaign. For one thing, I assumed that since I had served in Congress for six years, the people of Arkansas would know me. False. Outside the state's southern and central sections, my near-anonymity forced me to introduce myself almost as a newcomer. Little Rock television had not yet penetrated into the state's outer reaches. On top of that, I never honestly thought I would lose that race. Until then, with any challenge I took on, I moved to the task confident of victory.

Arkansas voters possess uncanny abilities. They see things for what they are, can spot a weakness, call a person up short when he deserves it, and reward a true winner who's earned the victory. And while I've been on the winning side more often than not, I needed to look closely at this, my first defeat. I had to take the electorate's verdict for what it was—a lesson to learn, more than a resounding wrist slap. In fact, an Arkansas spanking.

I also had to examine the harsh truth about money. McClellan brought it in from long-time supporters around the state. He outpaced me at every level. I received help from labor and respectable sums from Arkansas people, but the state's great cash tides flowed impressively toward McClellan. And I could see and feel it everywhere.

The old warrior knew the levers of power and influence, and was experienced in working them. The old guard—the Stephenses and the Darbys in the bank boardrooms—had quickly faced the truth about the runoff: I was only 16,000 votes behind, and Ted Boswell had garnered over 60,000 on his own. Once that writing appeared in giant letters on the wall, money statewide flooded into the McClellan campaign.

Finally, I think Arkansas voters were simply not ready for a major shift in Senate representation, at least not in my direction. Still, I knew a definite change filled the air, a determination to continue reforms Rockefeller and Bumpers had begun. Barbara and I had crisscrossed the state, covering thousands of miles. We sensed the strength of that liberating movement. Her stamina during this long campaign seemed unreal. But I had lost my timing. To play my part in that progressive movement, I would have to wait two years, and then run for governor.

Chapter 30
The Long Aftermath

Following the McClellan race, I abandoned politics, or politics abandoned me. I didn't care who was governor or president. I avoided reading the paper for months on end. I just wanted to be left alone and, like General MacArthur, silently fade away.

Don't ask me for an interview, I would tell reporters. I have nothing to say. No amount of Monday morning quarterbacking helped. A *Gazette* editorial the week following the runoff said I had been too cautious, and my House record showed too much shifting with political tides. I had "taken refuge in silence," it said, and this hurt my campaign. Who knew? I thought I had been anything but silent. Maybe the editorial was right.

I couldn't help looking at Ray Thornton, Jim Guy Tucker, Bill Alexander, and Ted Boswell. All but Boswell still had their political careers, and Ted could return to a lucrative law practice. In different ways, their careers were rocketing. The *Gazette* published a George Fisher cartoon after the runoff that perfectly captured my mood. He drew my face shaped like the sun on the horizon. The caption read, "Is it Rising—or Setting?" In my mind, that sun was going down. Fisher much later told me he regarded that cartoon as one of his best.

Lawyer friends in Camden graciously asked me to join their practice. And respectfully, I turned them down, fearing if I went back home, I'd never leave again. Something—I wasn't sure what—waited for me. Barbara and I knew we would bring our boys back to Arkansas. Staying in Washington, and joining a law practice or a lobbying firm, held no appeal. I had seen too many Congress members take that course after retiring or being defeated. They left their roots behind. I didn't want to go there.

By September, we had sold our Arlington house, buying a Little Rock home at 315 Ridgeway, in the Hillcrest neighborhood. The price was $35,000. We contracted with a group of moonlighting firemen to knock out and replace walls, then paint and fix it up, including repapering rooms and sanding floors. We installed central air conditioning and heat. With Barbara's magic touch, the house glowed, a Hillcrest jewel.

Byron Freeland and I set up a tentative law office in downtown Little Rock's Worthen Building. A young friend just out of law school, Byron would become a distinguished lawyer. We decided, on my return to the state, that hanging out a joint shingle would fit both our budgets.

The service station operators' association sought my services, but not many others came knocking. Some people speculated the labor unions fed me a six-figure retainer, but my only regular fee came from Don Tyson at Tyson Foods, $600 a month. Still, I was grateful for that. After the McClellan race, financial institutions wouldn't touch me.

Bill Overton and I fished every north Arkansas river and went to Razorback football games. The Red Cross asked me to serve as their annual drive's honorary chairman, and the Jerry Lewis Telethon drafted Barbara to help.

The good personal news: Barbara, the three boys, and I became a family—almost for the first time.

Until the Congressional session ended, I regularly returned to Washington, packing up loose ends and helping my staff find jobs in other House offices or downtown. I realized what low esteem political colleagues show for one just defeated. They tossed long, distant looks, diagnosing me as an Untouchable. Old friends ducked into cloakrooms to avoid eye contact. Politicians develop a herd instinct. Survival depends on abandoning victims. Or, closer to home, we silently agonize over distant relatives who wear out their welcome: when will they *leave?*

Not all my old friends stood apart. John Paul Hammerschmidt, my Republican House colleague, proved one of my warmest supporters during this period. He seemed to instinctively understand what I was going through.

Birch Bayh was another sympathetic colleague. An Indiana senator who had come in 1962 (whose son Evan now serves in that seat), Bayh stood among the most encouraging and welcoming Washington friends I can recall. He had defeated Homer Capehart, a well-established Republican, in a race very similar to mine. But, of course, with different results. He had called me during the runoff, wishing me luck. I took the call just as I was rushing out the headquarters door, running late. Ernie Dumas, the *Gazette* reporter covering the campaign, heard me on the phone. The next day, he published a short squib describing the friendly call.

A couple of weeks after the runoff, Senate members took a charter plane to Senator Allen Ellender's funeral. A stalwart McClellan colleague, Ellender had visited Arkansas on the Senator's behalf only a few weeks earlier. He had preceded McClellan as chairman of the Appropriations Committee.

On the plane, Bayh approached Senator McClellan, telling him he hoped to secure an Appropriations Committee spot. He asked Senator McClellan to consider him for the vacancy.

McClellan reared back in his seat, remarking, "Well, Senator Bayh, have you spoken to your friend David Pryor about this appointment?"

Arkansas's senior senator seldom missed a piece of pertinent information or an opportunity to use it. But things sometimes work out fairly. In the long run, Birch Bayh did get his committee seat.

My House term would expire on January 3, 1973. On a return trip to Washington, the afternoon flight from Little Rock first stopped in Memphis. Very few people were onboard. A large, rumpled man got on, taking an aisle seat directly across from me. I couldn't believe my bad luck.

There sat Mississippi's James O. Eastland, a long-time Senate member and one of McClellan's best and oldest friends. He had just won re-election in a hot campaign. Hoping he would not recognize me, I hid behind the newspaper.

A row of small bourbon bottles, the one-shot miniatures that airlines offered as cocktails, sat in front of him. He puffed on a huge cigar (smoking on commercial flights was legal then), and the cabin quickly filled with his smoke.

Soon after takeoff, he reached across the aisle and slapped my leg. "Say," he asked in a loud voice. "Aren't you that SOB who nearly beat my friend John McClellan?"

"That's me, Senator," I said.

He crawled over me, sitting by the window. He began a detailed rendition of his role in the McClellan race, which he referred to as "the Arkansas Showdown."

Eastland told me Senator McClellan had called him, sometimes more than once a day, during the runoff. He was ready to pull out of the race. But Eastland and Senator Ellender of Louisiana had talked him into seeing it through.

Eastland laughed heartily. He talked about how, during the runoff, he had landed at Little Rock's Central Flying Service with a shoebox full of cash for McClellan's campaign. Passing out loose cash, like allowing cigars on passenger planes, was still allowed in the '70s. In the airport hangar, he had delivered the cashbox to Justice Jim Johnson. Then he flew back to Jackson. "Lord only knows what happened to all that cash," Eastland mused.

This was all news to me. Of course, I wanted to hear more. But at that moment Senator Eastland's cigar ashes fell, setting fire to his tie. The flight attendant ended the conversation by dousing him with water.

One Saturday morning that October, I drove south on Little Rock's University Avenue, taking Dee, Mark, and Scott to a YMCA football game. Stopping at a traffic light, I noticed, in the next lane, a car with a badly faded "Pryor for Senator" sticker on the back windshield. I asked Dee to roll down the window, then shouted to the driver, "Sure do appreciate your help in that election. Thanks for keeping that sticker on your car."

The driver looked back and said, "I'm from out-of-state. This is my mother-in-law's car, and, whoever that guy was, I'm sure glad McClellan beat him."

Chapter 31
On the Road Again

My purgatory came in 1973. Neither fish nor fowl, I possessed no interest in running for anything. I concentrated on healing and reuniting with my family. Planning a political future remained out of the question. Still, everyone I saw wanted to stop and discuss the race.

Late that fall, I attended Camden's annual Chamber of Commerce banquet. It pleased and surprised me to see the guest speaker: Dee Brown, best-selling author of *Bury My Heart at Wounded Knee*, published three years earlier. Though born in Louisiana, Dee grew up in Stephens, a few miles south of Camden. We always thought of him as a Ouachita County native son.

Dee's book has inspired many readers, but his talk that night has stayed most vividly in my mind. To be truthful, the content wasn't what impressed me most. His uncanny, conversational manner inspired me then, and does still. His simple delivery skill helped restore my confidence and balance. Since that night, I have tried to adopt Dee Brown's method as my own. An orator? Maybe not. But a storyteller, yes.

As the year ended, people wondered who would run for office in the spring and summer. Senator Fulbright was up for re-election; after 30 years in the Senate, he was expected to draw no opposition. Only Dale Bumpers, rumored to be restless and sensing a dead end as governor, might stand an outside chance of matching up with him.

At that time, Arkansas governors served two-year terms with no term limits. With a good record and considerable luck, a governor could be re-elected over and over. Faubus, after all, held the office for 12 years.

Speculation rose concerning my readiness to make another race, that I had licked my wounds long enough, paid my campaign debts, and needed a new challenge. That scenario's problem was that I wasn't ready to make another statewide race. The '72 marathon had extinguished the fire.

The Internal Revenue Service was auditing a number of my major Senate race contributors. They were also auditing me. Word got out that any Pryor campaign contribution would likely raise a red flag. In a small state like ours, news travels quickly. So much for hopes of raising new-campaign money.

Having politics embedded in my system, however, I couldn't entirely separate myself from a future race's prospects; if not mine, then someone else's. I tried to talk Dale Bumpers into running—more than likely without opposition—for another term as governor. Then, at his election-night victory celebration, he could announce his candidacy for the 1976 presidential race. He would run from Charleston, his hometown, with his national campaign headquarters over his father's old hardware store.

The whole plan seemed a little hokey but exciting. I even talked to DeLoss Walker, his Memphis advertising confidant, mastermind of Bumpers's initial gubernatorial race, when he began with only 1% name recognition. In defeating both Faubus and Rockefeller, Bumpers brandished a vote-getting ability second to none.

My idea excited DeLoss, who urged me to lay out the plan to Bumpers. I did just that, hoping he would pass up challenging Fulbright and run for president. Bumpers and his entire family had loyally supported Fulbright throughout the Senator's tenure. Bumpers's decision would also provide more time for me to consider a run for governor.

A highly astute politician, Bumpers logically concluded he should challenge Fulbright, or someone else would—and win. Polling data showed the victor could hold the Senate seat for 30 years.

But from my conversation with Dale, I could tell he was seriously considering my presidential proposition. "Let me think about it," he told me.

Soon after that visit, Barbara and I joined friends on an Aspen trip, our first snow-skiing venture. It was mid-January, 1974. My second day on the slopes, I broke my ankle. I spent the rest of our adventure laid up on the sofa, my leg covered with a huge plaster cast.

A few days after returning to Little Rock, a blood clot formed in my leg. Rushed to the hospital, I stayed for a week until the clot dissolved. One night, the nurse entered my room and asked, "Do you want to take a phone call from a W. R. 'Witt' Stephens?"

Of course, I did. Mr. Witt and I had spent years as friendly adversaries; while never close, at least we had agreed to get along. By then, perhaps the state's richest man—next to Winthrop Rockefeller—he had played a major role in all Faubus's campaigns and recently in McClellan's race against me. What could he possibly want with a hospitalized, has-been politician, his right leg shackled in a cast?

I recognized the gravelly voice on the line. "Are you going to run for governor?" he asked.

"I'm not sure, Mr. Witt," I said. "But right now, I don't think so."

"Well, if you do," he told me, "I'm going to help you. I helped beat you last time, and I owe you one."

For a moment, I thought I was hallucinating from the Demerol.

A day later, Barbara drove me home from the hospital. As we headed up Markham, the car radio aired Dale Bumpers's voice, announcing for the U.S. Senate. I saw the old Rialto's screen, the cowboys leaping to their horses, the great race beginning.

Dale had actually flown to Iowa, but after spending his Saturday in a snowbound Holiday Inn, he was back home before dark. He later confided to me he just didn't have the deep desire—that "fire in the belly"—required of devoted presidential candidates. Jimmy Carter went to Iowa, and then to New Hampshire. I've always said that could have been Dale Bumpers. Carter, Bumpers, and Reuben Askew of Florida stood as the trio of progressive governors synonymous with the "New South."

Two weeks later, cast off my leg, Barbara and I gathered with family and close friends in our Ridgeway home's living room. Surrounded by the press, I announced for governor. I was 39 years old, and knew that time would not wait. I also knew that Lt. Governor Bob Riley would soon enter the race. He recently had undergone open-heart surgery, but the state knew him as a tough survivor. He could prove a strong opponent.

Sure enough, Riley soon donned a yellow turtleneck sweater, declaring in a news conference he had entered the race to win. I felt certain Faubus, my nemesis for 20 years, would announce in a matter of days for the late-May primary.

Faubus joined the race on March 30 at Little Rock's Camelot Inn. He mentioned a growing drug problem in schools and public-school funding, but mainly he came out against me. Pryor is controlled by "selfish outside interests," he charged, "and as a 23-year-old newspaper editor he supported integration of Central High School." Five days later, the *Democrat* asked whether the state was ready to return to those fearful days of 1957, declaring of Faubus, "this sly old fox has visited the hen house too many times before."

We leased an old, yellow-brick building, located mid-block on Center Street, as our headquarters. Formerly housing law offices, it would be demolished soon after the campaign, making room for the new Stephens, Inc. headquarters.

A cast of tried and true Pryor people came together once again. Barbara designed brochures, orchestrated ideas, schedules, and plans to turn out the votes. She laid the foundations for the race. We had no cell phones, e-mail, or fax machines then. But our statewide network communicated beautifully.

Normally, a political headquarters becomes disorganized and dysfunctional, run by volunteers, well-meaning but with easily-bruised egos. Faubus always said a candidate's greatest obstacle to election was the headquarters itself. Ours proved the one exception—it ran like a new Chevy on a freshly paved highway.

Late one Saturday night, a graffiti artist without much talent, using a tall ladder and harsh paintbrush, spelled out in big letters, "F— Pryor," or something as sinister, on the building's north side. The message stood out prominently, visible to eyes at least three blocks away.

The following Monday, Don Tyson, chairman of Tyson Foods in northwest Arkansas, came to the headquarters for a campaign finance meeting. He complained about the graffiti eyesore, demanding someone remove it immediately.

A couple of days later, Don called from his Springdale office, asking if the offensive lettering had disappeared. Sorry, Don, we told him. No one had found time to take it down or paint over it.

Don gathered up Billie Schneider, by all accounts the staunchest Democrat in north Arkansas. They stopped at a hardware store south of Fayetteville, bought a dozen cans of yellow spray paint, and flew in a Tyson plane to Little Rock.

Don and Billie climbed up on the headquarters roof, painted out the obscenities, and within two hours Don was back at work in Springdale. For Tyson, campaigns are like that: if you want something done, then you do it yourself.

The 1974 Democratic gubernatorial candidates included Orval Faubus, former six-term governor; Lt. Governor Bob Riley, highly decorated war veteran and political science professor; and David Pryor, former state legislator and three-term Congressman, recently defeated for the U.S. Senate. The Republicans would soon nominate Fort Smith's Ken Coon, a long-time party activist.

The race between Senator Fulbright and Governor Bumpers, however, captivated everyone's attention. Fulbright stood as a decades-long fixture in

Arkansas politics. As the youngest president of the University of Arkansas and a 30-year member of Congress, he had become a household name, not only in Arkansas, but around the world. As Senate Foreign Relations Committee chairman, he had gained notoriety for opposing the U.S. role in Vietnam, challenging both the Johnson and Nixon administrations. Many considered him one of the country's leading thinkers, especially in world affairs.

Many veterans' organizations openly challenged Fulbright's loyalty and patriotism. Some Arkansans also considered him out of touch and aloof. But his followers were fiercely loyal, and when the campaign got under way, they quickly sprang into action.

Since 1970, Bumpers had become known for his extraordinary communication skills, his ability to recall names, and devoted energy to one-on-one campaigning. The public also respected him for his intelligence in dealing with statewide issues. He presented a dramatic contrast to the erudite Senator Fulbright, the Rhodes scholar, educator, and world-renowned statesman. During his two terms as governor, Bumpers had also been blessed with a bustling state economy, and a strong agricultural community with record crops and high prices. He had spent millions building a network of community colleges and vocational schools.

The governor's race took a route totally unlike any I had ever run. Faubus renewed the charge that labor bosses controlled my every move. But by that time, threats of outside union influence reached unconcerned ears. Richard Arnold had begun his strikingly similar barrage eight years earlier, repeated with intensity by McClellan, but by 1974, little response came to such a charge. Fanning the 1972 Senate-race flames, Faubus also brought up gun control and amnesty, but neither issue caught on.

Faubus's strong support base from the 1950s and '60s had disintegrated. He acknowledged this by continually attacking former friends who were deserting him and coming over to my campaign.

"A certain number of would-be governor-makers," he charged, "met in a small hotel room in Little Rock and conspired to elect the next governor of Arkansas." He openly denounced Witt Stephens and John Cooper of Bella Vista for their betrayals.

Faubus also carried baggage from what the *Gazette* called his "scandal-wracked administration" as governor. The Central High School crisis and administration scandals had taken their toll. He still smarted from losing to Bumpers in 1970, and my early announcement for governor had made it possible for me to gain support from many of his earlier backers. Chief among these was Sheriff Marlin Hawkins, Conway County's acknowledged political boss.

In many people's minds, I remained a question mark. The southern 20 counties I had represented in Congress stood solidly in my column, and the Senate campaign had added to my statewide name recognition. But would that be enough? Was David Pryor considered controlled by labor bosses? Was he only an opportunist looking for the next job? Did he really want to be governor, or just use this as a stepping stone to the Senate?

On a hot May night, as Barbara worked the crowd, I joined a bevy of candidates under Friendship's oak trees at a large Clark County rally. The speakers included those running for sheriff, county clerk, and justices of the peace. We were each given five minutes.

Kenneth Coffelt represented Faubus, who was speaking in northwest Arkansas. Coffelt was a flamboyant lawyer and, like Foster Johnson, something of a perennial candidate.

"Look over there at David Pryor," he shouted and pointed directly at me. "Just look at him, folks. Why, he's nothing but a political cripple."

I didn't like that description, but I smiled. I knew that, whether you're a Razorback or a politician, people in Arkansas watch to see if you can take a hit and get back up.

Every Democratic primary campaign traditionally closes the night before the election in Benton, on the Saline County courthouse grounds—in the hotbed of union activity.

That night, Bumpers, confident of his looming victory, held back from charging Fulbright with anything more than being out of touch. When Fulbright got up to speak, a cluster of veterans conspicuously jumped up, folded their lawn chairs, and stomped off. His speech that night clearly signaled his final political stand. The die was cast. I couldn't help being reminded of when, at age 10, I had seen one of his first political speeches on Camden's courthouse steps. Tonight I was probably seeing his last.

After my speech, Virginia Johnson, Justice Jim's wife, rose to speak for Faubus. But she took her text on David Pryor, what she repeatedly called his "liberal" record, and the way labor bosses had controlled his entire career. And on and on. Her charges grew so outrageous and openly racist, I asked permission to refute what she had said. With a burst of energy I hadn't felt during the entire campaign, I lit into Virginia Johnson's charges from every direction—my voting record, the labor ties she falsely described, and my strong record in civil rights legislation.

I loved stirring up the audience, waving my arms and reminding them how her husband, Justice Jim Johnson, had called them "a mess of trash" only two years before in the McClellan race. The crowd rose up in a solid shout, and Virginia needed protection just getting out of town.

I hoped to take the primary without a runoff. Sure enough, I brought it off with 52% of the vote. The *Dumas Clarion* had predicted that, barring some big mistake like the misguided McClellan debate, Pryor would take the nomination in the first primary. Twenty years had passed since the Faubus-Cherry election, and Francis Cherry had been dead for nine years. I had just defeated Orval Faubus—his old nemesis—and Lt. Gov. Bob Riley. In those days, the Democratic nomination was tantamount to election.

* * *

That Democratic-primary night in June 1974, our supporters gathered in the Camelot Inn's ballroom to view the results. Barbara and I took the stand amid cheering from all sides. It's the kind of victory celebration you always dream of—a hot ballroom with screaming friends and supporters. We had Pryor family members from all parts of the country. It seemed half the state had gathered in that raucous room.

I took out a piece of paper, put on a serious tone of voice, and announced to the crowd, "Ladies and gentlemen, friends and supporters, in the last few minutes, I have had the privilege of sending the following telegram. It was addressed to Mrs. Francis Cherry, Jonesboro, Arkansas. 'Dear Mrs. Cherry: The score is settled.'"

The crowd went wild. Clearly, the majority gathered in that ballroom couldn't know about my experience exactly 20 years earlier with Governor Cherry. Family members and a few old friends might remember my driving him around the state. But they could never have known that, on a hot summer night in 1954, I had resolved someday, somehow, to settle a score with Orval Faubus.

At the same time, any Democrat there considered a win against Faubus, from any opponent and for any reason, a milestone. And, in some way, it represented a long-delayed vindication of Francis Cherry.

Almost immediately after reading that telegram to the crowd, I began to have serious second thoughts. In my mind, it suddenly had become an unnecessary grandstand play, a mean-spirited victory boast. A modest thank-you to my supporters would have been more appropriate. And a lot more like me. I've never liked prancing around in the end-zone, a frenzied action of self-congratulation at another's expense. I began feeling terrible about my statement—nothing but a cheap shot. I could only hope people would forget it.

My regret has never entirely left me. For years to come, my numerous encounters with Orval Faubus proved sometimes contentious and hostile, often friendly, seldom openly angry. We viewed each other with a mix of curiosity and respect. Our family backgrounds and upbringing differed in almost every conceivable way. We came from separate regions of the state, emerging from our early years with distinct ideas about government and politics, even our views of humankind. Over the years, we took long looks at each other. We laced our agreement to *get along* with a rich and complicated thread of regard.

Years later when I was in the U.S. Senate, I was scheduled for a speech in Cabot at a Confederate cemetery. I called Governor Faubus, asking if he wanted to ride up there with me. Governor Frank White had appointed him director of the Office of Veterans Affairs, and I had noticed on the program that Faubus was scheduled to say a few words.

"This is David Pryor," I said on the phone. "How're you planning to get to the cemetery on Sunday?" He said he would drive up, and I asked him if I could give him a ride. "We can go together and swap stories," I told him. We had a great trip, going over old battles and skirmishes and a few peace treaties as well. I had opposed just about everything he ever did, and he knew it, but you'd never have sensed that on the afternoon ride we took together, to and from that event.

Years later, when I had open-heart surgery, Governor Faubus came to the medical center and asked to visit me in intensive care. The nurse on duty kept out all visitors, including the longest-serving governor in Arkansas history. So he scribbled on a scrap of paper, "David, I came by to see you. I helped beat you in 1972, and then you beat me. I hope between us that bygones will be bygones. Orval E. Faubus."

His framed note hangs on my office wall.

In November, I defeated Ken Coon, the Republican candidate. Overnight

I began to assemble a cabinet and start the intense task of defining a legislative program. By January, our entire legislative agenda had to be ready to go.

Barbara and I began the tough planning for a move from one house to another. We had lived on Ridgeway for only two years, and it had become a comfortable home. Dee, Mark, and Scott—14, 11, and eight years old, respectively—would be changing schools. We would have to sell the Hillcrest house we had come to love and move to the governor's mansion, where we knew our lives would not be entirely our own.

I was inheriting a state treasury with no money, and looking at a country engulfed in a severe economic recession. But with all this uncertainty, and with so much behind us, I felt for all the world like an excited and grateful Willie Nelson: on the road again.

Chapter 32
The Once and Future Governor

Gentlemen, let me introduce today's guest. He's my son,
David Pryor, and one day he will be governor of Arkansas.
                    —Edgar Pryor, Camden Rotary Club, September 1951

The night before my January, 1975, inauguration, I made phone calls to Arkansas's three most recent governors. I asked if they had any advice for me.

Faubus said two things. He hoped that, for my sake, I never had to experience a night when the state executed a prisoner. A governor, or anyone else, should never have the responsibility for another man's life or death. Second, he felt we both probably would have agreed on many issues, if it hadn't been for the people around us. "I've always thought we could have gotten along pretty good," he said. Then he added, "Well, good luck."

Two former governors offered strikingly similar advice, warning not to act in haste. Dale Bumpers said his experience revealed that very few things needed immediate attention. Take a day or so to make up your mind, he advised. "My worst decisions in office were made in haste."

Sid McMath nearly echoed that. "Most of the time," he noted, "the popular thing to do at the moment is not the right thing to do." McMath's final counsel was to "remember the people who put you there."

My swearing-in ceremony took place in front of the Old State House on Markham Street, a downtown Little Rock landmark—the exact spot where, 17 years later, Governor Bill Clinton would announce for president. A bitter-cold day, the front lawn's fountain had frozen over. Carlton Harris, the Arkansas Supreme Court's chief justice, administered the oath. Miss Lily Peter, the state's poet laureate, read a poem encouraging all present to "keep Arkansas a land of beauty and gracious living."

We sped up the proceedings so the crowd could scurry back inside. I had asked Edward L. Wright to act as master of ceremonies. A distinguished attorney and future president of the American Bar Association, he whispered to me at the ceremony's beginning, "Please don't talk too long. These people are cold."

Fourteen years earlier, I had served as a colleague with many state legislators now preparing for the upcoming session. I gladly reestablished these relationships, knowing that, in the weeks ahead, I would depend on their support.

I knew they wondered what kind of chief executive I would make. They had known me as a legislator, sometimes a rebellious one. But a legislator and a chief executive are different animals. One calls for compromise, the other for acting on his own. Would I be capable of saying "No" when I disagreed with them?

Their looks clearly asked this question, as well as others: How much can we get away with? How and when will we begin testing our former colleague?

Arkansas was facing its toughest budgetary decisions in many years. In his last weeks as governor, Dale Bumpers had called the legislature into special session, finding appropriate ways to spend a sizeable state-budget surplus. He acted in a cooperative spirit and for fundamentally sound reasons. Still, spending that surplus made governing hard for those of us starting a new session.

The lame-duck governor and the legislature expanded state buildings and established vo-tech schools and campuses around the state. Years later, when I recounted this story to unbelievers, Bumpers would acknowledge spending those extra funds in the last days of 1974. Then he would add with a laugh, "But Pryor put his name on the plaques and cornerstones at all those schools." The chilling fact was that the lack of funds forced me to veto legislation establishing two community colleges, one in Mena and the other in West Memphis.

I called Bumpers when I heard about the spending activity. "Listen, for Pete's sake," I told him, "if you're calling the legislature into session to start spending money, and I'm not left with much, why don't you go ahead and spend it all? Having nothing is better than having just a little. I want to be able to say we don't have a penny. Otherwise, if you leave me with only a few million, I'll have every group in the state wanting the little bit that's left. And all I'll be doing is saying 'No!'"

On top of our state's depleted surplus, the entire nation had been suffering a recession since the end of 1973. A year later, it was just beginning to reach Arkansas.

The phrase, "muddle through" won't bring cheers, but that describes our approach in my first year and a half as governor. We practiced caution when creating any new program or extending any old one. I coined a corny phrase— "poor but friendly"—and soon tee shirts and coffee mugs abounded, pronouncing the Pryor slogan to everyone. I put out the word: we could fund no more community colleges or vocational schools. Plants were closing, and even a minor economic slowdown would require major belt-tightening.

Returning to government service also renewed one of my great pleasures—the privilege, and the fun, of working with the press. In Washington, a thousand miles away, you easily forget how people back home pick up their news, published and broadcast at the local level, by neighbors living down the street.

When governing in your own backyard, you're constantly reminded of how Arkansans value their daily lives: births, marriages and deaths, crop yields, county elections, and football scores. You also sense the natural instinct to write about the truth as you see it, which we call freedom of the press.

Mixing with local newspaper publishers and editors, and attending Arkansas Press Association conventions, resembled dropping in on someone's family reunion. At one APA luncheon in my first two weeks as governor, the crowd filled the Camelot Inn ballroom. The air of excitement there remains with me. So do valuable comments during the question-and-answer session following my speech. Members' words proved thoughtful and considered, not always sympathetic, but friendly, understanding, and congenial. I felt good about that session, not because I thought the state press would always support me—I knew the government-press realities—but because we had established a two-way dialogue, an honest exchange. I hoped that would last throughout my term.

Those days came before the *Arkansas Gazette* was absorbed first by Gannett and then the *Democrat*. Though often controversial throughout its existence, the *Gazette* had always led the way for the state's smaller papers—a stimulus for these local news sources to step from the shadows and take progressive positions.

These editors included Bob Newton at the *Warren Eagle Democrat*, Cone and Betty Magee at the *Cabot Star Herald*, Bob Fisher at the *Crossett News-Observer*, and Charlotte Schexnayder at the *Dumas Clarion*. Also Paul Buchanan in Batesville and J. E. Dunlap in Harrison. Bob McCord in North Little Rock. John Ward in Conway. The list goes on. The *Pine Bluff Commercial*, smaller than the *Gazette* but in many ways every bit as gutsy, took stands that reflected independence, conscience, and conviction. Ed Freeman, owner of the *Commercial*, stood as a courageous publisher who never shied from controversy.

Press attention often roams as a strange and unpredictable animal. Before being elected governor, I had served as a legislator for over a dozen years, first in Arkansas and later in Washington. As one of many lawmakers, you could often hide in the crowd, or had to work hard to get press attention. I had to adjust to a governor's life in a fishbowl. My new post suddenly thrust me into full view of the entire state. This new way of life affected every member of our family, but Barbara had to make the necessary adjustment first.

Two weeks before my inauguration, she had her long blond hair cut into a short bob with tight curls, known as a "natural" or "Afro." It never occurred to her that this personal decision would prompt such a swift and mixed public reaction.

The press immediately ran picture panels showing her hairstyle before and after, along with extended commentary on what her haircut might mean to my future political career. While a few conservative traditionalists raised their eyebrows, many younger women praised the new look, defending Barbara Pryor's right to wear her hair any way she pleased.

Years later, in fact, Hillary Clinton wrote how Barbara had served as a model to her and others, showing ways a public figure, especially an elected official's wife, should conduct herself.

But the public's glare took its toll. Some months after moving into the mansion, Barbara began pulling away from the public, cancelling appearances and scheduled appointments. She went into private counseling to help her heal from several years of grueling pressure.

As she explained then, she almost daily had to respond to campaign workers, staff members, friends, committees, task forces, and extended family. Ever on call, the resulting effect could only be termed exhaustion. Her doctors suggested extended rest as the one and only remedy to ensure full return.

The year proved long and arduous for both of us, and for our family. Dee was 15, Mark 12, and Scott nine. On November 27, our 18th wedding anniversary, we began a trial separation. Barbara moved to our Lake Hamilton home in Hot Springs—a recent purchase for a family retreat—a lovely house surrounded by pine trees with a wide front yard running down to the lake. She planned to spend time there while our boys stayed at the mansion, attending school in Little Rock.

She needed open-ended time to herself. While I regretted the separation, I understood this need to re-establish her identity, so often threatened over the years. I did what I could to encourage her in these efforts.

Barbara has always possessed an impressive inner core of self-assurance. But through years as a housewife, young mother, campaign confidante, and growing public figure, that part of her character had been challenged to the breaking point. In this way, she mirrored many women her age, raised to play the part of a willing and loyal consort.

As a way of restoring her intellectual discipline, she enrolled in courses at the University of Arkansas at Little Rock, plunging into an academic schedule demanding preparation and study. Our sons actually enjoyed seeing this strain of determination they had never realized in their mother. So did I. We saw Barbara growing in ways she had never felt allowed to demonstrate during many years of nurturing us, overseeing our home, responding to a constant, unrelenting schedule. These demands had left no room for privacy or the creative world she needed.

In the spring of 1976, when the electoral season began to roll around and a re-election campaign loomed, Barbara returned to the governor's mansion, clearly ready for whatever might come her way. Or I should say *our* way. Her manner took the familiar form of past campaigns, but she possessed a new and different bearing never shown before. No longer simply the politician and elected official's loyal sidekick, she had become her own person.

The following summer, Barbara produced a movie, "Wishbone Cutter." She arranged the funding, chose a cast and crew, and found the right locales for shooting scenes on the Buffalo River. The picture starred Joe Don Baker, Sondra Locke, and Slim Pickens. In 1978, it went into international distribution.

Barbara had proved herself an accomplished person who had undergone an internal test of will, coming through it as a woman in her own right. Because of this independence, our relationship has grown ever stronger. Together, we learned a new reality of holding public office: whether we liked it or not, our personal lives—private as well as public—would come under the news media's scrutiny. They increasingly saw public officials' lives, in every sense, as "news."

Chapter 33
Pulling it All Together

A few days after my inauguration, I stopped in the South Main drugstore near the mansion. Bringing my purchase to the woman at the register, I thought, "What the heck, I'll give her a thrill. She probably hasn't seen a real governor before."

I greeted her with a grin and a friendly hello. "I'm David Pryor," I told her, "and this is my first time in the store."

"Is that right?" she asked. "You live around here?"

Those early weeks in office, I expected to wake up every morning facing serious fiscal threats and policy decisions involving life-or-death emergencies. Somewhat to my surprise, that's not usually how a governor's agenda works.

We spent an astonishing amount of time distributing season passes to the Oaklawn Race Track in Hot Springs. Every year the Racing Commission gave the governor's office 12,000 free passes. We'd then dole these out to legislators, elected officials, and other friends and constituents.

I'd provide each legislative member 25 passes to distribute to constituents. Not that anyone saved big bucks by having a pass—track admission was only $1. But folks liked the prestige of approaching the gate, flashing a pass from the governor. This yearly distribution effort always created a frenzy.

My first controversial decision centered on a State Highway Commission appointment. The coveted influence and autonomy given each commissioner made these posts a hot commodity, desired by state leaders, local politicians, and even hangers-on. Each of the five highway districts amounted to a local empire, as commissioners possessed unilateral power to spend money and determine highway priorities in their respective areas. On top of that, their appointments lasted a full 10 years.

The 10-year term held by Maurice Smith of Birdeye, in eastern Arkansas, soon would expire. Otherwise, he would come up for reappointment. Orval Faubus had placed Smith on the Commission. During my campaign, I strongly argued that he could receive another term. He had openly supported my gubernatorial campaign, and his help proved a major asset.

But now I balked at giving one individual so much power, and for a 20-year period. Smith's huge popularity, and his sense of fairness and decency, all made the situation even more difficult. If he had displayed indifference to his eastern Arkansas constituency, or made an arrogant power grab, I easily could have moved against him. But he had compiled an exemplary Commission record. He was respected and revered.

Complicating things even more, the Delta region's county leaders remained solidly on his side, and a majority of House and Senate members signed a petition endorsing him. Every time I left Little Rock for points in eastern Arkansas, people confronted me, wanting to know if Maurice Smith would get another 10-year term.

On January 20, with only a few days in office, I spoke at the annual Chamber of Commerce banquet in Helena, the Phillips County seat. Maurice Smith sat near the head table. In my mind, he never took his eyes off me. I felt sternly under the gun. Several of his backers stopped by, expressing support for his reappointment.

As the banquet concluded, I noticed David Solomon seated at a back table. Solomon, a respected attorney and Harvard graduate, came from an old and prosperous family in eastern Arkansas. His trademark consisted of a stiff white shirt, a bowtie, and iron integrity. My mind always associated him with Atticus Finch, the father in *To Kill a Mockingbird*.

That night, he wore a blue tie with white polka-dots. He gave me a nod when our eyes met across the room. At that moment, the decision suddenly became clear and simple. Why hadn't I thought of him before? He's from the right part of the state and commands the trust of a wide variety of individuals and professional groups.

After returning to Little Rock around midnight, I called Solomon, got him out of bed, and told him I wanted to appoint him to the Highway Commission. Stunned, he asked if he could go back to bed and call me in the morning. He had never asked to be appointed, and no one had mentioned him as a possibility. But the more I thought about it, the more he seemed the perfect choice.

At 7:00 the next morning, he called, saying he would accept the appointment. I called Maurice Smith and told him of my decision. Equally surprised, and sorely disappointed, he took the news like the gentleman he was.

That year, the highway appointment became only my first encounter with Maurice Smith's family. A few weeks after I had named David Solomon to the Highway Commission, Maurice's wife led an energetic, well-organized effort to establish a state commission on spinal-cord injuries.

I felt we needed state-sponsored attention to spinal-cord injuries. But I questioned whether we should require a separate state government arm, even advisory. I thought this could proliferate into similar commissions addressing bodily injuries and physical disabilities, and I wanted to avoid an endless struggle over funding them.

But Maurice and his wife, determined advocates, lobbied hard for the legislation. Maurice visited the capitol nearly every day during committee deliberations.

Their dedicated interest had been ignited when a Smith family member suffered a spinal injury, requiring medical care unavailable in the state. Sympathetic to the Smiths' motivation, I offered whatever help I could, short of setting up a state commission.

In the end, despite my objections, the legislature overwhelmingly passed the bill. I reluctantly vetoed it, and the next day the lawmakers overrode my veto—the only override I experienced as governor.

The Solomon appointment became one of my toughest dilemmas as a new governor. The *Memphis Commercial Appeal*, which closely follows eastern Arkansas politics, accurately called the move "undoubtedly Pryor's most controversial appointment." I quickly learned how seemingly small issues like staffing and appointments always require inordinate time and patience. They all matter.

Soon following David Solomon's appointment, a similar instance arose in the state Department of Public Safety, ironically an agency always ripe for potential mishandling and conflict.

Reorganized shortly before I came into office, the Department seemed to be making progress, but I sensed the need for new leadership. I appointed my friend Willis "B." Smith as director. We knew the State Police component needed special attention. Several entrenched state senators exercised far too much influence with senior police officers. I had received repeated information that troopers in the field reported to certain Little Rock law firms, allowing them to profit from personal injury and criminal cases. For instance, a police officer might issue a ticket or summons, then report the action to a superior, who would then tip off the law firm.

With retirement imminent for two top state police brass, I implemented a dramatic change in leadership. To nearly everyone's surprise, I passed over 15 captains, a lieutenant colonel, and four majors, promoting Lt. Doug Harp to colonel and naming him the State Police director.

The 34-year-old Harp served on the governor's mansion detail. When I decided to appoint him, I asked him to sit with me beneath a big tree in the mansion's back yard. He remained speechless when I told him my plan. Then he finally commented that he needed to drive to Hot Springs and talk to his parents about this surprise development. He'd let me know that night. When he did, his answer was yes. Doug Harp became the country's youngest director of a state police division.

These appointments set an important tone for my administration. I wanted the public to know I possessed reliable judgment and would give every appointment considered time and attention. What's more, my judgment and actions would not rely on influence from longstanding political loyalties and allegiances.

Faubus's record had been seriously blemished by a personnel scandal known as Pensions for Pals. I was determined not to scar my administration in such a way. My staff members—especially Shirley McFarlin and Parker Westbrook—relentlessly sought eligible people willing to serve on state boards and commissions.

Following their recommendations, in August, 1975, when Judge Lyle Brown resigned from the State Supreme Court, I nominated Elsijane Trimble Roy as the court's first female justice. In November 1977, when she became federal judge of the western district, I named Pine Bluff lawyer George Howard as the State Supreme Court's first African-American member. Justice Jim Johnson remarked to the *Gazette* that I would have appointed Idi Amin if I thought it would get me the black vote.

David Solomon wasn't my only controversial appointment to the powerful Highway Commission. Early in my second term, I named Patsy Thomason the first female commissioner to this admittedly male dominion of power. This placed her in a political lair that long had glared with suspicion at newcomers.

Patsy had worked as a legislative assistant to Congressman Wilbur Mills. A Rison native, she had established a long, active relationship with Cleveland County. She had a family home and voted there. But she was living in

Little Rock when I appointed her. This double identification with southeast Arkansas and, at the same time, the state's center, settled any argument that I must favor one area or the other. The rivalry was fierce between the two regions.

Patsy not only brought the Commission diversity and a foot in both sections of the state, but she also knew people from all over Arkansas. Despite some objections, none of them surprising or well-grounded, Patsy proved a good and solid choice, and an outstanding commissioner.

Bruce Lindsey, in his early 30s, served as my legal advisor during my early years as governor. He had worked for Senator Fulbright in Washington while finishing his law degree at Georgetown. He knew both the law and Arkansas politics. While in our office, he divided his time between defining legislative programs and studying for the state bar exam.

One day, a constituent called, asking to speak to the governor's "top legal aide," our Number One expert who fully grasped Arkansas law.

"He's not in today," the receptionist replied.

"How long will he be out?" the caller asked.

"Well, for the next three days," came the answer.

"He's on vacation then?"

"No. He's taking the bar exam."

Bruce Lindsey went on to become one of President Bill Clinton's top advisers and confidants.

Chapter 34
Getting Down to Business

Arkansas's elderly citizens, like those around the country, needed immediate help. Thanks to its intensive research and interviews, my team in January introduced a legislative series known as the elderly bills package. These provisions received strong endorsement from a new national organization, the American Association of Retired Persons (AARP), just getting under way with influencing Washington and state capitols.

One key legislative piece allowed citizens at least 60 years old to attend state colleges and universities free of charge. This measure placed Arkansas among the first states to take such a step. Unfortunately, several state college presidents tried to sabotage the program. They complained that freely admitting senior citizens would disrupt classes and academic schedules while running off students who feel awkward sitting next to someone their grandparents' age.

Early one morning, as I walked up the steps to the governor's office, I overheard one university president in animated conversation with a state House member. He urged the legislator to defeat the proposal. I clearly heard him say, "Our young people don't want to go to class with their grandmothers."

When I reached my office, I sent a staff member to invite that college president for a visit. Within minutes, we were across the desk from each other. I made my position clear to him. If I heard of any college officials trying to kill this program, they'd be looking for another job before the sun went down.

All opposition disappeared, the bill passed, and Arkansas's seniors could return to school tuition-free. Hundreds of citizens have taken advantage of this program.

Two prime issues emerged in my term's early weeks.

First, constitutional reform, an interest I had maintained since my freshman legislator days. Arkansas still operated according to a legal document written and ratified in 1874. Dueling remained legal. That alone should have offered sufficient evidence to write a new constitution.

A governor's salary of $10,000, set by the century-old constitution, defied belief. Dale Bumpers used to say he inadvertently left his first governor's paycheck on the upstairs dresser. When the maid saw it, she thought it was hers and quit.

I wanted to broaden our state's horizons and defined a new constitution as that effort's cornerstone. Citizens had refused to ratify a constitutional convention in 1968. Recalling that, I chose a shorter, more direct route.

I planned to appoint 31 of the 35 delegates myself, with two apiece named by the House and Senate. I promised to name a broad spectrum of citizens. But Paul VanDalsem, my nemesis from the Faubus years, argued that I would select only my prominent backers. At one point he asked, "Is there any way we can keep him from appointing all bankers?"

I hoped to get the constitutional convention moving and avoid a tedious election process in choosing delegates. We designated 60 days in the summer of 1975 for the convention to write the new document. A special statewide ratification vote would follow in September.

State Republicans challenged our selection method in a "friendly lawsuit" filed by Lynn Lowe, my 1966 opponent for Congress. Dr. Robert Leflar, the state's most respected legal authority and former U of A law school dean, argued our case before the State Supreme Court. Even with solid support from the legislature, on May 28 the State Supreme Court ruled my approach unconstitutional.

My second prime issue was state ratification of the federally-proposed Equal Rights Amendment (ERA). The cause had risen during the Bumpers administration, and I was more than willing to take it on. The ERA simply reaffirmed equality in the work place, and for all people—men and women. Thirty-eight states needed to ratify for the ERA to become a federal constitutional amendment.

But a number of opposition groups had frightened voters, claiming the amendment would force Arkansas citizens into unisex bathrooms, pushing women into showers with men. According to Phyllis Schlafley, head of the St. Louis-based Eagle Forum, the amendment would wreak havoc in the armed forces.

One cold January morning in my first month as governor, Senator Olin Hendrix of Antoine knocked on my office's back door—the one that led directly into the governor's conference room. Of course, I invited him in. An old-school politician who had served in the state Senate forever, he knew how the upper house worked better than anyone.

"Governor, I can't stay but a minute," he said, "but I have a few constituents out here I'd like for you to meet. Maybe shake hands with them and say hello."

I envisioned members of his Sunday school class, or maybe the family of a young person wanting to serve as a legislative page. Slipping on my coat and straightening my tie, with Senator Hendrix at my side, I stepped into the conference room. Several hundred angry women stood staring me down, many of them holding up anti-ERA signs.

He looked at the crowd, saying "Governor, these are a few of my constituents from southwest Arkansas. They want to have a few words with you, and I told them you'd be glad to address their concerns. Now, I don't want to be rude, but there's a committee waiting for me upstairs, so I have to go. Thanks for your time, Governor, and so long for now." Senator Hendrix disappeared through the double doors.

These women spat hostility in ways I had never seen before, on this or any other issue. I explained my position and took their questions, hoping I could survive the encounter. Of course, I didn't see Senator Hendrix for days. Many years later, I would run into him and ask my good friend, "Senator, where have you been? Are you still in that committee meeting?" Olin Hendrix, one of our state's great characters, made public service fun.

In my first term's early days, I determined to clean up the litter defacing roads and highways, vacant lots, and public parks throughout the state. Litter degrades us, and I'm obsessed with removing it. One morning soon after being elected governor, I stopped a car and confronted a group of young people who had just scattered paper wrappings along four miles of public highway.

"I've written down your license number," I told the young man at the wheel, "and you'll be hearing from the state police within the next day or so." From the looks on their faces, I'd made my point. Whether my rash action did any lasting good (I never turned them in), I hope I drove the lesson home.

To combat litter, I started a "Pick Up Arkansas" campaign, proposing a nominal tax on soft drinks, pet foods, tobacco products, newspapers, wrappers, and other materials. Tops on the list were styrofoam cups of all shapes and sizes.

The program included a small-business tax of 15 cents per $1,000 of sales, designed to return modest revenue to local communities for fighting litter. I especially encouraged city councils to dispose of solid waste like abandoned cars and refrigerators.

But some eager, young revenue department officers sabotaged the plan. They mailed out an incredibly blunt postcard notifying business owners: "Dear Arkansas Citizen, if you own a business, you have the possibility of going to prison for five years unless you pay ..."

They could not have assaulted citizens with a more hostile or confrontational message. As a result, the state's small-business people went into an uproar. Editorials condemned the Pryor administration's Gestapo tactics. The *West Helena Times* reported that these notices plagued local businesses "like an epidemic of Asian flu."

The legislature demanded a special session and repealed the litter tax. I still deplore the shabby trash piles lining our roads and highways. A modest fee on disposables remains a good idea. Ironically, in October 1977, the National Keep America Beautiful competition gave "Pick Up Arkansas" its first prize for state cleanup programs. Diane Lyons was my staff member who kept this effort alive. She never gave up in her determination to keep the state litter-free.

One morning, Senator Knox Nelson, Representative Wayne Hampton, and other powerful eastern Arkansas legislators paid me an unscheduled visit. They brought DeWitt's Wilbur Botts, an upstanding citizen and civic leader.

"Governor," Hampton said, "we want you to meet Mr. Botts. He's been our friend, and now he's yours. He gave your campaign $500 and helped carry the southern end of Arkansas County for you. Now he wants to be a part of your administration. We're going to leave you two alone, so you can work something out."

The two of us sat down. I explained how we were involved in education, health care, prison reform, industrial development, and many other public interest areas. What about tourism? We were getting into that in a big way.

"Governor," he said, moving his chair closer to mine, "it really doesn't matter to me what I get appointed to, so long as you get me out of DeWitt one night a week."

Not every call a governor receives ranks as official business. Early one Sunday morning, a Conway supporter, active in his local American Legion, called the mansion. He had spent the weekend at the Legion convention in El Dorado. On his way out of town, a law officer pulled him over, booking him on a DWI charge.

"My wife is going to be as mad as a hornet," he said. "But I hear you and Judge Edwin Alderson down there are real tight, and I wonder if you can help me out with him. If you could put in a good word, only you and me and the Baby Lord Jesus will know about it."

I helped out Wilbur Botts, but I couldn't do much for the Conway Legionnaire, even with the Baby Lord Jesus on his side.

Chapter 35
Prisons and Rivers

Conversations with former governors, judges, and legislators led me to fear that a major crisis might erupt in our state prisons. Physically old, the facilities needed repair. Deplorable conditions pervaded, including inadequate medical attention, no meaningful prisoner rehabilitation, and seriously overcrowded cell blocks.

The appalling prison conditions struck home my first year as governor. During the Christmas holidays, I took our three boys to Cummins to share dinner with inmates. I wanted to establish in their young minds an indelible imprint of prison life.

During Winthrop Rockefeller's administration, serious problems with prisoner abuse, past and present, came to light. The courts criticized prison conditions, one opinion suggesting that "evil men" ran the system.

I actually became very conscious of the prison issue as a child. Governor Ben Laney had appointed Dad to the prison board. Once or twice, Dad took me to board meetings, and I remember spending the night on two occasions at Cummins Prison Farm near Pine Bluff.

As a law student years later, I wrote a paper about the prison system. And as a Congressman, I stressed in a Crossett speech that, if the state didn't improve conditions, the federal government might have to take charge. Perhaps an outlandish statement, but it made perfect sense to me. Federal "takeovers" have always been anathema to local powers.

Both Governors Rockefeller and Bumpers had appropriated money to address the prison problems. They had started building new facilities, particularly for the women's prison. So they had made considerable progress since my 1940s visits. Still, the seemingly evil atmosphere permeating the system haunted me.

But that wasn't all. Six or seven of every 10 prisoners who left regularly returned. In addition to improving living conditions, I wanted to instigate education and training programs to quell this high recidivism rate.

Early in my first term, I asked a mansion security officer to drive me to Cummins one night after dinner. An hour's drive, we got there about 10:00 p.m.

I had visited years before during the daytime hours but wanted to see it in the dead of night. I wanted to surprise them, so no one could prepare for me.

Jaws dropped as we drove through the prison gates, and word spread like wild fire that the governor had just arrived. I also received a surprise. In the crowded barracks, I saw a friend from law school days 12 years earlier. He had taken money from a client's trust account and converted it to personal use.

After touring the facility's main areas, I talked with prisoners and officials, paid my respects to the warden, and returned to Little Rock.

The next day, two legislators—who considered the prison their personal territory—came to my office, disapproving of my surprise visit. I had invaded their turf, and they let me know it. Imagine the audacity of my visiting our state prison without their knowledge or consent.

But I had just begun. I reacted to their complaint by appointing a study commission to define prison problems and recommend ways of addressing them. We found appropriate lawyers, doctors, and psychologists to serve on the panel, and I called a press conference to make the formal announcement.

One new commission member drew the most press attention: a former prisoner. I considered him ideal. He could bring insights and share experiences no one else could touch. The morning after the announcement, Witt Stephens called, mad as could be, asking if I knew what I had just done. Of course, Mr. Witt was still the state's acknowledged political king-maker.

The former prisoner, now a commission member, had more or less "kidnapped" Witt Stephens years earlier. On a country road outside Prattsville, he had threatened to shoot him. Stephens begged the man to let him go, promising to set him up in business if he'd spare Stephens's life. After holding him for several hours, the man eventually let him go. In return, Witt Stephens bought him a lawnmower repair shop. In time, the man ended up in prison. Because of his exemplary record while there, we had picked him for the commission. At the end of our conversation, Mr. Witt commented, "You know, he's not a bad fellow."

Not many people knew that Witt Stephens strongly opposed the death penalty. He always said his mother interpreted the scriptures, claiming the death penalty was wrong. On more than one occasion, he pled with Faubus to spare an inmate's life from the electric chair.

Some weeks after my initial Cummins visit, I went back for the annual prison rodeo. A three-night affair, it represented the year's big event for prison officials, the wardens, and their staff. State Prison Board members, appointed by the governor, attended as special guests, along with hundreds of inmates' families and onlookers in the stands.

For male prisoners serving a life sentence, riding a killer bull meant little more than a momentary challenge. What's to lose? But for the women prisoners, few of them there for life, the rodeo meant humiliation of the lowest order. As officials lounged in the stands with beer and barbeque, teams of female prisoners involuntarily took part in the "greased-pig" contest. In their striped uniforms, they wallowed in the filthy, mud-packed rodeo arena. Forced to chase a pig soaked in grease, they struggled until the winner emerged with the squealing pig in her arms. Several rounds occurred for the public's entertainment.

The contestants' children, husbands, and parents sat in heavy silence while others hooted and cat-called throughout the contest, throwing paper plates and cups at the dirt-caked female inmates. The winning pig catcher received a carton of cigarettes.

When we returned to the mansion that night, I sat down and wrote a note to the Department of Corrections commissioner and wardens. The next morning, I asked Col. Doug Harp to deliver the note in person to the prison. "As long as I am governor," I wrote, "there will be no more 'greased-pig' contests at your annual prison rodeo. This event is humiliating, ugly, and with no justification whatsoever."

Some years later, I was flying into Little Rock. Just before we landed, my seatmate leaned over and asked, "Senator Pryor, do you remember me?"

I looked back and took in his whole bearing, the nice suit and the polished shoes, but couldn't remember ever seeing him before. "No," I said, "I'm sorry, I don't."

"I used to be in charge of special programs at the state prison. You fired me from that job many years ago," he said, "and you were right."

* * *

On a chilly, rainy May 2 of my initial year in office, the first of five planes loaded with Vietnamese refugees landed in their new home: Fort Smith's Camp Chaffee. Hundreds of us crowded against a chain-link fence to watch families— children, parents, and grandparents—disembark from a grey C141 transport plane, receiving their first glimpse of America.

The federal government chose Arkansas as one of three states to receive refugees from the war. Not everyone was happy about the selection. One young man was screaming at them, "Go home! We don't want you!" A few spectators yelled at me to do something about this invasion of foreigners. But the majority who turned out that day supported the decision to relocate refugees to Camp Chaffee. I knew when I heard the First Baptist Church choir sing "America, the Beautiful," that everything would be okay.

My brother Bill, the Presbyterian minister in Victoria, Texas, drove to Fort Smith, choosing a Vietnamese family for his church to adopt. Having presided as minister for several years, he had earned his congregation's enduring trust. Nonetheless, the elders strongly opposed his adoption plan, and Bill had threatened to resign. In time they relented. The family that returned to Texas with him became productive members of the community and Bill's church.

A few of the Vietnamese spoke some English, learned from being around Americans during the war. Still, the crowds bewildered them, as did the appearance of this strange country. Already medically screened, they were scheduled to stay at Chaffee for only two weeks. The federal government then would relocate them in regions around the country.

As I welcomed them, I also tried to prepare them. If they encountered unfriendliness or hostility, they should try to understand: like them, we are facing unknown circumstances ourselves. They should know that outspoken critics did not represent the majority of people in Arkansas or America. I hoped my comments somehow made sense to this mass of frightened refugees.

This potential problem turned into a successful eight-month effort without a single incident of misconduct. We started more than 50,000 Vietnamese on their path to becoming productive American citizens. I stood watching the following December when the final busload left Chaffee.

* * *

Throughout the 1970s, Arkansas's northwestern section enjoyed significant population and industrial growth. Housing nearly doubled. Jobs became available in trucking companies such as J. B. Hunt and in several Tyson Food poultry plants. Many found work in the area's numerous WalMart stores, or the company's Bentonville home office. For generations Arkansas's poorest sector, the northwest was fast becoming its richest.

Meanwhile, southern and eastern Arkansas continued to suffer periods of great economic stress. The Mississippi River's Delta region mechanized a major part of its agricultural production, but this couldn't maintain a viable economy. Population diminished, and revenues for local schools and health services fell drastically.

North central Arkansas, with its own financial troubles, began to look wistfully at its western mountain neighbors, envying the recreational advantages of their rivers and lakes. Developers seriously planned to create a water reservoir, hoping to bring in tourism and expand real estate opportunities.

Looking back to the federal Flood Control Act of 1938, regional leaders asked the Army Corps of Engineers to dam the Strawberry River in Sharp County's Bell Foley community. A rider attached to several early Corps projects provided a governor special power. If a governor felt a proposed dam would prove detrimental to the state, he or she could veto its construction.

A bruising fight had raged in the 1960s over a dam proposed for northwest Arkansas's Buffalo River. The project would impede one of America's most scenic, free-flowing rivers. The Ozark Society, a new action group, led a spirited fight against the dam. A number of the mountain counties' landowners supported the project, which would greatly enhance their land values. But Congress designated the Buffalo a national river, recognizing it as a major scenic treasure and stopping plans for the dam. The late William O. Douglas, justice of the U.S. Supreme Court and an avid outdoorsman, described the Buffalo as one of the country's finest natural resources.

The Bell Foley Dam project proved a less clear-cut issue. The Strawberry River was small and during the summer dry season often reduced to a trickle. It laced the dramatic significance of the Buffalo. Still, the two opposing sides grew active and loud. Emotions reached fever pitch.

Both Senator McClellan and Congressman Bill Alexander, who represented the First Congressional District, strongly supported the dam. The State of Arkansas pledged to spend from $6 to $10 million for its project share, a hefty sum for a strained state budget.

My attention didn't focus only on the financial cost. I was greatly concerned about the potential environmental damage to a pristine part of the state. I read every study published on the issue, talked to groups on both sides, and invited people with differing views to visit the state capitol and express themselves. One raucous meeting flared for most of one day, divided almost equally between business interests favoring the dam and local citizens opposing it.

Twice I rode in a National Guard helicopter over the river area, picturing in my mind its hills and gentle slopes submerged under water, surrounded by lines of gas stations, bait shops, and billboards. "Right below us will be a Dairy Queen and a used car lot," predicted Joan Vehik, our brilliant young staff assistant who briefed me on the project. These trips spoke louder than all the feasibility studies put together. On July 9, I vetoed the dam.

Some 200 phone messages came in almost immediately. Two contrasting calls reached the governor's office around 10:00 p.m. that evening. Still there after a long and arduous day, I answered the phone myself when nobody picked it up.

The first caller, an angry woman, demanded to speak to someone "no lower than the governor himself."

I told her, "Ma'am, there *is* no one lower than the governor himself."

Another call came from an old man who said that he had one question about my Bell Foley decision. I told him to go ahead and ask it. He said that in 1938, the Army Corps of Engineers had driven a steel pipe in his tomato patch and ordered him not to move it. They said one day they would survey for a dam, and the pipe would provide a reference point. For nearly 40 years, he had plowed around that pipe. Would it be all right now if he went out there and pulled that blankety-blank pipe out of the ground? I told him to go ahead.

In later elections, my decision to block the dam would cost me politically, especially in my 1978 run for the Senate. I lost friends, votes, and dollars, but I am still convinced that I made the right decision. Today, the Strawberry River flows as it did a million years ago, free and unobstructed.

Chapter 36
Europe, Labor, and Lindsey

Like governors in all states, I had a consuming interest in attracting industry and creating jobs. The Arkansas Industrial Development Commission (AIDC), founded in the 1950s and brought to full flower by Governor Winthrop Rockefeller, had achieved some success through 20 years of activity. I made every effort to continue that progress, build on practices already in place, and look for new ideas and directions.

Soon after I appointed Frank White director of AIDC, he proposed establishing a full-time office in central Europe. Other state commissions had opened liaisons of this kind, and Arkansas was getting left behind while neighboring states flourished with new and productive industries from abroad.

With a strong financial background, Frank had come to my administration from Commercial National Bank. He had attended the U.S. Naval Academy with my former law partner, Harry Barnes, and knew just about everyone in the state. At that time, he was a staunch Democrat and an active state Jaycees member.

Frank outlined the idea for an office in Brussels, Belgium, the '70s center of Western European commerce, especially the Common Market. It seemed the most likely city to attract industrial leaders looking to invest more than $36 billion somewhere in the United States, with a potential interest in Arkansas. Before I knew it, he had invited legislators and financial leaders to support a foundation for financing the project, supplementing whatever appropriations the legislature would provide.

We were negotiating with Beckaert Steel Company, a major wire manufacturer. Eventually Beckaert located a plant in Van Buren. Frank promised the trip to Europe as only the beginning of a long and lucrative relationship with other foreign manufacturers dying to build plants in Arkansas.

Barbara and I headed a delegation of 20 Arkansans—legislators, AIDC representatives, and financial leaders—who flew to Europe to explore opening a Brussels office. We made a side trip to Munich, visiting Siemens Industries, and on our way back spent two days in London. As guests at the American embassy on the historic Berkeley Square, we met with Ambassador Elliot

Richardson, who graciously received us in the embassy's impressive state reception room. When Senator Virgil Fletcher of Benton met the ambassador in the receiving line, he said, "Glad to meet you, Elliot. Who you with?"

* * *

Tension reigns for a seated governor, an omnipresent sense that at any minute some major operation might go haywire. Even if minor, it would be my responsibility to fix it.

One evening, a trooper rushed into the mansion's breakfast room. Pine Bluff's mayor was calling with an emergency message. All the firemen in town had just gone on strike, the shaky phone voice told me.

"I'm at the Number Three fire station by myself," the mayor said. "I'm literally the only person here. Now what do I do?"

I asked him to repeat what he had just said, and he did, word for word.

Within minutes I ordered an Arkansas National Guard company into Pine Bluff. Most of them came from southeast Arkansas and areas close to the town. They quickly learned how to operate the equipment and set up a schedule to deal with any fire emergency. For the next several weeks, the Guard manned and operated the fire stations.

Bill Becker, the Arkansas AFL-CIO president, called a press conference two days into the crisis, condemning my decision. He intimated I was a strikebreaker, a traitor to labor's cause. But I knew I had no other choice. Labor became cool to me after that, maintaining I had allowed the Guard to stay too long. But I would not remove them until certain the city was safe. Two years later, I lost labor's endorsement in my Senate race, largely because of the Pine Bluff firemen's strike.

* * *

In 1976, Arkansas celebrated America's 200th birthday with a combined display of hoopla, allegiance, and pride. Joe Purcell, the state's lieutenant governor, chaired the statewide Bicentennial Commission. He presided over a wagon train making its way through Arkansas. He also authorized a somewhat controversial Liberty Bell replica on the state Capitol grounds's north side; it took up a lot of vacant lawn space.

On the Fourth of July, Bruce Lindsey, the governor's office legal counsel, and I left the mansion before daylight. We crossed the river bridge into North Little Rock, made our way to Camp Robinson, and boarded a

National Guard plane headed for traditional eastern Arkansas picnics that would host thousands.

Most of these were family reunions in such towns as Piggott, Pocahontas, Corning, Rector, Paragould, and Portia. The Piggott mayor and city council were scheduled to meet us at the airport. I was to serve as marshal for the July Fourth parade downtown.

Our plane landed at Rector, the wrong airport, some 15 miles from Piggott. The pilots had flown back to Little Rock, and Bruce and I couldn't figure out where we were. Finally, just before the clock struck the parade hour, we decided we must be in Rector. We raced out to the almost isolated state road and flagged down a truck loaded with watermelons. We asked the driver if he would take us to Piggott. I sat in the truck cab and Bruce climbed on top of a watermelon stack. The farmer said, "Did anyone ever tell you that you look like Governor Pryor?" I told him unfortunately they had.

Bruce and I barely made it to the parade on time. When it ended, we drove in a state police car to five additional picnics, each one bigger and noisier than the previous one. That night, we stopped in Conway for a Faulkner County July Fourth courthouse ceremony, then attended a rodeo right outside of town. We were back in Little Rock by midnight. The watermelon truck made it on the national news that night.

* * *

While labor may have thought I had become conservative in my first term as governor, at least one person felt I had moved too far to the left, especially on the Equal Rights Amendment and abortion rights. Jim Lindsey one day, to the surprise of many, came down from the Ozark hills to run against me for governor.

A newcomer to Arkansas politics, Lindsey was a veteran of the sports and financial worlds. A Forrest City native, he had starred on the Razorback football team and spent several successful seasons with the Minnesota Vikings. After retiring from professional football, he established a home base in Fayetteville, fast becoming one of the area's more aggressive real estate developers. He had put together the Northwest Arkansas Mall and scores of apartment complexes.

When Lindsey announced his candidacy, everyone took him seriously. His wife hailed from a popular Jackson County family with extended connections around Newport. Jim used two main issues popular among the right—school prayer and ERA—as his campaign's primary building blocks.

If he had started campaigning earlier, and broadened his issues, Lindsey might have proved more of a threat. As things turned out, I received 312,000 votes to his 171,000. Frank Lady and "Tuffy" Chambers, two latecomers in the race, combined for 8,000. The race amounted to a diversion rather than a serious campaign, even though it required time, attention, and money.

The following January, some seven months after the primary, while in Fayetteville I paid a call on Jim Lindsey. He told me he really opposed me for a second term because of abortion. He considered my position far too liberal.

My Republican opponent, Leon Griffith, had defeated Joe Westin in the primary. He ran with almost no money or support in the general election. I received 85% of the vote and wondered why it wasn't greater. Republicans had trouble fielding candidates for any state office, unlike elections today when the match-ups have become more even. Which reminds me of Camden in my early days, when the only Republican in town was Skidmore Willis. I think he stood as the only Republican in all of Ouachita County. I once asked Dad what a Republican was, but he didn't quite answer my question. "You'll know soon enough," he said.

Chapter 37
The Coon Dog

The Arkansas Plan represents my singular, most time-consuming project through two terms as governor. And the most controversial. The idea began in 1976. I was talking one night at the mansion with Steve Nickles, a doctorate-in-law candidate at Columbia University and a close family friend. Steve was one of the smartest people I'd ever known.

We were discussing possible items for the 1977 legislative session, chiefly local government financing's effect on state revenues. Our original idea involved state revenue-sharing for local governments while, at the same time, allowing counties to raise taxes. Increasing local revenues—or not—would depend on the voters. In any case, the state would end its traditional aid to cities and counties and focus purely on state concerns.

Those early discussions grew into a yearlong series of scrapes and struggles involving nearly every organization and public forum in the state. In the end, the Arkansas Plan in no way resembled what Steve and I had first discussed.

We reasoned that state turnback to cities and counties, plus education aid, sapped most state revenue. That left very little for health and social services, child care, and elderly aid. Yet the state should support these legitimate areas.

We optimistically assumed voters would replace state funds with county and local monies. Local leaders would encourage citizens to pass taxes to support local services. We banked on commitments from newly formed quorum courts, recently approved by Amendment 55 and slated to begin meeting in January. One of my first acts as governor involved establishing a Department of Local Services, bringing together several state agencies and offices that formerly had worked independently. Ron Copeland, former Texarkana city manager, headed the new department, bringing considerable experience for meeting local communities' needs. Bill Gaddy on my staff, who knew state government more thoroughly than anyone in Arkansas, coordinated our local initiatives with the new department.

We worked in secrecy while putting the Arkansas Plan together. We felt that if one item reached the press and public the whole stack of cards might collapse. I asked Steve to prepare a memo detailing the plan and suggesting a timeline. We held a budget retreat at Petit Jean, the state park near Morrilton, in May 1976.

Then I met with close personal friends and advisers at the mansion on July 20, explaining the plan to them. The group's reaction was 100% negative. Not a single encouraging voice. They called the plan too revolutionary, too complex, and entirely unnecessary. It promised to anger every group with local-funding interests, with the state basically abandoning cities and counties when it should be *increasing* assistance.

My closest political friends pointed to elections coming in 1978. Senator McClellan would almost certainly retire. If I had any political future, it lay in the U.S. Senate. But this plan would send me back to being a lawyer. Why jeopardize my political future with this foolhardy idea? It would never work, even if it passed.

The more critics complained, the more determined I became to see it through. Late that summer, I organized a Hot Springs retreat with personal staff and agency heads. We decided what to keep in the plan and what to drop. In an August 14 press conference, I mentioned that I was considering a plan to lighten local government's financial burdens. Nothing more than that. I also spoke of home rule, in the same breath discouraging any increased state sales tax. A *Gazette* follow-up article referred to a possible local-option tax, setting off more speculation.

On October 5, a small group of staff and agency directors held a dress rehearsal at Little Rock's Cajun's Wharf. By that time, open opposition was appearing in newspapers and among legislators. In some quarters the cries grew shrill. That night, I compared our situation to an encircled wagon train under fire, warning my team the barrage would come from all sides. But after a couple of weeks, I assured them, the attacks would die out, and we'd win.

Hair-raising, naïve wishfulness. I presented the plan on Monday night, October 11, to a legislative joint session in the House chamber. We sent special invitations to county and local officials—I think they all showed up—and encouraged the public to watch the statewide TV broadcast. The Little Rock channels carried the speech live. All very high drama. One of my closest legislator friends told me after the speech, "I don't understand a word of it—but I'm for it all the way."

The time had come, I announced, to restructure the relationship between state and local governments and, in particular, permanently change their fiscal connections. State government could not continue to act as a giant school board, city council, and county government. I admitted that the plan was complex. Because its parts overlapped, I stressed, it had to pass as a complete unit. Otherwise, the whole plan would be greatly damaged.

For the first few days, legislators seemed cautiously optimistic, at least on the surface. On the other hand, teachers regarded the plan—as one teachers' association official put it—"a complete copout." In no time, the teachers' group withdrew its endorsement of my re-election as governor.

The Municipal League, the Association of Counties, and the State Highway Department all predicted disaster. Soon the county judges joined the fray, followed by the state colleges and universities. By that time, most legislators, even those who seemed encouraging at first, had dropped by the wayside. An editorial by the *Gazette*'s J. O. Powell called the plan "the most hare-brained scheme in governmental financing to be seriously proposed in Arkansas in the last quarter century."

On November 16, at a Mountain Home courthouse meeting, I put the local-option idea this way: "Let the people decide if they want to buy a new coon dog or a new shotgun, or buy a new local service. Maybe a new fire truck. Maybe hire more policemen." The first to pick up the coon dog image was, naturally, George Fisher, the *Gazette* cartoonist. He made a cottage industry of me with a smiling, but clearly lazy, coon dog at my feet. From that day on, this high-flown design for remaking state government possessed a notorious designation: the Coon Dog Plan.

We held eight regional meetings in the state's major cities from November 17 through the first week of December. I intended to stir up the public, hoping that they would press their legislators to support the plan. Our meetings differed in every single instance, some quiet and attentive, others more like a pep rally before a ball game. We found partisan cooperation, along with expected occasional skepticism.

One night in Harrison, we ran into a sudden winter snow squall. Wayne Eddy, who was driving that night, stopped in the middle of the highway so we could help an elderly woman. Her pickup truck had a flat tire. Wayne and I spent nearly an hour digging through snow and ice, risking life and limb in that storm. When we finally finished changing the tire, she said, "Thanks. And if I wasn't a Republican, I'd vote for you."

Earlier in the month, the nation's voters had elected Jimmy Carter president, closing Richard Nixon's Watergate scandal and its aftermath. But back home, none of our crowds supported the Arkansas Plan the way we hoped. Most already saw a good working relationship between state and local governments. So if it ain't broke, why fix it? Meanwhile, we were traveling the state, describing a problem people didn't believe existed.

In my opinion, those regional meetings proved worthwhile. Even if the public didn't grasp the plan's details—and, admittedly, they were complex and confusing—I saw an enlightened public awareness of state and local government. This was unquestionably new and different. People were taking an active interest in how their cities and counties functioned, and how these local entities related to the state and federal governments. They also learned ways to take part in their government on every level. They showed a grasp of issues and a hunger for information that inspired me in every town we visited.

The failure of the Coon Dog Plan was a disappointment, but I wouldn't mind going back to it—if I could do a few things differently. For one thing, I'd make an early effort to consult legislative members and interest groups. In my determination to keep the plan confidential, I shut out critics who might have supported me, had they understood the plan before I announced it. Also, I would accept early sectional changes, alterations, and compromises instead of insisting on a self-contained package. It's easier digesting small bites rather than devouring the whole meal at once. Of course, you can't rewrite history.

Opening its session in January, the legislature took up our complicated array of bills. Over the next two months, we saw three separate versions of the plan, each more and more watered down.

In the first week of March, a series of House amendments had cut the plan to pieces. One version of a home rule bill finally allowed counties to propose sales taxes, and a new formula for equalizing school funds passed in separate legislation. But these were pathetic remnants of our elaborate design for change.

While my political advisers predicted doom for me, I'm glad to report their failed projections. In 1978, a year after my lofty home rule hopes went down in flames, I won a tough U.S. Senate race. During that battle, no one mentioned the Coon Dog Plan.

Chapter 38
The Die is Cast

In 1977, Senator McClellan addressed the Arkansas General Assembly. I didn't quite know whether to attend and hear him or quietly retreat into my office downstairs. We had not spoken during the five years since our fierce Senate battle. I felt it might create an awkward situation if he saw me in the House chamber.

So I compromised. I called his Little Rock staff and invited him to visit my office when he finished his address. He accepted my invitation, and we had a cordial visit, drinking coffee and discussing mutual hometown friends in Camden.

That was the last time I saw or spoke to Senator McClellan. He died later that year, on November 28, at his Riviera Apartments home in Little Rock. He was 81. I made quick arrangements to visit his wife Norma at their apartment the night of the funeral.

Exquisitely choreographed ahead of time, the meeting included detailed steps for the way our talk would start and end. A state trooper would drive me, and I would be ushered to a back room for our private talk. As governor, it was up to me to fill the vacant Senate seat. One year remained before the general election to permanently fill the position. At a certain point in my conversation with Mrs. McClellan, I was to offer the "McClellan seat" to her. She would express her thanks, but turn it down.

That's not exactly the way things turned out. In the first place, I had lived only two blocks from the McClellan home in Camden. Our relationship with her, while never close, had always been cordial, even through the heated 1972 campaign. Barbara and I had always called her Norma.

Despite her somewhat regal bearing, Norma McClellan was down to earth and approachable on any subject we had ever discussed. That evening, following the Senator's funeral earlier in the day, she could not have been more gracious. Our visit was not the stiff and formal confrontation others expected. I don't believe either one of us thought it would be.

As we sat down in the small room, almost knee-to-knee, 15 or 20 friends and family were milling about. She said, "David, would you be more comfortable if this conversation were just between us? I can ask these people to leave."

I told her that suited me fine. She quickly stood up, asking everyone to please go into the next room and out into the hall while the two of us talked.

Then we were alone. I began by telling her how sorry I was at the Senator's death. I even suggested that five years earlier, in some unfortunate way, I might have shortened his life, forcing him through that rigorous re-election battle.

She stopped me there. "You didn't shorten his life at all," she said. "In fact, you added years to it. That campaign gave him new energy. He was an old warrior, you know, and he loved recounting details of that race."

Then she reached out and took my hand. "I know what you're supposed to say, and I know what I'm expected to say, too," she explained. "And I appreciate what you're about to suggest. But I'm through with politics, and my plan is to move to North Carolina to be near my family. Thank you for coming by to say hello, and give my love to Barbara."

* * *

McClellan's death marked a critical milestone in Arkansas politics. Only a week earlier, apparently robust and in good health, he had announced he would not run again for the Senate. One of Arkansas's most formidable icons was gone. The heartbeats of younger aspirants went to full throttle.

I received more than 70 viable names for replacing Senator McClellan. They ranged from Wilbur Mills and Sid McMath to J. W. Fulbright, Oren Harris, and just about every practicing lawyer in the state.

On December 9, I called Kaneaster Hodges, a Newport attorney and long-time friend who had worked on my legislative team in 1975. A licensed Methodist minister, he is still a prominent lawyer and farmer in Jackson County. In our phone conversation, I said I wanted him to succeed Senator McClellan.

He came back with a whole raft of reasons for turning me down. He had a young family, extensive farming operations, and a law practice. There was no way he could pick up and move to Washington. I asked if he wanted to deny his children the chance to say their father had served in the U.S. Senate. Did he want to keep them from spending a year in the nation's capitol, visiting the Smithsonian, and learning firsthand about the world's greatest government? I asked him to think about it overnight.

The next morning, I called him back. He said he would do it. I made the announcement that afternoon, and Kaneaster Hodges was sworn in the next day in Washington.

The minute he landed at National Airport, he found himself immersed in the Panama Canal controversy. Should the U.S. ratify treaties divesting its responsibility for the canal? The issue had become white hot. President Carter faced a reluctant Senate, and the debate promised to consume an enormous amount of their time and effort.

Both sides back home—pro and con—charged that I would exercise control over this new, young senator, and that he would follow my instructions and vote to ratify the treaties. The truth is I never once discussed with Hodges how to vote on the Panama Canal, or any other issue. He quickly adapted to the Senate and was highly respected for his work ethic, his humor, and his uncanny ability to make lasting friends.

* * *

Meanwhile, Arkansas's political scene was bustling, an inevitable result of Senator McClellan's death. Late that year, I invited Attorney General Bill Clinton to drive with me to Hot Springs where I would speak to a tourism conference. For two hours we talked in the car, discussing issues ranging from our views of Arkansas politics to our plans for the future.

Our conversation carried no particular intensity, but I did sense an air of personal sparring from both of us. Without mentioning it, we both knew a Senate race loomed. Recent polls showed him in an even match with Congressman Jim Guy Tucker, who represented Arkansas's Second District. At the same time, my Senate-race polling numbers appeared slightly healthier than theirs.

In all likelihood, I told him, I would run for the Senate, leaving the governor's office wide open for someone like Arkansas's young attorney general. He was only 31, hungry, and developing an extensive political base. The governor's race would likely begin in a few weeks or months. I told him I thought he would be the favorite.

The Associated Press had already speculated Clinton would run for governor, but he had not commented one way or the other. "Get ready," I told him. "This is your chance. You can become the state's youngest governor ever, and you can stay there for a long time."

Several of my closest friends were growing wary of the young, ambitious Clinton—a caution that continued in my camp for years. They felt it inevitable that some day we would seek the same office.

For reasons I can't fully explain, this potential match-up never concerned me. We shared too many of the same friends and similar positions in the political center. I sensed a mutual respect so real that only the most bizarre circumstances would pit one of us against the other. In the course of time, that sense proved true. We never did compete for office and remained friends.

On the other hand, Jim Guy Tucker, then 34, could some day become serious competition. Smart, ambitious, and articulate, he had won the 1974 attorney general's race following a credible record as prosecuting attorney of Pulaski and Perry counties. We also had mutual friends, including labor, teachers, and the Arkansas Democratic Party's progressive wing. This overlap proved true for central Arkansas and many surrounding counties.

People often said that Tucker reminded them of a young John F. Kennedy, square-jawed and with an infectious smile. In 1977, the national Jaycees had named him one of the country's 10 outstanding young men. As early as mid-November, an *Arkansas Democrat* columnist observed, "Jim Guy Tucker is the most serious threat to Gov. David Pryor in a potential Senate race." A University of Arkansas poll showed him with a 10-point lead over me.

Congressman Ray Thornton, 49, loomed as another potential Senate candidate. He had been my friend since University days, when he ran successfully for student body president. I had watched him campaign on the library steps, strumming a guitar, calling himself "Cowboy Ray Thornton," asking for our votes. He had gone to Yale, and was then a second-year law student. He was also a tough campaigner, a trait I clearly remembered as 1978 rolled around.

Thornton was serving as attorney general when I announced against Senator McClellan in 1972. I had given him advance warning that I would leave my Fourth Congressional District office and seek the Senate. He took the early jump, campaigning to replace me and defeating Richard Arnold in his second run for the seat.

In Congress, Thornton distinguished himself on the House Judiciary Committee, taking part in hearings and voting to impeach Richard Nixon. Stepping down from Judiciary, he took a seat on the Agriculture Committee, strengthening his position back home.

Not only a formidable speaker and vote-getter, Ray Thornton also possessed a powerful family connection: he was the nephew of power broker

"Witt" Stephens and his brother Jack. Ray's mother, Wilma Stephens Thornton, was their sister. A wealthy family, they had always remained close in their personal and political ties.

Strategically based in Grant County at the state's center, Ray could run for any race he chose. He was blessed with talent, family, money, and location. He also had hired DeLoss Walker, the Memphis-based strategic public relations expert who had helped make Dale Bumpers a household name. Walker began working with Bumpers in 1970 and had managed his 1974 campaign against Fulbright.

Thornton hinted at a Senate announcement on November 3, stating publicly he would not seek another House term. We all knew what that meant. The next day someone asked me to comment on Thornton's statement. I made clear that retirement was not my option. But I had not decided whether I would run for the Senate or another term as governor. I actually had decided. But I wasn't ready to let everyone else know.

Congressman Bill Alexander of Osceola had considered entering the Senate race, but he announced in early January he would seek a sixth term representing the First District. The other Senate candidate turned out to be A. C. Grigson, 51, a Texarkana accountant and former high school teacher who had never held public office. He said that, when people got to know him, they would see him as Senator McClellan's logical successor.

* * *

By year's end, Tucker and Thornton appeared on the verge of announcing for the Senate. As a seated governor, I had reliable sources relaying daily information from around Arkansas; they consistently reported that the two men were ready. A race between a governor and two seated Congressmen would result in a political tornado.

The open Senate seat also created a domino effect among people wanting to fill two congressional seats, an open governor's slot, and possibly an attorney general vacancy. A stampede seemed imminent for one or two, possibly four, vacant positions—unprecedented in Arkansas history.

We quietly began the Senate race January 13 when I visited Lake Ouachita to inspect the damage from a severe ice storm. The next day, still making no formal announcement, we rented a campaign headquarters—our third Little Rock location in six years—this time at Second and State Streets.

Our first campaign finance committee meeting took place the night we returned from inspecting frozen Lake Ouachita. James H. "Bum" Atkins, my long-time friend, agreed to come on as finance chairman. The next day, I attended a Nashville Chamber of Commerce banquet, followed by the 50th anniversary of Camden's paper mill. Then McGehee's "Farmers' Day" and the engineers' banquet in Little Rock, where I introduced Oklahoma Governor David Boren. After that, Russellville, Lake Village, Van Buren, Springdale, Malvern, Hot Springs, and Conway.

* * *

Why was I putting myself through this killer schedule? Since my earliest interest in politics, I had considered the U.S. Senate a special place. Serving as a senator would be the best job in the world. The best job for *me*, at any rate.

My unsuccessful attempt at defeating Senator McClellan had only made the pursuit more attractive. Maybe I needed to redeem myself. Opportunities to seek an open Senate seat come rarely in a person's lifetime, especially in the South where turnover has traditionally proven rare. I had to do it, and I was ready. Of equal importance, Barbara was ready. Both of us knew full well the gruesome schedule that lay ahead, and the stress it would place on our lives.

Ray Thornton announced on January 10. Two days later he said that Archie Schaffer, Dale Bumpers's nephew, would come on as his campaign manager. Schaffer had directed all of his uncle's campaigns, and served as his administrative assistant in both Little Rock and Washington.

Bumpers quickly made it clear: Schaffer's heading the Thornton campaign in no way indicated Archie's uncle's preference. Still, the appointment sent immediate notice of a real contest. I should get my own organization in shape—and fast.

With Thornton definitely in the mix, I wanted to gain support from as many Stephens people as possible, or at least to neutralize them. My first strategic move was to secure Wayne Hampton's help. The state representative from Stuttgart, he was a powerful legislator and a supporter during my four years as governor.

Hampton was also a former member of both the Highway and the Game and Fish Commissions, and long-time ally in Witt and Jack Stephens's banking and investment businesses. In fact, they had placed Wayne on their Farmers' State Bank board in Stuttgart. For years he had also ardently supported Orval Faubus.

On Friday night, January 8, I spoke at the Gillette coon supper, an annual must for any Arkansas politician planning to stay in office. Everyone shows up for this first post-New Year's celebration. Just as it ended, I caught up with Wayne on our way to the door. I asked for a quick visit before I drove back to Little Rock. He suggested we meet in front of the courthouse in half an hour. The state trooper pulled our car up next to his, and Wayne got in the back seat with me. That night was country dark, as Barbara would describe it.

Wayne liked being addressed directly and without protocol. "Wayne," I said, "I need your support in my race for the Senate. We've been off and on in different camps, but I admire and respect you, and you've been an ally since I've been governor. I need you."

Wayne didn't hesitate. "Governor, there's a vacancy coming up on the Game and Fish Commission. Are you committed to anyone for that appointment?"

"Do you have somebody in mind?" I asked.

"Yes, my son Rick," he said.

"I'm committed now," I told him. "That appointment is his."

I announced Rick Hampton to the Commission on January 11, as a replacement for Kaneaster Hodges, who had to resign when he went to the Senate.

Word spread that the Hamptons had clearly thrown their support to David Pryor. Many found it hard to believe, but apparently true, that Wayne would cross the Stephens brothers and not support Ray Thornton. Four days later, Wayne picked up the local paper and read he had been dropped from the Farmers' State Bank board.

Politics, as they say, does make strange bedfellows. Sheriff Marlin Hawkins became another early member of the Pryor campaign team. In fact, he had supported me in the 1972 Senate race, and in 1978 he proved even more determined. His total domination of Conway County politics was legendary. "Go to every funeral in the county," he would advise young politicians. Another rule: "Don't burn your bridges; you never know when you might need to cross back over the river."

Sheriff Hawkins was a "Yellow Dog Democrat." In 1972, he even came close to carrying the county for George McGovern against Richard Nixon. The Saturday night before the election, he called me and asked, "Do you think I should bring in the county for McGovern?" The only reason he didn't was that he feared Arkansas would go heavily for Nixon, and Conway County would stand alone in the Democratic column. This might hurt his county, so he called off his people the night before the election. By a small margin, Conway County came in for Nixon.

Sheriff Hawkins didn't much believe in election reform. He said that whatever it takes to elect Democrats to public office, that's where he would end up. He had called me during the McClellan race to pledge his support, much to my surprise. He was sure that Senator McClellan was actually a Republican in Democrat's clothing. That's when he broke with the Stephenses.

On February 18, the Pryor living room once again became the setting for a political announcement. A few days before, Barbara had sent word to close friends and family about an important news conference taking place at the governor's mansion.

As always, she and our three boys stood with me. In an indirect allusion to Thornton and Tucker, I stressed how, in my experience as governor, I had come to know all of Arkansas, not just parts of it. "I've been there," I said.

Only one question from the press still comes to mind:

"How will this Senate race differ from the one in 1972?"

My answer: "This time I'm going to win."

Chapter 39
Back to the Hill

Polls were shifting in all directions. Five days after my announcement, one poll showed me with 65%, Tucker with 27%, and Thornton with 13%. At another point, I was down by 1%, with Tucker leading and Thornton third.

After holding a rally at Little Rock's Camelot Inn, Thornton came on strong in a third poll. He introduced a series of impressive, folksy five-minute radio interviews that ran every three hours. Called "Coffee with Ray," each little show gave him an opportunity to answer one or two questions. That's just time enough to impress people but not get into serious trouble. Why hadn't I thought of that?

Even though my four years as governor had left scars, I felt I had proved a decent steward of the public's trust and had achieved a solid record. I had seen the state through a mean recession without raising taxes, presided over a scandal-free administration, and had made solid, widely diverse appointments. We had helped protect the environment, brought balance to state office-leasing activity, and prevented private influences from penetrating prison and state police decisions. On top of all that, I would be leaving the state with a $40 million surplus.

On the other side of the balance sheet, I had to accept certain disappointments as well. Teachers' salaries had not risen significantly, state colleges and universities were seeing only nominal growth, and labor unions remained dismayed at my calling out the National Guard during the Pine Bluff firemen's strike.

Thornton's entering the race forced me to share my base in the 20-county southern tier. We had each served as the Fourth District's representative in Congress. Finally, even though David Solomon had performed impressively as a highway commissioner, lingering resentment existed in the east for my not reappointing Maurice Smith.

Normally during our campaigns, Barbara and I would politick together as a couple. Extremely effective and a great listener, she was crucial to each campaign. She could regale small groups with stories about living in a fishbowl and, at the same time, raising three sons and performing the first lady's duties. Even now, I find it hard to believe that she could balance those demands at the same time. She possessed superb political instincts and an ability to analyze human behavior.

As March turned into April, we found a need to split up our efforts, scheduling ourselves in different towns, often at opposite ends of the state. We worked long days at factory gates, coffee shops, civic club lunches, and chamber dinners from early morning through the night. Barbara always had a sixth sense about our trouble spots and how to fix them. She carried in her head the names of friends in each town. She could rattle off our county coordinators and not miss a soul.

On April 15 at its Hot Springs convention, the Committee on Political Education (COPE), the AFL-CIO's political arm, endorsed Jim Guy Tucker. My appearance before the committee proved a tough confrontation, even openly hostile. In their statement, COPE members vowed to "permanently retire David Pryor from politics." Brushing aside Thornton's request for a dual endorsement, the committee focused squarely on Tucker.

Only minutes before my scheduled speech, my friend and machinists-union ally Tommy Landers found two union members mounting signs that read "David Pryor—Strike Breaker!"

"What are you guys doing with those signs?" Landers asked them. Tommy and I had slogged through many labor trenches together. We understood each other entirely.

"We're going to parade them around the convention floor when Pryor gets up to speak," one of them replied.

"You're not parading anything," Landers came back. "And if you try it, I'll whip your ass in front of the entire AFL-CIO convention."

The signs went in the dumpster.

My speech was mercifully brief, featuring only a few references to our shared concerns and successful fights together. Preempting any planned attack against me, I brought up the Pine Bluff incident, when I had replaced striking firemen with the National Guard. The union posited that using the Guard for two or three days made sense, but six weeks was not acceptable. My remarks fell with a thud. As soon as I left the convention center, a roll call, amid thunderous applause, endorsed Jim Guy Tucker. Bruce Lindsey and I stopped for a milkshake at the Dairy Queen and drove in silence to Murfreesboro, where I rode in the Pine Tree Parade.

Two weeks earlier, the Arkansas Education Association had also endorsed Tucker, even though Thornton's mother had been a career teacher and was still an active association member. For Tucker, these endorsements meant votes as well as money, workers, and foot soldiers in the weeks ahead. For me, it was an assault to my ego. For years I had enjoyed the support of organized labor and public school teachers. I couldn't help considering the votes for Tucker as bills of divorcement. At the same time, the *Blytheville Courier-News* noted that, even with this backing, Tucker's position didn't look all that good. In fact, the paper said, polls hadn't scored positive numbers for any candidate. In still another poll, I dropped two points, Tucker fell nine, while Thornton picked up six. We could count on no reliable predictions in this race.

A *Democrat* editorial suggested I had readily shed the labor badge, which I now saw as a liability: "Pryor may have decided to work toward the public divorce that the AFL-CIO so obligingly made final at Hot Springs." But that view was all wrong. I had long valued labor's support and lost it only with regret. At the same time—in spite of COPE's decision—I knew Arkansas's working people well and felt certain I would retain a big block of their votes. And, sure enough, I did.

Election day hovers as the strangest of all days for a politician. We simply pass time in one frivolous way or another until the polls close. Nothing else to say or do, nowhere to go, only a constant hush. We wait, and wait, and wait.

Unable to sit still, on election morning May 30, I campaigned on Little Rock's Rodney Parham Road. A state trooper approached, telling me I had an emergency call from the governor's mansion. I scurried home, thinking some terrible tragedy had occurred. In the mansion's driveway stood a process server holding a subpoena. A Fort Smith preacher was suing me for allowing a local theatre to show what he judged a highly pornographic movie (the title unmentioned).

I actually breathed a sigh of relief. I went inside, called key supporters across the state, took a long shower and a short nap, and then prepared for the returns. I figured we would know something in three hours.

But even at 9:00 that night no one could tell who would make the runoff. I had carried 36% of the vote, Ray Thornton 35%, and Jim Guy Tucker 34%. By midnight, some rural boxes remained uncounted, and in north Arkansas's mountain counties you could bet everyone had gone to bed. We would have to wait until late the next morning, with almost a guarantee of facing a runoff. So

I thanked my supporters, a huge crowd still gathered at the Sheraton, said good night, and went to bed.

Shortly after dawn, I slipped on warm-ups and went down to the kitchen. No one was there. I walked out to the state police security's guard shack. The one trooper on duty slept in his chair.

Going back inside, I called the Associated Press to see if I had won, lost, or made a runoff. By a meager few votes, I led the ticket with 199,000; Tucker ranked second with 186,000; and Thornton a hair's breadth third with 183,000. Grigson came in with 8,000. Tucker and I faced a two-week runoff. It would become the longest, roughest 14 days of my life.

That night, Barbara and I drove from the mansion to Central High School. We joined a huge crowd in a hot gymnasium, watching our son Dee and his fellow seniors walk across the stage to receive their high school diplomas. I couldn't help but go through my mental Pryor vs. Tucker playbook. At the same time, I wondered why I was putting myself and my family through yet another high-intensity political contest. Looking at Dee in his impressive cap and gown, I wondered if he didn't deserve a more normal father, somebody with an ordinary job and plenty of time to spend with his children.

Meanwhile, I clearly had to pick up as many Thornton votes as humanly possible. The next day, I called Ray for his help, telling him that Barbara and I were on our way to Sheridan, his hometown. He told me he wasn't yet ready to endorse Tucker or me, but he thought I would win a large number of his supporters on my own.

We worked the Grant County courthouse, interviewed with the Sheridan *Headlight*, circled the town square, and called on the bank. We headed back to Little Rock and began the phone calls to plan a runoff effort. Do I attack or wait to be attacked? What other races would share the ballot? I wanted a county-by-county analysis of all returns. Do we spend time and resources where we're weakest—or strongest?

The next morning, I opened my press conference with a discussion of Tucker's record, suggesting he voted more often with northern liberals than with southerners closer to home. The *Northwest Arkansas Times* sneered that my comments resembled "an old-fashioned Dixiecrat-style attack."

The next day, Tucker said he would not criticize my record and intended to campaign on the issues. A *Democrat* analysis suggested that, by consistently referring to me as "David," he hoped to kill me with kindness. Our exchanges remained relatively civilized for the next two days.

Then on June 5, Tucker held a stunning press conference. He asserted that Jack Williams, my campaign manager, had approached Dr. John Pickett, Public Service Commission chairman. Tucker charged that Williams had asked Pickett to favor the Arkansas Oklahoma Gas Company in an upcoming rate-increase decision. The gas company was owned by Witt Stephens, Thornton's uncle and, since the runoff, my supporter.

Tucker's implication was clear: David Pryor was willing to interfere in a rate case as a favor to a wealthy backer. In fact, I had never discussed the gas issue with Williams or anyone else. In any conversation with John Pickett, Williams acted strictly on his own. Williams admitted he had discussed the case with Pickett, his long-time friend, but only requesting a delayed decision until after the runoff election. He said he simply hoped to see the rate case taken out of politics.

At my request, Bill Wilson and Bill Overton met with Jack Williams to get the truth. These were two of the best legal and political minds in our camp—in the state, for that matter—and among my best and oldest friends. I trusted them to ferret out the facts and advise me on what to do.

Wilson and Overton reported back that I could safely deny any wrongdoing on Jack's behalf. An old and trusted friend, Jack was an astute Texarkana businessman who had worked hard in Miller County on each of my elections. Wilson and Overton suggested I call an immediate press conference in Little Rock and douse the fire. Following that, I should hold another press conference in Texarkana, affirming confidence in my campaign manager. Anything less would add fuel to Tucker's charges.

On Tuesday, halfway through the runoff period, I held my fifth news conference in six days. I said, while I didn't condone my campaign manager's actions, I wanted him to remain in charge of the campaign. I also called for a full investigation conducted either by Lee Munson, the prosecuting attorney for Pulaski and Perry counties, or by Bill Clinton, the state attorney general.

I didn't know whether my position had convinced the public. Meanwhile, Witt Stephens refused to get involved. "I'm down here trying to haul hay and take care of my cattle," he said from his Prattsville farm.

Munson held a news conference on Saturday, saying that, after five hours of interviews, he found no criminal laws violated and no wrong committed. We hoped the public was paying enough attention to take his decision to heart.

For the next two days, we flew from one airport to another, crisscrossing the state for rallies and press conferences. We cut new television and radio spots. My campaign, in spite of the Williams-Pickett glitch, seemed energized, hitting on all cylinders. Barbara and I, though bone-weary, took heart at our statewide supporters' unshakable loyalty.

On Tuesday night, less than an hour before the polls closed, I told an AP reporter: "I wouldn't bet two dollars on this election, win or lose." As things turned out, Ray Thornton never endorsed anyone, and Grigson called me "the lesser of two evils."

Very early on election evening, Hayes Sullivan called the governor's mansion. Results were in from his tiny home box in Burdette, Mississippi County, always a state bellwether. Everyone in town had cast their votes by 5:00 p.m., retiring for the night. Results: Pryor 63, Tucker 4.

I knew things would be all right.

The *Pine Bluff Commercial* saw it as a short night, after all, despite the runoff's sound and fury. The editorial correctly suggested that the difficult decisions had come in the regular primary two weeks earlier.

By some 55% of the vote, I had become the Democratic nominee for the U.S. Senate, carrying 58 of the state's 75 counties and receiving 262,000 votes to Tucker's 217,000. Even though Tucker had carried Pulaski County in the regular primary election, I took it by more than 5,000 in the runoff. Interestingly, the runoff vote total was down about 95,000 from the 577,000 cast on May 30. One analysis suggested that Tucker's charge against Jack Williams may have boomeranged.

A UPI reporter stopped me at the mansion's back door, asking how it felt to join a wave of "New South" Democrats in Washington. I told him I didn't feel part of any particularly new wave. I was glad the election was over, happy and relieved, and looking to buy a car. For the first time in four years, our family wouldn't have state troopers to drive us around. And I was trying to rake up enough money to place a down payment on a house. In Washington.

Photo Section II

George Fisher cartoon depicts Governor Pryor bruised and bandaged from one 1977 legislative session, hearing aide Don Harrell relay the media's suggestion that the legislature might return to a new session. Courtesy of UA Special Collections.

Governor David Pryor consults with Shirley McFarlin and Parker Westbrook outside the governor's office, c. 1977.

Campaign advertisement spoof (1984) based on popular movie Ghostbusters graphics, featuring (l. to r.) Tommy Robinson, candidate for Congress, David Pryor, candidate for Governor, and Bill Clinton, candidate for Attorney General. Photo courtesy of UA Special Collections.

"Controversial Issues" facing the state legislative Joint Interim Committee and Governor Pryor in January, 1977, included a representation of the small bag of funds available to solve the state's problems. Cartoon by Jon Kennedy. Courtesy of UA Special Collections.

Governor Pryor addressing students at Henderson State University, 1977. Photo courtesy Pryor family.

Pryor family photo following 1975 swearing-in as governor. (Left to right) Dee, Scott, Barbara, Mark, David, and David's Mother, Susie. Photo courtesy of UA Special Collections.

Governor Pryor inspecting Cummins Prison Farm, c 1978. Photo courtesy of UA Special Collections.

Vice President Walter Mondale visits with Barbara Pryor entering the White House, c. 1977. Photograph courtesy the White House.

Governor Pryor and Arkansas State Police dignitaries are given a tour of a customized Ward school bus for public safety education. Photo courtesy Pryor family.

Pryor as a delegate to the 1976 Democratic National Convention where he made the speech seconding Walter Mondale as the Vice Presidential nominee. Photo courtesy of UA Special Collections.

George Fisher's 1978 cartoon about the difficulty of running for the U.S. Senate while a sitting governor. Courtesy of UA Special Collections.

Don Harrell (l.) and Governor Pryor in the governor's office, state capitol building, 1977.
Photo courtesy of UA Special Collections.

Governor Pryor (center) with President Gerald R. Ford to his left, and representative John
Paul Hammerschmidt, 1975. Photo courtesy of UA Special Collections.

Reception for Congressman and presidential candidate Morris Udall at the governor's mansion. (Left to right) Arvajean Jordan of Russellville, President of Democratic Women of Arkansas, Barbara and David Pryor, Udall, 1975. Photo courtesy of UA Special Collections.

President Jimmy Carter greets newly-elected Senator Pryor at the White House, January 1979. Photograph courtesy the White House.

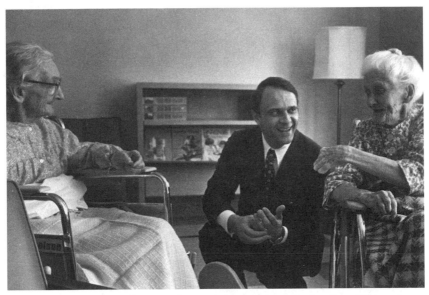

Pryor visiting with nursing home residents as his Senate Aging Study collects life-experiences and data from patients, coast-to-coast. Photo courtesy of UA Special Collections.

Pryor opens bags of mail in support of his fight for the elderly, September 11, 1980. Photo courtesy of UA Special Collections.

David Pryor (r.) and J. W. Wade, Jr., championing a "Taxpayers Bill of Rights" to give citizens respect and due process in dealings with the IRS, April 1, 1987. Photo courtesy of UA Special Collections.

Pryor (at podium) presents thousands of letters from citizens in support of Taxpayers Bill of Rights. Other Senators present include Al Damato, Harry Reid, Thad Cochran, Max Bauchus, Carl Levin, Charles Grassley. Photo courtesy of UA Special Collections.

Governor David Pryor chatting with U.S. Senator John L. McClellan, following the Senator's address to the General Assembly, 1977. Photo courtesy Pryor family.

Arkansas's U.S. House of Representatives delegation, c. 1971: (l. to r.) Bill Alexander, Wilbur Mills, John Paul Hammerschmidt, and David Pryor. Photo courtesy of UA Special Collections.

Pryor (l.) listens as his question is answered in a meeting of the Senate Select Committee on Impeachment. Fellow Senators Dennis DeConcini (of Arizona) and Howell Heflin (of Alabama) make notes. Photo courtesy Pryor family.

Pryor (right) is guest of NBC's Meet the Press, hosted by Bernard Kalb (center), September 22, 1985. Photo courtesy of UA Special Collections.

Pryor announcing bid for re-election to U.S. Senate, January 9, 1984, in the dining room of his mother's home in Camden. Photo courtesy of UA Special Collections.

Pryor's student interns and staff burn the midnight oil in preparation of hearings of the Senate Select Committee on Aging, September 18, 1980. Photo courtesy of UA Special Collections.

(Left to right) Federal Judge Henry Woods, Senator Dale Bumpers, Federal Judge Richard S. Arnold, and Governor Pryor visit following Woods' swearing-in ceremony, 1980. Photograph Courtesy Pryor Family.

Pryor being greeted by President Ronald Reagan in the Oval Office, 1982. Photo courtesy of UA Special Collections.

*Portrait of Arkansas former governors and lieutenant governor Winthrop P. Rockefeller, c.
2001. From left: Pryor, Clinton, White, McMath, Rockefeller, Faubus, and Bumpers.*

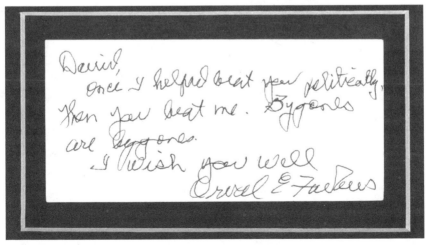

*When Pryor was in intensive care following his 1992 bypass surgery, former Governor
Orval Faubus left this conciliatory note when hospital staff denied him admission to Pryor's
ICU room. The now-framed note occupies a place of distinction in Pryor's office today.
Photo courtesy Pryor family.*

George Fisher, the beloved Arkansas Gazette cartoonist, immortalized Governor Pryor's proposed "Arkansas Plan" with a signature coon dog. When Fisher died in 2003, Pryor was asked to deliver one of two eulogies. Journalist Ernie Dumas delivered the other. Photo courtesy of UA Special Collections.

David Pryor with former Vice President Al Gore. Photo courtesy of UA Special Collections.

David Pryor speaking at the Kennedy School of Government at Harvard University, 2006. Photo courtesy of UA Special Collections.

Pryor family photograph, c. 2007. Back row (l. to r.): Judith, David, Jr. ("Dee"), Barbara, Adams, Jill, Mark. Front row: Scott, Devin, Diane, Hampton, Senator Pryor, Porter. Photo courtesy Pryor family.

Chapter 40
The Upper Chamber

By October 1978, the Pryor family's transition from Little Rock to Washington was in full swing. The Clintons were measuring rooms and designing drapes for the governor's mansion. We watched as the state capitol staff began their exodus to other jobs. Our budget proposals, prepared a few months earlier, became irrelevant. No one would pay attention to an outgoing governor's thoughts on anything, much less budgets, a farewell address, or advice to a new administration. Out with the old, in with the new ...

Among a mountain of cardboard boxes, I sat down one morning with Ed Penick in the mansion's east conference room. A member of one of Arkansas's oldest and most respected families, Penick served as president of Worthen Bank and Trust, an institution his ancestors established over a century before.

"Ed," I told him, "I've asked you to come by this morning to discuss a most embarrassing situation. In about two months we're moving to Washington, and I'm flat broke. My governor's salary for the past four years has put me below the poverty line, and we have to buy a house and a car. Would your bank make me a loan?"

Ever the banker, Penick said that he just happened to have a blank promissory note in his pocket, and within 15 minutes Barbara and I had co-signed a document that temporarily put us back on our feet. We were ready to go.

We traveled to Washington in mid-November. After long searching and detailed negotiations—interest rates were moving toward an all-time high—we settled on a house in Bethesda, Maryland. A neighborhood not too far from the Capitol, it featured good public schools and children close to our sons' ages. Dee was a student at Hendrix College in Conway, and Scott, 13, entered Western Junior High School, not far from our house. Mark opted to finish that fall semester at Central High School. For several weeks, he lived with the Houston Nutt family in Little Rock. He joined us for the spring semester, enrolling at Bethesda's Walt Whitman High School.

We were determined to hold on to the two younger boys for as long as they would let us. Of course, I knew this couldn't last forever. Our family was seeing the inevitable shifts and cracks that come with adolescence and growing up. We would have to see how this major move would change those things we couldn't control, even if we tried.

The first Saturday in December, we had held a "Moving to Washington" sale at the governor's mansion. But tons of furniture, files, and household items still waited to move with us. For years, the mansion had depended upon state prison inmates to make repairs and perform yard work. With the help of two inmates, Barbara, the boys, and I packed up boxes in the mansion basement, eventually loading them onto a U-Haul truck.

Within a week, following a thorough mansion repainting and cleanup, the Clintons moved in. In the upstairs family quarters, I had taped a large bottle of Tylenol to the bathroom mirror. My note said, "Dear Bill. Good luck. You're going to need this. David."

On January 15, 1979, Dale Bumpers escorted me down the center aisle of the Senate chamber, where Vice President Walter Mondale gave me the oath of office, inducting me as a member of the 96th Congress. A large number of Arkansans, and many living in Washington, joined us for a reception two blocks away at the Monocle Restaurant.

As soon as we had unpacked and settled the family in our new home, Barbara became immersed with Senate wives' activities, arts programs, the Kennedy Center, and Ford's Theatre. She was asked to plan special events for the Pen-Faulkner Awards, honoring distinguished fiction writers at the Folger Shakespeare Library. She also became active in the Motion Picture Association of America and, with its director Jack Valenti, began co-hosting a luncheon for Senate spouses. She had re-established her niche. In fact, a *Washington Post* society reporter wrote a story titled, "Welcome Back, Barbara" for the paper's Sunday edition.

My committee assignments turned out surprisingly similar to those I had held in the House 12 years earlier. Along with every new Senate member, I had asked for the Finance Committee and its jurisdiction over taxes, trade, and health legislation. This is the major action committee, a counterpart to the House's Ways and Means. But with seniority and previous commitments firmly in place, I would have to wait five years before landing that key slot. Instead, I was assigned to three other panels: Agriculture, Government Affairs, and the Special Committee on Aging.

That first Senate year, I learned the crucial need for patience. It would serve me for years to come. I also learned the nature of Senate decorum. The rules differed from those in the House. I would have to become familiar with new committee regulations, procedures governing filibuster, and a slower, more deliberate pace. The House's quick response and bluster simply didn't exist on Capitol Hill's other side. Entering the House chamber resembled walking into a gym during a fierce basketball game's final minutes. Heightened by intense competition, it proved always raucous and a little unwieldy.

Smaller, hushed, intimate, and in good taste, the Senate chamber possesses a sense of history so pervasive you feel tradition and heritage in the very air. The merest whisper will ricochet off the marble walls. That February, I delivered my maiden speech—a loud and ringing endorsement of American farmers, and concern for their struggles. Afterward, Senator Howard Metzenbaum of Ohio stopped by my desk and counseled, "No need to shout, David."

My thinking and actions had adjusted with age and experience as governor, but I hadn't charted a political philosophy of my own. My Senate campaign victory suggested that I fell somewhere between my opponents: Tucker (a liberal) and Thornton (a conservative). It was anyone's guess where I would land on most issues. In all frankness, I was asking that question myself.

Near the end of my first Senate year, The Christian Voice, a national conservative political lobby, rated me 14% on abortion, prayer in schools, and forced busing. The group gave John Paul Hammerschmidt, my Republican House colleague, a perfect score. Republican Ed Bethune, Arkansas's new Second District Congressman, received a 90% rating. Dale Bumpers and Congressman Bill Alexander each garnered 8%.

My heart sank when I read figures, percentages, and projections of this kind. It seemed that 1979 would become open season for assigning the Arkansas delegation either liberal or conservative ratings. I hoped Arkansans would judge me on each individual issue's merit, and how I voted. At the same time, I wasn't naive. I knew labels, ratings and percentages offered ready handles for defining any politician holding office.

I saw myself in tune with "progressive" to "liberal" Southerners such as Dale Bumpers and other Democrats. We had freed ourselves from the old Southern politics of race and segregation. But the political sands were shifting in the South and throughout the country. Conservative Republicans presented a rising force, especially in my region. Little chance existed that I could satisfy the so-called Christian right with its school prayer and abortion agenda.

When I came to the Senate, Jimmy Carter had served as president for two years, and his administration's newness was wearing thin. Our relationship wasn't warm—Carter was a tough person to get close to—but it remained friendly enough. We shared common ground: former Southern governors agreeing on most Democratic Party principles.

When Carter came to Arkansas in early 1976, running for president, I invited him to the mansion for breakfast. We sat around the family room table with my son Mark. After we had ushered Carter out the front door to his car, I turned to Mark and said, "You know, he's a fine person, but I feel sorry for him."

"Why?" asked Mark.

"Well, because he's out there thinking he can actually be president."

Mark said, "He's going to be president, Dad." It was a simple declarative sentence.

And I said, "What are you talking about?"

Mark, a seventh-grader, replied, "Just what I said. He's going to be president." With that, he took off for school, all confidence and assurance.

Carter was impressed when I later told him that story. Then, one night he called about some legislation he wanted me to sponsor. But before we started our conversation, he said, "Hold on. First I want to talk to Mark."

Jimmy Carter has remained an active, exemplary ex-president, advocating world peace, writing books on faith in politics, and taking part in Habitat for Humanity. In the White House, he made impressive progress on Middle East accords and advances in human rights.

But he surprised me sometimes, displaying an edgy, personal pride that contradicted my impression of a shy and unassuming gentleman farmer. Once, I joined other governors from rice-producing states, asking for an appointment to discuss P. L. 480, the Food for Peace program. We couldn't understand why we were having trouble scheduling the meeting, especially since our numbers included prominent Democrats such as California's Jerry Brown.

We found out later that Carter didn't want to provide Brown a press opportunity by visiting the White House. He still resented Brown, years after he had challenged Carter in the Democratic primaries.

Carter's administration experienced one of its lowest points with the fight over the Panama Canal treaties. When I arrived in 1979, he had just pushed through these unilateral agreements. Many conservatives considered this literally handing over, without any recompense, a valuable resource we should have retained.

Dale Bumpers and Kaneaster Hodges strongly defended the treaties. This demonstrated to me that Arkansas voters can tolerate their representatives' reasonable stances, even when they don't agree with them. "That vote will beat Dale Bumpers next time around." This general gossip traveled through the state's barber shops and court houses. But two years later, Bumpers won re-election by his strongest margin.

Arkansans in general care less about "liberal" and "conservative," and more about fairness and equal treatment for everyone. For many years, the state's voters gave Senator J. W. Fulbright a wide berth on foreign affairs. Not always agreeing with him, especially as the Vietnam War issue flared, they still respected his intelligence, integrity, and independence. The Fulbright name's association with Arkansas brought people a sense of pride. I could only hope their tolerance would continue during my Senate tenure.

* * *

In that first year, I received close scrutiny from the press, my colleagues, and voters who had sent me to Washington. This was no surprise. New senators are always judged by their voting patterns, alignments, committee work, floor speeches, and communication skills. It resembles a governor's fishbowl, except people care less about the personal, daily minutiae and more about our public statements and votes.

A geographic factor also comes into play: Washington sits more than a thousand miles from Little Rock. While the glare is intense, it lacks the steady spotlight shining every day on a seated governor. As governor, you're number one—as senator, you're one of 100.

It's critical for a new senator to choose a staff that's knowledgeable and responsive to constituents. This means answering the mail and returning phone calls. I was always a little amused—and annoyed—by new legislative assistants who wanted to "make policy" but thought they didn't have to return their phone calls. My friend Dan Tate, now a successful Washington lawyer, held his first Congressional job with Senator Herman Talmadge of Georgia. Dan recalled how one day Talmadge told him that he had heard good things about Dan's staff work.

"Everything's favorable," he told Dan, "except for one thing. I hear that you're always behind in answering the mail. It's piling up on your desk."

"Oh, Senator, don't worry about that," Tate replied. "It's just the nut mail."

"Listen, Tate," Senator Talmadge said. "Don't ever forget this. We couldn't get elected without the nut vote. Now get back to your desk and answer that mail."

I fortunately went to Washington with a handful of staff members already in place. Ray Scott, Bruce Lindsey, and Ann Pride took jobs similar to those mastered earlier in Little Rock. Vince Ancell, a member of the governor's mansion security detail, came on as a legislative correspondent. Active together in the governor's office, my staffers knew just about everybody in Arkansas. Even better, they knew me and my quirks. Still, we had to remind ourselves that these might be the same constituents, but we were now in a different place of doing business.

We also wanted to make my Russell Building office appear like home. This classic facility goes back to the 20th century's early years, with high ceilings, marble mantels, and large windows that afford sweeping views of the Capitol or downtown Washington. The expansive rooms even resemble an art gallery. With Barbara's insistence, we filled the suite with Arkansas artists' paintings, lent for indefinite time periods. This provided a unique means of showing off our artists' talents and generated considerable conversation among visitors from Arkansas and elsewhere.

We fortunately inherited Carmie Henry and Susie James, both former staff members in the McClellan and Hodges office. I convinced Doug Jackson—a film producer who had worked with Barbara, and with TV producers Harry Thomason and Linda Bloodworth—to move to Washington and supervise office operations. A master accountant and record keeper, he was also a fierce Pryor loyalist. He ultimately became an authority on military, intelligence, and security issues.

Henry Woods, a Hot Springs native and Capitol Hill veteran who had worked for Congressman Bill Alexander, joined the office early in my first year. A technology whiz, he took over organizing the back office. In no time, Henry became a master of mailing lists that included friends and interest groups.

Within hours of my floor speech or committee statement, he would target individuals and groups concerned about the issue, and send them copies.

Henry also put together a model intern program, a combination of training and instruction that, over the years, brought hundreds of college-age Arkansans to Washington. Most joined us for the summer term, but we also included students enrolled at Georgetown or George Washington University who wanted part-time Hill experience during regular school semesters.

With considerable coaxing, we convinced Anna Thomas to return to Capitol Hill and help us set up our office. Anna had worked for Senator Fulbright for many years, staying with him when he left the Senate to join a Washington law firm. Highly experienced in the State Department, she had served in Cambodia, and later in Lebanon, with the U. S. Foreign Service. Always a class act, Anna brought a calm, settling influence to our new, sometimes raw situation.

In the early 1980s, one senator told an informal group of Democratic colleagues he had a sorry staff. I've never heard anyone lambast his own staff in such a way. When he finished speaking, he asked us to provide names of possible replacements. The room remained dead still. Here was a colleague openly admitting his own failure, unable to put together competent people to serve his constituency.

I wasn't surprised that his staff was falling short. I was shocked that our colleague would demean his staff in such a public way. We understood when, in the next election, he joined the Former Members of Congress Club.

Sometimes competition arises between two senators from the same state, even when they're in the same political party. Maybe I should say *especially* when they're members of the same party. They compete for local press attention at home and try to outdo one another when introducing bills benefitting the state. At one point during my first Senate term, two strong-willed, northeastern same-state senators made no secret that they despised each other.

Fortunately, Dale Bumpers and I remained friends, Senate partners with similar Arkansas experiences and backgrounds. Maybe we differed in temperament and approach to legislation—even sometimes in government philosophy—but we had both served as governor, with firsthand knowledge of the state and its people. Perhaps even more important, Betty Bumpers and Barbara had shared much of the same history, not only as governors' wives, but as young women growing up in northwest Arkansas.

* * *

Bumpers became both mentor and colleague in our 18 Senate years together. I can't recall a time when we challenged each other. Which was good for me. Dale was eloquent in his arguments. A cardinal rule in Arkansas politics: never get up and try to speak after Dale Bumpers has had the floor.

I came to feel close to the Bumpers family as well. One night on the Senate floor, Senator Jeremiah Denton of Alabama tore into the Peace Links organization and its founder, Betty Bumpers. He couldn't have misunderstood more thoroughly this active coalition of prominent women dedicated to ending war and the hazards and costs of empire-building.

Denton was a former Navy admiral who had served in Vietnam and spent four years in a North Vietnamese prison. A staunch conservative, he had come to office in 1980 on a tide of pro-Reagan sentiment. His blistering floor speech attacked Peace Links as a Communist-inspired organization undermining our nation's strength.

It was late in the evening. I was in my office, listening to floor proceedings over the speaker when I heard this personal and unwarranted attack on Betty Bumpers. I raced to the Capitol on the subway, ran up to the Senate floor, and launched into a debate with Denton, questioning his facts and assertions. It never occurred to me not to defend Betty Bumpers and Peace Links, their work and accomplishments. I know that, if the tables had been turned, Dale Bumpers would have done the same for me.

Dale and I, of course, didn't agree on everything. For example, we took different positions on rationing gas. He favored it, believing it would help the nation. I opposed it, arguing it would hurt the state's farmers. I favored a 5% increase in defense spending, while Bumpers opposed it. And when I supported abolishing the Electoral College, he argued that small states were better protected with the system in place. I opposed producing nerve gas in Pine Bluff, and he said that he could support it as a deterrent to the Soviet Union's military designs.

But no animosity existed between us, and any question concerning a Bumpers/Pryor split was simply speculation. This held true even when political pundits and reporters attempted to drive a wedge between us.

A *Benton Courier* editorial raised the issue in early 1979. The writer said that, even though my early political runs were on the "liberal" side, when compared to Dale Bumpers, I could only be considered a "conservative."

Comparisons of this kind used to drive Bumpers crazy, he confessed at one point. "How can they say I'm liberal and you're moderate, or conservative?" he asked.

"I just talk slower, Dale," I told him.

The *Arkansas Gazette*'s Washington reporter Tom Hamburger, who later became a *Los Angeles Times* political writer, once drew a stark comparison between us. He said Bumpers found the Senate frustrating because he liked being a chief executive, and the Senate's seniority system irritated him. This description was accurate, although years later, Bumpers admitted that he came to like the Senate and how it operated. The longer he stayed, the more appealing the seniority system became.

On the other hand, Hamburger suggested I was living up to my image as "a nice guy," a master of political symbols, determined to offend no one. "Pryor," he concluded, "is getting excellent press and honing his political skills."

Dale and I were entertained by such contrasts. He liked to greet Arkansas visitors with me standing by his side, almost like an acolyte. "You want to hear about two really great and distinguished Arkansas senators?" he would ask the group, pretending to begin a bragging session. Then he'd draw surprised chuckles, saying, "O. K. Let me tell you about Hattie Caraway and Joe T. Robinson."

Chapter 41
Cars, Consultants, College and Soviets

During our first days in Washington, I dialed Bruce Lindsey, my legislative director, early one Saturday morning rousing him from bed. He and his family had just moved into their Alexandria home, and I thought he needed a break from unpacking boxes and crates.

"Bruce, if you're free for a couple of hours," I asked, "will you go with me to buy a car? I'm thinking of looking at an older model Mercedes that's advertised in today's paper. It looks really cheap."

"Sure," he said, "I'll be right over."

By that night, I had bought a six-year-old, dark-blue Mercedes. The dealer assured me this one-owner cream puff would drive trouble-free for years. Entirely on an impulse, Bruce bought a seven-year-old, light-blue Mercedes. For each of us, these lemons turned into total financial disasters, nearly sending both our families into bankruptcy. Within a year, I had thrown in the towel, asking my friend Bob Carver in Mena to send me a new Oldsmobile.

Two weeks after my swearing in, I took a cab one morning to my Russell Building office. (My car, of course, was in the shop.) A rainy day, few taxis were available, but I luckily secured one.

On our way down Connecticut Avenue, the driver spotted two men futilely hailing cabs from the sidewalk. He asked if we could offer them a ride. Maybe they were headed to the Hill. I said of course, and we picked up the two new passengers.

They were professional consultants working on a government contract. In the late 1970s, the role of private consultants, contractors, and advisers in government was just beginning to take off. Later known as "Beltway Bandits," they represented a new class of so-called specialists whose Capital Beltway offices surrounded Washington.

The two rain-soaked consultants were advising the Energy Department. As we rode, they discussed what fee they should charge. One suggested $12,000 as fair. His companion argued that, given their considerable talent and experience, they should double that figure.

"Let's ask for $24,000," he said.

"Yeah, you're right," the first one replied. "Nobody will ever know the difference anyway." They left the cab at a corner on Pennsylvania Avenue, disappearing into the crowd.

The taxi driver muttered to no one in particular, "Looks to me like I'm in the wrong business."

That conversation haunted me for days. I had heard how consultants arbitrarily did business, many of them hired without competitive bidding or accountability. I told Bruce about my cab ride, and we began studying the topic.

We discovered that consultants' price-gouging stood as just one abuse. Conflict-of-interest cases were even more prevalent. For instance, one consulting firm's director would evaluate a Pentagon missile system, even though he sat on the weapon manufacturer's board. More than simply a matter of over-spending, the consultant question also raised policy concerns. Who was making the government's decisions, a federal worker or an outside adviser? We also discovered a morale problem. A reasonably-paid government employee sat in the same cubicle with a consultant making three or four times the salary, with a year-end bonus, far richer health and retirement benefits, and almost no accountability.

Recently appointed chairman of the Subcommittee on Civil Service, I began hearings into this "invisible bureaucracy." A young man named Dan Gutman had just published a book titled *The Shadow Government*, which became a guide to our Energy Department investigations.

Knox Walkup—a capable young lawyer whose father had served as a Presbyterian minister in Helena, Arkansas—assisted us. A Harvard-educated law graduate, Knox had joined the committee staff under then-chairman Senator Jim Sasser of Tennessee. A bright and mild-tempered attorney who directed our strategic planning, Knox resembled a fierce bulldog when tracking down consultant and contractor abuses. Years later, he served for a time as Tennessee's attorney general.

Even the Carter White House admitted that government contracting had spiraled out of control. Carter had requested a list of all the federal government's outside consultants and contractors. Bert Lance, director of the Office of Management and Budget, observed that a thorough list would require an 18-wheeler just to transport the paper to the White House.

After a few of my Senate floor speeches and a couple of subcommittee hearings, people throughout government came around to our view. They began to see the pervasive nature of outsourcing labor normally performed by federal workers. We looked at this onion peeling as a first in exposing consultants—so massive they had become another, unaccountable level of government. *Time* magazine published a major piece labeling my target of concern "the shadow government," taking the phrase from Dan Gutman's book. While President Reagan had bragged about his administration's reducing the number of government employees, he had failed to reveal the rise in highly paid private consultants who basically took those federal workers' jobs.

I wish I could say my early stab at these abuses enjoyed some lasting success. But today's use of outside consultants has grown many times more widespread than in the early 1980s. While 1990s projects aimed at similar bureaucracy-reduction targets, they actually added fuel to the outsourcing process. Accountability took a back seat to what passed as efficiency, resulting in the new century's Blackhawks and Halliburtons.

* * *

My first spring in the Senate, Indiana Senator Birch Bayh asked me to join an effort to abolish the Electoral College. We wanted to provide direct election of the President and Vice President. I had supported similar efforts during my House years, but that movement had gone nowhere.

Senator Bayh's proposal, Senate Joint Resolution 2, was co-sponsored by a group of Democrats and Republicans including Ted Kennedy, Bob Dole, Jim Exon, David Boren, and Jacob Javits. States receive electoral votes based on population. We argued that direct popular elections would offer the most equitable process for electing the President and Vice President. One resolution provision required that any candidate receiving less than 40% of the votes would face a runoff.

In spite of our good intentions, the resolution proved short-lived. Orrin Hatch of Utah came up with his small-state defense of the Electoral College, and Daniel Patrick Moynihan of New York pleaded to keep the 200-year-old Constitution in place for the sake of stability. Still, it's little wonder young people become cynical about a government system that allows an Al Gore, with a popular-vote majority, to lose an election.

* * *

That summer, Barbara and I joined a group of senators traveling to the Soviet Union—my first official Congressional delegation, or "Codel." The group included Senators Richard Lugar of Indiana, Bill Bradley of New Jersey, Carl Levin of Michigan, Joe Biden of Delaware, and David Boren of Oklahoma.

Levin, Bradley, Boren, and I had only recently come to the Senate. This trip gave us a chance to get our feet wet in an international arena, and to learn from a new set of Senate colleagues. Since I had never visited any part of the Soviet bloc, I was anxious to go.

Our purpose was twofold. One was to test the waters of the Strategic Arms Limitation Treaty, or SALT, an agreement first signed by Gerald Ford and Leonid Brezhnev in 1974. We wondered if the accord remained alive. Our second purpose was to meet with Jewish dissidents who wanted to plead their case to parties—any parties—outside the Soviet Union.

The trip proved an eye-opener, particularly regarding the dissidents. Twelve Soviet Jews lived in Moscow's American embassy under the two governments' protection agreements. Embassies are internationally regarded as sovereign space and therefore neutral ground. The Soviets let the dissidents leave the embassy to visit our hotel, where we heard them describe their embassy life and existence outside the city's confines. I took special interest in stories of their families, and their continuing struggle to emigrate to Western Europe or the United States.

The Soviets allowed exactly an hour for us to confer, meeting in our hotel room. Everyone crowded in. Precisely at the hour's end, the dissident group's leader became nervous, urging his cohorts to return to the embassy. But several continued their spirited talk, hands waving in the air. Ten minutes later they were still there. For the dissidents to have the ear of several U.S. senators was a one-in-a-lifetime opportunity.

The hotel phones began to ring and didn't stop. Barbara would answer the phone, only to hear heavy breathing on the line, followed by an abrupt click. We went down the hall and found our American military attaché, an impressive young man with presence and authority. We asked him what we should do. He came back with us to our room, reached behind a chair, and with a swift gesture tore the wires out of the wall. "They won't be calling you again," he said.

As we escorted our guests toward the lobby, I realized I had left my glasses and rushed back to pick them up. When I reached our door, I noticed a very large man standing in a linen closet next to our room. He hovered, classically dressed as a spy: heavy trenchcoat reaching the floor, belt tied around his middle, and a dark fedora pulled down over his eyes. He peered through a wall slit that offered a full view of our bedroom where the meeting had taken place.

As I passed by him, he turned and looked at me, shock on his face. Not knowing an appropriate response, I gave a friendly but cautious wave and went on my way. I have always wondered what happened to the Jewish dissidents. Their situation, and our encounter with them, seemed to come out of another world. The stern atmosphere enveloping our meeting matched the still, drab streets of Moscow, where people lowered their heads in seemingly concentrated despair.

That trip brought home the Soviet government's full cynicism. Our SALT discussions revealed an internal war brewing between the Kremlin's hawks and doves. Five months later, when the Soviets invaded Afghanistan, we realized which side had prevailed.

Soon after we returned to the U.S., I introduced a bill calling for our country to boycott the 1980 Olympic Games, scheduled for Moscow, unless the games committee moved them outside the Soviet bloc. I argued that the Soviets would construct their Olympic facilities with slave labor and use the games to showcase their menacing system.

President Carter enforced a grain embargo against the Soviet Union. Later, the United States boycotted the 1980 Olympics altogether. This decision still reverberates among athletic and diplomatic circles, having come too hastily and with little regard for international relations. I knew we needed to take serious action, but I disagreed with Carter. I believed we should have pressed the Olympics Committee to move the games, but still take part. Most Americans, except those athletes who had spent years training for the event, generally accepted Carter's decision.

Chapter 42
A Matter of Ethics

Robert C. Byrd, the venerable Democratic majority leader, summoned me to his office late one Friday afternoon in January 1980. This invitation came as I still felt my way through the myriad federal issues and agencies. What could he have in mind to further complicate my job? Had I done something to anger this legendary Senate icon?

Still serving in the Senate in 2008, he remains a courtly Southern gentleman with patrician manners from another era. He's likely to lecture the entire Senate at midnight on Sophocles, or start a morning business hour quoting from Stephen Vincent Benet's *John Brown's Body*. The West Virginia Senator begins each day committing to memory a poem taped the night before to his bathroom mirror. Every two years, he reads his way through the entire *Encyclopedia Britannica*.

This is the stalwart mind I faced, stepping into his office that day, with some degree of trepidation.

"Now, David," he said when I took a seat, "we want you to join the Ethics Committee. Senator Quentin Burdick of North Dakota"—Senator Byrd always includes full title and pedigree—"has asked to be relieved of his duties. So there's a vacancy, and I think you're just right for the position."

Flattered by his invitation, I thanked him, but assured him that I was not right for that particular honor. "You don't want me," I told him. "You need a more senior member, maybe a former attorney general from one of the larger states, or a person more familiar with the rules and customs of the Senate."

"Not at all," he said. "You're the one for this distinction."

And with that he ushered me to the door, reassuring me it was highly unlikely that the Ethics Committee would establish a regular agenda. At the Democratic caucus's next meeting, he announced my new appointment.

Ethics Committee service hovers as an unwanted, thankless job. But nearly everyone with Senate tenure has to serve there. The panel monitors its peers' activities. In most cases, it becomes both judge and jury. Unique among Senate committees, it stands evenly divided between three Democrats and three

Republicans. This may appear to encourage fairness, but lacking a clear or predictable majority vote, it more often fosters frustration.

The day I met with Senator Byrd, I flew back that evening to Little Rock, staying the weekend at the Sam Peck Hotel. On the 10:00 news, I saw a brief shot of my colleague Senator Harrison "Pete" Williams of New Jersey.

The grainy image showed the Senator seated next to an Arab sheik who seemed to be handing Williams a sack of money. The camera cut to the news announcer, who revealed that the sheik was actually an FBI agent in disguise, and that a bribery case could conceivably involve Williams, seven other Congressional members, and 30 government officials. The Justice Department was determining overall involvement and would probably bring charges.

Within days, the Senate Ethics Committee received allegations against Senator Williams. For more than two years, we held hearings into the bribery case known as "Abscam," a press takeoff on the FBI's fake Abdul Enterprises, Ltd., set up to trap federal officials. Attorney General Benjamin Civiletti asked the Senate to hold off Congressional hearings until the government brought charges of its own. The committee considered this unacceptable, because the Justice Department had taken slow and inadequate actions.

I believed at the outset that the FBI had clearly overstepped its authority by entrapping Senator Williams and was taking an inordinate amount of time resolving the case. In addition, the Justice Department leaked information to reporters, which amounted to trying the case in the media.

Speaking to the Arkansas Press Association's annual convention, I described the FBI's release of information as "not a leak, but a torrential downpour," jeopardizing both Congress's and the courts' abilities to deal with any alleged wrongdoing. The FBI *used* the press, I said, and editors and reporters should know better than to fall for such shameless manipulation.

To my surprise, this speech caused a minor firestorm among the Arkansas press. John Robert Starr, the veteran *Democrat* columnist, suggested that I had become obsessed with Abscam, acting more like a trial lawyer than a U.S. senator. This pretty much summed up the reaction I received from the state's other editors.

Maybe Starr was right. Maybe I had gone too far. But I wanted the committee and the press to treat Williams fairly. In particular, I wanted information released from proper sources at the proper time, not in some underhanded way that would compromise Senator Williams's right to due process.

Senator Williams had learned of the investigation on a Sunday evening when he and his wife hosted a small dinner party. He had left his house, running to a neighborhood grocery store. When he returned, newspaper and television reporters had flooded his front lawn. One cameraman actually climbed a tree and peered into the bedroom window. The FBI had tipped them off.

Despite Senator Byrd's assurance that no Ethics Committee agenda lay on the horizon, we spent seemingly endless time on the Williams matter. Even with the government's bumbling mistakes, and the defense's claims of unfairness, Williams's guilt remained clear.

A New York grand jury indicted him on nine counts of bribery, conspiracy, and conflict of interest. Our committee's tensions steamed at an all-time high. We all knew Pete Williams well. Yet we were passing judgment on an obvious series of ethical breaches. In the Committee, I voted with the majority to expel him—clearly our only choice. But before the full Senate took final action, Williams wisely submitted his resignation. This occurred in early March 1982, more than two years after our hearings had begun.

On the night the news broke that he had resigned, I met *Gazette* reporter Tom Hamburger at the Madison Hotel to grab a late sandwich and discuss defense spending. Walking into the dining room, we saw Senator Williams, his wife Jeanette, and his legal team sitting at a back table. They were deep in conversation and, I'm certain, despondent. Seeing me, Williams's wife suddenly stood up, pointed at me, and shouted, "You're not fit to shine my husband's shoes!"

Jeanette Williams understood every aspect of her husband's trial. A former secretary to Hubert Humphrey, she had worked as a Senate Labor Committee senior staff member. I had known and respected her. But this night, I saw no reason to engage in conversation or argument. Emotions ran too high. I regretted that we had been forced to vote, and I felt frustrated by our drawn-out review of the Williams case. I had complained on the Senate floor, not defending Williams, but criticizing the FBI's bumbling entrapment tactics and questioning whether the bureau's proper functions included purview over such activities.

But I also knew our committee had made the right decision and that Williams was correct in resigning. Senator Russell Long of Louisiana pled Williams's case before our committee and the full Senate. He won my enduring admiration, showing great loyalty for his long-time friend and displaying courage in championing a losing cause.

I did not know my Senate Ethics Committee participation had just begun. The Williams case proved only a mild prelude to the far more absorbing, time-consuming investigation of the Keating Five, a group of my fellow senators caught up in a savings-and-loan scandal.

This case, which broke in 1989, actually went back to business activities in the early 1980s, when the Federal Home Loan Bank Board clamped down on savings and loan associations' real-estate investments. Irvine, California's Lincoln Savings and Loan had collapsed in 1989 after over-extending its investments. Its chairman, Charles H. Keating, Jr., received the lion's share of the blame. Keating claimed unfair treatment from the Home Loan Bank Board, particularly its former chief, Edwin J. Gray.

Gray maintained that several U.S. senators had asked him to give the Lincoln board a break. He said that, if he seemed to come down hard on Lincoln, he was reacting to undue pressure from Senate members. It turned out that Keating had provided these senators a total of just over a million dollars in campaign contributions.

Both the State of California and the U.S. Justice Department began investigating, and the Senate Ethics Committee opened hearings to determine the extent of the senators' involvement. We again spent nearly two years reviewing evidence and questioning our colleagues and a host of witnesses regarding their relationships with Keating. Almost every morning at 9:00, I would meet my staff attorney, John Monahan, a Georgetown graduate and a bright star on his way up. We would settle in for a full day of testimony in the Hart Building hearing room. We took time off only for Senate roll-call votes.

Fallout took various forms for those senators known as the Keating Five. Senator Alan Cranston had already announced he wouldn't run again in 1992. Dennis DeConcini and Don Riegle served out their Senate terms, retiring in 1994. People expected John Glenn to suffer difficulties resulting from the committee's mild reprimand, but he soundly defeated Mike DeWine in 1992, going on to retire in 1999.

John McCain bitterly resented being included in the Keating number. Later, he described his experience with the Senate Ethics Committee as more excruciating than his five years in a North Vietnamese prison. From the beginning, he maintained his innocence, asking that his name be stricken from the list.

Senator Howell Heflin of Alabama, the committee chairman, insisted that we give full attention to McCain's involvement. I agreed with that decision. I even made a point of saying that McCain should welcome the committee's full disclosure.

McCain was infuriated with me. For the next five years, he refused to speak to me or acknowledge my presence on the Senate floor, in meetings, even in the dining room and on elevators.

In October 1996, on my final day in the Senate, I cleared my Senate-floor desk, inscribing my name inside my desk drawer with a felt-tip pen—a custom long recognized by retiring Senate members. I was adding my name to a distinguished list including, most recently, Kaneaster Hodges and John L. McClellan.

I looked up and saw John McCain crossing the chamber, heading toward me. I cringed, fully expecting him to unload a final angry charge. He was known for having a rather explosive temper.

Instead, he pulled me up from my chair, asking if he could give me a hug.

"I've acted wrongly toward you for the past five years," he said, "and I want to apologize."

That reconciliation remains a moment I'll always recall as a surprise, but also with a sense of genuine gratitude. Partially out of his Keating-affair involvement, McCain has gone on to sponsor serious reforms in campaign finance laws. The McCain-Feingold legislation aimed to require more campaign-finance disclosure from candidates.

Chapter 43
Strangers in a Strange Land

One issue dogging my first Senate term involved the Defense Department's proposal to manufacture chemical weapons at the Pine Bluff Arsenal. It became such a hot issue that my longstanding relationships with Jefferson County friends and supporters threatened to completely unravel.

Confrontation ignited in April 1980, when a Pine Bluff citizens group came to my office, announcing that the Department of Defense planned to build a nerve gas production facility somewhere in the country. They wanted the facility for Pine Bluff. Clearly it would boost the economy and provide much-needed jobs.

This idea existed nowhere on my agenda, in part because the United States had not produced chemical weapons since Nixon's ban in 1969. But this issue ran deeper for me. I simply and naturally opposed nerve gas production. Also, stored nerve gas already existed, enough to kill every man, woman, and child in the world 20 times over.

Nothing would have pleased me more than assisting the Pine Bluff economy. I explained how I had teamed with them on every past project from highway construction, to moving the railroad away from downtown, to opening a new International Paper plant, not to mention protecting the city as governor during the firemen's strike. I fully understood the position spelled out by the mayor, county judge, and Chamber of Commerce. But I reminded them that, as governor in 1978, I had opposed the earliest suggestion of manufacturing chemical weapons in Arkansas. For me, nerve gas—its manufacture, use, or even existence—remained a moral issue. It was wrong.

President Carter's proposed 1981 budget included about $2 million for long-range planning of chemical weapons production. While the budget listed no specific actual production, some House members confided that Congress might add another $20 million for that purpose.

Carter's heart clearly opposed nerve gas production, and his budget prohibited the government from developing a new production schedule. But the Army had repeatedly attempted to circumvent the administration, appealing directly to Congress. I didn't like the looks of the Pentagon's maneuvers, and told the Pine Bluff team—my friends and long-time supporters—exactly where I stood. If you want jobs, I said, let's find something else and move it into the complex.

Dr. Matthew Methelson came to my aid with expertise, commitment, and considerable courage. A Harvard biochemist, he knew more about the subject than anyone in the country. We toured the Pine Bluff arsenal several times, and Pentagon research-and-development staff provided classified briefings.

They planned a new weapon using a binary formula: two chemicals, harmless on their own, would combine when a munition fired, producing lethal gas. They assured us of safety measures, and that these two chemicals remained "clean" weapons when kept separate from each other. I simply didn't believe what they were saying. I made that position clear, even though my Jefferson County friends hoped I could be persuaded. After all, Beryl Anthony, the Fourth District congressman, strongly favored the project; so did Dale Bumpers, though with somewhat less enthusiasm. Among the three of us, we simply agreed that I would disagree.

Complicating my relationship with Pine Bluff leaders, Dallas's Vought Corporation announced it would begin manufacturing missiles in Camden, bringing Ouachita County hundreds of jobs. Thrilled by the news, I still felt the certain chill from raised eyebrows among Pine Bluff civic leaders and the Chamber board. Had I favored Camden, my home town, over Pine Bluff?

The Pentagon eventually abandoned plans to produce binary weapons at the Pine Bluff Arsenal or anywhere else, but that decision took years. The House seriously stabbed at banning chemical weapons, first in 1982. It rejected the Reagan administration's $54 million item to begin production in Pine Bluff. When the vote came up, I went over to the House floor, soliciting whatever votes I could against nerve gas production.

Republican Congresswoman Millicent Fenwick, the grand lady from New Jersey, said before the final vote: "It is a disgrace to our country to even think that we could spend money, when we don't even know where to find it for children's lunches, for poison gas." This was one of her last statements on the House floor. She ran for the Senate that year, losing to Democrat Frank Lautenberg.

Ironically, the Senate in two floor votes had already approved binary weapons. On both occasions, Vice President George H. W. Bush came to the Senate chamber, breaking the tie on Pryor amendments by voting in favor of production. These were the only tie-breaking votes Vice President Bush cast in his term. After the last vote, he lightheartedly asked me if I would please not bring up my nerve gas amendment again. It seemed that every time he voted to break the tie, he got a distressing phone call from his mother. "She's on your side," he whispered.

Even after working feverishly against appropriations for nerve gas, I never knew whether my enduring opposition proved instrumental in the administration's abandoning its production. Probably their change of plans involved a number of factors, chiefly to abandon such an odious project on principle.

* * *

The first week of May 1980, the White House informed Governor Bill Clinton that 7,500 to 15,000 Cuban refugees would soon arrive at the Fort Chaffee military base. The administration also communicated this to John Paul Hammerschmidt, the Third District congressman, Dale Bumpers, and me.

This blunt notice came as chilling news, partly because the base had been used only for National Guard summer camps since 1975, after the federal government had relocated the last Vietnam refugees. We did not expect to see it operating again on such sudden notice.

The news also shocked us. We learned that many Cuban refugees had undergone routine deprivation and torture as the Castro regime's political prisoners. A number were known criminals. Very few could identify U.S. sponsors who might assume responsibility for permanent housing and employment. What's more, they had entered Florida under the most perilous circumstances, many of them challenging the sea in rafts and small boats.

Up to 1,200 could come to Chaffee every day, the first wave likely to arrive within the week. Arkansas stood as the only state outside Florida designated as a resettlement center.

Clinton appointed staff members to coordinate the refugee program. Bumpers and I both assigned people to go to Chaffee, providing federal cooperation. I sent Carmie Henry, a Vietnam veteran who knew more about the Pentagon, the Corps of Engineers, and the federal bureaucracy than almost anybody I knew.

Days later, nothing seemed to quell a riotous situation. Seething numbers of refugees set fire to four buildings, threw rocks and clubs, stormed the main gates, and barricaded dormitories. Well-organized gangs of rioters threatened local residents living near Chaffee, and gun sales in the area skyrocketed.

Even though the Carter administration sent in 1,400 Army troops, with another 600 promised, nothing indicated that all sides could reach an accommodation. We leveled criticism at the administration for failing to grasp the situation's seriousness and its lack of support for Arkansas officials trying to deal with the problem.

Our frustration grew because the Carter administration would not define who held authority to restrain the refugees. "I am extremely disgusted at the White House," I told the *Springdale News*. Arkansas had become a dumping ground for the unwanted. In purely political terms, our state's 1976 support for Carter's presidency ranked second only to Georgia. Was this our reward?

Bill Clinton and the governor's office suffered most from the administration's failure to provide security. Also, Clinton was personally determined to reach a solution on his own. My impression was that in hoping to solve an impossible situation and come up with a ready plan for a settlement, Clinton over-managed the crisis. While having the best intentions, he needed to let the Carter people and the Army bear the brunt of that rapidly deteriorating situation.

Frank White's defeating Clinton months later certainly resulted, at least in part, from the Cuban refugee situation. In July, the administration floated a trial balloon, suggesting it would send additional Cuban refugees to Chaffee. Our delegation, led by Bill Clinton, responded with a resounding "No."

* * *

At 3:00 a.m. on Friday, September 19, 1980, a Titan II missile, buried deep outside Damascus, Arkansas, exploded. The blast killed one worker, injuring a score of others. More than 1,400 people evacuated the area, most of them south to Conway. The Air Force assured us it detected no toxic gases or radiation in the atmosphere. This information temporarily calmed us, but it hardly relieved families and neighbors having to return to their homes, facing dangerous threats of a recurrence.

The explosion resulted from an accident the afternoon before. A technician on a routine assignment dropped an eight-pound wrench some 70 feet to the missile silo's floor. The wrench punctured a fuel tank, setting off a chain reaction ending with the deadly blast eight hours later. The silo housed a 130-foot intercontinental ballistic missile carrying a nine-ton nuclear warhead several times stronger than the atomic bomb dropped on Hiroshima.

Only weeks before the blast, I had joined Nancy Kassebaum and Bob Dole, both senators from Kansas, introducing a bill to provide early-warning signals to meet this kind of emergency. The Senate had passed the bill, but the Air Force had contended, incredibly as it turned out, that early warnings were unnecessary. In the hours after the fuel tank's puncture, but before the explosion, the county sheriff acted as a modern Paul Revere. He drove through the countryside, warning residents with a bullhorn that they should leave their homes and seek safer ground. This was their only early-warning system.

Vice President Walter Mondale happened to be in Hot Springs the day of the explosion, speaking to the state Democratic convention. None of us could get a satisfactory report from Washington about the Damascus explosion, so we asked the Vice President to intervene. We stood around his room at the Arlington Hotel, watching and listening as he called Secretary of Defense Harold Brown. Mondale requested a full report on the incident, asking in particular if precautions had been in place. And were these actual warheads?

Brown dodged Mondale's questions, trying to avoid blame, explaining that a Defense Department study was under way. But Mondale, frustrated by this bureaucratic obfuscation, insisted on the whole story. I watched as the Vice President made repeated pleas for a simple, straight answer. In time, he finally came away from the phone with the details we could not pry from the administration.

He said these were, in fact, live warheads. I spoke with reporters both from Arkansas and around the world, expressing our citizens' concerns, and the need for a warning system.

An Air Force report, issued early the next year, assured us that the Arkansas missile system was basically safe but potentially hazardous. Not reassuring. In May, the Air Force announced it would not rebuild the Damascus complex, saying the $225 million project cost was too high. Nevertheless, a year after the explosion, an early warning system was installed for six of the remaining 17 silos.

The Pentagon phased out the Titan missile in 1983, replacing it with a new MX system. The Reagan administration finally deactivated the missiles in 1987, declaring the property government surplus. The silos were filled with concrete, and the fields returned to meadow. No one around Damascus regretted that return.

Chapter 44
"The Great Communicator"

President Ronald Reagan's 1981 entry onto the Washington scene brought about changes in tone and manner. With any new administration, the city and the government (in a sense, the city *is* the government) always undergo distinct alterations, particularly when a new political party assumes power. Most people call the switch a "seismic shift."

One surprising Arkansas development involved Justice Jim Johnson's overture. He wrote Congressman Ed Bethune that he was "more than willing" to serve in any capacity suitable with the new Reagan administration. He then publicly tried to secure a U.S. Parole Commission spot, quickly gaining Senator Strom Thurmond's endorsement.

South Carolina's Thurmond chaired the Senate Judiciary Committee, which reviewed presidential nominees to the commission. He had worked with Jim Johnson in the 1950s, both supporting state sovereignty commissions to assure Southern racial segregation.

Dale Bumpers and I raised a furor over Justice Jim's ill-conceived recognition play. In fact, I promised Thurmond that if this scheme went forward, I'd filibuster the appointment. His candidacy quietly vanished within a week.

* * *

With some reluctance, I went along with Reagan's push for 1982 budget tax cuts. I also thought his spending-reduction proposals, however severe they appeared to my fellow Democrats, made sense.

I found other aspects of Reagan's agenda troublesome from the beginning.

First, he had opened his 1980 presidential campaign in Philadelphia, Mississippi, where 16 years earlier Klansmen had slain three civil rights workers. What kind of message was Reagan sending? I was fearful that Reagan or Thurmond, or even Justice Jim, would revive nostalgia for a racist South's "good old days." We were now living in a New South of promise and hope, and we had to defend it.

I also actively opposed Reagan's military buildup. I had always thought— naively, as it turned out—that since the days of Harry Truman, the Army and

Air Force had removed themselves from politics, and that a senator's voting record would not factor into making military decisions.

I was wrong. As I would soon learn, the Pentagon knew in detail where I stood on every issue. All military branches kept liaison staffs in the Senate Office Building, helping with constituent casework and answering questions about the state's military bases. They also kept files of our votes, and what we said, on every key military issue.

They knew that I opposed the B-1 Bomber and favored arms control. They certainly recognized my opposition to producing nerve gas. I had consistently questioned defense contractors' influence on national security and spending decisions, and military and industrial officials' revolving-door syndrome. I had taken to heart Truman's warning against an overblown military operating on bloated budgets, and Eisenhower's warning against a military-industrial complex.

My calling attention to military issues had taken off in 1981. I spoke out against the Defense Science Board, a "standing committee" of research specialists originally formed in 1956. Hailed as critical to our Cold War efforts, the board advised the Pentagon on science and technology development. Its work mainly involved arms agreements, basing modes for the MX Missile, submarine warfare, and weapons procurement. A board statement defined professional and unbiased objectivity as necessary qualifications for service.

Operating for nearly 30 years, the board had become entrenched with members clearly involved with conflicts of interest. Many were experts in military affairs, defense matters, science, and business. Others, however, were retired military officers, former public officials, and industrial executives conducting Pentagon business, including close ties to consultants with huge contracts.

The board exhibited a classic example of the good ol' boy network. A 1983 Inspector General's report defined the board membership's entanglements. Equally disturbing was the Pentagon's defensive response to the IG's report on procuring weapons prior to testing. The head of military research and engineering called the IG's findings biased and inaccurate, demanding that future evaluations be kept from public view. In other words, don't mess in our playpen.

After seeing the Pentagon's reaction, I pointed out on the Senate floor that this confrontation demonstrated clearly why Congress should keep its eye on the military-industrial complex. Only the week before, the Senate had passed a bill I sponsored creating an independent weapons-testing office, now certainly shown as necessary. For too long, improperly tested weapons such as the B-1 bomber and Abrams tank had been rushed into production. I also threatened a move—if the Defense Science Board did not change how it conducted business—to delete its funding from the 1984 defense appropriations bill. At that point, Senator Henry "Scoop" Jackson of Washington raced to the Senate floor, defending the Defense Science Board. I still picture him pushing his way through the double doors, taking a firm place behind his desk, ready for action.

No one knows whether my warning worked, or if the Pentagon even paid attention to a junior senator who didn't sit on the Armed Services Committee. But in May 1984, I received indications of the military's interest and suspicion. A top Air Force officer asked to meet with me to discuss "areas of mutual concern." My race for a second Senate term was just heating up, and the Pentagon was paying attention.

General James P. McCarthy sat in my office explaining how he considered many of my positions "anti-military." His studied precision held my concentration. I questioned whether the Pentagon considered my voting record in any systematic way. He said it did. I asked him to give me an example.

"The B-1 Bomber, for instance," he replied.

I asked him what other "anti-military" issues he had in mind. A young colonel at his side produced a two-page printout: 17 items listing my floor statements and votes. They knew, as I did, that keeping such dossiers on members of Congress was illegal. They also knew they had overstepped. The issues ranged from nerve gas and defense contractors to Pentagon hiring practices, the MX missile program, and finally the B-1. The printout reminded me of FBI files maintained to pin down spies.

Given my record and cynicism toward wartime profiteers, maybe I shouldn't have been surprised. But the Pentagon's excessively thorough research stunned me. I've no doubt these kinds of lists appeared against me during my campaign later in the year. I'm also certain the Pentagon targeted other members of Congress opposed to the huge spike in military expenditures.

At one point that fall, I called the president's weapons program "insane," adding that the Pentagon's brand of arrogance challenged the imagination. The military made poor decisions, executed by contractors with no-bid government jobs. These interlopers handed over submarines with cracked hulls and tanks breaking down every 30 miles. Military decisions, I complained, came in isolation, with no recourse, no second opinions, and no room for dispute.

Once again I openly attacked the Defense Science Board in a speech on the Senate floor. I emphasized the board's conflicts, including its makeup largely of retired admirals and generals in cozy relationships with defense contractors. This time, Senator Scoop Jackson didn't bother to counterattack. Maybe he had given up on me.

But I wasn't out of the administration's crosshairs. Two days after I made that speech, President Reagan invited me to the White House. He had proposed selling five Airborne Warning and Control System planes, or AWACS, to Saudi Arabia, and wanted them in an $8.5 billion defense equipment package. We had already become the world's leading arms dealer, just as we are today.

When his White House aides called, asking me to meet with him, I reminded them of my opposition, just in case they had forgotten. Four months before, along with 53 other senators, I had signed a resolution calling on Reagan to cancel the sale. I questioned the project's wisdom on every principle. Could we trust the Saudis with this equipment? How did we know they wouldn't turn around and sell the AWACS to the Soviet Union or Libya?

The president's people said they understood my opposition, but insisted I come anyway. It would be a one-on-one session and wouldn't take long. This was my first personal encounter with President Reagan, and I wanted to experience "the great communicator" firsthand. Our meeting took place only hours before the afternoon's scheduled AWACS vote.

I wanted to discuss several items during our session. I planned to encourage him to make another try at a SALT treaty, even though SALT II had apparently failed. Still, it was worth making a renewed revival effort. I also hoped he would cut nothing more from his Health and Human Services budget; he had left hanging programs for the elderly, disabled, and children's nutrition. Finally, I would encourage his appointing a farmer or small business person to the Federal Reserve Board vacancy coming in January.

Our meeting took place upstairs in the family quarters and lasted about 15 minutes. It was cordial but a little stiff. As we sat down, the president said he hoped I would vote with him on the AWACS sale. I told him I appreciated his interest, but I just couldn't do it. I respectfully asked him not to waste any more time with me. I knew he was busy, and I frankly remained on the opposite side.

As a good-will offering, I presented him a cookbook from the recent Arkansas Rice Festival in Weiner. Somehow I thought this would break the ice between us.

He got up and began to usher me to the door. As I was leaving, I spotted a red telephone in the corner. I pointed to it and asked, "Mr. President, do you ever talk to Mr. Brezhnev on that phone?"

He looked a little startled. "No, I never have," he said.

I asked him, "Why don't you pick it up and ask him to meet with you somewhere, or go fishing, and talk things over?"

"Oh, no," he said, "they wouldn't let me do that."

"Who wouldn't let you?" I asked.

"Well, I guess the State Department," he said. "They wouldn't let me."

Then maybe I got a little impertinent, but I couldn't resist. "You're the President," I told him. "You're not the State Department. You've been elected to settle things. They haven't been elected to anything. It seems to me the trouble now is that nobody talks things out. We speak through intermediaries and the press, and there's a lack of real communication."

"No, they wouldn't let me do that," he repeated.

In the end, the president thanked me for my point of view, adding he hoped I would change my mind on AWACS. There was no opportunity to bring up my questions. I wondered if the session seemed as odd to Ronald Reagan as it did to me.

While my relationship with Reagan was cordial but distant, I felt genuinely at ease with Vice President George H. W. Bush. Even though they shared a common, conservative point of view, Reagan and Bush differed in nearly every way. Reagan's Midwest and Hollywood background contrasted sharply with the New England blue blood that defined Bush and his father, Prescott Bush, a U.S. senator during the 1940s and '50s. George H. W. Bush and I had come to the Congress together in 1966, when we had chaired our respective freshman caucuses. During his term as vice president, Bush occasionally invited our former freshman-class House members to dinner at his home on the Naval Observatory grounds.

For most of 1981, I had supported parts of the Reagan program, along with other Democrats who later turned away from Reaganomics. During the Carter administration's final years, history's highest interest rates nearly brought the country to a standstill. No Democratic efforts to boost the economy seemed to work. Seeing the government's lethargy firsthand from the Senate, I was willing to try Reagan's new tax plan.

Democrats in general, with some caution, allowed the new administration the benefit of many doubts. The 1980 Republican election sweep, costing us our Senate majority, had shocked us.

In a bizarre and unfortunate way, Reagan received a great deal of personal sympathy and support after March 31, when John Hinckley shot and wounded him and his press secretary, Jim Brady. Congress and the nation fully supported Ronald Reagan, his family, and his administration, as we should have. From a purely political standpoint, in the weeks following the Hinckley assassination attempt, Reagan could have passed just about any legislative program he wanted.

I never gave full-fledged support to Reagan's programs. As 1981 ended and a new session got under way, I developed serious second thoughts about his major revenue provisions. So did most of my Democratic colleagues. We seemed to get our breath back. The Senate Democratic Policy Committee appointed me to chair a task force on Reagan's economic program, dubbed the New Federalism. But by mid-year, I found myself opposed to the president's plan. I came to favor Senator Fritz Hollings's suggestion that we freeze the 1983 budget at the same level as 1982's. This made better sense than anything we were getting from the administration.

My misgivings toward Reagan went beyond economic policy and race; they included doubts about his capacity to govern. He seemed to fall into a Nixonian syndrome, almost a paranoia, I hadn't seen during his first year in office. His advisers were pulling him away from press conferences. They made White House access, never easy in his administration, more and more difficult.

What had seemed a charming modesty in Reagan's shy character, even an official coyness, now looked more like open hostility to anyone who questioned his judgment. I found this rigid unwillingness to compromise a growing part of the right-wing Republican ideology.

I returned to the liberal-conservative definitions following my 1978 election. Still not wanting to be pigeon-holed neatly into either category, I drew distinctions. What made up a "liberal consciousness," and what was "conservative"?

In that regard, one of Richard Yates's *Arkansas Democrat* columns particularly impressed me. Yates was a Hendrix history professor who contributed regularly under the title, "The Old Professor," covering a wide range of political subjects.

Years earlier, Yates had written a series of letters to the *Arkansas Gazette* under the pseudonym, "Hardscrabble." For some time, no one knew the writer's identity. No one, that is, except his history students. These occasional pieces appeared for years, most of them taking a liberal slant and dealing satirically with the Faubus administration.

His 1982 column showed how "liberalism" still thrives in Arkansas and the nation, even though most people deny being liberal or agreeing with that philosophy. Since Roosevelt's New Deal, he said, "liberals" were seen as un-American, starry-eyed, and economically naive or ignorant. Conservatives like to picture liberals as living at a way-station on their journey to socialism or communism.

The irony, as Yates described it, rises because so-called liberal programs have traditionally won the people's hearts and votes. Try taking away food and drug regulations, or farmers' credit breaks, or regulating stocks and commodities, or wage-and-hour legislation, or Social Security, or welfare—and you'll see that most people truly are "liberal." No "conservative" would dare dismantle Medicare, or Social Security, or rural electrification.

In my view, these simple historical facts described the "conservative" Reagan administration's dire effect on our economy and our people. Reagan wasn't just spouting hackneyed conservative rhetoric; he and his administration really wanted to repeal the New Deal.

The turning point for me came later in March when Senator John Glenn visited Little Rock to speak at a Democratic Party banquet. I had flown down from Washington with John and Annie Glenn. As the former Mercury astronaut piloted his plane, we discussed what he would likely say in his speech.

"The $1 trillion national debt will certainly go up," he predicted. "It's time this administration took responsibility and stopped blaming everyone else. President Reagan is doing to the farmers of America what Colonel Sanders does to chickens."

Glenn's speech was exactly what I—and the Arkansas people—needed to hear. He systematically dissected the Reagan program, showing how it intended to disenfranchise the very people who depended on and trusted the government.

The next month at a Fayetteville news conference, I took my text from Glenn's speech. I predicted outright that economic and social calamity would result if Reagan's budget passed. It would increase the deficit, taking money out of circulation, threatening to raise interest rates to 30%. Reagan would have to compromise, I stressed. A $25 billion cut in Pentagon spending would be a good place to start.

For the next year, I focused increasingly on military program growth under Reagan, and the Pentagon's failure to become accountable. One of my heroes became Republican Senator Chuck Grassley of Iowa, a maverick conservative. He had grown extremely frustrated by the Pentagon's intransigence. At one point early in his tenure, he pulled up in the august United States Department of Defense's public parking lot, stalking inside to confront Army specialists who had brushed him off time and again. These officers had consistently refused to let a young and brilliant Pentagon whistle-blower testify on Capitol Hill.

Using Grassley's investigative technique as a model, I discovered highly sophisticated weapons sent into the field with virtually no early-performance testing. As expected, information came to me, not with Pentagon approval, but in spite of their efforts to conceal it.

The General Accounting Office released data showing 10 completely untested weapons programs, totaling $10 billion, currently in full operation. Even more maddening, developers and promoters officially approved performance of defense systems they had designed and manufactured themselves. I suggested this resembled teachers allowing students to grade their own papers.

In early 1983, the Pentagon started a fresh drive for nerve gas production. The line item was part of a massive defense bill that, in my view, begged for cuts and revisions. Senator John Tower, the Armed Services Committee chairman, challenged all Senate members, asking for "volunteers" willing to accept defense cuts in their home state. Exercising his strong and customary arrogance, he felt certain no one would accept his invitation.

As soon as Tower made his challenge, I raced to the Senate floor, requesting removal of $158 million for producing chemical weapons in Pine Bluff. If the administration wanted to be even further responsible, I stressed, it could cut the entire $8 billion program. I stated further that Defense Secretary Casper Weinberger should resign. The next day, Weinberger, who I considered a willing instrument of the Reaganites, came to see me in my office. Before our official meeting began, he whispered that Mrs. Weinberger agreed with me.

Immediately responding to my floor speech, the *Pine Bluff Commercial* complained that, as usual, I displayed more feeling than thought. Even though I might infuse a measure of good will into any situation, the editorial said, I reduced political thought to its lowest common denominator.

By the time that opinion hit the stands, the Arkansas press was portraying me as a primary detractor of the Pentagon and the entire Reagan administration. I felt comfortable in that position. The Reagan administration was simultaneously cutting taxes, starving needed domestic programs, and providing a blank check to the military. This combination of fiscal irresponsibility and insensitivity to human need was no accident.

In a speech late in the year, I called it unforgivable for Ronald Reagan to avoid lowering the federal deficit. "The country is hemorrhaging," I said, "and the man in charge looks the other way."

The Little Rock Rotary Club invited me to speak at a noon luncheon. I decided in my speech to challenge the Pentagon's inflated budget and waste. I attacked war-profiteers, unaccountable contractors and consultants, and the military-industrial complex's growing culture and influence. To my surprise, this room full of conservative business leaders gave me a standing ovation.

* * *

On Saturday, February 11, 1984, Republican Congressman Ed Bethune announced for the Senate in Searcy, his hometown. In his speech, he called Ronald Reagan's re-election "the most important race in my lifetime." He had gone to the White House a week earlier, Bethune added, to discuss his possible candidacy with the president. He also wanted to see if Reagan was as willing as Bethune to fight for what's important. If the Republican Party lost its hold on the government, he warned, the country would become ruled by Walter Mondale, Tip O'Neill, the labor unions, and other liberal interest groups. He concluded by quoting Albert Schweitzer: "The discovery of purpose is the discovery of power." I thought this was a little dramatic but truly was indicative of an ideologue.

I had expected Bethune to run against me. Since his 1978 election to the House, he had moved steadily to the political right, closely aligning himself with Reagan and the Republican Congressional leadership.

Bethune's role model was Congressman Jack Kemp of New York, a leading spokesman for supply-side economics. According to the supply-siders, cutting taxes stimulated economic growth, which in turn raised more tax revenue. Even back in the 1980 Republican presidential primaries, George H. W. Bush had defined Reagan's plan as "voodoo" economics. In practice, Reaganomics did appear based more on voodoo rituals than sound economic theory. However good his intentions in the early '80s, Reagan rocketed the budget deficit while weakening the federal government's ability to meet its basic obligations. But in serving the Pentagon, he was a gold-plated answer to prayer.

Bethune carried a copy of *Megatrends*, John Naisbitt's 1982 handbook of economic and social theory for conservative Republicans, a Kemp favorite. Early in the campaign, Kemp appeared in Fayetteville, proclaiming that electing Bethune to the Senate would help "spread the gospel." Ernie Dumas, in a *Gazette* column, said that after Kemp, Bethune stood as the purest exponent of supply-side economics and the New Right.

Ed Bethune and I had agreed on a number of issues while in Congress, chief among them a struggle against nerve gas, supporting farm bill provisions, and backing new bankruptcy legislation. We had known each other in law school, and Barbara and Lana Bethune were friends; our children had enjoyed each other's company on many Washington occasions.

Still, despite his 1981 public comment that I was his "good buddy," I sensed he would run against me if he could secure Republican-establishment backing. He got it.

Barbara and I had announced for re-election a month earlier, on January 9—a small reception for friends and family at Mother's Camden home. Still, it took me awhile to concentrate on the Senate campaign. Since Bethune wasn't officially in the race then, I didn't mention his name or formally acknowledge any expected opposition. My only personal comment came in answer to charges from Bob Leslie, the Arkansas Republican Party chairman. The day before, he had called me a socialist.

Following my announcement, Barbara and I drove to Fayetteville to celebrate Mark's 21st birthday on the University campus. Even with Ed Bethune breathing down my neck, I distinctly felt other, more important issues demanding my attention. For the next month, I put campaign planning on a back burner.

On Friday, February 10, the night before Bethune's formal announcement, Mother suffered the beginnings of a fatal stroke. Walking with friends into Camden's Whiteside Elementary School for a potluck supper, she fell on the sidewalk. The doctor arrived and, seeing the situation's gravity, immediately sent her by ambulance to St. Vincent Hospital in Little Rock 100 miles away. She died four days later, on Valentine's Day, at age 84.

Two days later, we held family graveside services in Camden, followed by a memorial at the Presbyterian Church. My brother Bill, a Presbyterian pastor living in Victoria, Texas, spoke at the service. Everyone hopes there's a heaven, he said, but what is *hope* for most of us was *certainty* for her.

Half the people I had ever known in Camden and Ouachita County filled Mother's house after the service. The gathering seemed more like a celebration than a funeral, truly appropriate considering Mother's range of friends and her full and active life. She had touched so many lives, and in so many ways. It was impossible for me to believe she was gone.

The morning had been cold but clear. Then, just after sunset, a huge storm swelled with lightning and thunder. I remembered what Mother had said about the crowds of people gathered at our house in 1952, the night she and Bill drove in from Temple, Texas. Dad had died earlier in the day, and she had expected to find the house dark and empty. But seeing all those people in the yard, she realized what it meant to be a survivor.

That's what I would learn—once again—in the following weeks and months: what it means to be a survivor. I would now be entrusted not just to carry on but to find new heights and challenges. Barbara and I knew we would leave the next day for Washington, gather our forces, and launch yet another campaign. What we didn't know was that it would be my last.

Chapter 45
The Last Hurrah

Ed Bethune stood out as an impressively formidable candidate. A former FBI agent, he possessed the distinction of being Arkansas's second Republican congressman since Reconstruction. His 1972 loss to Jim Guy Tucker for attorney general clearly showed a political career just beginning. The same year I went to the Senate, Bethune won the tough Second District Congressional race against Doug Brandon, a successful Little Rock businessman and popular state legislator. As a hard-driving campaigner, Brandon ran a strong race.

Determined to make his Senate run a referendum on the Reagan administration, Bethune brought in the Republican Party's leading national lights. The rush started when Vice President George H. W. Bush dedicated the John L. McClellan Memorial Veterans Hospital in Little Rock on May 4, followed by a $1,000-a-head breakfast for Bethune. Bush returned in August, on his way to the Republican national convention in Dallas, taking part in Pine Bluff's bass masters tournament.

After that May visit, I knew that Arkansas was in for a long and steady stream of Washington "visitors." Over subsequent months, more than 20 senators and cabinet members followed Bush. They ranged from Don Regan, the Treasury Secretary, and Agriculture Secretary John Block, to former President Gerald Ford and Senators Orrin Hatch, Bob Dole, Jake Garn, Howard Baker, and John Tower.

Those senators were colleagues of mine whom I saw every day on the Senate floor. In spite of close friendships, however, a genteel truth exists in politics: one's fellow senators will more than likely enter your state and, assuming you belong to a different party, campaign against you. No exceptions, no questions asked. I understood their visits on Bethune's behalf, writing them off as attempts to gain a Republican Senate seat. Understanding the process, in most cases I didn't take their invasions personally.

Many Senate members, however, consider these visits highly personal. They take copious notes, filing them away sometimes as simmering grudges that last for years. During one of Robert C. Byrd's re-election campaigns in West

Virginia, his new Republican colleague Alan Simpson of Wyoming came in and stumped for Byrd's opponent. State papers gave extensive coverage. When the campaign ended, with Byrd safely back in the Senate, he summoned Simpson to his office. He held up a sheaf of newspaper stories detailing Simpson's West Virginia attacks against him. Now victorious, Byrd reminded Simpson how he still chaired the Senate Appropriations Committee, with considerable power of the purse. Simpson, a savvy campaigner and politician, got the message. He issued an effusive apology. Apology made, apology accepted.

Coincidentally, Byrd had committed an incursion of his own in 1974, coming to Arkansas to campaign for J. W. Fulbright against challenger Dale Bumpers. Of course, Bumpers had yet to become a Senate colleague, so circumstances were not quite the same. But when Bumpers did arrive in Washington, Byrd found himself awkwardly having to welcome the new Arkansas senator and fellow Democrat. Several observers thought their initial Washington relationship a little frosty. Still, the U.S. Senate's mutually respectful nature allowed Byrd and Bumpers to become close friends, working together for the next 24 years.

One circumstance exists where Senate colleagues' campaign competition—even the friendliest encounters—is simply not permitted: if a Senate majority leader faces opposition back home, and the challenger encourages the minority leader to work against him. That potentially sticky situation rarely materializes. The two leaders know they have to work together every day.

A recent exception came when Republican majority leader Bill Frist of Tennessee traveled to South Dakota to campaign against minority leader Tom Daschle. Frist explained that he only stumped for Dashle's opponent, John Thune, not against Daschle. No one bought this bogus explanation.

There's another unforgivable sin among senators: breaking one's word. Occurrences of this kind, extremely rare, become a permanent scarlet letter among fellow members. Everyone else in "the club" soon learns about the breach, and tends to remember it for a long time. Because of something basic in their DNA, senators usually get along. But this gene may sometimes not be shared by overzealous staff members who drive wedges of discontent and discord.

As my 1984 campaign heated up during the summer, Senator Ted Kennedy of Massachusetts came to me one day. Harold Jinks of Piggott, head of the

Arkansas Senior Democrats, had invited him to address their Hot Springs convention. I had known Harold for many years, working with him on legislation dating back to my House years. We had put together a senior intern program in my Senate office, bringing two or three active, elderly Arkansans to Washington for several weeks. Among the first of that group, Harold at age 75 had broken his arm sliding into home plate, a member of our softball team, the "Pryorities."

Harold Jinks was a hard man to turn down. Kennedy, intrigued by the invitation, told me he knew of my tough race with Bethune, so he had declined. Aware of his unpopularity at the time among Arkansas voters, he didn't want to compromise my campaign. A Kennedy appearance could possibly complicate my chances, and he knew it. My Senate colleague proved generous in his decision—and correct in his intuition.

* * *

Out-of-state visitors represent a mixed blessing. Football veteran Rosey Grier showed up for a Bethune fundraiser, probably a safe bet among most state voters. He was popular as an athlete, and as a Republican. Then came evangelist Jerry Falwell, who also endorsed Justice Jim Johnson, a candidate for chief justice of the Arkansas Supreme Court. Earlier in the year, Johnson had switched to the Republican Party, announcing against Jack Holt, Jr., who defeated Johnson handily in the general election.

It's hard to say whether Falwell helped Bethune, but he drew a crowd. Chances are good that he solidified Republican support from the state's evangelicals. Falwell's major political influence had come in 1980, when he claimed that his support put Reagan in the White House. Still, even four years later, his appeal among conservative voters remained strong.

Bethune capped his outsiders list with Ronald Reagan's visit the weekend before the Tuesday general election. Naturally, we were all concerned about this most popular president's appearance and the inordinate amount of time he planned to spend in Little Rock.

This was no quick touchdown followed by a hasty exit. He flew in on Friday afternoon, spent the night at the Excelsior Hotel, and spoke at an enormous Saturday morning rally. We questioned why he would pay so much attention to one Senate race when he was involved in his own re-election campaign.

There were two possible explanations. One was that he had nothing better to do. According to the polls, he had little to worry about from his opponent, former Vice President Walter Mondale. The second was that his campaign wanted him out of any major spotlight during the campaign's final three days. Arkansas remained a safe haven, far from California and New York's overheated media. Advisers saw little chance for an offhand comment to damage his run at the last minute. Whatever he said in Little Rock likely would get short shrift from the national press. In any case, our pollster Tubby Harrison, a prominent Boston-based Democratic consultant, suggested later that Reagan's visit cost me three percentage points in the final vote.

Over that weekend, and for days leading to it, I was convinced that Reagan would inflict major damage. That Saturday morning, crowds gathered outside the convention center on their way to the president's rally. We were driving across town to the airport. I was scheduled for rallies throughout eastern Arkansas and the Delta, beginning in Blytheville, and I was geared up for a long day. I watched the lines of people wrapped around the building and stretching across the Arkansas River bridge. I thought, "They're going to get in that convention hall and hear one of the most popular presidents in the country's history praise my opponent."

Reagan naturally gained extensive coverage in all the state papers and on local television. He reminded the overflowing crowd that no one should take a Republican victory for granted. "President Dewey told me we should never be complacent," he added with his customary sly grin. Then he begged the 13,000-strong audience, "Don't send me back to Washington alone."

Reagan flew back to Washington that afternoon, not alone, but with his enormous entourage. His stopover probably did cost me the three points Tubby Harrison suggested. But I believe the constant tide of Washington Republicans and officials, flying down to Arkansas for fundraisers and press conference endorsements, damaged Bethune's campaign.

Outside politicians and stars have never successfully told Arkansans how to think or vote. That year would prove no exception. We don't snub visitors. Far from it. Time and again when I was governor, we brought in tourists from every state, and from countries worldwide. We demonstrated genuine friendliness and open arms. But we also boast a stubborn resistance to outsiders who try to manage our politics. We Arkansans will make up our own minds, thank you.

Senator Gary Hart and Vice President Mondale both came to Arkansas during 1984, but they campaigned for the national ticket rather than my re-election. Bethune, on the other hand, pulled out all the Republican stops, and in his own name. "The turkey was over-cooked." That's how I described to a *Gazette* reporter Bethune's lineup of invading supporters.

Chapter 46
"I Owe Arkansas Everything ..."

Early in the campaign, Bethune hitched his wagon to the Reagan train. He
pointed to a *Congressional Quarterly* 1983 profile showing my voting
against Reagan 77% of the time, highest in the Senate. At one point, he said I
was "scaring people to death" by criticizing the president and harping
continuously on high interest rates. Most of my anti-Reagan votes involved
Pentagon issues—nerve gas production, new weapons systems, operational
testing, and military reforms.

Bethune also insisted I followed Tip O'Neill as a tax-and-spend advocate
and fan of big government regulations killing individual initiative. He emerged
from a camp led by Newt Gingrich, Jack Kemp, and other ambitious young
Republicans hoping Reagan would help them replace Democrats with a strong
conservative ideology. These fellow Republicans assured Bethune he could beat
this liberal Pryor and spread the Reagan message to Arkansas.

But two problems came with that strategy. First, Arkansas had never been
a coattail state. If Bethune had looked carefully at our political history, he
would have realized its fierce independence. He also seemed to forget that in
1968 Arkansas voters had returned J. W. Fulbright, a moderate-to-liberal
Democrat, to the Senate; elected Winthrop Rockefeller, a seasoned progressive
Republican, as governor; and endorsed George Wallace, an ardent
segregationist and leader of the American Independent Party, as president.

Second, Bethune preached ideology to people who cared more about their
everyday problems—gas prices, rural electrification, and farmers' credit—than
the latest theoretical essays on supply-side economics. In nearly every campaign
speech, I asked farmers to compare our two records. Bethune had voted against
all the Rural Electrification Administration's expansion efforts, and he had
opposed giving farmers credit they needed to borrow in the market. Using
Megatrends as his text, he argued for the theoretical and abstract, while I tried
to point out what seemed practical and hands-on.

Bethune also charged that I had linked myself to North and Midwest forces
strengthening themselves at Arkansas's expense. Yet he never defined what

those forces were, or specifically where they operated. Ernie Dumas wrote in one *Gazette* article, "It may be hard to persuade many Arkansans that David Pryor is trying to sell them down the Ohio River." During this campaign, I hit on a slogan that became a recurring theme of my Senate term: Arkansas Comes First.

Bethune charged I was "distancing" myself from the national campaign of Walter Mondale and Geraldine Ferraro. While that was overstated, it had some validity. I was a long-time supporter and friend of Mondale. In fact, he had asked me to make one of his seconding speeches at the 1976 Democratic Convention. I was honored to do it. I had worked with Ferraro for two years on Pentagon overspending issues. Her House terms had been defined by strict objections to bloated military budgets and war profiteers.

But I was running a race of my own. An old political principle states you can run only one race at a time. My hands were plenty full, and Mondale knew it. Also, Mondale knew I stood with him. He came to Arkansas in August and again in October for an electric-cooperatives regional meeting. Far from setting myself apart, I greeted him on both visits, publicly stating my support for the Democratic ticket. I also disagreed with Bethune's charge that, when Mondale picked Ferraro as his running mate, he had written off the South.

The familiar conservative vs. liberal issue continued to come up. In May, the *National Journal*, a widely respected Washington political publication, defined the Arkansas Congressional delegation as the most liberal among Southern states. On top of that, it noted my composite record on 97 economic, social, and foreign affairs votes, saying I was even more liberal than Dale Bumpers. Being identified as a super-liberal in 1984 proved uncomfortable.

Such articles always renewed Bumpers's jests over annual comparisons of our voting records. He maintained our voting patterns remained nearly identical, but Arkansas analysts always classified him a liberal and me a moderate. While I didn't dispute the published voting patterns, I wondered if their effect would hurt me with more conservative voters. Once again, I trusted Arkansas voters' essentially good judgment, knowing charts and graphs were unlikely to persuade them. In the end, they would decide on their own. What matters is the unique and unwritten bond between one public official and the single constituent. Not only is most politics local, it's also personal.

Bethune and I met in one, brief television debate—more like a conversation—with him in Fort Smith and me in Fayetteville. We also held an

August 10 statewide radio debate at an Arkansas Broadcasters Association convention in Hot Springs. We spent most of the hour discussing Reagan's second- and third-year revenue cuts and indexing income tax rates. Paul Greenberg, writing in the *Pine Bluff Commercial*, suggested I demonstrated more energy and assertion than he had ever seen. Maybe, he said, I had decided after the McClellan debate in 1972 that I would never again sit passively and let an opponent cut me up. Greenberg's comment echoed my friend Dooley Womack's warning that I'd better not let Bethune "slice me up like a piece of boarding house pie."

In October, following a session with the Jacksonville Chamber of Commerce's governmental affairs committee, I ran into Bethune as he entered the meeting room. He stopped me and pointed directly in my face.

"Are we going to debate again, or not?" he asked at the top of his voice. "Why not?" he repeated. And then again, "Why not?"

I could feel my blood beginning to boil. Eager members of the press surrounded us, their pencils and tablets poised. For a couple of seconds, I couldn't decide what to say.

"You run your campaign, Ed, and I'll run mine," I snapped. Then I offered to mail him a tape of our earlier Hot Springs debate. That must have worked. It stopped the conversation.

Bethune ran a vigorous personal campaign from the time he announced in early February. In June, his "Walk Across Arkansas" took him over 20 miles, from Lake Norfork to Bull Shoals State Park. The next month, he spent nine days traveling the Arkansas River Valley by truck, tugboat, train, and foot. He walked from Subiaco to Paris and drove a tractor to a peach orchard near Clarksville. With his wife Lana, he walked from Bella Vista to Bentonville, and from Fulton to Texarkana.

The "Walk" as a campaign device never held much appeal to me, or seemed to have enough effect to make the effort worthwhile. At one campaign stop, a young Third District Congressional candidate asked my opinion of the campaign walk. "It's fine," I told him, "if you're looking for the armadillo vote."

Wanting to hold off public campaigning as long as possible, I didn't formally launch a full-fledged re-election drive until August 28. People get tired of looking at politicians every day, and hearing the same issues bantered about. What starts as a discussion often winds up being a whining bout.

We held a Camden fish fry for 1,300 people, planned and executed by our long-time friend Bob Justice. Then we tracked down another 400 supporters to sponsor neighborhood parties for my 50th birthday, which came on the next day. My brother Bill drove up from Texas, representing me at the Harrison home of J. E. Dunlap, the *Harrison Times* publisher. With a full two months left in the campaign, the first week of September left ample time to run a solid race.

Similar to all my past campaigns, this one became a family event, with Dee, Mark, and Scott working the crowds like old pros. When Barbara and I wanted the unvarnished truth, they became excellent advisers in judging our television spots or assessing reactions to speeches. As always, Barbara proved the true soldier in every detail of planning and following through on events. She established eye contact with every voter she met.

The race became especially important to Mark, cutting his political teeth on rallies and press conferences where he learned the important art of speaking with the press. He took off a semester from the University to campaign on his own, visiting 40 counties and filling in at rallies when I couldn't get there. He also kept a daily campaign journal.

At one stop, someone asked Mark about the Republican-leaning Third District, and he said the Pryors weren't giving Ed Bethune an inch. "We'll fight tooth and nail for the Third District," he said. And he was right, even though we knew it as a Republican stronghold since it elected John Paul Hammerschmidt in 1966.

One reporter in Heber Springs asked whether Mark felt displaced touring Arkansas, since he actually lived in Washington with his parents. "My house may be in Washington," he said, "but my home—and my heart—they're in Arkansas." At one point he admitted—presciently, as his life has turned out—that he found politics fascinating, but he didn't know whether he could ever do it for a living. A footnote: after serving in the state legislature and four years as attorney general, Mark went to the U.S. Senate in 2002.

Relief came in the 1984 campaign, seeing no apparent holdover from the more brutal 1972 and 1978 races. For one thing, the McClellan encounter had taken place a full 12 years earlier. Even the longest political memories tend to fade, for the most part, by that time. Also, Democrats tend to stick together, especially those of the "Yellow Dog" variety, and Bethune, a former Democrat himself, was running on a solidly Republican platform. I received support from former adversaries Paul Berry and John Elrod, who had directed the McClellan campaign, and from Ray Thornton, my 1978 opponent, and his campaign manager, Archie Schaffer.

Bethune carried four counties in northwest Arkansas and White County, his home. I carried the other 70. The strong returns heartened me, giving me confidence that my standing with Arkansas was solid. Even though I was hopeful throughout the campaign, I honestly did not expect to receive such a landslide vote.

"I owe Arkansas everything ..."

That's how I started my Excelsior Hotel speech late in the evening on Tuesday, November 6, as the returns came in. My statement was true, not only here at campaign's end, but in the years leading to it. And since then as well. I had won the Senate race by nearly 57%, getting just over 500,000 votes to Congressman Ed Bethune's 370,000.

By any standards, this stood as a solid and gratifying win. Still, I knew receiving 60% of the vote presented no reason for cockiness or taking our hard-won victory for granted. You may be elated by results, and for very good reason. But you must remember the morning after the returns, four out of the first 10 people you meet voted for somebody else.

Chapter 47
The Right Place

I was entering the most productive period of my public life. In many ways, it proved also the most satisfactory—and the most frenzied. Those years, from 1985 through 1996, curiously combined packed, busy days with full and comforting assurance of my place and time. With secure Senate tenure and another campaign's pressure lifted, I honestly felt for the first time that whatever happened could not threaten me. It was simply meant to happen.

I also came to believe it's not adoration we seek in public life, but simple respect from those we serve. It's important to work with them, and to have them recognize that we've done our best. Along with this assurance came a reminder that I should not take myself too seriously. Self-deprecation seemed always natural for me, but now it became more real, and more important, than ever.

Here I was in the Senate, where I had always wanted to be. Yet the forces that brought me back to that hallowed ground could have sent me in any direction. As hard as I had worked to hold onto my Senate seat, no manifest destiny dictated my race's outcome against Ed Bethune. I could still be editing a Camden weekly newspaper as easily as practicing law. I recognized a combination of hard work, good luck, and instinct for opportunity had defined my career.

I also rested comfortably with my own ambition, that quality which people consistently condemn in politicians. A variety of factors motivate anyone elected to public office, ambition among them. Look at Abraham Lincoln and John F. Kennedy. And both the Presidents Roosevelt. They became political idols, but their ambition was enormous. In their way, Dr. Jonas Salk, Mahatma Ghandi, Martin Luther King, Jr., and Sam Walton—weren't they all ambitious?

No doubt, friendships formed those Senate years proved cornerstones of that good luck and satisfaction. Dale Bumpers became easily my closest confidant, due to both our Arkansas connections and our simple pleasure in each other's company. We managed to play off quirks and curiosities in each other's character. Bumpers, the great raconteur, often entertained colleagues in the private senators' dining room, spinning stories using me as a foil. And no one could better laugh at himself, or at me, than Dale Bumpers.

At the start of my third Senate term, I decided to run for secretary to the Democratic Conference. The job amounts to assisting the majority leader in tracking senators' votes and likely positions on legislation. I asked Dale to nominate me at the caucus's next meeting. He said he'd gladly accommodate me, but he wanted to know exactly what the Democratic Conference secretary *does*. "Absolutely nothing," I told him. "Great," he said, "you'll be perfect for the job."

I was forming strong friendships with other senators as well, many destined to last for years. These colleagues included, to mention only a few, Sam Nunn of Georgia, Jay Rockefeller of West Virginia, Jim Sasser of Tennessee, Michigan's Carl Levin, David Boren of Oklahoma, Bennett Johnston of Louisiana, Thad Cochran of Mississippi, Warren Rudman of New Hampshire, and Chuck Robb of Virginia. Don Riegle of Michigan and I had entered the House of Representatives together in 1967. At that time, he was a Republican. But now, several years later, we were Democratic seatmates on the Finance Committee. My friend Chris Dodd was my Senate chamber seatmate.

Montana's Max Baucus became a close colleague, at one point asking me to campaign for him in Bozeman, at a large breakfast for senior citizens. Glad to help in his re-election, I met with his campaign staff before the breakfast to get an idea of his opposition.

"What are the charges against Senator Baucus so far?" I asked.

The answers sounded an old refrain: "They say he's too liberal for Montana, that he's become a friend of Ted Kennedy and the likes, and that he's out of touch with the state." These charges mirrored those that Republicans leveled against just about any seated Democrat.

Several hundred seniors showed up for the breakfast, and I introduced Senator Baucus to the crowd.

"How many of you have been to Washington, D. C.?" I asked. About half of them raised their hands.

"And did you go by and visit with Senator Baucus?" Several hands went up.

"How many of you remember that sign on Senator Baucus's desk that proudly proclaims, 'Montana Comes First?'"

Again, several hands shot up in the air, along with general applause throughout the room that grew louder when I announced, "And now, Montana's favorite son: Max Baucus."

Max whispered to me as he came to the podium, "I don't have that sign on my desk."

"You do now," I said. A quick call to the Senate carpenter shop produced the sign that still sits on Senator Max Baucus's desk today.

* * *

In early February 1986, Levin, Boren, and I headed a Congressional mission to the Philippines—part of our government's commitment to assure their president's fair election. Since the end of World War II, the United States had considered the Philippines a necessary stability base in the Pacific. The Reagan administration actively supported Ferdinand Marcos in his attempt to win another six-year term. Opposing him was Corazón Aquino, the popular widow of Senator Benigno Aquino, assassinated three years earlier.

National elections had occurred February 7, six days before we arrived in Manila. Marcos was rather grandly declaring himself the winner, but distinct evidence of rampant fraud existed. An earlier U.S. delegation led by Senator Richard Lugar of Indiana had roundly condemned the election results.

Lugar's report led to a U.S. Senate resolution denouncing the questionable Marcos victory. When we arrived at Clark Air Base outside Manila, the country was in lockdown, Manila's streets eerily deserted by seven million citizens. They had stayed cloistered in their homes, fearing a revolution protesting the fraudulent election.

The three of us stepped directly into the controversy, almost without knowing it, when we met with Cardinal Sin and Corazón Aquino's deputy, Jose Concepción, at the Cardinal's residence on February 15. The same day, Marcos formally claimed that he had won, and Cardinal Sin found himself chief peace broker between the two factions. We backed the Lugar findings of fraud, informing the Cardinal that many of our colleagues supported Aquino and her opposition's challenge. Whatever peace Cardinal Sin could bring to his country's strife would receive Congress's full backing.

Unfortunately, Reagan's insistent support of Marcos complicated our stand. We wanted to avoid, if possible, the appearance of U.S. divided loyalties, even while recognizing that Marcos had clearly committed fraud.

Cardinal Sin greeted us with confidence and grace—a true church leader and consummate politician who saw what needed doing and was willing to influence its achievement. I was impressed by his calm manner in the face of national unrest threatening to become panic. He assured us that attempts at fairness would succeed. In the end, the will of the Philippine majority prevailed. Corazón Aquino's success came in large part through Cardinal Sin's tireless efforts. Our role had been to demonstrate that the United States Senate solidly backed Aquino and the forces of democracy.

Marcos nevertheless held an elaborate inauguration for himself on February 25. It turned into a mock ceremony poorly attended, taken seriously only by his closest comrades and military puppets. When it ended that evening, he went into exile in Hawaii with his wife, Imelda, leaving behind garish evidence of their luxurious lifestyle. Included in this display were several thousand pairs of Imelda Marcos's shoes that became symbols of her husband's reign. Corazón Aquino soon became the seventh president of the Republic of the Philippines and a strong ally of the United States.

* * *

My relationship with Oklahoma's David Boren went back to our years as governors of neighboring and sometimes competing states. Arkansas had defeated Oklahoma in a classic Orange Bowl confrontation in 1978, a hotly contested game. The generally-accepted opinion had held that Oklahoma would hand us a stinging defeat.

Their coach was Barry Switzer, a native of Crossett, Arkansas, and a former star player for the Razorbacks in the late '50s. His series of swaggering public statements made clear an Oklahoma victory would crown his impressive career. Adding to the bowl-game excitement, Boren and I announced public challenges at press conferences a week before the game.

Our informal delegation from Arkansas arrived in Miami two days early, braced for a humiliating outcome. The odds lay heavily against Arkansas. To help build morale among his underdog team, Lou Holtz invited me to a practice workout. Maybe a few words from the governor would do some good.

It's still unclear what moved the Razorbacks to play their near-perfect game. To everyone's surprise, including that of nearly our state's entire population, we defeated Oklahoma by a whopping 31-6. Early the next morning, an expensive 10-gallon Stetson arrived at the mansion, along with conciliatory best wishes from Governor Boren of Oklahoma. The hat, a gigantic model in the best Stetson tradition, was humorously too large to wear. Because it symbolized my longstanding friendship with Boren, I later brought it to Washington, displaying it atop my Senate office bookcase.

With his good nature and high-spirited personality, David Boren proved a ready target for practical jokes. A couple of years later, I had a chance to return a kidding gesture. Sitting at the back of an American Airlines plane, I waited impatiently with other passengers for takeoff from Washington's National Airport. The plane wasn't moving, and we were growing tired and fidgety. Finally, attendants hustled a rushed and frantic David Boren onto the plane and into a first-class seat at the front.

After we had left the ground, I scribbled a note, asking the flight attendant to give it to Senator Boren. I wrote that I was Jim Blaine from Pryor, Oklahoma. I had seen him hold up the plane, then take his seat in the first-class section. I wanted him to know that, as recipients of Social Security and as struggling Oklahoma seniors, my wife Myrtle and I would never vote for him again. I added that, while sitting in the Senate gallery earlier that day, we heard him proclaim that "even Social Security recipients may have to sacrifice to help pay off the national debt."

Boren and I both changed planes in Memphis. When I came through the gate, I saw him nervously pacing up and down, waiting for "the Blaines" so he could explain himself. He showed me the note he had received. He wanted simply to assure them that he never flew first class and had taken that seat only because the economy section was filled. He even wanted to explain himself to me.

"Where did you say they were from in Oklahoma?" I asked.

"Pryor," he said, and in a flash he got both the point and the joke. "You blankety-blank. I should have known," he added, as he stormed off.

Boren and I maintained such a strong friendship that, during the late 1980s, our wives even entered a business relationship. Molly Boren, a major political asset to David, brought to Washington not only a distinctive background as attorney and state judge, but also a strong talent for interior design. It didn't take long for her to team up with Barbara in founding a design enterprise. It became a thriving business during the late 1980s and into the '90s. They called the two esteemed senators in now and then for "consultation" and to deliver furniture. Boren left the Senate amid enormous popularity, becoming the University of Oklahoma's much-revered president.

* * *

Staff changes, which always occur during and after a campaign, had actually started in 1984, at the Senate race's beginning. In 1979, early in my first Senate term, Skip Rutherford had given up a Fayetteville banking career to direct my Little Rock office.

Skip had spent five years tirelessly traveling the state, holding informal hearings in court houses, meeting with local editors and reporters, and visiting with elderly people in nursing homes and hospitals. He had proved both popular and creative. For instance, when we faced the possibility of Congressman Tommy Robinson's announcing against me in 1984, Skip sent a roomful of balloons to Robinson's son, who had entered the hospital for minor surgery. We didn't know how much this might have dispelled Robinson's plans—or if he had ambitions for my Senate seat at all—but Skip maintained that, one way or the other, the nice gesture couldn't hurt. Shortly after this, Tommy announced for governor.

Frank Thomas had joined the campaign staff in 1984. He took over directing the state office, a demanding job, after Skip joined Mack McLarty at Arkansas Louisiana Gas Company. Frank had covered the governor's office as a television reporter for Little Rock's Channel Seven. He knew state politics from that side of the desk. Years later, when I retired from the Senate, he joined Stephens, Inc., as their vice president for public affairs. Frank was backed up by Kelly Robbins, an energetic young political organizer from Hot Springs who brought a high level of enthusiasm to the Senate office.

Another major staff addition was Portia Porter, the daughter of Al Porter, a long-time Little Rock activist in the black community. A recent graduate of Oberlin College, Portia brought to her job a quick intelligence and a commitment to improving people's lives. That's what struck me about her first of all. She was ideal for taking on health and education issues, plus the ticklish social questions like prayer in schools, abortion, and school busing. Portia was both patient and wise in meeting constituents from Arkansas who came to Washington, many with strong views on these issues.

One of these visitors led the Arkansas chapter of FLAG, an acronym for Family, Life, America, and God, an organization active in social issues. The woman came to the office in October 1987, expressing support for Robert Bork, whom Reagan had recently nominated to the Supreme Court.

Some weeks earlier, I had announced my opposition to Bork's nomination, based on his record as a judge on the District of Columbia Court of Appeals. His consistently reactionary decisions attempted to roll back civil rights progress. I also objected to his self-righteous and arrogant professional conduct. Controversy swirled around his nomination. Even Governor Bill Clinton, a former student of Bork's at Yale Law School, came to Washington to testify against him.

The FLAG representative questioned my opposition to Bork. But before our meeting, she was asked to sit down with Portia to present her arguments, and leave her written material with us. We usually met this way with constituents if I was in a committee hearing or on the Senate floor. The visitor could define the issues with a staff person, then follow up with me. A constituent had never balked at this informal procedure.

But the woman from FLAG held back when she met Portia. Soon it became obvious that she felt tentative expressing her concerns to a young African-American woman. Nonetheless, in time she agreed to speak with her.

"I'm impressed," she said as they sat down in Portia's office, "that you seem so clean, and that you're dressed so nicely. I can see that you're a credit to your husband, and your race."

Portia ignored her tone and manner. Instead of reacting as she might have wanted to, she moved directly into hearing the woman's views.

The FLAG leader's arguments had no effect on my opposition to Robert Bork. My vote against him proved one of the most controversial but satisfactory and justified votes on presidential nominees during my Senate tenure. The other two came when George H. W. Bush nominated Clarence Thomas to the U.S. Supreme Court and John Tower as defense secretary.

All three nominations attracted nationwide attention, and in each case I stated firm and repeated opposition. Bork's hearings became so acrimonious that the term "borked" came to describe anyone who receives stiff Congressional scrutiny in hearings and then gets voted down by the committee. The long-time critical voice against personal injury litigation, Bork went on to sue Yale University in early 2007 after he fell on a speaker's platform at New York's Yale Club.

Despite George H. W. Bush's public comment that Clarence Thomas was the country's best-qualified Supreme Court nominee, anyone who looked closely at his record could see he was woefully unprepared for the job. Also, like

Bork, he lacked judicial temperament. His ascension to the Court resulted from the heroic efforts of Senator John Danforth of Missouri. Years earlier, he had hired a much younger Thomas in the Missouri attorney general's office.

As for Tower's nomination as secretary of defense, he should never have been nominated in the first place; even he came to realize that. An overwhelming sadness prevailed at the end of the vote. He had served over a quarter-century in the Senate, in the end discovering he had few friends and even fewer supporters.

Chapter 48
A Front-Row Seat

Tax reform became the docket's first item following my 1984 re-election. As a new Senate Finance Committee member, I gained a front-row seat at this great Washington tribal dance, sometimes resembling a three-ring circus. With competition always keen for a committee seat, I began laying necessary groundwork even before the 1984 election. I became familiar with upcoming issues and talked with current members about what they hoped to achieve.

The committee selection process belonged almost exclusively to the committee chairman, Russell Long of Louisiana. He tracked me down one afternoon only minutes before my Jonesboro Rotary Club speech.

"What do you think about televising the Senate?" Long asked over the phone without a word of greeting. I knew he adamantly opposed putting Senate floor proceedings onto closed-circuit television. A strict constructionist on Senate rules, he fought nearly all attempts to change or modernize floor procedures.

"I think just like you do, Mr. Chairman," I told him.

"That's what I hoped," he said. "You just got appointed to the Finance Committee." And he hung up.

In addition to holding fast on Senate rules and tradition, Russell Long strictly read the Finance Committee's agenda and the purpose of levying taxes. His thinking ran strikingly similar to Arkansas's Wilbur Mills, the House Ways and Means Committee chairman. You weren't just dealing with revenue, Long used to say. You're engaged in helping human beings through social change. He most often put it as "acquiring social and economic justice through the tax code."

One day in 1990, Senator Long attended a Pryor fundraiser at the Democratic Club. Seeing the extended line of people trying to get in the door, he put his arm around me and said, "Ain't it good that so many people are still interested in good government?"

Russell Long's father, Huey P. Long, had barnstormed through Arkansas in the summer of 1932, helping elect Hattie Caraway to the U.S. Senate. Together they made over 30 stump-speech appearances, railing against Wall Street's robber barons. The Depression had devastated Arkansas, and Huey's charismatic and flamboyant message brought hope to crowds totalling 300,000 people who heard him speak. In the end, Hattie Caraway won, becoming America's first female U.S. senator ever elected in her own right.

Experts predicted that in 1985, Congress and the White House would agree on the most sweeping tax-code revision in three decades. The time was ripe. Any tax-law changes, any cuts or attempts at simplicity, would begin and end in our committee.

I had to find a full-time tax lawyer with intellect, educational background, and political savvy. I interviewed a host of the best-trained Washington attorneys, and several from Arkansas. A surprising number wanted the position, even when it would mean leaving a lucrative career with a law firm or lobbyist concern.

I soon decided the person must know Arkansas and our peculiar differences in geographic, financial, political, and social structures. I chose Tom Courtway, a graduate of Hendrix College and the University of Arkansas law school, who was completing a master's in law at Georgetown.

Tax-bill hearings got under way the week after Memorial Day 1985, and lasted all summer. I kept thinking about Wilbur Mills, the many years he had carried in his head the most minute tax-law details, and the subtle changes made in nearly every congressional session. We now planned a major overhaul of those longstanding provisions.

What struck me most were the horror stories we heard about the Internal Revenue Service's treatment of taxpayers. The abuses that came to light that summer went beyond bureaucratic indifference and unnecessary paperwork, although these two concerns proved serious enough. I was dismayed by IRS agents' intimidation and bullying, aimed not only at individuals but at small businesses.

I became determined to attack these IRS abuses. In September, I sponsored, and the Finance Committee approved, a proposal placing the burden of proof in all tax disputes on the IRS. This seemed fundamentally fair. Historically, in disputes with private citizens, all other government agencies were responsible for the burden of proof. Only the IRS had been exempted. But we found considerable opposition from the tax "industry" and top revenue officials.

The Finance Committee passed the Tax Reform Act of 1986 the following May. Among other things, it reduced income tax rates from an unwieldy 15 down to two—28% and 15%—broadening the tax base. It also reduced tax shelters for the wealthy and expanded provisions for pensions and Individual Retirement Accounts. Most important of all, it attempted (without success) to simplify the code so that average taxpayers could read and understand it. Even then, it turned out to be a confusing mess, perhaps more complex than before we began the "reform." So it goes in Washington. Nothing seems to change.

After 16 months of hearings, deliberations, wrangling with the Reagan administration, and incessant lobbyist visits, we gave final approval to the Tax Reform Act on September 27, 1986. Mobs of well-heeled lobbyists had gathered daily outside the Finance Committee. That led the Dirksen Office Building's second-floor hallway to become known, appropriately, as Gucci Gulch. And this was picked up as the title of an insightful book, *Showdown at Gucci Gulch*, by Jeffrey Birnbaum and Alan Murray. The eyes of Washington focused on this single hallway. The most subtle thoughts expressed in those committee deliberations reached across Capitol Hill, spreading to the inner sanctums of Wall Street and the world's financial markets.

The tax bill dominated my schedule that summer and into the fall. In fact, it remained that year's only major "game in town" for most senators and their staffs. The action proved so intense that it overshadowed even the earlier Reagan tax bill, known as Kemp-Roth, in 1981.

Because of my almost total absorption in the committee, Barbara had stayed at our Little Rock apartment for most of the summer. She planned to return to Washington at the end of September. She was especially concerned about her younger brother, David Lunsford, who had been admitted for depression to the Bridgeway Hospital in North Little Rock. Only 33 years old, he had started a round of doctor-prescribed medication and faced a promising future. He seemed to be pulling out of the deep despair that had led to his treatment.

But a day or two before Barbara's scheduled return to Washington, David took his life on Bridgeway's hospital grounds. Barbara was with him when he broke away from her, climbed up a tall oak tree, and leapt to the ground from a top limb. It was a paralyzing moment for Barbara, who stood helplessly as he fell at her feet.

Our family's entire activity came to an abrupt halt. What could anything in our busy schedules mean in the face of David's final rash act? We were devastated.

Barbara's older brother, Porter Lunsford, had died of leukemia in 1970 when he was 33 years old. Even knowing that Porter's death was imminent and couldn't be prevented, we had never fully become reconciled to his loss. Porter was a fun-loving brother to Barbara and an irrepressible wit, very much like his father. Now, nearly 20 years later, David had died at the same age, and under such tragic circumstances. There was no way we could have anticipated his suicide, or prepared our reaction to it.

We were once again heartbroken the following summer, in July 1987, when my sister Elinor's son, Matt Ozment, also took his life in Little Rock. In the face of such despairing moments as these, public life's demands quickly take on a vastly diminished importance.

Trying to explain these actions took second place to providing support for both surviving families. I still think of David and Matt, two of nature's gentle spirits, as young men—both still boys, in many ways—who loved their full lives. But at some inexplicable point, those lives took a tragic turn toward depression and despair. Could any of us have foreseen what was happening in their minds, or altered their final actions? These were the questions our families asked ourselves over and over. Even these many years later, final answers with any satisfactory and lasting comfort are still to come.

Early in the morning of Matt Ozment's memorial service, Federal Judge Bill Overton, my long-time and closest friend from law school, died of cancer at his Little Rock home. Doctors had diagnosed his illness two years earlier. The last months of his life were filled with brief and frustrating setbacks, followed by determined efforts to return to work. He showed a consistently heroic refusal to give in to his illness. As a federal judge in 1982, Overton had struck down the infamous Act 590, the so-called "Balanced Treatment Act," requiring Arkansas public schools to teach creation science. His decision remains a victory for clear-thinking people in Arkansas and throughout the country.

A brilliant lawyer and judge, Overton was governed by an inner core of no-nonsense practicality. He brought to this earthiness a finely tuned sense of humor. Once, on a fishing trip in Canada, we found ourselves on an immense lake when a fierce storm came out of nowhere. Our small boat tossed and turned in every direction, but there was only one life preserver onboard. I thought this a good time to put a professional question to him, at least half in jest. "Who is more important," I asked, "a U.S. senator or a federal judge?" He didn't hesitate: "That Indian guiding this boat!"

The two of us sat on his front porch only a few days before his death. In a very weakened voice, he asked me to come closer. He said he wanted to tell me a secret. When I moved nearer to him, he said, "Pryor, I want you to know something."

"What is it, Judge?" I asked.

Barely audible but with a smile, he said, "Women lawyers are better than men lawyers."

Bill's wife Susan asked me to speak at his memorial service. The First Methodist Church in Little Rock overflowed with friends and relatives of the Overton family, along with nearly every judge and lawyer from around Arkansas. This was probably the most difficult public speech I recall ever making. Bill Overton was not only a brilliant attorney and federal judge, he had been my close friend, adviser, fishing partner, and confidant for more than 25 years. I think of him every day.

Chapter 49
A Walk in the Woods

At the end of 1987's summer recess, I returned to Washington with new resolve and sense of purpose. Still shaken by personal loss and the demands of a time-consuming job, I determined to shape my life's direction. I also knew the difficulties this would involve.

The Democrats had regained a Senate majority in 1986. I chaired the Senate Subcommittee on Oversight of the Internal Revenue Service, a small but crucial arm of the Senate Finance Committee. The title, though cumbersome, meant that I could monitor the IRS in all its questionable, overreaching activities. More than that, I received an opportunity to provide taxpayers with rights and protections they'd never known before.

With the 1986 tax-bill hearings still fresh in my mind, I could recall numerous IRS abuses. Using tactics any creditor would envy, federal agents could legally wipe out a bank account, or seize a carpenter's truck, or close down a small business—and the individual citizen possessed no recourse.

In one case, a 10-year-old California girl had to forfeit her total savings of $694 because her parents owed back taxes. Similarly, the IRS had taken $173 from an Iowa farmer's three small children when their father sold his farm to pay his income tax. Hundreds of similar horror stories whetted my appetite to challenge the federal agency's unaccountable actions.

The new W-4 tax form loomed over all these individual abuses. The IRS hailed it as a marked improvement in taxpayer fairness. The problem was that no one, including agents and department heads, could understand or explain the new form. Not even members of the tax-writing Finance Committee could fill out the jumbled-up W-4. Of course, we were receiving thousands of complaint letters.

A prime example of IRS bullying tactics came with agents' treatment of Judge Harry E. Claiborne, Nevada's chief federal judge. Claiborne, a McRae, Arkansas, native and 1937 Ouachita College graduate, was recognized as one of the Southwest's best criminal defense attorneys. Known by Nevada lawyers as "the Arkansas preacher," he was also a legendary storyteller who drew on early experiences in rural Arkansas and Mississippi.

In 1984, Claiborne was convicted of tax evasion, the first sitting federal judge found guilty of a crime. He began serving time in an Alabama prison, and the Senate set up a special 12-member committee to hear his case. The panel questioned whether he should be impeached and agreed he should. After a closed floor debate, the Senate endorsed the committee's recommendations and impeached him. As a committee member, I heard all sides of the argument. While I could not defend his questionable conduct—no one even tried—I found it equally impossible to justify the actions of the FBI and IRS in obtaining information to convict him.

Judge Claiborne had proved amiss in IRS dealings, but he was not a criminal, and he did not set out to defraud the federal government. His chief fault lay in over-dependence on tax advisors and financial consultants. He maintained that a vengeful Justice Department framed him for his balanced treatment of criminal defendants. This might well have been true.

From my view, the FBI hounded Judge Claiborne to humiliate a high-profile tax offender, in this case a federal judge. An anonymous caller to my office, identifying himself only as a government agent, said he had joined other officers who entered and ransacked Claiborne's home without a proper search warrant. I couldn't shake the memory of seeing Judge Harry Claiborne led by federal marshals from the Senate floor in handcuffs and leg irons. They then shoved him into a van at the U.S. Capitol's front steps. He served 17 months in a federal penitentiary, where he managed the prison greenhouse.

* * *

A Taxpayers Bill of Rights had hovered in the back of my mind since the Finance Committee hearings that summer of 1986. As chairman of the IRS Oversight subcommittee, I had become well-positioned to begin pushing for such a bill. My primary goal was simple and direct: give the taxpayer the benefit of any possible doubt in disputed cases, and place the burden of proof on the IRS.

These were hardly new objectives. Another Senate Finance subcommittee had held hearings on these issues over a decade earlier. It concerned me that, despite past good intentions, Congress had written no meaningful legislation, much less passed and signed a bill into law.

From 1987 through 1989, our subcommittee heard more than 200 witnesses of IRS abuse and the need for reform. We received repeated details of IRS agents employing over-zealous, heavy-handed, and often illegal methods.

Large numbers of agents regarded delinquent taxpayers as "deadbeats," and property seizures were not only allowed but encouraged. One Los Angeles revenue office boasted a wall sign reading, "Seizure Fever—Catch It!" A Baltimore IRS office memo reminded agents that low seizure rates and few criminal referrals could affect employee salaries and benefits. This "macho mentality" seemed to define IRS seizure methods.

Our initial witnesses were IRS whistle-blowers willing to testify about abuses. These agents constantly spoke of fearing to question their superior officers' authority or conduct. In one hearing, IRS Commissioner Lawrence Gibbs assured us that agents were trained and severely curtailed in their aggressive activities, making any bill of rights unnecessary. All employees received handbooks clear in their disciplinary guidelines, he insisted. I argued that changes should occur in the *law*, not in some Internal Revenue Service manual.

My principal allies were Democratic Senator Harry Reid of Nevada and Republican Senator Chuck Grassley of Iowa. In addition to shifting the burden of proof, we called for a new inspector general's office in the IRS. We demanded a requirement that the federal agency send written statements of charges and complaints—similar to the reading of Miranda rights—to any citizen under investigation. We extended taxpayers' response time from 10 days to 30 and guaranteed an individual citizen be represented by an attorney or a certified public accountant. The bill also assigned a taxpayer's ombudsman to each IRS district office, a provision the IRS strongly opposed.

Confronting skepticism from all sides, I welcomed support and encouragement from any place I could find it. At one point, a key provision needed the strong hand of Senator Lloyd Bentsen of Texas, the Finance Committee chairman. Without his support, the amendment surely would fail. Bentsen was a friend, but he played his cards close to his chest. It was never safe to take his support for granted. One afternoon he came to me on the Senate floor. He asked if I still headed that small Governmental Affairs subcommittee on post offices, and did the subcommittee still name new Federal buildings and other government facilities. I told him both counts were true.

"Well," he said, "an old friend and supporter of mine down in Corpus Christi has been diagnosed with terminal cancer. He's a war hero and a leader in the state and community. His name is Hector P. Garcia, and that post office is about to be finished in Corpus. I was wondering ..."

"It's done," I told him. On January 27, 1987, the Hector P. Garcia post office was dedicated in Corpus Christi, Texas. This occurred shortly after my tax provision passed the Senate Finance Committee, with the full endorsement of Senator Lloyd Bentsen of Texas.

That November, the committee approved the Taxpayers Bill of Rights, but the bill died at year's end. This came as no surprise, since there was strong opposition to reining in the IRS. Most of the objections came from the Reagan Administration, strongly determined to kill the legislation, or at least water it down. But even some Democrats proved less than enthusiastic, fearing tax revenues would suffer.

My staff lawyer at this time was Steve Glaze, a native of Little Rock and an impressive tax specialist who saw this legislation through many stages of rewriting and to its final form. The following March, after hard lobbying on my part, the committee voted it out a second time, and the Senate passed it in October. In one of President Reagan's last public appearances of his second term, he signed it into law in November. The bill marked the first time Congress had approved legislation giving rights to taxpayers without adding powers to the Internal Revenue Service.

* * *

A group of Arkansas business leaders and Arkansas State Chamber of Commerce officers decided in 1987 that the state should push Arkansas products and technology abroad. This was the age of *glasnost*, when Mikhail Gorbachev committed the Soviet Union to accountability, open discussion, and freer trade with the West. Our party was pulled together with help from Graham Catlett, a Little Rock businessman excited about opening exchange programs with the Soviet Union. Graham believed an economic mission by top Arkansas entrepreneurs was the ideal place to start. He had enlisted the splendid services of another young and ambitious entrepreneur, Vince Insalaco. Barbara and I were asked to lead the delegation.

The group included a number of distinguished Arkansans: Sam Walton of WalMart, Don Tyson of Tyson Foods, Cecil Cupp from the State Chamber of Commerce, James "Bum" Atkins, Mack McLarty, Melvyn Bell, and Walter Smiley. All of our party flew first class except for the Pryors and the Waltons, who flew coach. We spent a week in Moscow conferences followed by another two days in Leningrad, now once again St. Petersburg. The Soviet Committee on Youth Organizations hosted us, providing escorts and translators for our visits with government officials and business leaders.

The primary target was an emerging capitalist class eager to lift the Russian economy back on its feet. A trip highlight involved touring Gum, the huge state-operated department store near Red Square. Sam Walton shared detailed suggestions for marketing the store's products; later in the day he gave the WalMart cheer in our Moscow hotel's lobby. Bill Keller, the *New York Times* Moscow correspondent (later the paper's executive editor), covered our visit, and in particular Walton's entrepreneurial demonstration.

* * *

Soon after this trip, I was privileged to take a much-touted Walk in the Woods. Here's how it came about. A late '80s informal meeting with timber industry leaders renewed my concern about clear-cutting in the Ouachita National Forest. The long-recognized custom of leveling large swaths of forestland had always struck me as causing permanent damage.

One forestry expert described clear-cutting as an ecological trauma without precedent in nature, second only to a major volcanic eruption. The practice destroys buffer zones that prevent flooding and removes forest canopies protecting wildlife and natural growth.

Since the 1930s, the U.S. Forest Service had seemed more interested in helping the timber industry than in managing forestland for wildlife habitats and human recreation. The federal agency had even built roads to accommodate lumber companies, which amounted to an enormous industry subsidy.

Such close and longstanding relationships had resulted in higher industry sales. The Forest Service had kept a portion of those proceeds to patch up damage caused by the cutting itself. For years, this procedure had received a series of environmentally sound names like "meadow restoration" and "wildlife openings." But it was clear-cutting pure and simple, by any definition the quickest and most efficient way to destroy a forest.

The Forest Service caught Arkansans' attention in 1986, announcing that it wanted to produce 200 million board feet a year from the Ouachita National Forest, a wide stretch of rolling woodlands that runs from eastern Oklahoma to central Arkansas. This meant clear-cutting, in effect decimating more than 35 varieties of hardwood and softwood, leaving thousands of acres denuded and bare.

Following my conversations with timber industry leaders, I wondered if we might find some middle ground for agreement among the environmentalists, the timber industry, and the government. Fully aware that the lumber and paper industries have traditionally been among Arkansas's major employers, I had to strike a delicate balance between them and the environmentalists who had become galvanized by the Forest Service's scorched-earth plans.

In August, 1990, I wrote a letter to U.S. Forest Service chief Dale Robertson, asking for a moratorium on all Ouachita National Forest clear-cutting. Somewhat to my surprise, he responded favorably, suggesting a field inspection to discuss the matter.

This invitation led to a "walk in the woods," as the press came to call it, outside Perryville with Robertson and Ouachita Forest Supervisor John Curran. I knew they had to protect the Forest Service's interests, but I was also familiar with Robertson's background as a Bald Knob native and University of Arkansas graduate. Surely he would understand the opposition to clear-cutting, and might even agree to an action plan that would protect the forests. Adding to the political and financial mix, we also had to consider the local school districts that would lose revenue from timber sales.

Carmie Henry of our staff drafted the sensitive agreement that would satisfy all parties concerned. He masterfully spelled out terms of a Forest Management Plan that covered nearly two million acres. It later became national policy. Under our proposed agreement, clear-cutting could only occur to protect trees against disease.

The forestry association quickly objected to the moratorium, stating that it side-stepped all the Ouachita Forest's management directives. They also accused me of caving in to the Sierra Club and the Ouachita Watch League. But in time they agreed with our plan and projections, especially as public opinion shifted in our favor. Our agreement led to the Ouachita National Forest becoming the country's first federal woodland to ban the clear-cutting practice.

Chapter 50
The Graying of America

Michael Dukakis lost to George H.W. Bush in the 1988 presidential election, but the Democrats retained Senate control. In the general election, however, Senator John "Doc" Melcher, a Montana Democrat, lost. That meant I would become chairman of the Senate Aging Committee. I was sorry for my good friend, but at the same time I became eager to take on an ideal challenge, considering my interest in aging issues since my days in the House of Representatives.

For staff director, I chose Portia Porter Mittelman, who fit perfectly due to her knowledge of issues touching the country's elderly population, particularly in Arkansas. She became the first African-American female to direct a Senate committee staff. Her assistant, Chris Jennings, had worked on the committee for Melcher. Chris had perhaps the widest background on health concerns of any Senate staff person.

Chris seemed hesitant about taking the job when we first discussed it by phone. I was in Little Rock, and he was in his Washington office, preparing to move out with the remainder of Melcher's staff. I asked how serious he was about staying on.

"Well," he said after a long pause, "there's this one consideration I have to deal with." I asked him to tell me about it.

"I'm going into the hospital in two days," he said. "You see, I'm donating one of my kidneys to my brother."

I said, "You're hired." Chris later went to work for Hillary Clinton. Today, he is one of Washington's most respected contributors to the cause of universal health care.

As a member of the Aging Committee, and long before taking the chairmanship, I had sponsored hearings on catastrophic and long-term care insurance. These began in 1986 in Fort Smith. Along with Senator William Cohen, my Republican colleague from Maine, I had expanded these investigations to include rural health problems. We found that hospitals situated away from urban centers were in dire need of primary care personnel and equipment. Also, they received lower reimbursement rates under Medicare than hospitals in cities.

Leading up to a reauthorization of the Older Americans Act, we found a dismaying recurrence of violence among grandparents raising children and grandchildren. This occurred amid drug and alcohol abuse. Hearings on these and related social concerns proved especially effective when we held them in regional settings such as Little Rock and Portland, Maine. Witnesses became more willing to testify at home than in Washington, D.C., tossed in the federal bureaucracy's uncertain waters. We discovered bravery among whistle-blowers similar to the courage shown during our hearings into IRS abuses.

We also found that many organizations claiming to benefit the aging were actually money-making schemes, preying on unwitting elderly citizens. This abuse first came to my attention in a Little Rock grocery store. An elderly man showed me a letter from some fly-by-night organization, the letterhead indicating an official U.S. government agency. It asked that he send $10 to save his Social Security checks.

Hundreds of thousands of unsuspecting seniors were falling for these scams. The United Seniors Association, along with Citizens for Better Medicare, maintained extensive mailing lists. They solicited elderly people's funds but rarely worked on legislation or improving conditions for the aging. Direct mail expert Richard Viguerie, who began his career working for evangelist Billy James Hargis, was a prime instigator in these efforts. So was James Dobson, who went on to head Focus on the Family. Together, they ran organizations that I called "fright factories," heavily financed by the nation's leading pharmaceutical manufacturers.

Most of our Aging Committee's attention, in fact, focused on the pharmaceutical industry's growing influence. By the 1980s, this powerful collection of major corporations greatly profited from the elderly population's medical needs. Our efforts to gain information, however, proved very difficult. Many of the leading drug companies refused to answer our questions or claimed scheduling conflicts prevented them from appearing at our committee hearings.

One leading pharmaceutical company's chairman actually wrote, "We believe that a hearing is not an appropriate forum in which to elucidate the very complex issues you raise." While these companies chose not to testify at a Senate hearing, they were sharing openly with investors their enormous, even outrageous profits. Legitimate profits can be justified, but we were targeting the industry's wholesale profiteering by abusing America's most vulnerable population.

The pharmaceutical companies constantly stressed the money they spent on researching and improving drugs. But in fact, while they spent $9 billion on research and development, they put $10 billion a year into marketing, advertising, and lobbying. Products billed as breakthrough innovations too often turned out to be "me-too" drugs, copying brands already on the market. Today that practice has only grown worse.

From 1980 to 1989, drug prices rose 88%, but company taxes shrank during the same period. The Labor Department estimated that, in one month, prescription drug costs increased 9.2%, more than double the rise in the Consumer Price Index. Making matters worse, U.S. wholesalers' prices on 100 of the most widely prescribed drugs ranged 32% higher than those in Canada.

One morning I had breakfast with the president of a major pharmaceutical company. My friend and former colleague, Howard Baker of Tennessee, represented the company in Washington and suggested that we three meet for a conversation.

"What do you want of us, Senator Pryor?" the company president asked.

"Just give the American consumer the same price you sell your drugs for in Canada," I replied.

"Oh, but that's impossible," he said. "It would be too complicated."

A doctor in Smackover sent us a bag of "loot," gifts received from pharmaceutical companies hoping he would recommend their products to his patients. We sent the contents to Andy Rooney, the CBS "60 Minutes" commentator. He devoted his Sunday evening segment to the "loot."

Rooney said every day is Christmas in a doctor's office, where drug companies' chairmen play Santa Claus. Manufacturers were sending full sit-down lunches three times a week to key doctors on their lists. They provided resort vacations to medical specialists and called such trips "continuing education." Pointing to our Aging Committee's hearings, Rooney suggested, "You shouldn't invite Senator Pryor and the president of any drug company to the same dinner party."

In 1990, I introduced what became explosive legislation that set the pharmaceutical industry on fire: the Pharmaceutical Access and Prudent Purchasing Act, or PAPPA. It was intended to end the prescription drug price spiral. A simple and direct effort to assist Medicaid, the largest single purchaser of pharmaceuticals, the bill enabled state Medicaid programs to negotiate with manufacturers to lower drug prices.

This tool would have given Medicaid officials the same negotiating authority already available to the Departments of Defense and Veterans Affairs. We even had endorsements from the three leading retail pharmacy groups—the nation's local drug stores. They argued that, at last, the manufacturers could play a meaningful role in containing costs for their customers.

In no time, the pharmaceutical companies published newsletters defining my bill as cumbersome and complicated, scientifically unsound, harmful to Medicaid recipients, and unlikely to save anybody money. An official of the Pharmaceutical Manufacturers Association, or PMA, the industry's lobby group, issued an op-ed article even claiming the legislation was unconstitutional.

Struggles with the pharmaceutical companies continued through my remaining Senate years, from my Aging Committee chairmanship's beginning until I retired in early 1997. We never fully reconciled our differences.

I introduced a generic drug bill in 1996. That was the last straw as far as the drug manufacturers were concerned. I wanted to close a loophole to the General Agreement on Tariffs and Trade, or GATT. It forced makers of generic drugs to wait an unconscionable 20 years before releasing a product that competed with a brand-name drug. Ted Kennedy of Massachusetts and Paul Simon of Illinois supported my bill. Industry lobbying proved fierce and constant, and once again their side prevailed. This final effort came in the summer before my retirement. By then, I must say that defeat had come to feel customary.

My experience on the Finance Committee, working on the Taxpayers Bill of Rights, and struggling for direct answers from pharmaceutical manufacturers, brought home two invaluable truths: first, that special interest lobbyists' full power not only influences public policy, it often writes it, dictates its tiniest details, and determines its longevity and effect on our social structure; and second, because of the lobbying community's clever tactics, together with its almost endless fund supply, the public will probably never learn the extent of its influence.

* * *

My heart attack on April 15, 1991, put a quick stop to any active participation in Senate hearings and floor action. More to the point, I thought my life—both personal and professional—had come to a grinding halt.

Two days after the attack, the *Arkansas Democrat* ran a lengthy story titled, "Highlights of David Pryor's Life." Reading it made me think I was witnessing my obituary preview—the way Huck Finn, from his hideaway on Jackson Island, spies the search party trying to find his body washed up on the river bank.

My doctors performed angioplasty at George Washington University Hospital on April 22, and the next day upgraded my condition from fair to good. Uncertain what that meant, I decided it sounded encouraging, and willingly accepted the new designation. Later, Mark revealed to a reporter the family's primary concern: that the hospital please not give me a telephone.

Even though I was technically out of the action, things didn't come to a complete standstill. By that time, the Aging Committee staff was headed by Theresa Forster, a former member of my personal staff. She had left Capitol Hill to head a legislative program for a private home healthcare agency. She had worked with the Halamandaris family, two brothers and their parents who were national pioneers in designing hospice programs for the elderly. Her return to the Senate was a major boon to the Aging Committee.

Back in April, only a day after my heart attack, Majority Leader George Mitchell had introduced a bill on my behalf. It required states to adopt consumer protections for private, long-term care insurance. This followed one of the earlier recommendations by Congressman Claude Pepper's commission. It also gave me a policy issue to track during the long summer.

Lloyd Bentsen, chairman of Senate Finance, then introduced a Pryor bill easing small business employers' efforts to set up employee pension plans under 401(k) rules. Once again, I felt I was still taking part in Senate business and followed closely what turned into a major retirement question.

On the first of August, I made a video appearance before a Fort Smith hearing—my first public duty following my heart attack and several months of recuperation. It was also the first time a witness had offered testimony by satellite. A *Times Record* reporter stated that I looked "tanned but a little gaunt." I didn't know whether to be encouraged or depressed by that description.

* * *

Looking back on those years, I'm struck by the number of tax bills, public events, political pronouncements, even wars, which seemed to sweep through in quick succession. On August 2, 1990, Saddam Hussein invaded Kuwait, and five days later the U.S. sent troops to Saudi Arabia to assure stability at the border. The U. N. imposed immediate sanctions against Iraq. In late November, the Security Council passed a resolution stating that, if Saddam hadn't withdrawn by January 15, the U.N. would authorize the use of force against Iraq.

For two months after the invasion, Congress generally believed that Saddam Hussein would realize what he was up against and pull back his troops. The numbers were against him. By the end of August, more than 30 countries had joined the allied coalition, and a build-up of cruise missiles, fighter planes, and bombers awaited action. Saddam, however, refused to budge.

Early polls showed many Americans skeptical of military intervention, hoping that diplomatic efforts would succeed. When President George H. W. Bush doubled the original military force in November, Senator Sam Nunn held hearings to determine the administration's intentions. Surely some diplomatic ground hadn't been covered. But by year's end, the country seemed to support U.S. military action in the "first" Gulf War.

As talks failed between Secretary of State James Baker and Tariq Aziz, the Iraqi foreign minister, polls showed even more solid public support for war. The leadership shown by President Bush's commander, General H. Norman Schwarzkopf, proved a major factor in solidifying confidence. He became a national hero seemingly overnight.

In the Senate, we debated whether the nation should go to war over Kuwait. Democrats drew straws to determine the order for making our floor statements. No pressure existed to oppose the administration and unite against the war effort. Each senator was essentially an independent contractor. We caucused over one weekend and stayed in touch during the following days to determine existing support and opposition. Democrats' major speculation centered on senators: Al Gore, who ultimately voted in favor of Desert Storm, and Sam Nunn, who, in a hushed Senate chamber, voted against it.

In spite of our mission's overall acceptance, I questioned the wisdom of a military commitment on such new and uncertain ground. For that reason, I voted against Desert Storm and whatever military action it included. I believed that even a minor skirmish in Iraq and Kuwait could spiral into a major conflict beyond our control. The issue of time also concerned me. How long would this operation take, and how would we know when it was over? The administration, most of all the Pentagon, brushed these and other questions aside.

The Desert Storm attack began on January 17, 1991—the first war fought on live television. In fact, in a groundbreaking event, the start of combat operations was actually announced on CNN. More than a million ground troops, nearly half of them American, were involved in major fighting confined to Iraq, Kuwait, and the border areas of Saudi Arabia. The resolve of Iraq and its military had been so weakened by six months of economic blockades that it was a wonder its army lasted even 41 days.

President Bush declared victory on February 27. In the first week of March, our troops began to come home. We lost a total of 148 military personnel in the conflict.

Secretary of Defense Dick Cheney admitted later that Bush wanted Congress's authorization to enter the war, but it wasn't really necessary. Bush looked at approval from Capitol Hill as a minor inconvenience and in no way essential. The administration had Truman and the Korean conflict as a precedent for acting on its own. If the president hadn't been given permission from Congress, Cheney said that he would have recommended going ahead without it. It appeared, even then, that the legislative branch was at best an impertinence, a position that today the George W. Bush administration has repeated time and again.

Cheney's response has stayed very much in my mind during the several years of our current war in Iraq. It betrays a typical attitude on the part of Dick Cheney, the Defense Secretary then, and since the 2000 elections, Vice President of the United States. It occurred to me in 1991 that our country should be very sure of its intentions, and our preparations must include contingencies for any conceivable outcome. We possessed far better reason for confidence at that time than in 2003, when doubt and skepticism came to infect the national consciousness.

Those who, like me, opposed the 1991 war in Iraq nonetheless instinctively trusted our leaders, even while disagreeing with them. What's more, a concrete body of intelligence supported their military actions, and the Pentagon had made solid plans for any possible contingency. These assurances proved tragically absent when this country invaded Iraq in 2003. The added loss of confidence in our political leadership is a sad result of the administration's arrogance and incompetence.

Chapter 51
Friends of Bill

Bill Clinton announced as a presidential candidate on a bright Thursday morning, October 3, 1991, in front of downtown Little Rock's Old State Capitol. John Robert Starr, the *Arkansas Democrat-Gazette*'s managing editor, had been reminding Arkansas readers that Clinton had promised to serve out his term as governor, but Clinton explained over and over that he had traveled the state, asking everyone he talked to about changing that commitment. He claimed many times that they had given him permission.

Earlier in the year, Barbara and I had attended Vince Foster, Sr.'s funeral in Hope. A seasoned politician and businessman, he was the father of Vince Foster, who later joined the Clintons in the White House. During the service, I took out a funeral program, wrote "RUN!" on it, passed it down to Hillary Clinton, and whispered a request that she hand it to her husband.

A week before Clinton's announcement, John Daly, our best-known young golfing sensation, had just won the PGA championship, firing the sporting imagination of all Arkansas golfers. I said that I hoped Clinton, like Daly, would pull out his driver, tee up, and hit a long one. A corny metaphor maybe, but heartfelt and sincere. The attention and good will Clinton could bring to Arkansas would prove enormous.

That morning Clinton, our 45-year-old governor, announced to a cheering mob that he would help bring about a "new America." He promised to broaden opportunities for all. When the Associated Press listed the top Arkansas stories of 1991, Clinton's announcement and fledgling campaign ranked number one; listed second was the sad demise of the oldest newspaper west of the Mississippi, the *Arkansas Gazette*, its final major story being Clinton's entry into the presidential race; and third was our Arkansas troops' deployment to service in Operation Desert Storm.

Many in that October crowd had supported Clinton for almost two decades, since 1974 when he challenged John Paul Hammerschmidt, the veteran Third District Congressman. Though Clinton lost that first race, this dynamic young law professor, with a background as a Georgetown graduate and Rhodes scholar, established a base of fiercely loyal friends, particularly in the state's western and northern counties. Two years later, he became Arkansas's attorney general at 29 years old, the youngest person in the state's history to fill that office.

After winning the governor's race in 1978, Clinton was jolted two years later, losing to Frank White, a Democrat who turned Republican specifically to run for governor. Many editorial writers predicted a quick and regrettable end to Bill Clinton's promising career. They said, well, the Clinton bubble has burst. He'll never be able to pull those fractured pieces together again. Nearly all newspaper editors sounded his political knell.

But somehow Bill and Hillary Clinton found the strength and resolve to rise again, and two years later they regained the political capital everyone thought they'd lost. When he lifted from the ashes, he seemed a wiser and more thoughtfully seasoned Bill Clinton. In their second race, he defeated White by close to 75,000 votes—a hefty win in anyone's book—and he would never again let his guard down, or allow attacks on his record to go unanswered.

Many at the Old State House that October day of his presidential announcement were curious and unsuspecting bystanders. They weren't looking for any landmark moments or historic gestures. Media attention was generous by Arkansas standards, but the national press corps remained skeptical, even cynical, when Clinton said he would run for president. After all, George H. W. Bush was sporting a 90% approval rating that very day.

Through the rest of the fall, Clinton cultivated key players in the early primary states. He moved with a quiet precision I found impressive but not entirely surprising. Some 300 Arkansas Travelers, as they came to be called, made their way to New Hampshire by car, van, plane, and bus. Their message rang clear: "We're from Arkansas, and we're friends of Bill Clinton. We want to tell you about him." This steady stream got under way in January, and Barbara and I readily took part in the New Hampshire invasion. John Brummett, the *Arkansas Democrat-Gazette* columnist, said these friends had anted up "like donors to the Razorback Scholarship Fund."

Clinton's greatest challenge came from former Senator Paul Tsongas of Massachusetts, and for good reason. Tsongas had left the Senate in 1985 after an enviable record as a progressive Democrat with a surprising business bent. He not only came from New Hampshire's next-door state, he was highly regarded as a thoughtful, serious public servant and a brilliant lawyer. Late January's polls showed Tsongas well ahead, but Clinton running a respectable second. Health questions about his past battle with cancer pursued Tsongas all year. In time, unfortunately for his spirited campaign, he had to retire from the race. Tsongas returned to his law practice in Boston and died in 1997. His early death was a sad loss to his state, the Democratic Party, and the country.

On January 28, just weeks before the New Hampshire primary, a former Little Rock cabaret singer named Gennifer Flowers claimed on the front page of the *Star*, a tabloid newspaper, that she had carried on a 12-year affair with the Arkansas governor. All hell broke loose. Flowers had worked in Little Rock as a television reporter and had interviewed Clinton and other public officials a number of times. The press, even in Arkansas where she was known as a less than reliable journalist, gave her surprisingly more credibility than she deserved.

The following Sunday night, Bill and Hillary Clinton went on CBS's "60 Minutes" immediately following the Super Bowl. The television audience of 40 million viewers ranked as one of the largest ever recorded. Clinton acknowledged having been the cause of pain in his marriage, but he stated flatly that Flowers's allegations were false. Admitting that he had known Gennifer Flowers, he described her as nothing more than "a friendly acquaintance" who had interviewed him on local news stories.

The Clintons appeared remarkably calm and confident in the interview. He even seemed to enjoy himself, addressing every question with a helpful elaboration and leaving nothing unanswered. But despite his denials, and Hillary's warm assertions of faith in her husband, their campaign came to a virtual stop.

The next day Gennifer Flowers held a rowdy press conference at New York's Waldorf Astoria Hotel. The national press turned out in droves. Flowers confessed she had been in love with Clinton but was now sick of "the lying and deceit." When asked for his reaction, Clinton said that as far as he was concerned, the matter was closed.

It was just the beginning.

Chapter 52
The Comeback Kid

If New Hampshire's citizens hadn't heard about Bill Clinton earlier, they certainly knew about him after that wrenching weekend with Gennifer Flowers all over the news. Some media skeptics referred to him as a walking dead man. Others simply rolled their eyes. Few if any gave him the slightest chance to recover from Flowers's charges.

Clinton's resilience might have come from having lost two early political races. There's nothing that gets a politician's attention like losing a tight election. But in my view, his resolve went deeper than that. Clinton has never wavered, always believing in that enigma called the American Dream. He came literally out of nowhere and with nothing. But he defined himself as a person of intelligence and charisma. With unmatched determination, he found what he set out to achieve for himself and for the country.

There was something else. Clinton's political savvy assumes our country is split down the middle, no matter the issue. To win an election, or govern successfully, he has always planted his feet at that division's center, so he can move either left or right. He always leads from the middle.

* * *

Barbara and I visited New Hampshire several times in early 1992, doing everything we could to excite the cold but curious crowds. I can still see her trudging through the snow and loving every minute of it. Our collective plans worked in the end, but only after pulling out all the old political stops we could remember. Or maybe it was more like pulling teeth. When a man in the crowd yelled at me, "I don't like politicians," I called back to him, "I don't either!"

We took our campaign cue from Patty Criner, a childhood friend of Bill Clinton who had worked for me in the governor's office and had come to New Hampshire to set up Clinton's headquarters there. During the first weekend in February, I appeared on three radio stations in New Hampshire's southern half, making probably 10 stops along the way. In addition to considerable New England reserve, I found a surprising amount of anti-Bush sentiment. This in spite of Desert Storm, a struggle that received popular support from nearly everyone. In the end, the electoral decision turned on much more than the war. As Clinton's adviser James Carville said at the start of the campaign, "It's the economy, stupid."

A high point for Clinton's New Hampshire campaign came on February 18, when Arkansans for Clinton held a massive rally in Durham. Later, I told his press people about how Joe Purcell had been elected Arkansas attorney general in 1966. No one outside central Arkansas knew who he was, so he put together a newspaper ad, hoping it might stir up his campaign and get statewide attention. It sent the Purcell numbers through the roof. The *Arkansas Gazette* ad covered two full pages, listing names and home phone numbers of a thousand people living in and around Benton, his hometown. "We're Joe Purcell's friends and neighbors in Saline County," it said. "Please call us *collect* if you want to know more about this fine man."

Some of Clinton's professional consultants found the idea a little hokey. But the Clintons went for it. So we rounded up as many Arkansas Travelers as possible, asking them to sign the ad with their phone numbers. We even called many others still in Arkansas who were willing to put their names on the list. The ad ran in several New Hampshire papers and drew favorable reaction, plus an impressive number of phone calls.

On the following Tuesday night, the Clintons invited Barbara and me to join them backstage before the final New Hampshire rally. The election returns were just coming in. The huge crowd and charged atmosphere swelled with a feeling that something unexpected, maybe something very important, was about to happen.

At just the right moment, Clinton burst through the curtains and onto the stage. To a wildly cheering audience, and an incredulous press corps, he proclaimed himself "the comeback kid."

Tsongas won the New Hampshire primary, but Clinton had picked up a second-place momentum no one could stop. He crisscrossed the country, and the unknown Arkansas governor became better known every day. Stressful primary schedules sometimes required he appear in two places at once. So I ended up being a surrogate in Illinois, where he ran a strong first, and eventually in Connecticut. But my voice became irrelevant as the campaign took on a life of its own. I was filling up space. Any time I came back to the Senate, my colleagues acted quizzical yet respectful. I could see that they wanted to know more about this "comeback kid" who seemed to defy the laws of political gravity.

A minor cloud rose on the horizon when H. Ross Perot joined the race as an independent in April. I feared he would give refuge to those who didn't like Bush but were still skittish about Clinton. Renewing my old commitment to help change the electoral college, I filed a proposal in early May for a Constitutional amendment returning the presidential election to the popular vote, i.e., to the American people. Far-fetched as it seemed to many, the possibility lingered that Perot could split the vote, throwing the presidency's decision to the House of Representatives. It could even end up in the U.S. Supreme Court. Ironically, during the Democratic Convention in New York, Perot issued a public statement also calling for an end to the electoral college and returning national elections to the public. To no one's surprise, Perot pulled out of the race on July 14.

* * *

The Pryor family took a welcome recess from the political whirl that spring and summer. In fact, we called a temporary halt not once but twice. On May 9, 1992, David, Jr. married Judith Del Zoppo of Richmond Heights, Ohio, at a fine and traditional country wedding in Virginia. Our friends, the John Cooper family, made their North Wales Estate available to a crowd of family and friends from Arkansas, Ohio, and Washington.

Mark's wedding to Jill Guffin Harvey took place two months later, on July 4, at the First Presbyterian Church in Little Rock. In both events, coming so closely together, Barbara and I were happily reminded of what is truly important: the private and personal parts of our lives keep us somewhat sane and forever grateful.

Nonetheless, schedules and agendas remained outside our control. The Democratic National Convention, with all its raucous celebration of Arkansas's best, and the Clintons with their pack of political junkies behind them, would pour into New York City only a week after Mark and Jill's wedding.

Barbara and I joined a noisy crowd of Democrats on a special Amtrak train from Washington. When we pulled in to Penn Station, New York Mayor David Dinkins proclaimed that his city had always known how to throw a party. "But we're not just going to have fun," he said. "We're going to elect the new leader of the free world."

A week after the convention ended, George H. W. Bush launched his campaign with an attack on Bill Clinton as "the governor of a certain state located somewhere between Texas and Oklahoma." Even though I could recognize a glint of humor in his comment, I took Bush's remark personally enough to bring maps to a press conference, pointing out the president's error. For me, his attitude represented views far more telling than a mistake in geography. The voters simply weren't buying Bush.

For 12 years, the Republicans had controlled the White House, dictated policy, deepened the deficit, named federal judges, and set the agenda. Now it was the Democrats' time. The happy frenzy surrounding Clinton's inauguration flourished almost without precedent. Many compared it to the excitement of John F. Kennedy's 1961 inaugural.

The full sweep of Clinton's campaign and election didn't really hit me until his inauguration, when I watched firsthand the literal transfer of power from Bush to Clinton. For the first time in a long while, Clinton was making a speech that included nothing about air bases, highways, and government contracts. His famous memory for facts and statistics took a back seat to a more transcendent, almost spiritual vision of the years ahead. He spoke for only 14 minutes. That had to be a first in Bill Clinton's history.

Still, an undertow of negative and spiteful resentment remained. Many who had worked in the primaries, walked the streets, and sacrificed financial resources failed to sense that gathering storm. I remember one night seeing a street vendor on DuPont Circle, only a block from our house, selling buttons that said, "Impeach Bill Clinton."

He hadn't even been sworn in.

Chapter 53
The New Team in Town

Early in Clinton's presidency, an article in the *Wall Street Journal* described me as his closest Senate ally. I cringed at this designation but saw little I could do about it. The press liked to create matches, as well as highlight divisions.

The pundits enjoyed exploring the new president's association with anyone who might become his Paul Laxalt, the Nevada senator considered Ronald Reagan's best friend in the upper house. It had to be Bumpers or Pryor, they said. Laxalt even offered a word of caution to Bumpers and me together: "You're going to get a lot of people mad at you because their wife didn't get to sit next to Hillary."

Thomas Friedman, the *New York Times* columnist, suggested that Clinton and Bumpers mirrored one another as policy wonks with razor-sharp tongues and a spicy competitiveness. Pryor, on the other hand, he said, seemed more like a Clinton uncle. He decided we were both equally close to the new president. I suppose, in our very different ways, he was right.

Nobody needed to tell Clinton how to approach public policy, work a legislature, or write a bill. Certainly no one could tell him how to make a speech. I think Bumpers supplied him with tips on handling individual senators. I did a little of that myself, basing my advice on what I had experienced in both the House and Senate.

Only days after the November election, my doctors decided I needed to undergo by-pass surgery in Little Rock. I had delayed this since my heart attack in 1991, and I wanted to keep it as secret as possible. I didn't want people making dire predictions about my health, suggesting I had become too sick to carry out my Senate duties.

Trying to keep my surgery and convalescence a secret proved a joke. It became front-page news in Arkansas papers, especially in mid-November. Only a few days after the election, Bill Clinton and Al Gore came to visit me at the University Medical Center.

What's more, rest proved impossible. I faced requests for jobs, appointments, even meetings supposed to last "only five minutes." Many people

I hadn't seen in years suddenly became my best friends. Barbara and I were both fielding calls from former colleagues and strangers around the country. One former Congressman asked to be Secretary of Defense, and another knew he would be perfect at the State Department. Mack McLarty, Clinton's childhood friend from Hope, thought about Commerce but decided that White House chief of staff would make a better fit. Lloyd Bentsen called to say he had accepted Clinton's offer to become Secretary of the Treasury.

My one firm commitment was to help Hugh "Tater" Black become U.S. marshal in Arkansas's Western District. Following Tater's job nomination, a Justice Department spokesman called, saying Tater had done poorly on his physical. Maybe the position would place him in a precarious health situation. In fact, he concluded, the stress could kill him.

"Give him the job," I insisted. "He's going to die if he *doesn't* get it." He got the job.

Mike Espy, a young black Congressman from Mississippi, called not long after my surgery, as I still lay weak in bed. An up-and-coming Democrat from a state fast becoming Republican, Espy knew a lot about farmers' needs. His father had served as an Agriculture Department extension service agent in Crittenden County, Arkansas, in the heart of the Delta.

Espy expressed interest in the Secretary of Agriculture's job. He asked if I would talk to my friend Don Tyson about him. Don seemed to support Espy's appointment, though he wasn't passionately interested in anyone for that position. "If you and Dale can work with him, it's good enough for me," he said. Such was the endorsement of the world's largest poultry producer and a major force in American agriculture. Espy came on board, with dire consequences no one could have foreseen.

A new president traditionally enjoys a political honeymoon of three or four months. For Clinton, it became short-lived indeed: gays in the military, budget issues, appointments, the demands of high expectations. His short-term economic package immediately ran into trouble. He even had to account for a Los Angeles haircut that bottled up traffic for several hours.

Organized and well-heeled anti-Clinton efforts also began rising. In February, Jack Kemp and William Bennett joined other high-profile Republicans, announcing "Empower America," a movement to oppose the Clinton administration's every single proposal. An arm of the conservative

Heritage Foundation, the new group touted financiers including the Scaife family, who became long-time Clinton antagonists. Richard Mellon Scaife, an heir to the Mellon banking and steel fortune, also launched his "Arkansas Project." He hoped to track down any gleanings of a Clinton scandal.

I was not surprised at Kemp's alignment with this group, and certainly not at Bill Bennett's, who has always seemed to act as America's self-appointed scold.

Kemp and Bennett's allies included an impressive array of Washington arch conservatives: Jeanne Kirkpatrick, Reagan's U.N. ambassador; Vin Weber, a Minnesota Republican recently retired from the House; and Haley Barbour, a Mississippi lobbyist later elected that state's governor. Weber became the organization's president. To give the group official Republican Party credibility, Barbour signed on as the Republican National Committee chairman. This Republican team fathered what Newt Gingrich called the Contract with America.

I found that—at the end of the Bush administration—when Kemp left the Department of Housing and Urban Development, he had handed out $94,000 in bonuses to his agency's top political appointees. One had become Empower America's public relations director. A month after Clinton's inauguration, I stood before the Senate with HUD printouts in hand. I charged, "Jack Kemp's idea of empowerment is to hand out taxpayer dollars to lame-duck political hacks."

The vehemence of this speech frankly surprised even me. This rallying cry was my first, but hardly my last, foray into defending the Clinton administration's efforts. I knew that several anti-Clinton senators, waiting until the right moment, would come to the Senate floor and lambast the president and his administration. But once challenged, they would quickly vanish into the cloakroom, dissolving from view.

Republicans weren't the only opponents to Clinton's ideas and politics. During that first year, I found myself spending considerable time lobbying fellow Democrats on his behalf. This often involved simply hearing suggestions, complaints, and points of contention from Senate colleagues, then passing them on to Bruce Lindsey, Mack McLarty, or someone else at the White House.

New York's Democratic Senator Daniel Patrick Moynihan couldn't seem to bring himself to like Bill Clinton. His visceral reaction always surprised me, because they were both highly educated, intelligent, and, it seemed, similar in philosophies. Although from very different parts of the country, they had risen from financial deprivation and comparable family backgrounds.

A major disagreement over health care arose early in Clinton's first term. At one point, Moynihan exclaimed, "There is no health care crisis in this country!" Certainly that opinion totally opposed reality, not to mention what both Clintons were saying.

Hillary Clinton's task force on health care nevertheless addressed many problems Moynihan had defined and railed against. Even when the panel detailed its recommendations in public, Moynihan remained unwilling to support them.

The Clintons attempted to bridge the gap, occasionally inviting Pat and Liz Moynihan to private dinners at the White House family quarters. Nothing seemed to help. Moynihan would often go out of his way to stop me, saying, "Well, did you see what *your* president said this morning?"

His animosity remained a mystery to me. But I should note this: late in 1999, after Moynihan had announced he wouldn't run again, Hillary entered the race for his seat. She did this by appearing with him at the Moynihan farm in upstate New York. It seemed he and the Clintons had somehow reached a just peace. He died three years later.

* * *

In March 1992, at the presidential campaign's beginning, *New York Times* reporter Jeff Gerth wrote the first article in a series about a failed north Arkansas business venture. The issue would come to be known as "Whitewater." Initial installments drew only small attention, but by the time Clinton took office the media and his opponents began to show an interest. I still think some of Whitewater's appeal came from the rather exotic locale, a still undiscovered and unspoiled part of the state. A certain romantic image caught the reader's eye, a kind of Shangri-la that engaged older couples seeking a retirement haven.

Material for Gerth's story was fueled, researched, and financed by anti-Clinton forces both in Arkansas and across the country. Sheffield Nelson headed the team. A Little Rock attorney and former ArkLa executive, he had lost a governor's race to Clinton in 1990 and was seeking revenge. Justice Jim Johnson, still hard at work on the far right, also weighed in with scurrilous opinions. Clinton detractors in 1992 published nationally *Slick Willie: Why America Cannot Trust Bill Clinton*, a pamphlet by David Bossie and Floyd Brown, basically repeating Gerth's *Times* reports.

In time, details of Whitewater took on an importance they never warranted. Thanks to the *Times*'s relentless attention, a scandal of real proportions flared. The *Times*'s dogged pursuit of the story has remained a mystery for many people, including me. I've always connected it with Howell Raines, the paper's editorial page editor. He seemed to expect Bill Clinton to become *his* kind of left-leaning president.

Raines, an Alabaman who took over the editorial page in 1993, was a progressive only three years older than Clinton. He had supported the Democratic Party platform in 1992. He may have also felt jealous of Clinton's charisma and success. Whatever the reason, the *Times* would not let Whitewater go.

The Securities and Exchange Commission investigated Whitewater but never charged the Clintons or Jim and Susan McDougal, their business partners and long-time friends. Three separate inquiries also turned up nothing.

In early 1994, to address continuing questions about Whitewater, Clinton asked Janet Reno, his attorney general, to appoint a special counsel. Clinton's first choice excelled in character and background. Robert Fiske, a former partner in New York's Davis Polk and Wardwell law firm, took the job in January, 1994. A highly respected lawyer with a distinguished career as a litigator, he had been appointed U.S. attorney for New York's Southern District by President Gerald Ford.

Almost immediately after his appointment, Republican critics targeted Fiske, complaining he was being too easy on Clinton. In August, when his term as independent counsel ended, he was not reappointed.

Fiske's removal resulted from an agreement between Judge David Sentelle, head of the Justice Department's special division overseeing the independent counsel, and Sentelle's mentor, Senator Jesse Helms. Helms and his North Carolina colleague, Lauch Faircloth, had met with Sentelle for lunch in the Senate dining room in mid-July. The three were Republican Party leaders in North Carolina. Sentelle's wife had, in fact, worked as a receptionist in Faircloth's Senate office. Despite public claims that they had discussed only personal matters, including their prostate glands, the three agreed that Sentelle would name a new investigator for Whitewater. Fiske simply had to go.

They chose Kenneth W. Starr, a Texas native who had attended Harding College in Arkansas, a liberal arts school supported by the Church of Christ. Starr, a former judge and later solicitor general under President George H. W.

Bush, had become a partner in the prestigious Washington law firm of Kirkland and Ellis. He provided a perfect voice and presence for his conservative base. With a personal animus toward Clinton he never attempted to disguise, Starr pursued the case with incredible and relentless determination.

My direct involvement with the Whitewater scandal came only as a frustrated Senate member observing the Banking Committee's seemingly endless string of hearings. Republicans had taken over the Senate in 1994 and eagerly had begun whatever investigations of the Clinton administration they could justify. Banking Chairman Al D'Amato of New York promised to uncover what he termed the nefarious dealings by Bill and Hillary Clinton and their Arkansas partners in crime, Jim and Susan McDougal.

D'Amato actually began pressuring for these hearings in February the previous year. He spent three straight days on the Senate floor, asking why the Resolution Trust Corporation had not investigated the Clintons' banking practices. Either the Democrats would agree to hearings, he said, or the Republicans would bring Senate business to a complete stop. The federal government's "conspiracy of silence," he charged, had to end.

Several times I rushed to the floor to defend the president. At one point in March I even defended him against D'Amato on the Phil Donahue television show. When D'Amato released a blueprint for a second round of hearings covering a range of Arkansas officials and business people, I said on the Senate floor that his plan stood as "a declaration of war against the State of Arkansas."

The Republicans considered the Banking Committee the ideal arm for incessantly investigating Clinton, and they found D'Amato a willing leader. When the second round opened on April 24, 1996, he issued a total of 26 subpoenas. Those called included Clinton's lawyer David Kendall, Bruce Lindsey, former Clinton gubernatorial chief of staff Betsey Wright, Hillary Clinton's assistant Maggie Williams, and several members of Little Rock's Rose law firm.

At one point, I phoned Hillary, encouraging her to appear at the Banking Committee door the next morning, walk to the front table, and announce she had come to defend herself. "If you'll do this," I told her, "D'Amato and his gang will scurry for the exits." But attorneys in the White House didn't think much of my suggestion, and they advised her to keep her cool.

By the time these hearings ended in June, their 768 pages showed no criminal involvement on the part of either Bill or Hillary Clinton, or by anyone in the administration.

I'll never forget D'Amato's exclamation as the Whitewater hearings began to heat up: "It's payback time, baby!"

My colleague, Senator Chris Dodd of Connecticut, commented that D'Amato's investigations had proved "the most partisan and politicized hearings in the history of the Senate."

Chapter 54
A Small River in Arkansas

The Whitewater controversy finally reached an official end in 2000, four years after I had left the Senate. Robert Ray, Starr's successor, ruled that neither Bill nor Hillary Clinton had knowingly taken part in any criminal conduct. By that time, the Whitewater affair had filled the news for eight years. The federal government had spent $60 million. Hundreds of innocent people had testified before a special grand jury. At one point during the investigation, the FBI had assigned more agents to Whitewater than to the Oklahoma City bombing incident.

On July 20, 1993, our group of transplanted Arkansans lost a true friend and colleague. Vince Foster, a sensitive and brilliant lawyer with a wife, children, and an impeccable background, took his life in Fort Marcy Park across the Potomac River from Washington. I had known Vince and his father, a leading Arkansas insurance man who had been active in state politics. It was at Vince, Sr.'s funeral that I had sent the note encouraging Bill Clinton to run for president.

Vince's sister, Sheila Anthony, was one of Barbara's closest friends in Washington. Her husband, Beryl Anthony, had served in the House of Representatives from Arkansas's Fourth District from 1979 to 1993.

A native of Hope, Clinton's hometown, Vince had worked with Hillary in Little Rock's Rose law firm. He was among the many Arkansans who came to Washington with the new administration. His graduation address to the University of Arkansas Law School, delivered only two months before his death, described the legal profession's role in American society—perhaps the best commencement speech I have ever heard.

After months of prosecuting the Whitewater affair, Robert Fiske filed his preliminary findings. They included the firm assertion that the scandal had nothing to do with Vince Foster's suicide. Fiske made this clear statement shortly before his removal from his independent counsel position. Foster, he said, was an innocent and well-meaning young man suffering from an undiagnosed case of severe depression.

Fiske's views infuriated conservatives and contradicted a persistent and vicious campaign, continuing even today. This ugly plot insists that Vince Foster was hiding Hillary and Bill Clinton's complicity and guilt in Whitewater and other matters. The truth is that Vince remained troubled by complicated and private doubts, and by misgivings none of us will ever understand.

Three days after Vince Foster's funeral in Hope, my brother Bill died of amyotrophic lateral sclerosis, Lou Gehrig's disease, at his home in Bella Vista—a small town in Benton County, Arkansas, popular among retirement couples. Bill was 65 years old and a recently retired Presbyterian minister who had spent most of his professional life in Texas. Still in his twenties when Dad died, Bill took over the Chevrolet business in Camden while knowing, at the same time, that his call was to the ministry. He had picked up his young family in the mid-'50s, moved to Texas, and completed his theological degree at the Presbyterian seminary in Austin.

Never willing to let his mind rest, Bill moved to Benton County when he retired from the ministry, enrolling in law school at the U of A in Fayetteville. At the same time, he took up sculpting in a back room of his house. He rode to Fayetteville every day on a new motorcycle, a sleek model he had wanted to own all his life.

Bill's wife, Mary Lou, and their grown children fully supported his decision to strike out in a new direction for what was left of his life. Bill was always a nonconformist, even as the minister of conservative Presbyterian congregations. This streak of independence endeared him to his family and to the congregations he served. And to me.

None of us could have known, of course, how brief his time would be, or that he would live only a few months after the diagnosis. Bill's disease progressed with remarkable swiftness compared to many ALS victims. In the end, that proved a blessing for him and his family.

Bill always returned to Arkansas to work in my campaigns, putting up yard signs, sweeping out the headquarters, taking a low profile whenever and wherever he could. He would fill in for me, making a speech whenever my schedule became complicated, but he preferred standing in the back, watching the political scene develop without his help. I still miss my brother's counsel, his sense of humor, and his determination not to make harsh judgments of anyone, even when I'm only too willing to render a few. His special presence embodied a free spirit of intellectual energy.

Only months after Bill's death, his wife Mary Lou died in a car accident near her north Arkansas home.

* * *

Susan McDougal became a clear victim of Whitewater and its fallout. She was one of the only people who served prison time for being involved in the scandal. The truth is that she was caught up in a web of spite surely directed more at Bill Clinton than at Susan or her husband, Jim.

Susan was born in Germany where her father served in the military. But she was raised in Camden, where, at one point in my short legal career, I had represented her father. She attended Ouachita Baptist College. As a student there, she came to know Jim McDougal, her political science professor. They were married in 1976.

Jim McDougal had befriended Bill Clinton during their student years in Washington back in the '60s. When the Clintons returned to Arkansas, the two couples became close. The McDougals operated a small savings and loan association known as Madison Guaranty Trust in north Arkansas and developed a real estate project south of Little Rock.

Kenneth Starr and his Washington team demanded that Susan come clean about her dealings with the Clintons. She cooperated in good faith, turning over documents and information related to land investments and to Madison Trust. She also complied with demands to tell prosecutors everything she knew relating to the case. Dissatisfied with her testimony, Starr insisted that she describe the nature of her *real* relationship with Clinton. When she failed to relate what he wanted to hear, he charged her with contempt, then saw her bound, shackled, and sent to prison. She was eventually transferred to a series of women's prisons before Clinton pardoned her in the last weeks before he left office.

At one point in his investigations, Starr spoke to the West Little Rock Rotary Club. He detailed his prosecutors' work, and, at the end of his speech, asked for questions from the floor. Dr. Roger Bost, who had directed the health department under Dale Bumpers and later during my four years as governor, stood up and asked directly, "Exactly what is your mission, Mr. Starr?" At that point, Starr sputtered and stammered. He clearly could not come up with an answer and left the meeting.

The prosecution of Susan McDougal was political from the beginning, and because of that she became a political prisoner—a true miscarriage of justice and a classic abuse of our legal system. The federal government's raw power, when misused, can crush the life out of even our strongest citizens.

The taint of Whitewater didn't end with rumors concerning Vince Foster or with Jim and Susan McDougal. Agriculture Secretary Mike Espy became ensnared in the investigation's expanding web. Starr accused him of criminal involvement with Don Tyson.

Tyson had given willing support to Espy's appointment, but the two men hardly knew each other, even after Espy took office. Nonetheless, Donald Smaltz, a California lawyer who had represented the Teamsters as well as Ferdinand Marcos, was appointed as special counsel in 1994. He tried desperately to determine if Espy had made deals with Tyson Foods in exchange for sports tickets, lodging, and airfare. The charge was that Espy—in exchange for favors—had promised Tyson he would weaken food safety standards affecting the poultry industry. In reality, those who make their living selling chickens are the last people on earth wanting to see weak inspections. One bad chicken can close a plant down, sending the company's stock price into a serious downward spiral.

Espy was indicted in 1997 on 39 charges of receiving gifts and engaging in improper behavior. No one expected the case to last more than six months. By the time it got under way, Espy had already resigned from the Clinton cabinet and returned to Mississippi to practice law. Then in 1998, four years after the investigation began, including testimony from 70 witnesses and an expenditure of some $20 million, Espy was acquitted of all charges.

During the trial, Smaltz subpoenaed 2,000 Tyson workers who had filed injury claims against the company, some going back to 1990. He hoped to dig up whatever complaints he could against Tyson. Moving into the federal building in Fayetteville, he installed a dozen phone lines and sent out a fleet of official vehicles to track down any information on Tyson, whether it directly involved Espy or not. He struggled mightily to find anything on Espy or Tyson, no matter how trivial or irrelevant.

Espy had sent Tyson reimbursements through the mail for tickets, airfare, and hotel accommodations. Smaltz promptly filed charges of mail fraud, claiming that Espy had used the U.S. postal system for "criminal activities."

Because of my contact with both Tyson and Espy during the appointment process, our office telephone records were subpoenaed, along with letters, memos, and any other written and electronic material that might relate to the case. Leslie Chalmers and Pate Felts, my assistant and chief of staff, submitted all appointment schedules and phone logs. Attorneys from the Justice Department conducted extensive interviews with other staff members, including two lengthy sessions with me.

Barbara was called to come before a D. C. grand jury. She was ably counseled by James Hamilton, a veteran Washington attorney who was not allowed to attend any of the jury proceedings.

"What is your relationship with Don Tyson?" was among the opening questions.

"He's a long-time friend of my family, beginning with my parents, who were all living in Fayetteville," she said.

The questioning went on. "And did you attend his party in Russellville? Was Secretary Mike Espy present that evening? What did Mr. Tyson wear? Whom did he dance with? Who was the entertainment?"

Barbara answered each question in order, and to the final one she said, "The entertainment was by B. B. King and the wonderful Lucille."

"And who is the 'wonderful Lucille'?" asked the prosecutor, assured that he had discovered an embarrassing detail.

"B. B. King's guitar," Barbara said. The grand jury exploded in guffaws and adjourned for the day.

This exchange is only a small example of the carryings-on that characterized the Smaltz hearings. Not only a travesty, the investigation stands as one of the great, abusive fishing expeditions our judicial system has ever perpetrated. I was constantly reminded of a wise saying Dad used to quote when he was sheriff: "Be careful when you give a little man a badge and a gun."

Tyson's lawyers advised him to accept a plea of guilty, based on an 1879 law that had never been invoked before. He paid a fine of $6 million.

Tyson's corporate spokesman, Archie Schaffer, had been indicted by Smaltz for asking Espy—in a routine invitation—to attend an annual meeting of the Arkansas Poultry Federation. It happened to be scheduled on the same weekend as the house party to celebrate Tyson's birthday. Schaffer, who narrowly avoided being sent to prison, was finally pardoned by Clinton before he left the presidency. All over Arkansas, bumper stickers had mushroomed, reading "Free Archie!"

During that Christmas season, Donald Smaltz presented his staff members with a wristwatch inscribed "The Espy Matter," and featuring Smaltz's face. By the time the Espy trials finally ground to a halt, I had been out of the Senate for nearly two years, and the Whitewater affair seemed a long way off.

Chapter 55
The Long Goodbye

At 10:00 a.m. on April 21, 1995, Barbara and I—backed by our old and reliable team of Pryor friends and family—stood on the Capitol Hotel's balcony. I announced that I would not run for another Senate term. Current and former staff members packed the place, along with press and media, and political faces from all over Arkansas. C-SPAN covered the event live.

This decision had been building in my mind for a long time. I had first begun to think about retiring in 1990, when I was fortunate enough to win re-election without opposition. Or, as one prominent Republican commented, "Pryor always has opposition—he just doesn't have an opponent."

I found considerable appeal to ending my active political life without pronounced opposition. One day at the Democratic caucus luncheon, Terry Sanford, my Senate colleague from North Carolina, joked at my lacking an opponent: "I don't think I'd want a job that nobody else wanted."

In August, 1993, I first openly mentioned retiring in a C-SPAN interview. That was only speculation, but as I looked around, I saw many of my Senate colleagues making retirement plans: David Boren of Oklahoma, Sam Nunn of Georgia, Bill Bradley of New Jersey, Paul Simon of Illinois, Jim Exon of Nebraska, Bennett Johnston of Louisiana, Howell Heflin of Alabama, Nancy Kassebaum of Kansas, and Claiborne Pell of Rhode Island—all were deciding to move on for one reason or another.

The more I became aware of this growing exodus, the more sense it made for me to make a decision. The Democrats had just suffered an election disaster in 1994, losing both the House and Senate. I had been forced to give up my edge in committees. Frankly, I remained tempted to stay around and witness the party's return to full strength. Missing out on our efforts to regroup stood as my chief regret in leaving, but even that temptation couldn't make me stay. It was time to go.

The wisdom of this decision became even clearer when Dale Bumpers and I were having breakfast one day at Little Rock's International House of Pancakes. A waitress at the cash register had stared at us for some time.

Before we left, she said, "I'm sorry to bother you two gentlemen, but we've been having a discussion over at the cash register. Didn't one of you used to be sheriff?"

Only a few days later, another woman came up to me at the University Mall and asked, "Aren't you David Pryor?" I told her I was. "And didn't you run for something a while back?" I told her I had. "And did you win or lose?"

I had just turned 60 the year before, and was ready for a new life while I could still anticipate the promise of time, energy, and opportunity ahead. Despite a lot of speculation, the decision had little to do with my immediate health. The heart trouble four years earlier, and the resulting bypass surgery, seemed to have worked their way clear. There was no assurance of lasting good health, but my doctors remained optimistic about the recovery process. Best of all, I was feeling strong and energetic.

A phrase I had used numerous times during the 1972 McClellan campaign kept coming back: a U.S. Senate seat should never be considered one person's personal property. On top of that, I did not look forward to the endless days and weeks of fund-raising, airplane trips, and the frantic pace of a U.S. senator. I had never enjoyed raising money the way a number of elected officials do. In fact, I detested it. A few of my friends looked forward to getting on the phone and making calls to prospective campaign donors. I never did. I left raising money to others like Bum Atkins, my long-time friend and campaign finance chairman, or to Phil Herrington, or Truman Arnold, who had a magic touch in these endeavors. I also depended on Ann Pride in my office, who did the leg work when we were raising campaign funds. Raising money always seemed an occupational hazard, a necessary burden of holding office.

My reasons for retiring were complicated and not entirely clear. Steve Barnes, a long-time Channel Seven political newsman and stringer for *The New York Times*, wrote that maybe the Senate was no longer the place I had dreamed of as a boy, and that grandchildren are hard things to turn down. He figured that with three grandchildren growing up around me, I might have simply decided it was time to go.

This was pretty accurate guess work on Steve's part. When I first aspired to the Senate, people like John Stennis, Lloyd Bentsen, Tom Eagleton, Henry Jackson, and Warren Magnuson all shared a bond, even when they disagreed on specific issues and particular legislation. Willing to work together, they formed a collegial group. Over the years, such compatibility had too often fragmented into a series of personal agendas.

Jon Kennedy, the *Democrat-Gazette* cartoonist, was a little more direct than Barnes. He assumed my frustration in seeing the new Republican majority led by Newt Gingrich and his raucous House crew. The Contract with America, after all, was still fresh in everyone's mind. Kennedy's cartoon showed me surrounded by overfed, laughing elephants, sitting back and enjoying themselves like loud buffoons, while I was hunched over my desk, exhausted, and muttering, "I'm outta here."

Important family reasons urged me to pull back from my Senate career. While I didn't make a public case for them, they remained nonetheless real. One of these involved my concern for Mark, his health, and the possibilities for his political career. In 1994, he had challenged Attorney General Winston Bryant, who was seeking a third term. Mark's campaign floundered in part because he never convinced the public that Bryant should be removed from office. In addition, I've always thought the voters decided one Pryor was enough in public office. In other words, his timing was off, and in politics timing is always a primary factor.

The following year, Mark thought he had simply injured his leg playing pickup basketball. But his doctor discovered that, in fact, he had developed an advanced case of sarcoma. What we thought was a torn tendon turned out to be a deadly malignancy, usually found in young adults, and often fatal. Mark underwent 13 hours of surgery. For several months, he could not walk without assistance. His children were small, and his career as a lawyer or a politician had to be placed on hold. For several months, our family felt frantic.

Fortunately, with the help of excellent care, the disease has not recurred, and he is now cancer-free. At the time of Mark's diagnosis in 1995, however, I found very good reason to shift my priorities and begin looking toward Arkansas as a full-time home again. When Mark announced for the Senate in late 2001, and then took the Senate seat I had held, it became clearer than ever that my decision was right. Dee and his family had found a home in Washington, and by 2001, Scott and his wife were settled in New York.

Even after I announced my retirement, I still had nearly two years left in my term. During that time, I worked on new farm legislation with Thad Cochran of Mississippi, and a series of bills on military base closings with

Olympia Snow of Maine. Orrin Hatch of Utah asked me to co-sponsor a bill establishing pension plans for small businesses, which extended the work I had done earlier in the Finance Committee.

The following March, the University of Arkansas asked me to join its political science department and lecture on state politics and history. I considered it more like "holding forth." This suggestion struck me as exactly the right decompression move out of active political life. I commented how it would be fun to become a wandering ex-political figure and substitute on the teaching faculty. It also seemed the right time to announce that I would leave my papers to the University's Special Collections Division. I donated more than a thousand boxes that included material from my time in the state legislature, the U.S. House, the governor's office, and the Senate.

* * *

My last day on the Senate floor came on October 3, 1996, as the Senate prepared to adjourn for fall recess and the midterm elections. I dreaded this particular day and its ceremonial trappings, knowing exactly what lay in store. When Paul Simon of Illinois retired, all male members of the Senate wore bow ties on the floor for that day. It was a tribute to Simon's signature fashion choice.

Even though a senator's final chamber hours are always filled with warm and much-appreciated tributes, there's also a strong dose of genuine embarrassment. Barbara and my staff had already thrown a farewell reception in the Caucus Room of the Russell Office Building on September 18. Several hundred friends, staff, and fellow senators had shown up for that event.

But farewells on the Senate floor were a distinctly different thing. The floor speech that touched me most had been a talk Dale Bumpers gave a week before. As always, he managed to beat the crowd. Dale described the night when we first met at a large Democratic gathering in Little Rock. It was 1968, when I was serving in Congress and he was seriously considering a run for governor. He said that our appearance together gave him the idea of making his first campaign two years later.

Senator Strom Thurmond pointed out that he had always called me "sheriff" because he knew my father had been a county sheriff. This is true. In fact, I'm not sure Thurmond ever knew my real name. He did meet Dad when he came through Camden in 1948, campaigning for president on the Dixiecrat ticket. He didn't get very far with Dad, either. But Thurmond had a prodigious memory, and once something fixed in his mind, like a nickname or a distinguishing character trait, he never forgot it.

Robert Byrd was the last to speak. He described me as someone who never made "big noises like half a dozen grasshoppers under a fern," and added that I would soon be listening to "the crickets chirping in the Arkansas dusk, raising their noisy chorus to the rising Arkansas moon."

Senator Byrd's send-off impressed me as a fitting way to make my exit from the Capitol I had always loved. Now, after a long time away, I began the long trek home.

Chapter 56
Finding a Place

For any politician, divorcing yourself from the public stage is no easy task. Bringing the curtain down, when you anticipate no curtain call, makes it even harder. Many find it traumatic, especially those who for years have longed for attention, affection, and, above all, acceptance.

Over time, we become hopelessly spoiled by the trappings of public office. Someone always drives you to an event or picks you up at the airport. Someone always wants to care for you. All right, I know: your true friends are always there. But so are the supplicants.

In 1972, after my loss to John L. McClellan, I suddenly spun out into private life. For almost two years I was a fish out of water.

I left Washington in late 1996 under different circumstances. After two elections to the governor's office and 18 years in the Senate, I had restored the self-confidence lost after the humiliation of defeat. At age 62, I found myself beginning a new life chapter.

Dean Bernie Madison at the University of Arkansas's Fulbright College had followed up Chancellor Dan Ferritor's suggestion of a teaching assignment. He even designed a course and offered the title "Distinguished Lecturer on Public Policy and the Law." To tell the truth, I wasn't sure what that meant. But being on the University campus, my alma mater, and surrounded by energetic students and faculty, held distinctive appeal. It promised an entirely different world from Washington and Senate business. Barbara and I were ready to decompress, and she was going home to the hills she had known and loved so many years before.

For the next academic year, I led class discussions dealing with public policy on the state and federal level. We covered the realities of being a state's chief executive, allocating resources, facing tight budgets, and dealing with legislators. When I asked my students which part of the federal government interested them most, a few always replied without hesitation, "How do you get to be a lobbyist?" For the most part, I found the students became engaged not so much in politics *per se*, but in public service that appealed to them in a personal way. The great majority of them clearly wanted to pursue a career that could make a difference in the world.

Across the campus, Barbara took art courses from Arkansas fiction writer and artist Donald Harington. His novel, *The Choiring of the Trees*, has long been a favorite of ours. Her classmate was Archie Schaffer, the Tyson Foods spokesman then facing the series of trumped-up charges made by Donald Smaltz.

We rented a small apartment not far from the campus. It soon felt like home. Barbara, always a child of the Arkansas hills, was happy to get back to her roots in and around Fayetteville. That semester she was invited to write a short essay describing her favorite spot in Arkansas. It was collected in a book along with articles by Donald Harington, Dee Brown, Jimmy Driftwood, Helen Gurley Brown, Wayland Holyfield, Lucinda Williams, and other celebrated Arkansas natives. Published by the University of Arkansas Press, the book was called, *Somewhere Apart:"My Favorite Place in Arkansas."*

After considering all sections of the state, Barbara chose Cass, in the Boston Mountains on the Mulberry River, where her great-grandmother grew up. She described the dogwood and redbud trees hanging over the country lanes, and the hardwood trees' earthy colors of fall. She recalled the pig trails where bears used to roam. She talked about being a child and swimming all morning and afternoon in the rocky-bottomed river. "We learned to swim in the cold green water of the Mulberry River," she wrote. "There was a large hollow rock where my mother would bathe my little brother. Sometimes we stayed in the creek all day long, and Mother would make coffee in a skillet, and we would drink it out of tin cups."

Crossing the bridge over the Mulberry River has always brought a rush of memories from Barbara's childhood. Her relative, Champ Turner, had owned and operated the general store at Turner Bend. Her cousin Lonnie Turner has taken us to cemeteries in the hills around Mulberry, pointing out ancestors who lived there over many years. "These days," she wrote toward the end of her recollection, "when I turn off the interstate and onto Highway 23, no matter how tired I may be, I take a deep long breath of that clean mountain air, and I drink the fresh cool water and feel restored. I know then that I'm home."

The pace of our lives underwent a fundamental change. Sitting in our Fayetteville apartment, in front of a flaming fireplace, we watched Bill Clinton's second inaugural on television, beginning to sense the distance between Arkansas and Washington. That same month of January, as winter set in, I made a phone call searching for firewood. The man at the other end of the line said, "By the way, who is this?" I told him my name was David Pryor. He said, "That's funny. We used to have an old politician around here by that name."

The Fulbright College encouraged me to invite guests from Washington and elsewhere, stimulating discussion on public issues among students, faculty, and townspeople. Some of the speakers I brought in were Jack Valenti, president of the Motion Picture Association of America, and Senators Jim Sasser, Paul Simon, and Dale Bumpers. Richard Fenno, a University of Rochester political science professor and one of the country's foremost American political observers, traced various Senate campaigns reaching back to the 1970s. Fenno had written a profile of three 1978 Senate campaigns: those of Claiborne Pell, Paul Tsongas, and David Pryor. In a sense, he knew more about my first Senate campaign than I did.

I asked Fred Smith, an Arkansas native who founded Federal Express, to speak to students on the growth of the nation's transportation and delivery system. Smith's story comes right out of Horatio Alger, the mythical rags-to-riches American hero. He had come to me back in the late 1960s, when I was still in the House, explaining his detailed plans to set up a Memphis airline hub and fly packages overnight nationwide and around the world. I didn't laugh out loud, but in a nice way I predicted it would never work, and wished him well all the same. Despite my chilly reaction 25 years earlier, Fred Smith asked me to serve as a consultant for his international company.

My friend Phil Herrington asked me to join his investment firm as a managing director, and to work with him and my Camden friend James "Bum" Atkins. Phil assumed that I knew something about investments, or about being a managing director. At about the same time, the Fort Worth-based Corphealth Corporation asked me to help them extend group mental health coverage in the private and public sectors.

Working at the opposite end of the corporate spectrum, Winrock International, an agriculture organization based in Arkansas, named me to its board. Winrock, founded by the late Winthrop Rockefeller, is now a non-profit organization developing resources in rural areas around the world. Later, Heifer International asked me to join its board.

One advisory board appointment bore surprisingly mixed results. The Donald W. Reynolds Foundation asked me to chair an advisory committee to plan a regional geriatric center in Little Rock. The foundation wanted to attach the state-of-the-art facility to the University Medical Center. It was designed to become a model for other centers around the country.

I was pleased to work once again with Dr. Robert Butler, president of the International Longevity Center in New York and a professor of geriatrics at Mt. Sinai Hospital. Dr. Butler had worked as a close consultant to the Senate Aging Committee years before. For that reason, I was familiar with his worldwide reputation as a passionate physician and researcher. In addition, I knew him as a true humanitarian and had come to value him as a friend.

After chairing the advisory committee for some months, two foundation officials came to my Little Rock office. They said that since I had become chairman of the Bill Clinton Legal Defense Fund, I would have to resign from the foundation's advisory team. My high-profile identification with President Clinton would be seen as too political for me to serve on the Reynolds Foundation committee.

This was the first time in my life I had been fired from a job, even one I had taken on a part-time basis. The Reynolds officials' decision proved a genuine disappointment. I had looked forward to the mission aimed at benefiting the elderly population of Arkansas and nearby states.

* * *

The 1990s enriched our family life, with our three sons living part of the time in Arkansas and much of it in Washington and New York.

David, Jr., and Judith, who had married in 1992, became the parents of David Hampton Pryor III, my namesake, and found a home in Washington. David had operated an events business of his own and later acted as the Clinton administration's deputy chief of protocol. In 2001, he joined the legislative office of FedEx Corporation as vice president for governmental affairs.

Mark and Jill, living in Little Rock, had two children, Adams and Porter. After serving in the Arkansas House of Representatives, Mark was elected the state's attorney general in 1998. Four years later, he defeated incumbent Tim Hutchinson, a Republican from northwest Arkansas, and took the Senate seat I had held.

In October, 1997, Scott Pryor married Diane Benfonte of Long Island at the sprawling Virginia farm of our friends Nick and Mary Lynn Kotz. The Kotz family had been among our closest friends since Barbara and I first went to Washington. Their hillside lawn provided an idyllic site for the wedding. Scott had lived for almost a year as a cabin sitter in Alaska and had moved back to Washington to work in advertising and film-producing. When he moved to New York in the early '90s, he became a city dweller, living in the Chelsea neighborhood. He now produces television commercials. He and Diane moved to Scotch Plains, New Jersey, and their son Devin was born in 2006.

Barbara continued her engagement with the arts and home-and-office design. Even though officially retired from her interior decorating business, she continues to help friends in Arkansas and Washington, D.C. in designing their homes and offices.

Chapter 57
The Road to Albania

Early in 1999, the Institute of Politics at Harvard's John F. Kennedy School of Government invited me to become a Fellow. The Institute was conceived in 1963 immediately following President Kennedy's assassination. Drawing on the experience of many distinguished leaders in academics, government, and politics, it opened in the fall of 1966. The late Richard Neustadt, Columbia University's presidential historian and later a Clinton administration advisor, became its first director.

The Institute exposes undergraduates to philosophies and writings of public officials, journalists and authors, office holders, and government leaders. While focusing on government at every level, the Institute emphasizes *politics*, as its name suggests.

Harvard matched my satisfaction of teaching at the U of A with the chance to learn from the distinguished, international array of leaders and writers visiting the Institute. I received an opportunity to share my own experience as governor and senator in a weekly discussion group called "Everything (Well, Almost) You Ever Wanted to Know About Winning and Holding Public Office, But Were Afraid to Ask."

In early April 1999, when I had nearly finished my semester as a fellow, I was watching daily reports of Kosovo's growing conflict. Like many in the United States, I was moved and horrified by that divided country's human suffering.

The ethnic cleansing we witnessed on nightly television had begun the last week of March, when NATO started a bombing campaign against Slobodan Milosovic's Serbian government. Despite NATO's stern warnings, and those from our State Department's Richard Holbrooke, Milosovic had refused the terms of a proposed agreement between his government and the Kosovo Albanian delegation. Reacting to this outright rejection, NATO Secretary General Javier Solana ordered bombing to start on March 24.

In an enraged retaliation against NATO, Milosovic directed the Yugoslav army, controlled by the Serbs, to force natives out of their homes in Kosovo. What started as a small stream of refugees became a flood by the beginning of

April. Families were mercilessly uprooted in villages and driven from Kosovo into Albania, Macedonia, and Montenegro. Villagers who resisted, or who were thought to sympathize with the Kosovo Liberation Army, were summarily tortured, killed, or forced to flee for their lives.

I closely observed the news segment that followed thousands of women and children making their way, on tractors and by foot, hundreds of miles from Kosovo, trudging to whatever secure sites they could find. The first safe destinations were Albania's villages and towns.

I felt a call to take part in whatever humanitarian effort I could find. In my letter to the Institute asking permission to take off before semester's end, I confessed that I had been "too young to fight Hitler, and too self-preoccupied for the civil rights struggle in Selma, but this time I've got to do something." The Institute granted me an early leave.

Right away I called Brian Atwood, a former staff member of Senator Tom Eagleton and a Carter administration assistant secretary of state. Clinton had appointed him director of the Agency for International Development (AID), and his office was deeply involved in the refugee effort. I told him that I would willingly pay my own way. I could drive an ambulance, dig latrines, change diapers, prepare meals, or perform any other task that needed doing.

Atwood replied that unfortunately I was past the volunteer age limit. Besides, he added, didn't you have heart surgery a few years ago? He assured me that AID wouldn't touch me. But he gave me a number I might call at the International Rescue Committee in New York. He seemed to think I would get a fair hearing. He also offered to let me use his name.

The International Rescue Committee (IRC) was exactly where I needed to go. Founded in 1933 at the suggestion of Albert Einstein, it assisted refugees in the early days of the Nazi regime. Einstein never directed the committee's efforts, but he recognized its importance from the beginning. "Any intelligent fool can make things bigger, more complex, and more violent," Einstein wrote when the committee began its work. "It takes a touch of genius—and a lot of courage—to move in the opposite direction."

Moving in that opposite direction has remained the 75-year-old global organization's lasting purpose. On the ground wherever armed conflicts occur, the committee sponsors teams of relief workers to provide food, health care and, most of all, hope.

My initial call was frustrating at both ends of the line. But after an hour's conversation with two staff members, I finally got my message across. Very reluctantly, and with a touch of suspicion—why would this former senator want to spend his retirement in Bosnia?—they agreed to pass my name to their supervisors.

Some 48 hours later, I got a call from the head of an IRC office. "Can you be on a plane to Albania the day after tomorrow?" he asked.

My major worry became how to tell Barbara. As I nervously unveiled this scheme to her, she quickly grasped my plan. She was also fully supportive, even if a bit concerned about my safety. Always the true soldier, she gave me a thumbs-up.

Two nights later, on April 20, I was in a taxi going to Boston's Logan Airport for the flight to Albania. The cab driver was listening to radio reports of the Columbine School massacre that had taken place earlier in the day. He turned to me and screamed, over and over, "The world has gone mad."

The initial leg of my trip was to Zurich, where I was told all flights into Albania had been cancelled because of the conflict. Taking a chance, I flew from Zurich to Rome, waiting another two days for word from Albanian Air. Finally they put me on an ancient Russian-built plane that flew over the Adriatic to Tirana, Albania's capital.

For the next four weeks, I assisted teams of relief workers in setting up campsites and passing out needed medicine to a floodtide of refugees. I was assigned a dwelling with a married couple, both medical doctors, in a nearby room. He was an American with a degree from Johns Hopkins, and his wife was a native of Australia. They had temporarily given up their practice to join the Albanian relief efforts. I marveled at the humanity of people like this.

In the beginning, it seemed that I was in everyone's way. None of the team of doctors knew what to do with me. My first assignment was to negotiate with local tribal leaders in finding suitable locations for the camps, which would soon be overflowing. I was then sent on a two-day excursion by truck and van to Gramich, in southern Albania, hoping to find a place to set up another refugee community. Each 50-mile leg of the trip took nearly three hours because of the steep and narrow roads, the livestock blocking the highways, and the constant presence of displaced refugees. Driving after dark put us in danger of highwaymen, who often captured or robbed travelers for a few dollars.

At each stop, I was called on to work in the camp's supply systems, providing baby bottles, diapers, blankets, and food. At one point, 6,000 ethnic Albanians poured into an abandoned sports arena in Tirana, another 4,000 moved into a tobacco warehouse, and 2,000 filled a scrubby city park that had long ago lost its grass and trees.

Almost by accident, I met a group of seven doctors and two nurses, a part of the Flying Doctors of America. They had only recently arrived in the country and carried with them an enormous cache of donated pharmaceuticals in large military duffel bags.

The Flying Doctors was a new organization to me, but I soon learned of their history. Founded in Georgia in 1990, the group started out as a nonprofit and nonsectarian organization made up of doctors, dentists, chiropractors, nurses, and other health-care specialists. Their principle is modeled on care for the poorest of the poor, a mission defined by Mother Theresa.

Entirely without a sponsor, this team of physicians and nurses could find no one to direct or escort them from one region to another. They even had trouble locating the refugee camps they had come to serve. Since I had helped with setting up camps and moving supply teams, I knew the routes and locations. I volunteered to become a member of their team.

On our daily excursions, we established temporary stations where the doctors examined hundreds of bewildered escapees and refugees, mostly elderly men and women, as well as many children. Only a few were young and able-bodied men, as most males had either been thrown into Kosovo slave camps or conscripted into the Serbian army.

At each stop, we were besieged with requests from refugees who held photographs of brothers, fathers, and other family members. Every three or four days, I went to the makeshift center for the International Red Cross with names to be checked in our attempt to reunite families. Only once was I actually helpful in locating a missing person by matching his name with a photograph. This 12-year-old boy was reunited with his mother and sister after wandering the countryside for several weeks.

We assisted a 16-year-old boy suspected of being part of an opposition family. He had been forced to stand in the town square before his friends. Serbian army members then shoved a gun in his mouth, ordering him to put on a Serb uniform and swear allegiance to Milosovic. At that moment, a NATO tank lumbered into the square and moved directly toward the crowd, giving the boy a chance to escape.

At one location, some 50 curious bystanders watched as one of our dentists pulled the teeth of more than a hundred refugees, dropping each tooth into a galvanized bucket to onlookers' cheers. Albanians instinctively resisted using painkillers, even during these agonizing procedures. For most of them, this grueling activity amounted to entertainment. The scene in that stuffy room resembled live theatre.

One night at a camp operated by a Turkish relief organization, two 14-year-old girls disappeared from their family tent, never to be seen again. According to authorities, they were likely kidnapped and sold into the Eastern European sex trade.

The Albanians boasted that they had more Mercedes-Benz automobiles per capita than any other country. They rarely added that the cars were stolen from Greece and Italy and then smuggled by sea into Albanian ports. Most of them were also old, with motor and serial numbers scraped off. As many as 10 families would frequently pool their resources to buy one old Mercedes-Benz or any similar vehicle.

The Flying Doctors turned out to be a lasting inspiration to me and to those they treated. One physician in particular—Dr. G. B. Espy of Atlanta—continually motivated me and the members of his team. We have stayed in touch with each other since returning to this country. When they left Albania, the Flying Doctors donated large deposits of drugs to a Lutheran organization that pledged to dispense the medicines to refugees. Otherwise, there was a fear that these drugs could enter the black market, active throughout Albania. On their final evening, the team presented me an honorary membership and gave me a Flying Doctors jacket.

As I left for the airport to return to Boston, I asked the IRC driver to stop at a camp we had hastily supplied at an abandoned park. I wanted to make a final check on the project we had started only days before.

We stopped the car at the camp entrance as a young boy emerged from his family tent and gave me a long, uncertain look. He seemed to recognize me from my previous visits. Then he went back inside. In another minute, he came out and, with a smile, handed me an orange. Neither of us could speak the other's language, but in that moment words were unimportant. This was simply his way of saying thanks. I still have the orange, hard and shriveled almost beyond recognition.

The bombing ended on June 10 when Serbian troops began to withdraw from Kosovo, and Milosovic finally agreed to conditions defined by the international community. The siege had lasted 78 days.

There's a historical footnote. The United Nations continues to administer the region. For years, the U.S. and Europe have assured Kosovo's ethnic Albanians that one day they will stand on their own. But even now, years after the conflict, their autonomy is far from assured, even though on February 17, 2008, they declared their independence.

* * *

Sometime in the early weeks of 2000, word reached me that the Kennedy School wanted me to apply for Director of the Institute of Politics. My former Senate colleague the popular Alan Simpson of Wyoming had served out his term and was headed back west. The final decision depended on the approval of the Institute's board, Senator Ted Kennedy, and his nephew, John F. Kennedy, Jr. They had agreed to offer me the appointment only days before John, Jr., tragically died, along with his wife and her sister, in a plane accident off Martha's Vineyard.

At the end of that summer, Barbara and I moved into a two-bedroom apartment at Quincy House on the Harvard campus. New Quincy is an enormous building, eight-stories tall, which opened in 1959 as a symbol of the "new" Harvard. It stands in stark contrast to the traditional, neo-Georgian buildings that surround it. Some 500 undergraduates became our housemates— a special time and place for us.

As the Institute director, Alan Simpson had used his extensive connections in Washington to sponsor visitors from both Republican and Democratic ranks. I was responsible for continuing that spirit of bipartisanship. My purpose soon widened, however, to include lobbyists and writers, journalists and artists, in order to give students both a broad and deep understanding of U.S. political activity.

Senate and House members, most of them former colleagues, naturally formed the backbone of our public programs and seminars. We sponsored brown bag lunches, formal dinners, small receptions, sessions with "politics and pizza," and public lectures—any format that brought people together for group discussions. Whether the Harvard undergraduates learned anything or not, I certainly did.

After each two-year Congressional election, the Institute and the Kennedy School hold a series of orientation sessions for newly elected U.S. House members, led by current and former members of Congress and their staffs. In addition, the Institute's yearly mayors' conference draws public audiences of close to a thousand participants.

* * *

Throughout the morning and afternoon of September 11, 2001, the students, faculty, and staff gathered in the Institute's large, open forum to share concerns, condolences, even fears and uncertainties about our country's future. For everyone in the nation, this was a day of unspeakable tragedy. We brought in large television sets and made available whatever space we could for the growing numbers who found solace in others.

One remarkable comment I heard two days later remains lodged in my memory. Mike Murphy, a Fellow that semester, was having lunch with a group of colleagues in the Institute's dining room. Murphy had recently directed the 2000 presidential campaign of John McCain. He had a firm grasp of both Republican politics and foreign policy in the new Bush administration.

As we were taking our seats, Murphy said, "Well, get ready. We're going to Baghdad."

"Baghdad?" somebody asked. "Why Baghdad? Iraq had nothing to do with what happened at the World Trade Center."

"You may be right," Mike replied. "But that's where we're going."

Of course, he was right. As we are now aware, we went to Baghdad despite the evidence that Iraq had nothing to do with the attacks on September 11.

Some weeks later, former CIA Director John Deutch spoke to a Kennedy School forum attended by more than a thousand people. Someone asked if our military should make retaliatory moves and invade Iraq, as Bush had begun to suggest.

"Just remember," he answered, "any damn fool can find his way to Baghdad. It's getting out that's going to be hard."

Chapter 58
Back to School

In December, 2000, during the Clinton presidency's final days, the Clintons invited Barbara and me and our long-time friends Truman and Anita Arnold to be their guests at the White House for the Kennedy Center Honors. The president had appointed Anita as a Kennedy Center trustee, and for all of us it proved a special and event-filled weekend. Particular excitement reigned in seeing Hillary about to be sworn in as a U.S. senator from New York, and listening to her plan her upcoming inauguration into that special club.

Bill Clinton, the private citizen, hit the ground running when he left the White House in January. He moved into a Harlem office and settled into a new house upstate, in Chappaqua, New York. He laid out detailed plans for a Clinton Foundation to sponsor global initiatives in health and economic development. As Hillary was being sworn into office, the now-ex-president was staking out political territory of his own.

He also focused on the Clinton Center and Presidential Library in downtown Little Rock, on the Arkansas River's south bank. Abandoned warehouses and old supply buildings still dotted the 27-acre site. But when Clinton showed serious interest in the new library, the neighborhood took on a decidedly different air. At that point, pledges of money and public support poured in at a rate never seen before in Arkansas. Contributions of all sizes and shapes flowed in from around the United States and the world.

Renowned architect James Polshek designed the library to resemble a huge, glass railroad car, playing off its locally historic location adjacent to the old Rock Island Railway station and tracks. A nearby rail bridge was redesigned as a pedestrian walkway across the river; its sturdy iron rafters and poles suggested the Bridge to the 21st Century, a recurring symbol of Clinton's presidency. The library opened officially on November 18, 2004, with all former living presidents—Clinton, George H.W. Bush, Jimmy Carter, and Gerald Ford—in attendance, along with a guest list of dignitaries from around the world. They gathered outside, in spite of the worst torrential downpour in the state's history.

As a major component of the library complex, Clinton envisioned a graduate school of public service. The academic program's original plan went back to 1997, when he began his second term in office and started considering his legacy. Friends and staff looked at other presidential libraries and their graduate programs, but none seemed to match Clinton's vision. The Kennedy School of Government, the Truman School in Missouri, the Johnson Library in Austin, and the George H. W. Bush School at Texas A & M all trained their students primarily for government service. Their graduates found careers in state or federal agencies, and many of them went into teaching.

Clinton approached his school's mission differently. He wanted to prepare students for a wide range of service efforts in both the public and private sectors, domestically as well as internationally. When he looked closely at the possibilities, he found that civic engagement and global leadership made for compatible opportunities, whether they took place in the Mississippi River Delta or in Sri Lanka, India, or the Sudan.

He also wanted to avoid building the school on a major university campus, thinking that detachment from an academic environment would strengthen its offerings beyond just a teaching curriculum. He also preferred an urban setting over a remote, rural campus. The Little Rock waterfront, with its expanding office buildings, shops and restaurants, and a new regional library, proved in every way compatible with the Clinton plan.

Diane Blair, Arkansas history and political science professor at the U of A in Fayetteville, began work in 1997 to design an academic course connecting the new school with programs on the Fayetteville campus, the University of Arkansas at Little Rock, and the U of A School of Medical Sciences. She proved the right person for this job—well-known for her knowledge of politics and government and, with her husband Jim Blair, among Bill and Hillary Clinton's closest friends. She developed a program offering a master's degree in public service, requiring 12 graduate courses, five consisting of field projects.

As library construction progressed, the old Choctaw railway station became the clear choice as the University of Arkansas School of Public Service's future site. This gracefully designed station, built in 1895, had once served as a bustling arrival and departure point on the Rock Island line, but it had long been abandoned and left to crumble. Much to everyone's surprise, it had avoided demolition. After the Roy and Christine Sturgis Foundation gave $5 million toward restoring the structure, it became the Clinton riverfront compound's academic center.

Fortunately for everyone involved, Dr. Tom Bruce initially shepherded the school through the intricacies of educational bureaucracy and challenges of funding, staffing, curriculum development, and student recruitment. Tom Bruce and I had first met when I was governor and he was dean of the University medical school. He later spent several years in Battle Creek, Michigan, with the Kellogg Foundation, then came back to retire in Arkansas, or so he thought. He was immediately recruited to help found the Arkansas School of Public Health, using revenue from recent tobacco settlements. From there, he agreed to help make plans for the Clinton school, and received the title of associate dean. Tireless, totally committed, Dr. Bruce helped establish the new school's skeleton framework. His creative, public-service spirit gave the school the beginning lift it needed.

On several occasions, the former president returned to Little Rock to oversee plans for the library and the school curriculum's early stages. One evening, he was scheduled to speak at a major convention center event. About three hours before the reception, he asked me to join him in hitting a few golf balls. Nothing rigorous, he said, just a few holes before dark.

His large security contingent joined us. Plainclothes officers surrounded the golf course when we got there. Playing golf with Bill Clinton always takes a fair amount of time, but for some reason this round seemed to go on forever. It's his nature to stop along the way for shaking hands, stepping out for photographs—the usual public activities of a rock star.

I felt the long and tedious process had to wear particularly on a young couple following behind us. I could almost sense their exasperation at the long delays. As darkness came, the reception hour closing in, Clinton remained—as always—oblivious to time, and to the impatient couple behind us. Finally, as we approached the 18th green, I held back, offering an apology for the interminable delays.

"He doesn't get to do this often," I explained to the young couple. "Just hope you understand and won't hold it against him."

"Not to worry," the young man said. "We're Secret Service."

* * *

One morning in Fayetteville, Barbara and I were having breakfast at Gaylord's, a favorite spot, when my cell phone rang. Alan Sugg, the U of A president, greeted me with "David, we want you to be the dean of the Clinton School of Public Service."

I was highly honored, but I also felt unqualified, and told him so. At the same time, I offered to help him find the right person for the job. It was a brief conversation.

Barbara asked, "Who was that on the phone?"

"Alan Sugg," I told her.

"What did he want?"

"He wants me to be the new dean of the Clinton School."

"Are you going to?" she asked.

"No, of course not. I'd be a terrible choice."

"I think you should," she said.

"You do? Okay. I'll do it."

As always, Barbara was right. Her view was that President Sugg's offer might provide a professional and personal challenge. I went to his office and told him I'd take the post, especially since I knew that I would be working with Tom Bruce.

The transition from the Kennedy to the Clinton School created a vibrant contrast. The former was comfortably established, steeped in years of tradition and ivy-encrusted acceptance; the latter was new, not yet fully funded, but vigorous and exciting. My earlier experience at the Kennedy School's Institute of Politics provided valuable experience, and a base for making decisions in this new and different setting. Diane Kelly's steady guidance helped enormously. A tireless office manager, she possessed an instinctive ability to recognize potential problems and avoid them, or if they existed, solve them with ease. Once I became comfortable in the academic dean's role—a whole new arena for me— public service as a graduate discipline took on an entirely new meaning. It wasn't arts and sciences, or engineering, or law. But like these other fields of study, the school of public service established a set of learning principles and vocabulary all its own.

Working with Dr. Bruce and an outstanding faculty, we defined disciplinary courses in leadership and decision-making. Then, on a more specific, nuts-and-bolts level, we added seminars and lectures in public service's legal dimensions, and in communications for both print and electronic media. Along with our students, I was learning to appreciate the discipline behind social change. I began to see that a civilized society's progress calls for more than simply good intentions and personal commitment. To establish a new order of responsibility, we must first learn the tough historic lessons and tests our country has faced—and passed—in its efforts of public service.

Our first semester brought in 16 students with impressive backgrounds, both academic and professional. They were excited to discover a new program, untried and untested but offering considerable promise—the only academic curriculum of its kind in the country.

Time and again, we had to correct misconceptions that the Clinton school provided academic training in public affairs. It's public *service*, we continually reminded the press and visitors. The differences between the two are vast. Public affairs includes a wide range of politics, history, management, media, legislation, and governmental organization. Public service emphasizes personal and community efforts—both professional and volunteer—to improve the greater good at every level.

Since that inaugural year, the school has enrolled other students with experience in the Peace Corps, AmeriCorps, teaching, medicine, banking and finance, and most branches of the military. The second class came to 22 students. Each year since, the school has enrolled an increasing number of young men and women from all parts of the world. With degrees in hand—and in the face of the world's major challenges—these graduates have committed their lives and careers to a wide range of service organizations.

The school has also drawn a world-famous roster of speakers, dignitaries not only willing to visit but anxious to use the Clinton library and school as platforms for discussing history and public policy, and even for touting a recently published book. These visitors have included Henry Kissinger, Madeleine Albright (in fact, most of the former Clinton cabinet), Supreme Court Justice Stephen Breyer, Congressman John Lewis of Georgia, Senator John Edwards, and President Jose Maria Aznar of Spain.

Even though the Clintons possess the most solid Democratic credentials of anyone, the school has always included guests from the Republican ranks. In the first year, former Senator and Majority Leader Bob Dole delivered the opening public lecture. Last year, a record audience heard presidential adviser

Karl Rove place the current Bush administration into a context of American history. His appearance was moved from the school to the Little Rock Convention Center to accommodate an overflow crowd.

The credit for attracting this wide range of guest speakers and lecturers, and for giving them a platform at the Clinton school, belongs to Skip Rutherford, who had directed my state office during the early years I spent in the Senate. When I retired from the school in 2006, Skip was the clear and logical choice to succeed me as dean. He had taken part in the early planning of courses and curriculum, and he knew what Clinton wanted to achieve in setting up the public service agenda.

* * *

A year after taking the job as the Clinton school dean, I received a surprise call from my former colleague Senator Harry Reid of Nevada. We had not been in close touch since my retirement, but we were friends during my Washington years, and he was a stalwart associate in the Democratic caucus, even before he became the Senate's Democratic leader.

Senator Reid asked if I would consider a presidential appointment to the board of the Corporation for Public Broadcasting. He said that the White House had informed him of an open slot for a Democrat. As Senate minority leader, Reid could suggest nominees for the president's consideration. Would I like to add my name to the list of likely candidates?

After some initial research, I called back and told him that I would welcome consideration if he wanted to nominate me. This appointment offered real potential for active involvement in public media issues. The Corporation for Public Broadcasting (CPB) has long overseen fairness and integrity in programs offered by both the Public Broadcasting Service (PBS) and National Public Radio (NPR). While I had not worked directly with the board's members, I had known a number of PBS and NPR news commentators and editors, including the country's dean of television journalists, Jim Lehrer. Their public standing depended on the corporation and its pledge to support unbiased television and radio.

For the next year, the White House office of personnel went through the nominations, compiling biographical information, financial records, security clearances, and letters of recommendation. Finally, my name emerged, and President Bush nominated me in November 2006. Senate hearings and a confirmation vote soon followed.

The yearlong vetting process afforded me plenty of time to become familiar with the corporation's workings. Founded in 1967 and chartered by Congress, it protects public broadcasting from partisan pressure and offers a shield from extraneous political interference and control. The corporation's financial support comes from both private and public sources. These funds—nearly $400 million in 2005—are distributed to PBS, NPR, and hundreds of local public television and radio stations nationwide.

CPB traditionally has possessed little direct influence over programming on television or radio. It can't force either PBS or NPR to air a program the corporation has funded. The key is in its financing. It provides seed money for individual shows such as "Sesame Street" and "The NewsHour," while supplying grants to individual television and radio stations. National Public Radio's Diane Rehm, who recently visited the Clinton School, and "All Things Considered" are daily staples for millions of listeners.

When I came to the board in late 2006, the corporation had ended a protracted and public standoff with its current chairman, Kenneth Y. Tomlinson, a Republican and arch conservative first named to the board in 2000. A native of Galax, Virginia, Tomlinson had a background in journalism, having worked as a reporter on the *Richmond Times-Dispatch* and later as managing editor of *Reader's Digest*. At one time a correspondent in Vietnam, he was named the Voice of America's director during the Reagan administration. In addition to his varied professional career, Tomlinson raised thoroughbred horses on his farm in Fauquier County, Virginia, not far from Washington.

Tomlinson's agenda spelled near-disaster for the nonpartisan and revered Corporation. He tried to intimidate anyone who questioned his authority. Congress had made several previous attempts to eliminate the corporation's public funding, and Tomlinson's divisive tactics and bellicose demeanor did nothing to win friends for broadcast independence.

My tenure began a full year after Tomlinson had resigned under pressure, and the recovery work being done by this dedicated board and staff was really just beginning to take shape. I have been privileged to join in these efforts to rebuild confidence and trust. Tomlinson's onslaught had cast only a temporary shadow on a body of public servants determined to shield public broadcasting from that kind of political interference.

Public broadcasting remains an American treasure. Still, for some reason, 72 Republicans in the House of Representatives recently voted to cripple funding for the corporation, and thus for public broadcasting. What a senseless loss this would have been had their efforts succeeded—a loss for the majority of Americans who hunger for fairness in news analysis and to eagerly receive historical, cultural, and thoughtful perspectives. Fortunately for us all, these avenues of news and opinions remain protected and open, available to everyone in our nation.

Chapter 59
Voices of History

Shortly before I left the Senate, Barbara and I were invited to visit Louisiana State University. Senator Russell Long's friends were celebrating his years of service to the state, and we viewed with great interest his papers in the LSU library. Long had joined his family of Louisiana political legends, carrying on the legacy of his father, Huey, and his "Uncle Earl." I was flattered when the organizers asked me to speak, and I'm certain Barbara's close friendship with Carolyn Long, the Senator's wife, played a large part in my invitation.

Our friend Ted Jones of Baton Rouge included us on the guest list to tour the Old State Capitol Building. Ted himself was inducted into the Louisiana Political Hall of Fame. He is currently a chief benefactor of the state's political museum in Winnfield Parish, the home of Huey P. Long and "Uncle Earl."

The library's great collection of Louisiana oral history—rich in the state's brand of politics and public service—especially grabbed our attention during that tour. The late T. Harry Williams, Huey P. Long's biographer, started this collection in the 1930s. He and his wife had traveled to every corner of the state, interviewing people from all walks of life. Their collection resounds with stories and family histories, chronicles of towns and cities, and accounts of robust political campaigns that shaped the Bayou State.

Driving back to Arkansas from our two days in Baton Rouge, Barbara and I talked over what we had seen. We decided we should begin an oral history of Arkansas. In its early stages, it would resemble the Louisiana collection, drawing entirely from Arkansas's people and its history. I recalled from years ago a statement by Dr. Willard Gatewood, history professor at the University of Arkansas: "It is time we define ourselves, rather than letting everyone else do it for us." Certainly we possessed rich state traditions that needed to be recorded and saved. We also had an inactive Pryor campaign fund that could help launch such a project.

After weeks of discussion and planning, we announced a contribution of $220,000 to begin an oral and visual history center at the University of Arkansas, to be housed in the history department. In 2005, the Tyson family generously donated $2 million to financially stabilize the project. It received a name—the Barbara and David Pryor Center for Oral and Visual History—and a new and distinct location on the top floor of the Mullins Library.

Barbara and I have watched this program develop from an abstract concept to a bricks-and-mortar collection. We've always admired oral history and the way it captures local facts and figures, but its true and lasting worth lies in the telling of the tale. Bruce Lunsford, Barbara's father, stood among the great storytellers coming out of the Arkansas Delta; in a similar way, Susie Pryor, my mother, became known around Ouachita County for spinning yarns of her childhood and the town's early history. The stories were valuable and true, to be sure, but the way they told them easily doubled the fascination.

The first time I realized the power of spoken history came through a long-playing record narrated by the newscaster Edward R. Murrow. *I Can Hear It Now* reproduced 1930s and '40s live interviews, informal comments, and news accounts by both famous and unknown people. I marveled over and over at Winston Churchill's call to arms in World War II's early days, with Big Ben tolling in the background. I listened in awe to the frantic cries of an unidentified radio newscaster describing the dirigible *Hindenburg*'s explosion in 1937. My favorite speech was Lou Gehrig's "luckiest man on the face of the earth" farewell from Yankee Stadium on July 4, 1939.

Barbara and I discussed how we might collect interviews for the new center. We knew we wanted one-on-one recollections by people from all backgrounds and life experiences. We wanted Arkansans who had impacted our state, but also people whose lives otherwise would never be recorded in any other medium. We were also determined that these photographs and oral histories not become simply musty collections of unused artifacts tucked away on a library shelf.

Two major Arkansas oral histories already collected have involved interviews with editors, reporters, photographers, and staff people who had worked for the *Arkansas Gazette* and the *Arkansas Democrat*. The late Sid McMath and I had spoken with Hugh Patterson, former publisher of the *Gazette*, asking his financial support for the project. He and his family responded generously. Roy Reed, a former *Gazette* reporter who later worked with the *New York Times*, directed the *Gazette* interviews. With the support of *Democrat* owner and publisher Walter Hussman, Jerry McConnell, the

Democrat's former managing editor who had worked for both papers, brought together interviews with former *Democrat* employees.

Based on these and other tapes, we're finding that people's stories, when they're interviewed orally, differ greatly from their experiences related in written form. Interviews become social events, while writing remains solitary. Silence also plays an important role; a thoughtful pause or hesitation may bring drama to an oral interview but become lost in a written text.

In the big picture, oral history, visual history, and written history meld into one experience. It's called looking back. For me, the instinct to reach for the past involves a very personal dimension. Someone said the longer a public official has remained out of the public eye, the more honest and insightful he or she becomes. I can only hope this rings true for me, and for the set of memories I've offered in this book. In any case, I'm constantly tempted to look back and wish I could have done things differently. What about those decisions that came too soon or too late, or the names and faces forgotten, old friends slighted unintentionally, and speeches too long or not delivered at all? Especially in recent months, I've thumbed through scrapbooks and files of yellowed press clippings, letters and notes, calendars long out-of-date—all of them causing me to wonder where time has gone, and how I filled the hours and days allotted to me. Most of all, did I get it right? And, if not, where did I go wrong?

Some may proudly boast, "No regrets. I did it *my* way." Whenever I hear this claim, two reactions come readily to mind: first, I would love to know how that kind of naked self-assurance feels; and second I don't believe a word of it. Who doesn't look back without a twinge of regret, or even remorse, or at least a sense of curiosity? What if events around me had taken another twist or turn? And if they had, would I have played out my part in this pageant on the public stage in some different way?

For years now, I've regretted two missed opportunities in my political life. In each case, I had stored up considerable political capital, securing my investment in the public trust. Now I wish I had used some of that capital instead of letting conscience get trumped by expediency.

The first missed opportunity was the way I waited so long to oppose the war in Vietnam. I knew our country wrongly kept the conflict going, but I stayed the course, to use a current term, until late 1968. Second, I took a much too tentative approach to the early civil rights battles. I went about building my career as a lawyer, state legislator, and Congressman while all around me there surged an open and heroic struggle for equality.

Neither of these choices resulted from a lack of awareness or mistaken information, or a failure of will, or a weakened sense of commitment. In both cases, I knew what was happening, and I saw others take up the cause and make their stands. But in each instance, I failed to grasp the situation's enormity and its lasting importance to the country. Do I save my capital for a later time, or should I spend it now? I questioned then whether my single voice could possibly have made any difference. In retrospect, I wish I had become involved much sooner, and with more passion.

These two momentous public chapters were written many years ago, yet they still occupy conspicuous places in my memory. They remind me that those who elect us are always far ahead of those they elect. Looking for leadership, they want us to act—not simply *react*.

This said, it seems to me the public perception of our federal executive and legislative branches has reached an all time low. Instead of meaningful direction, we see a 30-second sound bite. The big money required to seek public office today creates an empty reservoir from which to draw strength or faith. Most Americans feel their voice being snuffed out by the selfish interests of power, influence, and wealth. In this process, healthy skepticism too often slides into deep cynicism. Our political vision becomes obscured while many of our nation's leaders vacillate, sweeping the vital issues of health care, education, and equal opportunity off the table.

An outstanding young Harvard graduate recently asked me to advise him on his future. Inspired to enter some form of public service, he wondered if politics might prove the right place to begin. I wanted to tell him it might be the right place to end. First, before anything else, try to find out who you are.

"If you try to become someone else, you'll fail," I told him. "And if you pretend to be something you're not, then you should choose another field. A politician's career is one of perceptions, and the people you serve will soon find you out. The public has an innate sense about who you are and what you believe. Too many politicians underestimate the intelligence of their constituents."

I've always admired my former colleague, Senator Claiborne Pell of Rhode Island. Even in the thick of his fiercest political campaigns, he had the will to say, "We don't pay enough taxes." He believed that government should do, not less, but *more*. For most politicians, a statement of that kind would end a political career, but Senator Pell had reached such a level of trust with voters in Rhode Island that they returned him to the Senate by huge majorities. A truly chosen few enjoy this communion of trust in public life. Most do not.

My calling has been politics. For whatever reason, I became a public person, and I have loved this work with a passion. My life's mosaic consists of the million miles and faces covering the canvas on my particular easel. It's almost impossible to lay down the brush and declare the painting complete.

The psychologist Erik Erikson believed that, among human behavior's greatest drives, were being wanted and needed. That's been my experience. I have been blessed by the best family on earth, and by people who have shared with me their tolerance and generosity, rewarding me with their confidence. It's been a great trip.

Index